The Conscious Universe

BY THE SAME AUTHOR

Felicitavia
When the Time Comes
The Ashram
Devi
Song of the Taino
The Jazz Master
In the Land of the Saints
The World is my Mistress

The Conscious Universe

A Commentary on
Shrii Shrii Anandamurti's Ananda Sutram

Devashish

InnerWorld Publications
San Germán, Puerto Rico
www.innerworldpublications.com

Copyright 2021 by Devashish Donald Acosta

All rights reserved under International and Pan-American Copyright Conventions. Published in the United States by InnerWorld Publications, PO Box 1613, San Germán, Puerto Rico, 00683.

Library of Congress Control Number: 2021951708

Cover Design © Devashish Donald Acosta

The photo in the front-cover image, "The Mirror of the Universe," was taken by the Hubble Space Telescope. It shows the Helix Nebula.

No part of this book may be reproduced or transmitted in any form or by any means, electronic or mechanical, including photocopying, recording, or by any information storage or retrieval system, without permission in writing from the publisher, except for the inclusion of brief quotations in a review.

ISBN 9781881717867

When the river born from the mountain cave, after crossing numerous plateaus and green and golden plains, merges into the blue waters of the sea, does that river die? No, it doesn't die. Nothing ever entirely dies. The rhythmic sweetness of the river lives on in the ocean's towering waves. Although human beings know this, they prefer to forget it. And because they wish to remain oblivious, they are overwhelmed by the pain of loss. From beginninglessness to endlessness, every entity lives eternally in supreme peace in the bosom of the Great. No one was ever lost, no one is ever lost, no one will ever be lost.[1]

— Anandamurti

Contents

Introduction	1
Chapter One	11
Chapter Two	108
Chapter Three	191
Chapter Four	253
Chapter Five	270
Afterword	325
Bibliography	328
Glossary of Sanskrit Terms	333
Roman Sanskrit Key	335
Notes	336

Introduction

THE SANSKRIT WORD FOR "philosophy," *darshan*, literally means "vision," in the sense of a direct, intuitive vision of reality. Rather than being solely an intellectual discipline, as philosophy is generally understood to be in the West, the pursuit of knowledge in its own right (from the Greek words *philo* and *sophos*, the "love of wisdom"), the word *darshan* implies spiritual knowledge. A true *darshanika* or philosopher in the Indian spiritual tradition is not an intellectual per se but a rishi, a sage who has attained the highest spiritual realization and who thereafter endeavors to translate that enlightened vision into the language of human understanding in order to provide his or her fellow human beings with a conceptual framework capable of giving direction and meaning to their lives. The Vedas and the Tantras, the two principle sources of Indian scripture, are generally regarded, at least in large part, as the work of enlightened sages, and thus they are also referred to as *áptavákya*, eternal truths—literally, those utterances that stem from the direct experience of the ultimate reality and which are capable of guiding us to that same experience.

Thus in the Indian tradition, the study of philosophy is not an intellectual exercise. It is one facet of the mental training that allows us to move from a state of ignorance to a state of enlightenment by guiding us in our efforts to discover the inherent meaning underlying each and every aspect of our existence and to use that burgeoning vision to accelerate our spiritual progress. It can be compared to a comprehensive map of reality. A map is not the territory. It is a proportional representation that helps us to move from where we are to where we want to go. Likewise, a spiritual philosophy or *darshan* serves as a particularly valuable tool with which to navigate the challenges of incarnate life as we make our way toward the same enlightened state from which that philosophy was born.

There is another word in Sanskrit, *ádarsha*, that is sometimes used interchangeably with *darshan* and which is derived from the same root, *drsh* (sight). *Ádarsha* is commonly translated as "ideology" or "ideals," but its literal meaning is "mirror." Like a mirror held up to reality, an *ádarsha* presents us with a reflection of the supreme truth that we can use to guide and illumine our actions as we move toward that truth, toward the goal of our human journey.[2] Without the guidance of a true *darshan* or *ádarsha*, our journey is almost sure to flounder. Without a reliable map or sound, comprehensive directions, we are bound to go astray, or at best to waste valuable time in circuitous detours that could have been avoided. Hence, different philosophical systems and religious ideologies and doctrines have evolved over the millennia in response to this inescapable need for an accurate compass by which to navigate the journey of our lives, and their teachings have been the principle guiding force behind our psychic and spiritual evolution during the long march of human civilization. From the mouths of philosophers, sages, and prophets have come the words by which we live our lives, even if we are largely unaware of their influence. From them have come the values that often go unquestioned and without which we would not be who we are today, for they have given us the measure by which we have learned to judge our experience. This has been true since the dawn of human civilization and it is even more true today, in a world of warring ideas vying for our hearts and minds, from the often-divisive teachings of institutionalized religion to the equally divisive materialist ideologies of capitalism and Marxism, profoundly influenced by a scientific worldview dominated by material reductionism. We are all in need of a reliable map, a trustworthy lens through which we can see and interpret the world, and this book is an attempt to present one such map, Shrii Shrii Anandamurti's *Ananda Sutram*.

Shrii Shrii Anandamurti (b. Prabhat Ranjan Sarkar, 1922–1990) was a modern Indian rishi, an enlightened sage whose teachings were fully conversant with contemporary scientific thought and yet fully grounded in the ancient traditions of Indian spirituality.[3] Though his teachings cover a vast panorama, their roots are firmly grounded in Tantra, and thus *Ananda Sutram* is a modern exposition of this ancient spiritual tradition. *Ananda Sutram* is a *darshan*, a work of philosophy. To call Tantra itself a philosophy, however, would be to limit both its scope and its historical importance. Tantra is first and foremost the science of human development that arose in the Indian subcontinent over seven thousand years ago.[4] Tantric philosophy is one aspect of that science. The practices of yoga are another, as is the well-known Tantric depiction of the human being's subtle spiritual anatomy, including chakras, kundalini, *nadiis*, and so forth. In a wider sense, Tantra refers to the spiritual culture of the indigenous inhabitants of what is now modern India and its immediate neighbors, a culture whose ideas and discoveries have had a huge impact on the spiritual development of our race, an influence that already in ancient times reached all the way to Europe in the West and to China in the East, from where it made its way to Korea and Japan. While modern Indian culture and spiritual thought is widely considered to be a continuation of the ancient Vedic civilization, which arrived in India from Central Asia through the Aryan migrations that according to genetic evidence began around 7000 BCE and finished about 3000 BCE,[5] the spiritual science for which India is rightly revered is primarily a legacy of the indigenous Tantric culture, which was absorbed by the invading Aryans over the course of several millennia. The Vedic religion that the Aryans brought with them from Central Asia was and is primarily ritualistic in character, propitiating the gods for prosperity and good fortune (much like our modern consumer society), whereas the Tantric teachings and techniques are more rightly considered a science, the science of intuitional practice, embedded within a particular philosophical framework. Both the Vedic and Tantric traditions are very much alive in modern India and in modern Indian thought. On the surface, they appear to have melded into one spiritual tradition (which many, if not most, Indians think of as Vedic without fully understanding its origins), and to some extent this is true, but beneath the surface the two traditions flow on like adjoining rivers who retain their separate identities though their waters often intermingle.

The core teachings of Tantra, which have long been absorbed into the wider current of Indian philosophical thought, unfold from one simple premise: that all of creation is the play of one universal Consciousness, singular in essence and infinite in its various manifestations, the eternal substratum of what is fundamentally a conscious universe. This makes it diametrically opposed to the modern reductionist model that dominates contemporary scientific thought, where consciousness is seen as a byproduct of matter, the fortuitous result of a random combination of elements, a largely unquestioned assumption that is both philosophically and experientially untenable.[6] Rather, matter is a transmuted form of Consciousness, a veil that hides from all but the most discerning eye the unity of existence. In effect, Tantra presents us with a unified field theory that subsumes the world of matter and the world of mind and which has been a part of human understanding for millennia. Unlike the ever-elusive unified field theory of modern physics, however, it is not a supposition according to the great Tantric masters and innumerable practitioners down through the ages but a verifiable truth that has been proven over and over again in the laboratory of human experience by mystics of various lineages who have gained access to the one infallible source of knowledge: the direct perception of reality (although "perception" is a dubious word choice for the realization of a truth that is both within and beyond the senses). And as with any science, if we replicate their experiments in our own inner laboratory, with practice and perseverance, we will also prove the truth of those teachings and attain to the same enlightened state.

For most of its history, the teachings of Tantra were passed on orally from master to disciple without being written down, even long after the invention of written script. Tantra was principally a *sádhaná shástra*,[7] a system of spiritual practice rather than an intellectual doctrine, and for this reason its teachings were restricted to its practitioners, who would learn it orally from their masters in strict secrecy and then pass it on to their disciples. But eventually many of the teachings were lost due to a lack of competent preceptors, and thus it became necessary to write them down. Even then, much of what was written was written in a twilight language that in large part continued to restrict the teachings to the various schools of Tantric practitioners, since without a skilled guide to interpret those teachings the uninitiated reader could not understand them.[8] These are the Tantric texts that have come down to us today: the sixty-four principle Tantras and a sizable number of related texts. None of these in their written form are more than two thousand years old, which has led many scholars to consider them much more recent than the Vedas and thus indebted to the Vedas, especially to the Vedanta, but the teachings contained in those texts are in fact far older than these scholars give them credit for and indeed had a considerable influence on Vedantic doctrine. This confusion is perfectly understandable, given the secrecy that has surrounded the Tantric lineage down through the ages and the fact that the Tantras weren't finally written down until long after the Vedas were.[9]

Ananda Sutram is thus a continuation of the Tantric tradition, a modern exposition of ancient ideas that adds new elements to a story that is still being written. If Tantra is a river that began in the Himalayan fastness some seven thousand years ago with Shiva, the first great Tantric master, *Ananda Sutram* follows the course of that river into the present day, somewhere in the Indo-Gangetic Plain.

Because the knowledge systems found in the Tantras and the Vedas originated in a time before the invention of written script, they had to be memorized in order to be passed down to future generations. For this reason, they were composed primarily in verse form (*shlokas*), where the meter served as an aid to memory, or in the form of *sutras*, which was the preferred form for philosophical works. The word *sutra* literally means "thread." In this context, it refers to the central thread that binds together a constellation of ideas, a short, succinct aphorism that functions as the kernel of a particular philosophical argument. A single work of philosophy, usually running no more than one or two hundred sutras (*Ananda Sutram* has 85; Patanjali's Yoga Sutras has 196), could be easily memorized, with each sutra functioning in much the same way as a mnemonic, thus allowing an individual easy access to the whole of that philosophy. The student would memorize the sutra and learn the argument or teaching woven around that particular thread. Having memorized the collection of sutras, the entire teaching would then be housed in their mind for exposition or further development. The six classical systems of Indian philosophy, for example, are each based on seminal texts written in the form of sutras, as are many other works of Indian philosophy, both spiritual and secular. To use a more modern analogy, we can compare sutras to the section headings in a textbook, where each heading is followed by a comprehensive explanation. By memorizing the section headings and assimilating their explanations, the student would then have the entire textbook at their disposal. This tradition of philosophical composition has continued on into modern times due to the many advantages afforded by this ancient literary form.[10]

Due to their extreme concision, sutras on their own can be exceedingly cryptic and at times almost unintelligible, and thus after the invention of written script, the tradition of writing commentaries based on the great treatises sprang up, with each commentator giving their particular interpretation of an important work, often using that text to support their own school of philosophy. To further the analogy from the previous paragraph, these philosophical textbooks in the form of sutras only became fully useful to students when accompanied by a suitable commentary. Arguably the single most influential philosophical work in the yogic tradition is Patanjali Yoga Darshan (Patanjali's Philosophy of Yoga), better known as the Yoga Sutras. Hundreds, if not thousands, of commentaries on the Yoga Sutras have been written over the more than two millennia since its composition, many of them lost or forgotten, and new commentaries are being published every year. But all of these owe a particular debt to the oldest existing commentary, commonly known as the "Vyasa Bhyasa" (Vyasa's commentary). Without the Vyasa Bhyasa, the Yoga Sutras might have remained largely unintelligible to future generations, and it is generally accepted that Vyasa's commentary is a faithful representation of the oral body of knowledge that accompanied the Yoga Sutras until Vyasa penned his text in the fifth century ACE, though it is not actually known how closely it adheres to Patanjali's original intent. Likewise, each of the six orthodox schools of Indian philosophy in what is commonly referred to as the Vedic tradition[11] — Samkhya, Yoga, Nyaya, Vashishta, Mimamsa, and Vedanta — is based on one or more canonical sutras, and each of these sutras is accompanied by a legacy of important commentaries, some of which have become canonical in their own right.

The present text, *Ananda Sutram*, was dictated orally by Anandamurti to Sushil Dhar in the spring of 1961 during the master's nightly walks with a small group of disciples in the outskirts of Jamalpur, where he would stop at the tiger's grave, a well-known local landmark situated in an open field. Sushil was responsible for bringing along a pen, paper, candles, and a glass to protect the candle from the wind, and Anandamurti would dictate two or three sutras a night, several nights a week, followed by a short explanation in Bengali. A conversation on the topic would then ensue during which the disciples would be free to ask questions. In response to one such question, Anandamurti said that the short explanation he had given and which Sushil had transcribed would be "enough to avoid others giving radically different interpretations in the future, as has happened with the Gita of Krishna and the Yoga Sutras of Patanjali."[12] The detailed explanation, he added, would be found in his discourses.

In effect, Anandamurti's short purports, which can be found in the original printed version, serve as *Ananda Sutram's* first commentary, the first and only irrefutably canonical commentary, having been dictated by the author simultaneously with the respective sutras. The next commentary on *Ananda Sutram* (which omitted Chapter Five) was written in the early 1970s by Avadhutika Ananda Mitra Acarya, an American disciple, and was circulated in manuscript form among students of Anandamurti's philosophy until it was finally published in 1981. In keeping with the spirit of Anandamurti's response to his disciple at the tiger's grave, it followed closely Anandamurti's original purports and added extensively from his printed discourses, those that had been translated into English at the time, as well as drawing from contemporary scientific thought and from different spiritual traditions. I first read a photocopied manuscript of her commentary in the summer of 1976 and it greatly enhanced my reading of the original text as well as my overall understanding of Anandamurti's philosophy, as it has no doubt for a great many readers, both before and since. This present commentary is the next in what I fully expect to become a long and fruitful tradition of interpretive work based on *Ananda Sutram*.[13] As with Ananda Mitra's commentary, I have taken the original purports as both a springboard and an organizational anchor. I have then tried to synthesize the more detailed interpretation that can be found in Anandamurti's collected works, the majority of which were not available to Ananda Mitra when she wrote the first "non-canonical" commentary, since at that time many of Anandamurti's works had not yet been translated into English and the master still had some eighteen or so years of extraordinarily productive work ahead of him. I have done my best to incorporate that "detailed explanation" directly into the body of the text, and wherever practical or useful I have added relevant quotes from his writings to the endnotes, especially on points of particular importance or emphasis or difficulty. In addition, I have made an attempt to situate Anandamurti's ideas in the context of the Indian philosophical tradition, particularly where similar or identical terms or concepts are interpreted differently and are thus in dialogue with each other, and at the same time I have tried to situate his philosophy in the context of contemporary scientific and social thought, thus reaching both into the past and into the present to find common ground between these different descriptions of reality. Wherever my interpretations of the material have gone beyond a simple synthesis of Anandamurti's own words, as found in his written texts, there are bound to be students of his philosophy who will have different and perhaps better interpretations to offer. It is my hope that this commentary will stimulate them to add their ideas to the philosophical conversation, whether in the form of lectures, videos, articles, commentaries of their own, or simple informal debate. As I see it, one function of any commentary is to stimulate new and hopefully better ideas or interpretations that will serve to enrich our collective understanding.

With respect to the original Sanskrit, since *Ananda Sutram* was dictated orally, as were all Anandamurti's printed works, which were either compiled from his discourses or dictated to a disciple, it seems that the author followed a recognized practice for the oral dictation of Sanskrit texts by dictating what modern Sanskrit scholars call a "disambiguated" version. Modern Classical Sanskrit in its written form follows very precise rules that were codified into their modern form by the famous grammarian Panini approximately 2400 years ago.[14] These rules include a wealth of orthographic changes, most notably the rules of sandhi, or word combination, that can make for significant differences between an oral and written text. The principal purpose of sandhi is to facilitate euphony. For example, in English we pronounce the word "cats" with a terminal *s* sound and the word "dogs" with a terminal *z* sound, even though they are both spelled with a terminal *s*, and we pronounce the word "the" differently depending on whether it is followed by a vowel or a consonant. These are examples of sandhi that are not reflected in written English. In Sanskrit, however, such euphonic changes are reflected in the spelling, which can make it difficult at times to recognize the original word or grammatical case, even in certain cases for scholars of the language. The transmission of a disambiguated text leaves far less room for confusion or the accretion of scribal errors, which was likely Anandamurti's intent, given that the disciples that took dictation and printed his books were not trained in Sanskrit. It was this original, partially disambiguated version that was printed in 1961 and which has come down to us today.[15] However, for the purpose of this commentary, I have introduced a written version of the text with sandhi and other minor corrections to make it easier for Sanskrit scholars and students who are used to reading Sanskrit literature that adheres to these written rules, which may have been how the author intended for the sutras to eventually be published, just as his oral discourses in languages such as Bengali or English would be modestly edited before appearing in printed form. For this, I am fully indebted to Professor Shaman Hatley of the University of Massachusetts who was kind enough to prepare this "ambiguous" version in both Devanagari and Roman script. This is followed by a fully disambiguated version—the spelling one most commonly encounters in a Sanskrit dictionary—alongside a word-by-word translation. Rather than use the IAST romanization system that is commonly used by many Sanskrit scholars, I have used Anandamurti's own romanization and included a key, which includes the IAST equivalents where they differ. Where Sanskrit words have been absorbed into English without any significant semantic alteration, such as "rishi" or "chakra," I have used the English dictionary spelling. However, I have kept as Sanskrit terms, complete with italics and diacritical marks, those Sanskrit words that have been assimilated into English with some loss or change in meaning, or whose use in English differs significantly from Anandamurti's use of the word, such as the four *varńas* that are introduced in Chapter Five.

Regarding the structure, *Ananda Sutram* is divided into five chapters that Anandamurti left unnamed. Each chapter has its own distinct focus, however, ranging from the cycle of creation in Chapter One to Anandamurti's social philosophy in Chapter Five, and I have tried to make that focus clear in the short introduction to each chapter, rather than adding chapter titles that were not in the original. As with most sutra literature, the text may appear to have a certain disjunctive quality that is particular to the form. While there is an obvious logical sequence between certain sutras, especially those grouped around a single theme, others may seem at first glance to be disconnected from the preceding or following sutra. There is, however, an underlying logic to the sequence of sutras in the various chapters that I hope will become clear to the reader as the text unfolds.

Chapter One

I regard consciousness as fundamental. I regard matter as a derivative of consciousness. We cannot get behind consciousness. Everything we talk about, everything that we postulate as existing, requires consciousness.[1]

— Max Planck

IN CHAPTER ONE OF *Ananda Sutram,* Anandamurti describes the *brahmacakra,* the "cycle of creation" or cosmological system. The chapter begins, as logic dictates, with the definition of the Supreme Being, Brahma.

शिवशक्त्यात्मकं ब्रह्म ॥ १ ॥

I.1 *shivashaktyátmakaṁ brahma*

shiva, consciousness; *shakti,* operative principle, power or force; *atmakam,* composed of; *brahma,* the great

"Brahma is composed of Shiva and Shakti."

It is an axiom of Tantra that the nature of the macrocosm is reflected in the microcosm. "What is here is there; what is not here is nowhere."[2] In other words, if we examine our individual nature, we can see in microcosmic form the macrocosmic processes at work. All our experience devolves into two distinct modes: consciousness and the dynamic manifestations of which consciousness is the quiescent witness—in short, our *awareness of existence.* We are aware of our sense of self, the motions of our mind, and the ever-changing play of the material universe, but our awareness itself is motionless and unchanging. These two facets of experience appear to be separate and distinct, and in terms of our experience of the world they are, but if we examine them more closely we find that they cannot be separated, any more than we can separate the two sides of a piece of paper. All that we witness, be it thought, emotion, or material object, exists within a field of cognition that the ancient Indian sages called *brahma*, the Great, so called because it encompasses all of existence. Without cognition or consciousness there is no experience and thus no mind or matter, for neither mind nor matter can be experienced apart from consciousness. And since neither can be experienced apart from consciousness, since both are therefore fully dependent on consciousness for their existence, they are and can only be an expression of consciousness, just as ocean waves, being dependent on the ocean for their existence, are an expression of the ocean. This is our individual experience, if we examine it closely, and our individual experience, our individual nature, is the mirror of the macrocosm. Thus Brahma is known as the "One without a second." It is best described, however, as being the composite of two principles, for this is how we experience reality—as consciousness and the objects of consciousness. This division of Brahma into two distinct principles can be looked at from a purely philosophical perspective as a conceptual device, but it is also an accurate reflection of incarnate experience, one that is necessitated by the mind's confinement within the bounds of duality. Hence the macrocosm, or Brahma, as we know it, consists of consciousness, *shiva*, and its inherent power of manifestation, *shakti*.

As Anandamurti highlights in his short commentary, consciousness is the ultimate substantiation of existence. The existence of the material universe is perceived in the mind, but without consciousness, the witnessing entity, those thought-waves would remain unsubstantiated. We are aware of our thoughts, be they perceptions of physicality or abstract rumination, and we are aware of them because we have within us the faculty of consciousness, the power of cognition, which is distinct from our thoughts and which provides the screen, so to speak, on which they appear. This distinction between consciousness and thought is a common source of confusion, especially among those who are unfamiliar with Indian philosophical and spiritual traditions. "I think, therefore I am," postulated René Descartes, the "father of modern philosophy," as he is sometimes referred to in the West, but awareness continues unabated even when all thought ceases, a fact that has been proven time and again in the laboratory of individual spiritual experience, and it is a testament to how endemic this confusion is in human thinking that even so influential a philosopher as Descartes was unable to differentiate between thought and consciousness.[3] The same fundamental failing underlies all materialist thinking. Materialists are convinced of the primacy of matter. They contend that matter exists independent of consciousness, and they try to convince us, in their grasping for speculative straws, that consciousness is a byproduct of matter. Apparently, they make this contention without realizing (or at least, without admitting) that all their statements, conclusions, and speculative logic are mere thoughts, rising and falling like waves within their minds, and that without the faculty of consciousness to witness those thoughts, they would not and could not exist. Even a cursory examination of human experience is enough to prove beyond the slightest shadow of a doubt that consciousness is the sole independent entity. Without consciousness, there is no awareness of thought, and without thought there is no perception or conception of matter. Take away matter and thought remains. Take away thought and consciousness remains. Take away consciousness, however, and nothing remains. Thus both matter and thought are fully dependent on consciousness and are hence transitory or ephemeral in nature. Not so consciousness, which, by its very independence and its unique position as the ultimate substantiation of existence, is eternal in nature. It is like a mirror that reflects our thoughts, just as the mind is like a mirror within a mirror in which we see reflected the varied perceptions of the material universe. Take away the original mirror and all reflections disappear.

This is a truth we all recognize on a subliminal level, even if we have not yet made the effort to turn our awareness within and decipher the inner hieroglyphics of the self. We say that we are conscious beings, and in truth we cannot even imagine existence without consciousness, but what does it actually mean when we say we are conscious beings? Many, perhaps most, people take it to mean that we are conscious because we have the capacity for thought and self-reflection. But a careful look inside will demonstrate to anyone who makes the effort, and who is able to develop sufficient clarity of mind, that we are conscious not because we think but because we are aware of our thoughts, even that most subtle of all thoughts, the "I am," the pure sense of existence. We know that we exist because there is something inside us that is aware of our existence. That something is consciousness, the atman or the soul. Every one of us, whether we recognize it or not, is aware of the truth that the ground of our being—and thus of all being, of being itself—is consciousness, and from this stems our sense of indivisibility from the soul, for we cannot be separated from consciousness. Nothing can be separated from consciousness, nor can consciousness be divided. It cannot be separated into my consciousness or your consciousness, though each of us connects to that singular ground of being through our individual minds. That Consciousness is Brahma, the soul and fabric of the universe, and while it is the motionless witness of existence, the substantiation of all that is, it also has the capacity to manifest itself in innumerable dynamic forms through its inherent power, or Shakti.

शक्तिः सा शिवस्य शक्तिः ॥ २ ॥

I.2 *shaktih sá shivasya shaktih*

shakti, force, power, energy, cosmic operative principle; *sá*, she, this; *shivasya*, of Shiva

"This Shakti is the power of Shiva."

Shakti, the power of Shiva, is the kinetic or immanent counterpart of Consciousness.[4] That is, Shiva is *skaktimán*, powerful. Think of a man lying motionless in profound slumber. He has the capacity or potential to awaken from his slumber and enter into a state of motion, a state in which he is capable of prodigious feats. That capacity for activity, that inherent power, is present but unexpressed in the sleeping man. It remains in a quiescent state until he awakens and begins to manifest his dormant potential. Similarly, the capacity for self-manifestation is inherent in Consciousness, and that innate dynamism, or Shakti, is what gives rise to existence as we know it. One of the most famous images in the Indian spiritual tradition is that of the great spiritual master Shiva ensconced in profound meditation. As long as Shiva remains absorbed in pure Consciousness, in a state of absolute inner tranquility, he remains motionless. But the moment he opens his eyes and begins to stir, he begins to express the infinite creative potential that had been hitherto unexpressed. Either way, it is the same Shiva, whether at rest or in motion.

Perhaps the most common analogy for "Consciousness" in Indian philosophical literature is that of an ocean, the ocean of Consciousness. In its quiescent state the ocean is motionless and undifferentiated. But the moment it begins to stir, that is, the moment waves arise in that infinite expanse, differentiation becomes apparent. One wave can be contrasted with another and they can thus be experienced as separate entities. But no matter how varied these waves, whether we call them mind or matter, they are nothing but the motion of the selfsame ocean and cannot exist apart from it. There remains only one entity, one ocean, whether it is quiescent or tossed by waves, and the inherent capacity of the ocean of Consciousness to go from a state of absolute motionlessness to a state of motion is its Shakti, its power of expression, the force of Consciousness by which that Supreme Intelligence conducts the infinitely varied activities that make up the cosmos, from the whirl of a spiral nebula in the depths of space to the photosynthetic glow of a green sulfur bacterium in the depths of the ocean, clinging to the stone walls of a hydrothermal vent. Thus, if we are to understand the nature of existence, we must examine this manifest power in its own right.

What is the primary function of Shakti? It is to transform the hitherto quiescent Shiva. Any transformation of Consciousness is, in effect, an act of bondage, the imposition of form on the formless, Consciousness in its pure state being unbound, the one independent, unchanging, eternal entity. Thus the role of Shakti is to bind Consciousness, and by doing so, to give birth to the creation. Hence Shakti is traditionally addressed as *sá* or "she" in Indian spiritual discourse, symbolic of its creative function. Another word for Shakti is *prakrti*, from the root *kr*, "to do," and the prefix *pra*, "forth" or "onward." "*Prakrti* is that whose nature is to cause or bring about an action."[5] Its closest English equivalent would be "procreator," or "procreatrix," with the English prefix *pro* similar in form and function to the Sanskrit prefix *pra*. Thus *prakrti*, the primal energy of creation, takes the material of Consciousness and fashions it into the manifest universe.

When it is seen as a separate principle, then the creative matrix, *prakrti*, must logically be a blind force. Just as electricity requires human consciousness in order to power our lights and appliances, *prakrti* cannot act in the absence of Consciousness. If Consciousness turns away from *prakrti*, so to speak, if Shiva closes his eyes in motionless meditation rather than witnessing his creation, then *prakrti* has no choice but to remain quiescent as well. *Prakrti* is thus a conjunctive agent rather than an absolute cause. In philosophical parlance, every object in this universe, be it material or psychic, has a material cause and an instrumental cause, as well as a conjunctive agency that links the two. The material cause is the substance from which the object is formed; the instrumental or efficient cause is the agent that has made the object or allowed for it to be made; and the conjunctive agency is the power by which the instrumental cause shapes that substance into its present form. This is commonly explained through the analogy of a potter fashioning a pot from a lump of clay. The clay is the material cause, being the substance from which the pot is formed; the potter is the instrumental cause, being the maker of the pot; and the potter's artisanal skill and effort, as channeled through the potter's wheel, is the conjunctive agency, the power by which the clay becomes a pot. Consciousness, being the only independent entity and thus the ground and substance of being, is perforce the material cause. Being the one immutable, eternal entity, it therefore follows that it is from Consciousness that the variegated forms of this manifest universe have arisen. And since Consciousness is the substantiation of all that exists, the source of mind and of all subsequent agency, it is necessarily the instrumental cause as well, for without its witness-ship nothing can take place. In other words, it is Consciousness that transforms itself into the myriad forms of the manifest universe, just as the sleeping man awakens and transforms his hitherto inert body into the forms and waves of motion. And the power by which Consciousness transforms itself into these myriad forms is its Shakti or *prakrti* or maya, as it is variously known in the yogic lexicon.

This Shakti or *prakrti* is further characterized as consisting of three distinct principles or modalities, known as *guñas* in Sanskrit. The word *guña* literally means "binding thread" or "binding rope." It is also used in the sense of "attribute" or "qualification." The binding action of the *guñas* is what gives rise to the myriad attributes of the expressed universe. Thus Shakti or *prakrti* is trivalent. Its function is to bind Consciousness, and that binding action manifests in three different modalities, all of which are present though not necessarily active at the same time. *Sattvaguña*, the first of these three principles, is commonly translated as the "sentient" force, symbolized by the color white, *rajoguña* as the "mutative" force, symbolized by the color red, and *tamoguña* as the "static" force, symbolized by the color black. Together they give rise to the experience of duality. *Sattvaguña* represents one pole, *tamoguña* the other, and *rajoguña* the intermediary struggle or transition between these two poles.[6] We live in a world of duality—night and day, dark and light, sound and silence—because everything in this manifest universe is a product of the interplay between the three *guñas*. In order for duality to manifest, there must be three principles, the two poles and the constant mutation or movement in one direction or the other, since nothing in this universe is static, and in fact we cannot conceive of the universe otherwise. We think of existence in terms of light and dark, hard and soft, ignorance and wisdom, and the infinite shades of transition between these opposing poles. We find the same three principles at work in the rise and fall of temporal manifestation. Everything is born, maintains its existential flow for some period of time, and then dies or disappears, whether it is a solid object that lasts for millennia or a fleeting thought that vanishes before it is even noticed. When *rajoguña* prevails in the struggle for existence we see the radiance of *sattvaguña*, but when *rajoguña* wains and *tamoguña* begins to dominate, activity gives way to staticity and eventually to death.[7] Thus all expression in this universe, be it material or psychic, every wave in the vast ocean of existence, is Consciousness under the varying degrees of the influence of *prakrti*, just as the waves and floating slabs of ice are varied manifestations of a single ocean. Or to put it in the simplest terms, everything we experience is *prakrti* as witnessed by *puruśa*, consciousness.

This division of the Macrocosm into *puruśa* and *prakrti*, Shiva and Shakti, has been an indelible feature of the Indian philosophical landscape for thousands of years, although the understanding of these concepts has evolved over the millennia. In the old Vedic texts, the word *puruśa* was used to refer to the male supreme being, and *prakrti* was used to refer to nature, a meaning the word has retained until this day in the Indian languages descended from Sanskrit. We can imagine the sages of antiquity contemplating the workings of nature and recognizing the interplay of the three *guńas*, gradually refining their understanding of the relationship of consciousness to nature and natural law. By the time of the Mahabharata, some 3500 years ago,[8] as highlighted in the Bhagavad Gita, which forms one section within one of the eighteen books that comprise the great Indian epic, the fundamental roles of *puruśa, prakrti,* and the three *guńas* in the creation were well established in Indian spiritual discourse, and these terms have come down to us today with essentially the same meaning. *Prakrti* by then was understood not to be nature per se but the original cause or principle of which nature as we know it is the effect. Thus Anandamurti refers to nature and its laws as *prakrti's* "style of operation."

Not long before the Mahabharata, Maharishi Kapil formulated the world's first formal philosophy, Samkhya.[9] The word *samkhyá* means "enumeration" or "number," and its use is indicative of Kapil's profound intuitive realization that there was an underlying mathematical order to the creation, a realization that Pythagoras came to independently nearly a millennium later in Greece and which now forms the basis of modern physics' understanding of the universe.[10] Kapil enumerated the creation into twenty-four successive *tattvas* or factors, beginning with *prakrti* and proceeding stepwise through the creation of mind and matter, and his cosmology was by and large adopted by subsequent schools of Indian philosophy along with Samkhya's fundamental terminology and tenets.[11] While Anandamurti also adopts the basic terminology of Samkhya, he has refined and in some cases redefined those concepts to a degree that markedly differentiates his teachings from other systems of Indian philosophy. Samkhya considered *prakrti* to be separate from *puruśa* and conceptualized them as equally independent and eternal forces that combine to give rise to the universe. In addition it recognized one eternal *prakrti* and an infinite number of separate eternal *puruśas*. It is here, right at the beginning, so to speak, that Anandamurti's philosophy differentiates itself from Kapil's, in effect entering into dialogue with this most ancient of all philosophical systems and with subsequent schools of Indian philosophy as well, since each of these schools has interpreted these fundamental philosophical concepts according to their own lights. Samkhya is rightfully considered to be a dualist philosophy, as is the closely allied Patanjali Yoga Darshan, so closely allied that it is also referred to as Seshvara Samkhya, theistic Samkhya. This dualistic conception of the creation is perfectly understandable, since *prakrti*, as we experience it, appears to have dominion over *puruśa*, depriving Consciousness of its freedom—the all-powerful goddess dancing on the inert body of Shiva, as is often depicted in the Indian artistic tradition—but nothing can happen without the presence of Consciousness.[12] Samkhya considered Consciousness to be a catalytic agent but did not recognize its role as the instrumental cause. It attributed both the instrumental and material causes to *prakrti*.[13] Shiva, however, does not cease to be sovereign when he stirs from his motionless trance. The dormant, unmanifest Shakti is sheltered within Shiva when Consciousness remains in its pure transcendental state, and even when *prakrti* appears to have Consciousness under dominion it remains a subordinate, dependent entity. This is borne out by the fact that no state of manifestation is permanent. Even the seemingly indestructible atoms that make up matter have a beginning and thus an end to their material form, and what is impermanent cannot be independent. This impermanence of all form is of supreme importance in the human quest for spiritual enlightenment, and it is the proof of *prakrti's* dependence on *puruśa*.

In the process of creation, as Anandamurti describes it, elaborating a chain of causation that was hitherto absent in Indian philosophy and which will be explored in subsequent sutras, *prakrti* gradually binds Consciousness, imprisoning it within the walls of form and thereby robbing it of its inherent freedom. Consciousness in its pure, unaltered state has no attributes, no qualities. It is unbound and ever-free. It is not subject to the *guńas* and is thus beyond duality. In the language of philosophy, this unbound state is called *nirguńa*, "without *guńa*." But once *prakrti* becomes active, *puruśa* or Shiva begins to take on attributes under its influence and Brahma becomes *saguńa*, "with *guńa*," beginning with the subtlest of all attributes, the sense of existence, the first evolute of *prakrti* in Kapil's list. This binding process continues to grow in intensity until Consciousness reaches a state of maximum bondage, what we experience as the world of solid matter, a state in which there appears, at least upon cursory examination, to be no expression whatsoever of Consciousness. At this point, *puruśa* reverses course and starts curtailing the freedom of *prakrti* to bind it, until Consciousness finally reverts to its characteristic unbound state, the state of perfect freedom. Thus there are two phases in the march of *prakrti*: the extroversive phase, in which Consciousness is gradually bound tighter and tighter by the noose of *prakrti*; and the introversive phase, in which the dominion of *prakrti* is gradually withdrawn, until Consciousness ultimately becomes free from its influence. Anandamurti calls the extroversive phase *saińcara*, a Sanskrit word that means "outgoing movement," and the introversive phase *pratisaińcara*, which means "incoming" or "returning movement." It is in these two phases that we see the effect that proceeds from the marriage of *puruśa* and *prakrti*.

तयो: सिद्धि: सञ्चरे प्रतिसञ्चरे च ॥ ३ ॥

I.3 *tayoh siddhih saińcare pratisaińcare ca*

tayoh, of the two; *siddhi*, fulfillment, realization, substantiation, proof; *saińcare*, in the extroversive or centrifugal movement; *pratisaiṇcare*, in the introversive or centripetal movement; *ca*, and

"Their fulfillment is found in *saiṇcara* and *pratisaiṇcara*."

The Greeks considered the universe to be perfectly harmonious, a material expression of an underlying perfect order, and thus they called it *cosmos*, which means "order," for the opposite of *cosmos* — *chaos* — was nowhere to be found. Atheists are wont to tell their theistic counterparts, "If God exists then show me," a variation on the ever-popular, "Prove it." The simple answer to such a demand is, "Take a good look around you." The greater part of the creation is too subtle to be perceived by the senses, even with the help of the most powerful instrument, but in every instance it leaves traces that tell of its existence. We cannot see an electron, even with the help of the most powerful electron microscope, but we can see the traces it leaves, proof of its passage.[14] A tracker in the forest knows that an animal has passed because of the tracks it leaves. An electron does the same. It leaves minute tracks by which its properties and activity can be analyzed. Similarly, in 2013 the existence of the Higgs boson was "confirmed" by analyzing mountains of data generated by the Large Hadron Collider on the Swiss-French border, when accelerated particles were made to collide violently under controlled conditions. That data revealed traces of the Higgs boson. *Puruśa* and *prakrti*, Consciousness and its creative force, are too subtle to be perceived, but their footprints are everywhere we turn, and we don't need a particle collider to generate the necessary data. A simple look at the universe is enough.

Saiṇcara is the inanimate or macrocosmic phase of creation, the progressive formation of the material universe — from space and energy to the densest elements in the periodic table. Human beings have been looking at the universe for as long as we have been here, and we have expended untold effort in trying to figure out how it works. To discover its laws so that we could take advantage of those laws. Ever since our cave- and plain-dwelling ancestors discovered that certain rocks chipped in certain ways and were thus ideal for making stone tools; that friction generated heat, which could then ignite dry wood and brush; that round objects rolled and things you dropped, drop. Laws. An underlying order that governs the functioning of the world around us. Wherever we look we are faced with a vast intricate order. We often take this for granted but we shouldn't—not if we are going to dip our toes in the waters of philosophy. Everything in the physical universe displays order and at a level of complexity that is absolutely astounding to an inquiring human mind, so much so that we have been studying this order for millennia and are still only scratching the surface of that understanding.

Take a simple rock or a piece of metal, the densest objects we commonly encounter. Delve down into what appears to our senses to be a piece of inert matter and we find that there is nothing inert about it. The atoms and molecules that make up that structure are each a universe of motion in and of themselves, a universe that follows certain laws, whether it be the orbit, charge, and spin of the electrons, the forces that hold the nuclei together, or the way atoms combine to form molecules, which then combine to form particular substances or structures. Both metals and nonmetals interact with their environment in certain characteristic ways. They undergo contraction and expansion in response to certain stimuli and react in unique ways in the presence of other elements or substances. The great physicist Jagadish Chandra Bose famously demonstrated this in his laboratory in the first decade of the twentieth century:

> "To my amazement, I found boundary lines vanishing, and points of contact emerging, between the realms of the living and the non-living. Inorganic matter was perceived as anything but inert; it was a thrill under the action of multitudinous forces.
>
> "A universal reaction seemed to bring metal, plant and animal under a common law. They all exhibited essentially the same phenomena of fatigue and depression, with possibilities of recovery and of exaltation, as well as the permanent irresponsiveness associated with death."[15]

Bose showed that the same reactions that occur in living tissue were also present in the various metals with which he began his experiments, markedly so in more sensitive metals like tin, and less so but still clearly visible in less sensitive metals like platinum. The response of the living and nonliving to various stimuli was so strikingly similar that when Sir Michael Foster, a veteran Cambridge physiologist on a visit to Bose's lab, picked up one of his records of electrical response and Bose asked him what he thought it was, he said, "a curve of muscle response, of course."[16] When Bose told him it was the response curve of tin, he jumped out of his seat in amazement. He then urged Bose to communicate his discovery to the Royal Society, of which Foster was secretary at the time. That paved the way for Bose to present his findings in May, 1901, and these would form the basis the following year of his book *Response in the Living and Nonliving*.

In his peroration, Bose had this to say:

> I have shown you this evening autographic records of the history of stress and strain in the living and non-living. How similar are the writings! So similar indeed that you cannot tell one apart from the other. We have watched the responsive pulse wax and wane in the one as in the other. We have seen response sinking under fatigue, becoming exalted under stimulants, and being killed by poisons, in the non-living as in the living.
>
> Amongst such phenomena, how can we draw a line of demarcation, and say, here the physical ends, and there the physiological begins? Such absolute barriers do not exist.
>
> Do not these records tell us of some property of matter common and persistent? Do they not show us that the responsive processes, seen in life, have been fore-shadowed in non-life? That the physiological is related to the physico-chemical? That there is no abrupt break, but a uniform and continuous march of law?[17]

We commonly consider such reactions to be purely mechanical, but that does not explain their existence, and explain it we must. As Bose alludes to in his peroration, what we call mechanical is in fact an expression of intelligence at its most rudimentary level, which in turn betrays the presence of consciousness in its most veiled form, for as we have seen earlier, intelligence cannot exist independent of consciousness. If there were no latent consciousness whatsoever in these elements, they would not and could not react to their environment. They would be truly inert, something that is unthinkable in the manifest universe. Similarly, everything in nature relates to its environment in certain specific ways that fall into definable patterns. When a paired photon reverses its charge, its partner instantaneously undergoes a charge reversal, even if the two photons are kilometers apart and moving in the opposite direction at a velocity approaching the speed of light. Everything exists in relationship to everything else, and all movement in relationship is an expression of order and thus an expression of consciousness, from the simplest electron in orbit around its nucleus to the planets in orbit around their suns with their respective gravitational pulls.

Study any branch of physical science and you will see the same phenomenon at work. The universe is ordered down to the very last detail, from the movements of celestial bodies to the behavior of subatomic particles. Logic dictates that something cannot come from nothing—only nothing can come from nothing. Something has to come from something. The effect is potential in the cause and the cause is traceable from the effect. The potential for a specific manifestation has to be present in order for that specific something to manifest. Immense energy is released when an atom is split because that energy is already present in the atom. Order is the footprint or trace of intelligence. A lesser manifestation of intelligence implies that there is a greater intelligence from which it is born, although it would be patently naive to consider the unimaginable complexity of the cosmos as a lesser manifestation of intelligence, seeing as it is far beyond the grasp of even the most brilliant human mind. Intelligence is inherent in the physical universe, manifesting as an immense fabric of intricate order, but the better word is "consciousness," for consciousness is the source of intelligence, as we can see by examining our own small portion of the cosmos. The intelligence of human thought is only possible because our minds are illuminated by the light of awareness, because they function within a field of cognition. Order is an expression of intelligence, which is itself an expression of consciousness, the cause buried in the effect but ultimately discernible to the inquiring mind.

If we follow the progression of the Big Bang, modern science's closest theoretical approximation to *saiṇcara*, we find the successive appearance of energy, space, gas, light, and celestial bodies. Eventually portions of these celestial bodies coalesce into planets, which then cool enough for liquid and solid matter to make their appearance. The vast, ordered complexity of the cosmos from the Big Bang onward, when considered in its entirety, from the subatomic to cosmic levels, can only come from an underlying intelligence far beyond human imagining, an intelligence that is cosmic in character, and that intelligence in turn can only come from Consciousness, for without Consciousness there can be no intelligence. Thus, by tracing our way back from the effect to the cause in this outgoing movement, we find the proof of *puruśa* in a world that prima facie consists only of *prakrti*, for as modern physics has demonstrated, all matter can be reduced to energy in certain characteristic patterns that may or may not come within the scope of perception. And energy, as we know, is a blind force. It cannot express order without some intelligence to guide it, and at the macrocosmic level that macrocosmic intelligence is visible everywhere we turn, clear evidence of the inseparable conjunction between *puruśa* and *prakrti*.

The counterpart of *saiṇcara* is *pratisaiṇcara*, the animate or microcosmic phase of creation, the world of living beings—or more accurately, the world of individual minds. From the most primitive manifestation of life to the most advanced, we see the progressive manifestation of consciousness. Or rather, the progressive revelation of consciousness, its liberation from the bondage of *prakrti*. In primitive unicellular organisms, the same intricately ordered but formerly inanimate substances are transformed into the building blocks of life. Hydrogen, oxygen, carbon, sulfur, water, salt—the same substances floating in a constantly changing soup, but now they manifest life, and life manifests as a conscious control of matter. The simplest unicellular organism performs hundreds if not thousands of functions, intelligent functions: absorbing nutrients and excreting wastes, rejecting harmful matter, cell replication, autonomous movement, and on and on and on. Indeed, at the molecular level, the simplest living cell performs hundreds of thousands of functions, each with a specific purpose that is perfectly integrated into the overall needs of that cell. If we take a close look at the production of proteins and amino acids in a living cell, it resembles nothing more than an intricately orchestrated workshop, an assembly line of extraordinary precision. We attribute these behaviors and cellular processes to instinct, but what is instinct but a manifestation of mind at its most primitive level—or rather, at its least conscious level. As we gradually move through more and more complex life-forms, we see an increasingly conscious manifestation of mind—the development of emotions, learning, self-serving behavior—until we get to the human being and the appearance not only of subtle abstract thought, but more importantly, of self-awareness, the capacity to know that one is a conscious being and thus to endeavor to understand the nature of consciousness, as the reader is doing at this very moment. This endeavor gradually takes the human being beyond the intellect and into the realm of intuition, the final gateway to Consciousness, and eventually to the enlightened state.

Anandamurti begins his short commentary to this sutra by stating that "the existence of any entity is realized through its actions, its thoughts, or its witness-ship, with witness-ship belonging to *puruśa* and the other two substantiating factors primarily to *prakrti*; and thus *prakrti* is substantiated as the origin of the flow of thought and action when it becomes one with objectivity."[18] All manifestation can be reduced to these three arenas: the vibrations or motion of energy and matter, *saiṇcara*; the psychic world of individual minds, *pratisaiṇcara*; and the witnessing consciousness that beholds them both. And thus it is through *saiṇcara* and *pratisaiṇcara* that the existence of Brahma, the play of *puruśa* and *prakrti*, is realized, for it is in *saiṇcara* and *pratisaiṇcara* that the nature of Brahma is on full display.

The same *prakrti* that dominates the material universe also dominates the processes of life, but as life evolves, we see *prakrti's* hold upon Consciousness gradually lessening until it becomes the lightest of veils in the most highly evolved human beings. Consciousness becomes matter in the inanimate world, becoming veiled from view but retaining its ordered nature; and in the animate world, mind evolves out of matter as a vehicle for Consciousness to gradually free itself from the bondage of *prakrti*, until it regains its characteristic unbound state. This is the observable footprint, the ubiquitous manifestation of the inseparable interplay between *puruśa* and *prakrti*, between Consciousness and its creative force.

परमशिवः पुरुषोत्तमो विश्वस्य केन्द्रम् ॥ ४ ॥

I.4 *paramashivah puruśottamo vishvasya kendram*

parama, supreme; *shivah,* consciousness; *puruśa,* consciousness; *uttamah,* highest; *vishvasya,* of the universe; *kendram,* center

"The Supreme Consciousness, *puruśottama*, is the nucleus of the universe."

As we have seen, everything in this universe is an expression of an implicit order, from the subatomic systems that comprise matter, following the inexorable laws that govern their existence, to the whirl of planets holding fast to their orbits in the depths of space. Everywhere we turn we see a vast web of intricate, interrelated systems, and even where we fail to perceive the presence of structure or system and label it as chaos, there is an underlying order to that apparent chaos that we fail to grasp with our intellect. It is a characteristic of the ordered nature of the universe that everything belongs to certain systems and is in turn composed of other systems. The existence of a system presupposes a center or nucleus, whether perceptible or imperceptible. Due to the intelligent provenance of the creation and its subjection to the law of duality arising from the presence of the three *guńas*, we are unable to conceive of anything that goes beyond the bounds of structure, and we are unable to conceive of any structure or system that does not have a center. Indeed, in the absence of a center a structure cannot maintain its existence. "Things fall apart; the center cannot hold, mere anarchy is loosed upon the world," William Butler Yeats famously wrote in the aftermath of the First World War. But even then, the various components of a disintegrating structure become integral parts of other structures. The atoms that make up a decaying body are absorbed into other bodies, the human being who loses his family is absorbed into other social circles, and even death does not put an end to the bonds of relationship, as we shall see in Chapter Three.

This is just as true in the psychic world as it is in the world of matter. Social relations have structure, human thoughts and emotions follow ordered patterns, as chaotic as they may seem at times, and even the most experimental novel or music or visual art betrays an underlying order, despite the artist's best efforts to the contrary and regardless of whether or not we are capable of comprehending it. The center of a story, for example, is its premise, whether implicit or explicit, and the various elements of the story are inevitably connected in some visible or invisible way to that premise. In other words, they revolve around the nucleus of the story in much the same way that the Earth revolves around the Sun due to the Sun's gravitational pull.

All these different systems are caught up in the eternal dance of relationship, and there is one supreme system to which they all belong, the cosmological system, which Anandamurti calls the *brahmacakra*, the ever-revolving wheel of *saiṇcara* and *pratisaiṇcara*, involution and evolution, the cosmic systole and diastole, the outgoing and ingoing breath of the universe. And what holds it all together, the center of this vast cosmological order, is the witnessing Consciousness from which the universe has sprung. Consciousness is the only fixed entity in creation, the only motionless entity. It is the one entity that performs no action, that undergoes no change, and thus it is by definition the center or nucleus of everything that moves, which is all of existence. The center of any rotary system is by definition a fixed or stationary point, and in this universe of *saiṇcara* and *pratisaiṇcara* the only stationary existence is Consciousness. The physical universe, as scientists have long known, does not have a physical center. But it does have an ideational center. On the individual level the center of the physical universe is the observer, the individual witnessing consciousness, or *jiivátmá*. On the macrocosmic level, the witnessing Consciousness is known as *paramashiva* or *puruśottama*, Supreme Consciousness, but Consciousness is one and indivisible, and these are only apparent distinctions, labels given to Consciousness that change as our vantage point changes.

One of the analogies Anandamurti uses to describe this nuclear Consciousness is the atomic system. Another is our planetary system. Just as electrons revolve around the nucleus of the atom and planets around the Sun, so does each and every manifestation of the universe, whether animate or inanimate, revolve around the nuclear Consciousness. Some of these manifestations are gradually moving away from the nucleus, without ever escaping its gravitational pull. This is the phase of *saiṇcara*, during which Consciousness is gradually metamorphosed into increasingly dense, inanimate forms. Others are gradually moving toward the nucleus, like an asteroid caught in the gravitational pull of a huge planetary body, decreasing its radius with every revolution. This is the phase of *pratisaiṇcara*, where the individual mind gradually proceeds toward Consciousness as it passes through more and more developed life-forms.

Perhaps the most popular analogy for this in Indian literature is that of Krishna and the *gopis*, the female cowherds of Vrindavan. At night the *gopis* would congregate by the banks of the river Yamuna to dance to the music of Krishna's flute. They would dance in a circle around their beloved Gopala, and when the night came to a close, each would be convinced that they had been dancing alone with their Krishna all night long in the eternal dance of love. In the same way, each and every entity of this universe, whether animate or inanimate, is dancing around the cosmic nucleus, drawn by the power of the cosmic flute. Attraction is the law of the universe, the force of gravity being one material expression of that law, as are the other three fundamental forces of modern physics. The electrons and planets remain in their orbits due to the power of cosmic attraction, and so does every animate and inanimate being, from the tiniest speck of cosmic dust to the most exalted sage absorbed in the trance of divine meditation. All revolve around the one universal center, even as they take part in other, minor systems, and in the end they all merge back into Consciousness, bringing the cosmic cycle full circle.

प्रवृत्तिमुखी सञ्चरो गुणधारायाम् ॥ ५ ॥

I.5 *pravrttimukhii saiṇcaro guṅadháráyám*

pravrtti, inclination or tendency for manifestation, desire; *mukhii*, toward; *saiṇcara*, extroversive or centrifugal movement; *guṅa*, binding principle; *dháráyám*, in the flow

"*Saiṇcara* is the extroversive movement within the flow of the *guṅas*."

In its pure state, the nuclear Consciousness at the center of the cosmological order is unbound and immutable, a sea of perfect tranquility. But once the creative potential of *prakrti* becomes active, the cycle of transformation that we experience as the creation begins to unfold. This is not to imply, however, that creation has a beginning or an end. Just as the division of Brahma into *puruśa* and *prakrti* is a mental construct that allows us to better comprehend a singular entity that is ultimately beyond comprehension, the idea that the creation has a beginning is a device that allows the mind to better comprehend its transcendental nature. Time is a function of the microcosmic mind. More specifically, it is the mental measurement of events, the mind's mapping of action.[19] Consciousness is beyond the mind and thus beyond the reach of time, but we have no recourse other than to talk of a beginning when trying to conceptualize an infinite, timeless reality, since the mind is incapable of grasping either infinity or timelessness. Consciousness is eternal and hence the creation is also eternal, a continuous ebb and flow from the nuclear Consciousness in which *puruśa* remains ever-free, even while apparently undergoing bondage. Consciousness is both bound and unbound at the same time, both temporal and atemporal—being infinite it cannot be limited to one or the other—but for the sake of understanding, we must allow our mind to impose a starting point to the creation, while at the same time recognizing that this starting point is atemporal.

This point of origin is known as the *kámabiija* in Sanskrit, the seed of desire. It is from the *kámabiija* that the creation blossoms forth, impelled by Consciousness's inherent desire for self-expression, its *icchāshakti*, the activating alchemy of *prakrti* that wakes *puruśa* from its metaphorical slumber—the will and power of Consciousness being one and the same. Like the sleeping man in sutra I.2, whose potential for action is awakened from its dormancy when his sense of self-awareness returns, Consciousness begins to stir. Because the quiescent *puruśa* is motionless and unchanging, this incipient movement is necessarily extroversive in character, a movement toward manifestation, as denoted by the word *pravrtti*. *Vrtti*, an important word in the yogic lexicon, means "occupation," "tendency," or "mental modification," and the suffix *pra* carries the sense of "onward." The occupation of the mind is thinking, and thought is thus a modification of Consciousness, the original substance. Hence *pravrtti* here refers to the inclination or urge of *puruśa* to manifest itself through mental modification, and that progressive movement is centrifugal or extroversive in nature, leading away from the quiescent state of the nuclear Consciousness and toward greater and greater expression. It is thus *pravrttimukhii*.

This outward movement that propels Consciousness toward ever-increasing self-expression is effected by the three binding principles of *prakrti*, beginning with *sattvaguńa*, the sentient force and the strongest of the three *guńas*. *Sattvaguńa* imposes on Consciousness the sense of self-awareness, the knowledge of existence, known as *mahat* or *mahattattva* in Sanskrit. Consciousness in its unqualified, unbound state is not aware of itself. It is pure awareness, nothing more. The sense of existence is a quality, a mental modification. In order for Consciousness to be self-aware, it must have an object. It must become *aware of itself;* that is, the sense of existence becomes its object. It has gained the *knowledge* of *existence*, the knowledge of "I." Remove the "I" and Consciousness reverts to its unalloyed, objectless state, beyond all qualities, all modification, completely unconditioned. While this is impossible for the mind to fully comprehend, it is something we can intuit through deep introspection. We know that we exist. How do we know that we exist? Because there is something within us, a cognitive faculty, that is aware of our existence. That sense of existence is an object for which our consciousness is the subject, the ultimate and supreme subject. Remove the sense of I, the feeling of existence, and that awareness remains, but for lack of an object it is no longer aware of anything. It is, as it were, lying in tranquil blessedness, motionless and unfathomable.[20] But the "moment" *prakrti* begins to exert her influence over *puruśa*, Consciousness undergoes a subtle metamorphosis. It becomes self-aware and is thus no longer the pure objectless Consciousness. It is now the witness of its own existence. In this sense, Consciousness has "awakened," a poetic trope that can serve to enliven our understanding.

The three *guńas* of *prakrti* exist in an endless flow of mutual transformation that will be explored in detail in Chapter Four. In this process of transformation the power of *sattvaguńa* gradually wanes and *rajoguńa*, the second of the three *guńas*, starts to exert itself. *Rajoguńa* further qualifies *mahat*, and due to its influence the sense of doership or authorship arises, which is known as *aham* or *ahamtattva* in Sanskrit. The "I" of "I exist" now imbibes the potential for action. *Aham* is the singular first-person pronoun in Sanskrit, the equivalent of the Latin *ego*. *Aham gachhami*; "I go." The feeling of existence on its own, the pure "I am," is not capable of action. In order for it to act, the sense of authorship must be present, and this implies a further qualification of Consciousness. Not merely "I" but "I do."

Anandamurti makes the point that these first two stages are purely theoretical. Due to the presence of *aham*, Consciousness becomes capable of action, but no action can be carried out without an object. In order to think, one must have a thought. In the absence of thought, the capacity for thought is purely theoretical or potential. But in the flow of the *guńas* the dominance of *rajoguńa* gradually wanes and *tamoguńa*, the static principle, begins to assert itself. *Tamoguńa* is responsible for the objectivation or demarcation of Consciousness. When Consciousness takes on form it is called *citta*, the objectivated portion of the mind, whereas *aham* and *mahat* are *citta's* subjective counterparts. *Citta* literally means "mind-stuff," the nontangible, nonmaterial substance we call "mind." Without *citta* there are no thoughts, no mental content, merely the potential for thought. But with the formation of the cosmic *citta* due to the influence of *tamoguńa*, the qualification of Consciousness is no longer theoretical. The cosmic "I"—or Cosmic Mind, as it is often referred to in

Tantra and yoga—is now fully functional. Under the influence of *tamoguńa*, the thought waves of the Cosmic Mind gradually take shape in the ocean of Consciousness, leading to the formation of the material universe, a process that begins with the appearance of three-dimensional space and ends with the formation of solid matter, a process we will examine in detail in Chapter Two. This is *saiṋcara*, the inanimate phase of creation, the gradually increasing crudification or densification of the thought waves of the Macrocosmic Mind under the increasing influence of *prakrti*, resulting in the formation of the manifest universe. It is the centrifugal or analytic phase of creation in which the One becomes the many. This power of *prakrti* to bring *puruśa* under its dominion is known as *avidyámáyá*. *Avidyá* means "ignorance," literally, "not-knowledge." In its centrifugal action, *prakrti* is the force that serves to veil Consciousness by giving it form, thus creating ignorance of the true nature of reality. It has two aspects, its veiling action and its centrifugal movement, known as *ávarańii shakti* and *vikśepa shakti* in Indian philosophy.[21]

These three functional layers of mind, *mahat*, *aham*, and *citta*, the metamorphosed forms of Consciousness, also comprise our individual or microcosmic minds, which in turn allows us to better understand the nature of the Macrocosm. The same "I" that gives rise to our sense of existence is capable of action, and that same "I" takes the form of the content of our minds, the different thought waves generated and witnessed by the ego or thinker. It is for this reason that human language has three fundamental forms of speech: subject, verb, and object, corresponding to *mahat*, *aham*, and *citta*. This is true at the microcosmic level and it is equally true at the macrocosmic level. Just as our individual consciousness, or atman, is the witnessing counterpart of the tripartite functioning of our minds—"I see an elephant; I feel happy; I want world peace"—at the macrocosmic level, Consciousness is the witness of the functioning of the Macrocosmic Mind. But while Consciousness is one and indivisible, there are distinct differences between the macrocosmic and microcosmic minds. While the microcosmic mind is unilateral and multipurposive—we can only think one thought at a time and we have many desires—the Macrocosmic Mind is multilateral and unipurposive. It generates an infinite variety of simultaneous thought waves but behind all its thought waves there is only one desire: the welfare of all created beings, which ultimately lies in the attainment of liberation from *prakrti* through the process of *pratisaiṇcara*. And while our individual thought waves have no material substance, the thought waves of the Cosmic Mind comprise the manifest universe and all the living beings that inhabit it.

A useful analogy for the *saiṇcara* phase of creation is that of a high-speed fan or a jet-engine turbine. As long as the fan or turbine is at rest, the blades are clearly visible. There is no motion to distort or veil its fundamental nature. But once the turbine begins to rotate, almost imperceptibly at first and then gradually faster and faster, its appearance begins to change, and when it reaches maximum velocity it appears once again to be motionless—but now the blades are no longer visible. What is visible is at best a shadow or ghost of its original self. But while the blades are now hidden to the naked eye, the full power of the fan is easily perceptible in the form of wind and sound. Similarly, Consciousness in its original state is motionless and without qualities. But once it begins to vibrate under the influence of its inherent Shakti or power, it undergoes an apparent change, first into mind, and eventually, as the rate of vibration increases, into matter, until the material universe is fully manifest with its innumerable qualities and the original substance is hidden from view. The world then appears as the shadow or ghost of Consciousness.

We look at this shadow-form, this ghostly apparition, with our physical eyes, and matter appears to be static, and on the surface it is, since it is under the bondage of *tamoguña*, the static force of *prakrti*, which gives matter the appearance of stasis. But if we look with our inner eyes, the eyes of understanding, an endeavor the efforts of modern science have made considerably easier, it becomes evident that the inanimate world is actually in a state of constant motion, constant vibration—the denser the substance, the more rapid the vibrations, that is, the shorter their frequency or wavelength.[22] What appears to be static only appears to be so because its vibrations have gone beyond the bounds of perception. Thus we discover that the essential nature of the manifest universe is motion or energy—Shakti. The word for "world" or "universe" in Sanskrit is *jagat*, which means "that which is in constant motion." That motion at the macrocosmic level is a product of a constant process of involution that has resulted in the gradual formation of planetary bodies through a continual process of solidification, a phenomenon that is going on right beneath our feet in the molten core of our planet. Even this very earth that shelters us is constantly changing, an inexorable part of the "great systole and diastole of growth and dissolution."[23] And yet, just as the turbine never ceases to be a turbine, just as its blades undergo no actual change, whether the turbine is at rest or in motion, Consciousness remains Consciousness, regardless of its apparent change of state.

To continue with our analogy of the motionless Shiva in a state of profound inner absorption, at a certain point his sense of self-awareness returns, followed by his ego-sense or sense of authorship, and as a consequence he begins to stir. He gets up from his meditation and prepares to begin his day, which reaches its zenith in the intense activity of his creative endeavors, where his innate power of self-expression is on full display. His consciousness, once perfectly objectless and quiescent, is now witness to the full sum of his energy or Shakti in action. But that now-intensely active Shiva, whose powers never cease to amaze us, will not stay active forever. At a certain point his thoughts begin to turn homeward, drawn by the inescapable allure and unfathomable peace of his inner abode, and eventually the charm of activity begins to lose its once-irresistible appeal.

निवृत्तिमुखी प्रतिसञ्चरो गुणावक्षयेण ॥ ६ ॥

I.6 *nivrttimukhii pratisaiṇcaro guṇávakśayeña*

nivrtti; repose, return, cessation, absence of desire; *mukhii*, toward; *pratisaiṇcara*, introversive or centripetal movement; *guña*, binding principle; *avakśayeña*, by the waning

"*Pratisaiṇcara* is the introversive movement due to the waning of the *guñas*."

The *saiñcara* phase of creation reaches its culmination with the formation of solid matter, the zenith point in the flow of *pravrtti*. The five sensible forms of matter—ethereal, aerial, luminous, liquid, and solid—are now fully expressed and the imposition of qualities on the formless *puruśa* can go no further. The imprisonment of Consciousness within the bonds of matter has attained its final form, and it is at this point that *puruśa* begins to withdraw *prakrti's* freedom, thus initiating the return journey back to the nuclear Consciousness, to its original unbound state, in the phase known as *pratisaiñcara*.

The word *nivrtti* means "repose," the cessation of all modification or manifestation. There comes a time when Shiva begins to wind up his labors and make preparations to return home, when the power to the turbine is switched off and it gradually starts slowing down on its way back to its original state of rest. Neither can remain in motion forever. Once Consciousness has reached a state of maximum qualification or maximum densification, it begins to free itself from the bondage of the *guñas*, gradually increasing its expression until it returns to the unqualified, unbound state of perfect repose. This is the fundamental cycle of creation without which the creation would not be complete, the ebb and flow between activity and quiescence that is mirrored in the diurnal movements of day and night and in the sleeping and waking cycle of living beings. But whereas the imprisoning of Consciousness plays itself out at the macrocosmic level, the liberation of Consciousness takes place at the microcosmic level, through the medium of living beings. From the womb of matter arises an endless parade of individual minds undertaking the journey of evolution, progressing through higher and higher lifeforms until they attain a human body and acquire the capacity to merge their minds into the objectless state. It is not a reverse or retrograde movement, which would imply the withdrawal of the cosmic thought waves, but a true cycle. At the macrocosmic level Consciousness is continually being transformed into matter, and at the microcosmic level matter is continually being transformed back into consciousness through the evolutionary medium of individual living beings with their microcosmic minds.

Pratisaiñcara is thus the centripetal or synthetic phase of creation in which the many proceed toward the One under the waning influence of the *guńas*. Here *prakrti* is known as *vidyámáyá*, the force that confers knowledge or *vidyá*, that is, the force that serves to reveal Consciousness, to reveal the true nature of reality. It also has two aspects, its revealing power and its centripetal movement, known as *samvit shakti* and *hládinii* or *rádhiká shakti* in Indian philosophy.[24] In the animate world, living beings arise not out of nothing but out of matter, which is a condensed form of Consciousness, and consequently undertake an evolutionary journey through the coordinated activities of body, vital energy, and mind that will eventually require them to shed their individual egos in order for the consciousness they shelter to achieve its ultimate unbound state. This formation of the individual ego-self and its ultimate dissolution is the mechanism by which Consciousness attains liberation from the bondage of *prakrti*. In effect, *prakrti* is being drawn back to *puruśa*. It exerted its power for a time, reveling in the magical play of creation, but eventually the attractive power of that supreme bearing draws it toward the state of *nivrtti*, the cessation of all its activity.

The Buddhist philosophers contend that the individual self or soul, the *jiivátmá* in Sanskrit, is an illusion. And in a certain sense this is true, since the individual self is not a permanent reality—it is a relative truth, a temporary phenomenon, a cage through which Consciousness looks out on the world. But it is also the mechanism through which Consciousness frees itself from bondage, and in the attainment of freedom, individuality is left behind. This is a difficult terminus for the individual ego to come to grips with, at least until the pull of the supreme state becomes so powerful that the sense of individuality begins to feel like the cage that it is, the final and eventually unbearable impediment to real freedom. The urge to do spiritual meditation is the natural outcome of the expansion of Consciousness, the natural expression of *puruśa's* urge to liberate itself from all that stands in the way of its freedom, and individuality is the last vestige of its bondage. Thus it is not the ego that provides the impulse to do spiritual meditation but Consciousness. It has imprisoned itself in its creation and in *pratisaiṋcara* it frees itself from that self-imposed bondage through the progressive manifestation and ultimate surrender of individuality.

This is the eternal dance of Consciousness: thinking itself into bondage and then freeing itself through an endless progression of individual living beings. It can be compared to a writer writing his character into a difficult predicament and then freeing her. Before the writer can free his character from prison, he first has to put her in prison, and from there the drama of her journey toward freedom keeps us on the edge of our seats. Nor is there any end to the number of possible twists and turns in the same overarching plot. The Divine Author goes on writing tale after tale of imprisonment and freedom throughout eternity, and it never gets old. Every living being's journey toward freedom is entirely unique and ever-new, and yet it never ceases to be the same journey.

दृक् पुरुषो दर्शनं शक्तिश्च ॥ ७ ॥

I.7 *drk puruśo darshanaṁ shaktish ca*

drk, seer, witness, cognition; *puruśa*, consciousness; *darshanaṁ*, act of seeing; *shakti*, force, power, energy; *ca*, and

"*Puruśa* is the witness and Shakti is the act of seeing."

Shakti, as mentioned earlier in this chapter, is often depicted dancing on the inert body of Shiva in Indian art and literature, an effective symbolization of the import of this sutra. Consciousness performs no action. Rather, it is the witness or substantiation of the activity of *prakrti*. Here the word *darshanaṁ*, "seeing," implies all afferent and efferent action, all movement of thought and matter, not only the act of perception. All manifestation is due to the influence of the *guṅas*, and thus the dance of the universe at all levels, whether mental or material, perceptible or imperceptible, is the dance of Shakti on the motionless body of Shiva. But while Shakti is the one and only actor in this universe, none of its actions can take place in the absence of Consciousness. Thus its entire dance—from the imposition of the sense of existence to the explosion of a supernova to the words of an enlightened sage—is dependent upon Consciousness.

In his explanation of this sutra, Anandamurti reprises the chain of substantiation in the briefest of terms as it proceeds through the various stages of mind: *citta*, *aham*, and *mahat*, the objectivated portion of the mind and the two subjective portions. This is an important cornerstone of his philosophy and is best understood by tracing the act of perception as we experience it, keeping in mind that our microcosmic minds are a mirror of the Macrocosmic Mind. It is in the act of perception—or rather, in the unclouded discernment of the act of perception, which becomes possible through deep introspection—that we can come to know the true nature of existence.

Whenever we perceive a material wave arising in the cosmic *citta*, our mind reproduces that wave as if it were a photographic plate. As I look out at the tree in front of my window, the light reflected from the tree strikes my eyes and forms a mirror image on the retina, which then raises a corresponding wave in the optic nerve, which in turn transmits that image to the visual cortex of my brain. But in order for me to see that image, my mind must attend to it. If my mind fails to do so—if it is asleep or unconscious or in a coma, for example—then I won't see the tree, even if my eyes are open and the image reaches the visual cortex. In order for the tree to register in my consciousness, my mind must also reflect that image, much as the retina did in the initial stage. Once that image has formed in my mind, I can then recreate it without the need of my eyes through the power of memory.

In Anandamurti's lexicon, it is the *citta* that receives and stores the image. The brain is the material vehicle that allows perception to take place, but if the *citta* does not perform its function there can be no perception—a sleeping or unconscious man will not hear somebody walking past him even though his ears are perfectly functional. In this stage, the *citta* is the substantiation of the auditory image. Even if the *citta* takes the form of the image, however, perception cannot occur if the *aham* does not attend to that image. A person can be awake but be so absorbed in a particular thought that they don't see or hear a person walking past. Under hypnosis, however, that perception may be recovered. In this case, the *citta* performed its function but its subjective counterpart, the *aham*, did not substantiate the perception—that is, until the person was placed under hypnosis. We become aware of a particular perception when the *aham* attends to it. Hence in this stage *aham* is the substantiation of *citta*. In the next stage, the mind becomes aware of its authorial function; it does not merely perceive but recognizes the act of perception. For this, the sense of existence, the pure "I am," must be present, and thus at this deeper level of subjectivity, *mahat* is the substantiation of *aham*. Going even deeper we find that there is something within us that knows that we exist. That is our consciousness, the true witness and the ultimate substantiation of existence.

Thus, through deep introspection, it is possible to discern the difference between consciousness and mind. This particular discriminative ability is called *átmánátma viveka* in Sanskrit, the ability to differentiate atman or consciousness from non-atman.[25] What commonly happens, however, is that we confuse *drk*, the witnessing entity, with *darshanam*, the faculty of sight. In the Mundaka Upanishad there is a well-known analogy that illustrates this point: two birds are perched in a tree; one eats the fruit of that tree while the other merely watches.[26] Here the bird that witnesses the action is indicative of Consciousness in its unaltered or supreme state, while the bird that eats the fruit represents the tendency of our individual consciousness, or *jiivátmá*, to identify with the object of attention—in other words, our failure to differentiate between *drk* and *darshanam*. This is the fundamental confusion that gives rise to our sense of separateness and has commonly been identified in Indian philosophy as the cause of suffering, as for example in the Yoga Sutras of Patanjali.[27] Consciousness, when it is not confused with *prakrti*, is known as *paramátmá*, Supreme Consciousness; it is known as *jiivátmá* when it is caught in *prakrti*, the *jiivátmá* being the reflection of *paramátmá* in the microcosmic mind. The moment our individual consciousness is freed from the modifications of mind, however, it recovers its identity with the infinite Supreme Consciousness.

With the development of *átmánátma viveka* comes the realization that the mind, in and of itself, is not conscious. It only appears to be so due to the conflation of consciousness and thought. In actuality, there is a distinct difference between consciousness and mind.[28] Our thoughts, perceptions, and emotions are waves that appear within the field of consciousness. They are no more conscious, in and of themselves, than are the words that appear on a computer screen. They are like the moon that appears to be self-luminous but which actually shines with a borrowed light, or an expanse of water that shines when it reflects the light of the sun or moon. Thus, in this sutra Anandamurti takes a closer look at the nature of consciousness so that we can learn to separate it from the act of thinking—from thought itself—an attainment that is supremely difficult to achieve, so much so that the central tenet of Western philosophy, "I think therefore I am, " is a testament to this confusion.

Let us now look at this confusion stage by stage. Suppose we examine a rock and become fascinated by what we see, to the point that our attention becomes completely absorbed by the striations on its surface, the varied flecks of color, its texture and hardness. For those few moments of total absorption we are not aware of ourself, or even of the act of seeing, but only of the qualities or characteristics of the rock. We have not ceased to be a conscious being—otherwise we could not be conscious of the rock—but during those moments of intense focus we are not aware of ourself as the subject. In other words, our consciousness is identified with the object of perception. The same can happen with our body. Our attention can become so absorbed in a painful or pleasurable sensation that for some moments it dominates our consciousness. To a greater or lesser extent, our mind—and hence our individual consciousness, which is the substantiation of our mind—is identified with that physical sensation. *Aham* is active—without *aham* there can be no perception as we know it—but in those moments our consciousness is largely identified with our *citta*. Inevitably, however, our *aham* reasserts itself and we become aware not just of the object or sensation but of our actions and reactions, and the thoughts that lie behind them, the ongoing narration of our experience that is forever playing in our mind. Our consciousness is no longer absorbed in *citta* but is once again largely identified with *aham*, which is how we generally spend the greater part of our day.

Suppose we are busy attending to our work, focusing on what we are doing. We may be engaged with the outside world—working in the garden, driving, teaching a class—or our work may be largely internal—studying for an exam, trying to come up with a solution to a problem, or simply indulging in a pleasant daytime fantasy. Either way, our consciousness tends to be absorbed in what we are doing or what we are thinking, that is, it tends to be identified with our sense of authorship, our ego-self or sense of individuality, our *aham*. One reason why movies are so enticing is their ability to take our consciousness for a ride in the marvelous theater of our imagination, a theater conjured into existence and presided over by *aham*. Whether we are working or socializing or playing in the fields of our imagination, our consciousness tends to spend the better part of its time absorbed in the activities of *aham*. Sometimes we are so absorbed in what we are doing that we forget who we are at that moment, as for example, when we get so caught up in a movie that we forget that we are enjoying a work of fiction. At other times our capacity for self-reflection kicks in. We come out of that imaginative trance and become aware that we are watching a movie. We may even take notice of how that onscreen experience is affecting our emotions, playing havoc with our pulse rate. This awareness of *aham* is made possible by the presence of *mahat*, the next level of substantiation, our underlying sense of existence that forms the backdrop for our sense of individuality, the screen on which it is reflected.

Now let us imagine that we are sitting on a deserted promontory looking out at the ocean as the sun begins to set over the horizon. It is so beautiful, so peaceful, that our mind grows quiet and we begin to feel the pure joy of being alive, the pure joy of existence. Perhaps we do some meditation and our mind quiets even further, and when we open our eyes we feel a sense of mute wonder bordering on rapture. We are no longer caught up in what we are doing or what we are thinking. We are aware of nothing more than the rapturous glow of being. For those few priceless moments, our consciousness is no longer absorbed in *aham* but in *mahat*, the pure sense of existence that lays behind and beyond the ego-self. It is such a blissful experience because in that moment our mind is temporarily freed from the heavier restraints of *prakrti*. When the mind is active or agitated, our consciousness naturally gets absorbed in the activity of *aham* and *citta*, but when the mind grows quiet it begins to experience the transcendental bliss of existence, the characteristic nature of *mahat,* and it is then that we arrive at the threshold of resolving the confusion between *drk* and *darshanam.*

What is it that allows us to be aware of our sense of existence? What is it that is aware not of *who* we are but simply *that* we are? Even the sense of "I am" is a modification of consciousness. What is the screen on which this mental modification appears, on which all mental activity appears? In order to answer that question we have to be able to separate the witness from the sense of I, *mahat* from the witnessing consciousness. And this is not truly possible until *aham* becomes relatively quiescent or inactive. As long as the mind is tossed by waves, our consciousness will be to a greater or lesser extent identified with the thinker of those waves and with the waves themselves. But as the waves settle and *mahat* is freed from its substantiation of the modifications of the mind, the sense of individuality is gradually transcended and the fundamental confusion between *drk* and *darshanam* disappears. The state of perfect quiescence of *aham* and *citta* is known as *savikalpa samadhi* in yoga and Tantra, the trance of determinate absorption in which we fully realize the true nature of reality.

गुणबन्धनेन गुणाभिव्यक्तिः ॥ ८ ॥

I.8 *guṅabandhanena guṅābhivyaktih*

guṅa, binding principle, quality, attribute; *bandhanena,* due to the bondage; *abhivyaktih,* expression

"Attributional expression unfolds due to the bondage of the *guṅas.*"

Consciousness in its pure state is without qualities, but when it comes under the influence of *prakrti* it undergoes modification and that modification is expressed through the imposition of qualities on the formless, unqualified *puruśa.* Thus the word *guṅa*—literally, "binding rope" or "binding principle"—also means "quality," since the bondage of *puruśa* equates to the imposition of qualities, the imposition of limitation on the limitless. True freedom in the cosmic sense is freedom from qualities.

In the *saiṇcara* phase of creation, that qualitative imposition begins as a result of the influence of *sattvaguña* and the consequent imposition of the sense of existence, the cosmic *mahattattva*, followed thereafter by *rajoguña* and the formation of the cosmic *ahaṁtattva*, and finally *tamoguña*, which gives rise to the cosmic *citta*. With the formation of the cosmic *citta*, every subsequent vibration in the cosmic body is subject to the influence of all three *guñas*. Even in the initial or theoretical stages of the formation of the cosmic *mahattattva* and *ahaṁtattva*, the unexpressed *guñas* are present in latent form, since *prakrti* is at all times the composite of the three *guñas*. But with the formation of the cosmic *citta*, all three *guñas* are fully active and remain active throughout the creation, varying only by degree. The dancing goddess may at times seem serene and buoyant in her movements, at other times frenetic, and at others lethargic, depending on whether her mood is dominated by *sattva*, *rajas*, or *tamas*, but her every gesture carries traces of the other two *guñas*.

The trivalent nature of *prakrti* can be compared to the three channels that combine to form the millions of colors that appear on a television or computer screen. We have all had the experience of sitting entranced in front of a high-definition screen, our attention captivated by the marvels of modern cinematography. It may be a nature documentary, a newsreel from the other side of the globe, a romance, thriller, or daytime drama, but whatever the subject matter, the on-screen experience transports us into different worlds, one after the other, a dizzying expansion of the world we see outside our window. The variety of expression seems infinite, and yet all of it is the play of three simple colors—red, green, and blue, which not coincidentally are the three colors detected by the three types of cones or photoreceptor cells in our retina. Expand that screen to encompass the entire universe and we find the same principle at work. Hidden behind this vast, unfathomable panorama we find the play of three fundamental principles. Rather than the red, green, and blue of an RGB screen, the traditional colors ascribed to the *guñas* are white, red, and black, where white represents one pole, the full-color spectrum of *sattvaguña*, and black the other, the absence of color of *tamoguña*. Every expression in the manifest universe is a composite of these three channels, and the infinite gradations within each of the *guṅas* give rise to the infinite variety of qualities, both perceptible and imperceptible, that define those expressions. *Sattvaguṅa*, the sentient force, gives rise to the qualities associated with lightness, expansion, subtlety, happiness, and peace. It functions to reveal consciousness, to promote the consciousness-ward movement. Its opposite pole, *tamoguṅa*, the static force, functions to demarcate and thus veil consciousness. It engenders the qualities of stasis, heaviness, lethargy, ignorance, and contraction. *Rajoguṅa*, the mutative force, produces the qualities of mutability, restlessness, and dynamism. In *rajoguṅa* we find expressed the inherent movement toward one pole or the other, toward the light of *sattva* or the darkness of *tamas*.

In the involutionary or inanimate phase of creation, the centrifugal movement of *prakrti*, *avidyámáyá*, continues to further qualify *puruśa* after the initial formation of the cosmic *citta*, and in the process there is a corresponding increase in attributional expression. This increasing attributional expression is seen in the gradual formation within the cosmic *citta* of the five fundamental factors—ethereal, aerial, luminous, liquid, and solid. Whereas the first two stages in the formation of the Cosmic Mind were dominated by *sattvaguṅa* and *rajoguṅa* respectively, the formation of the cosmic *citta* is dominated by *tamoguṅa*, and since the function of *tamoguṅa* is to demarcate Consciousness, it brings Consciousness within the bounds of physicality. The metamorphosis of Consciousness is no longer theoretical and hence is no longer purely psychic. With the formation of the ethereal factor, the waves of matter begin to take shape within the Cosmic Mind. The Cosmic Mind now has an object, and that object has attributes over and beyond the sense of existence and the sense of authorship that are characteristic of the cosmic *mahattattva* and *ahaṁtattva*.

As the bondage of *tamoguṅa* grows, the interparticular space continues to decrease, leading to increasing friction, and the combination of the external binding pressure of *tamoguṅa* and the corresponding increase in internal friction gives rise to greater and greater attributional expression. This is a principle we are all fully acquainted with in our individual lives, even if we are not familiar with the elementary laws of physics. Less space, more friction. More friction, more expression. It is the difference between sitting alone in a vast open space and sitting with fifty other people in a crowded room. With the formation of ethereal factor, we get three-dimensional space, energy, and the quality or inference of sound, but there are gradations within *tamoguńa*, as within all the *guńas*, and thus there are gradations within ethereal factor as well. The ethereal factor is indivisible and imperceptible, being beyond the scope of even the most advanced scientific instruments. It is, as we shall see in Chapter Two, the very fabric of space. But due to the external binding force of *tamoguńa*, space continues to undergo compression, and eventually the ethereal factor reaches a point where it is converted into aerial factor. This is a continuum rather than an abrupt transformation, as is the case with each of the subsequent factors. The gradual appearance of aerial factor out of the womb of ethereal factor can be seen through the gradual expression of the inference of touch and additional attributes that were not present in ethereal factor. Thus there are portions of space that are less dense than others, having been more recently transformed into ethereal factor out of the cosmic *ahaḿtattva*, and other portions that have become so dense that they are in a transitional stage between ethereal factor and aerial factor.

This process of gradual contraction and increasing attributional expression continues through the formation of solid matter. Out of the aerial factor arises the luminous factor and the inference of sight; from the luminous factor arises the liquid factor and the inference of taste; and from the liquid factor comes the solid factor and the inference of smell. We have five senses because there are five inferences and thus five perceptible forms of matter, a concept we will explore more fully in the next chapter. Within each of these different factors there are varying degrees of bondage, but what remains constant is that the greater the bondage, the further along the continuum we go, the greater the attributional expression.

Anandamurti points out in his commentary, however, that this does not mean that *prakrti* has grown in force. What increases is not the power of *prakrti* but the variety or diversity of expression. Ethereal factor is unvaried in nature, but by the time we get to the solid factor and the various planetary bodies, we encounter a seemingly infinite variety of attributes. *Prakrti's* power is now spread throughout the five fundamental factors and the five inferences they emit. An ocean can have one huge wave or an endless variety of smaller waves of different sizes, strengths, and duration, but in either case the power of the ocean remains the same. Thus the attributive power of the ethereal factor, which carries the sound inference alone, is equal to the attributive power of solid matter, which carries all five inferences. Hence the expressive power of the sound inference emitted by the solid factor is significantly weaker than the power of the sound inference carried by the ethereal factor, which is why a person who loses one sense sees their other senses grow in power. The person's sensory capacity remains the same but it is now distributed through four senses instead of five. The attributional force of *prakrti* remains the same, whether that force is divided among five different inferences, as it is in solid matter, or whether it is expressed through the single inference of sound.

गुणाधिक्ये जडस्फोटो भूतसाम्याभावात् ॥ ९ ॥

I.9 *guṅádhikye jaḋasphoto bhútasámyábhávát*

guṅa, binding principle; *ádhikye*, due to excess; *jaḋa*, matter; *sphotaḥ*, bursting; *bhúta*, created object, fundamental factors; *sámya*, balance; *abhávát*, from the lack of

"Due to excessive pressure of the *guṅas* and a loss of balance between the fundamental factors, *jaḋasphotaḥ* occurs."

In these next two sutras we reach the endpoint of the *saiṇcara* phase of the creation and thus the full elaboration of Anandamurti's Tantric cosmology. The word "cosmology" has been experiencing a revival in recent decades within the fields of astronomy and physics, especially astrophysics, and it remains the most apt word with which to describe Anandamurti's sweeping description of the formation of the universe.

With the appearance of the solid factor under the ever-increasing influence of *prakrti*, we find matter condensing into the various celestial bodies. However, the constant pressure of the binding principles of *prakrti*, specifically *tamoguña*, does not end here. *Tamoguña* continues to exert its binding force, decreasing the intermolecular and interatomic spaces and giving rise to denser and denser forms of solid matter and consequently to greater and greater friction within those solid bodies. This process of gradual densification, which began with the imposition of self-awareness on pure Consciousness, has two possible finalities. Either that celestial body will achieve a stable state of structural solidarity, paving the way for the appearance of living organisms, or else a lack of balance between the five fundamental factors (primarily an excess of the solid factor) will deprive that celestial body of the necessary conditions for life, and with the continuing pressure of *prakrti,* the process of densification will reach such an extreme that the built-up exterial force cannot be contained and that structure will either explode or disintegrate. This explosion or disintegration of solid matter and its concomitant transformation into subtler factors, especially the ethereal factor, is referred to as *jadasphota* by Anandamurti. It is in effect a recoiling of the cosmic thought waves.[29]

It is important to emphasize here that the gradual contraction of matter, beginning with the first expression of the ethereal factor, that is, with the first expression of the material universe, automatically leads to an increase in internal clash or friction between its relative constituents that is expressed in the opposing forces of attraction and repulsion, what Anandamurti refers to as the interial and exterial forces. All interaction in the universe, from the macrocosmic level to the quantum level, is governed by the interplay between these two forces. The four fundamental forces of contemporary physics are all different expressions of attraction and repulsion, whether it be the gravitational force, which keeps us from flying off our planet; the electromagnetic force, which governs the chemical behavior of matter, centered around the attraction and repulsion of unlike and like charges; the strong force that binds together the atomic nucleus; or the weak force that flips quarks up, down, and sideways. Wherever we look in the realm of *saiñcara* we see the inescapable dance of attraction and repulsion. In the Sun above our heads, gravity pulls inward while its burning gases push outward, and every ordinary substance we touch is either attracted or repelled by magnetic fields. The origin of this ubiquitous attraction and repulsion is the binding force of *prakrti*, which is expressed within the realm of duality as *vidyámáyá* and *avidyámáyá*, the centripetal and centrifugal forces, the force that liberates Consciousness and the force that binds Consciousness, physical law being a reflection of the interplay between the *guńas*. Nor is this principle limited to the material world of *saiṇcara*. The interplay between these two forces is equally on display in the psychic world, the world of *pratisaiṇcara*. All manifestation is movement, whether physical or psychic, and all movement is governed by attraction and repulsion. In Anandamurti's view, however, these twin forces are best understood in the context of a single law, the law of attraction, for *prakrti* is controlled by *puruśa*, being the expressive power of Consciousness, and behind that expression lies the eventual, inevitable attraction of all created beings toward the source of the creation. For this reason, Anandamurti refers to repulsion as "negative attraction," in much the same way that modern physicists use the term "negative entropy," and it is not unreasonable to think that physicists will one day succeed in their efforts to merge the four forces into a single force: the law of attraction.

This progressive contraction and consequent increase of friction within an object cannot go on forever. Matter cannot get denser and denser ad infinitum. If it doesn't reach a stable state then its destiny is to disintegrate, either through explosion or through gradual disassociation of its constituent parts due to the localized dominance of the exterial force. We are familiar with the first type of *jaḋasphoṭa* in the form of supernovae and with the second in the gradual disassociation of cosmic bodies (partial *jaḋasphoṭa*), being seen in dead planets, certain stars, and according to some astrophysicists, in black holes as well. The different types of supernovae have been studied extensively by modern physicists, and their observation goes back thousands of years to Indian and Chinese astronomers. We are less familiar with black holes, but modern research supports the conclusion that they begin with the collapse of a celestial body, and logic dictates that they will eventually undergo some form of *jaḋasphoṭa* (such as what is known among quantum gravity theorists as a Planck star).[30] This has led some contemporary physicists to wonder if the Big Bang was not in fact a Big Bounce, a model supported by recent research in loop quantum gravity.[31]

This "stirring up" of the cosmic thought waves liberates enormous amounts of energy, and it is one factor in the persistent thermal disparity of the universe,[32] the continual presence of nonequilibrium states that are integral to the formation of new stars and to the eventual appearance of life, an endlessly repeating process that functions as a kind of ongoing cosmic regenesis. Some modern physicists, unable to see beyond the second law of thermodynamics, believe that the universe as a whole is heading inexorably toward a state of maximum entropy, and some still ascribe to the nineteenth-century notion of the eventual or at least theoretical heat death of the universe as postulated by classical physics.[33] Anandamurti does not agree. The postulation that the universe could eventually reach a state of absolute stasis is contrary to the fundamental nature of manifest existence, and *jadasphota* is one of the internal mechanisms by which the Macrocosm maintains the eternal dynamism of the creation. In addition, the universe is neither a closed system nor an irreversible system, as is universally assumed in contemporary physics. New matter is forever being created in the process of *saiṋcara*, and as we shall soon see, the solid factor is forever reverting back into mind and ultimately into consciousness in the eternal flow of *pratisaiṋcara*.

Anandamurti refers to *jadasphota* as "negative *saiṋcara*," since the solid factor is transformed into subtler factors in direct opposition to the natural flow of *saiṋcara*. He points out, however, that the subtler factors created by *jadasphota* can never go beyond the bounds of matter—the subtlest form they can take is the ethereal factor. Immediately thereafter, those disassociated portions retake the normal path of *saiṋcara* under the ever-present pressure of *prakrti*, eventually reaching once again the state of solid factor. Were *jadasphota* to lead to matter reverting to mind-stuff or *citta*, it would mean the withdrawal of the thought waves of the Macrocosmic Mind. This would be equivalent to the cessation or suspension of macrocosmic activity and the end of creation, which is both illogical and impossible given the nature of *saiṋcara* and *pratisaiṋcara*.

On a smaller scale, nuclear explosions are another example of *jaḍasphota*, as is the natural wear and tear of physical organisms, whose structural balance is maintained through the replenishment of those disassociated elements through the intake of food, water, light, air, etc., and the basic concept can be applied metaphorically to social structures as well, although that is beyond the bounds of cosmology.

If we go back to the preceding sutra, we find Anandamurti's cosmology entering territory that has no parallel in Indian philosophy—nor in any other philosophy, for that matter. It does have certain parallels with modern physics; however, there are significant differences as well. Two of those differences are pertinent to both this sutra and the preceding one. The first of these is the assignation of a point of origin to the creation—as we have seen earlier, the Macrocosm is beyond the purview of time, time being a function of the microcosmic mind, and thus the creation can have no beginning and no end. The second fundamental difference is modern physics' essentially static view of the universe, its failure to take into account the role of Consciousness in the creation (the forward-looking views of some of the pioneers in quantum mechanics notwithstanding). This static view of the creation—the idea of the conservation of matter and energy—does not admit the possibility of the continual creation of new matter out of Consciousness and the continual reversion of matter into consciousness, which, as we shall soon see, is the key to the genesis of the universe, to both *saiṇcara* and *pratisaiṇcara*.

गुणप्रभावेन भूतसङ्घर्षाद् बलम् ॥ १० ॥

I.10 *guṅaprabhávena bhútasauṇgharśád balam*

guṅa, binding principle; *prabhávena*, due to the influence; *bhúta*, fundamental factor, created object; *sauṇgharśát*, friction, clash; *balam*, energy

"Due to the influence of the *guṅas*, friction occurs within the fundamental factors and energy arises."

As was mentioned in the previous sutra, the external pressure of *prakrti*, by gradually contracting matter, gives rise to opposing interial and exterial forces — that is, to clash or friction expressed as attraction and repulsion, as for example, in the interplay between negatively and positively charged subatomic particles or the tendency for atoms and molecules to attract each other at large distances and repel each other when they get too close. This interplay between the interial and exterial forces, pushing and pulling against each other, is otherwise known as *bala* or energy, and energy in its different forms — kinetic, mechanical, electromagnetic, etc. — is present in every expression of the material universe in differing proportions. The moment the ethereal factor comes into existence in the cosmic *citta* under the influence of *tamoguña*, the waves of motion arise and motion is synonymous with energy.

Another word for energy in Sanskrit is *práña*, a word many readers will be familiar with, and where there is matter there is *práña*, no matter how subtle that expression of matter be. Essentially, "matter is nothing more than bottled-up energy."[34] Or rather, the same substance we call "matter," whether it be in solid, liquid, luminous, aerial, or ethereal form, can be seen as either matter or energy, depending on the lens we are looking through. The finer the lens, the more the "illusion" of solidity breaks down. A lump of iron turns out to be composed of atoms in constant motion, which are themselves composed of finer particles, and those finer particles under more intense scrutiny dissolve into patterns or quanta of energy, "elementary excitations of a moving substratum."[35] Thus one of the meanings of the word *shakti* is "energy," for all expression in the manifest universe is due to the binding influence of Shakti, and all the waves stirred up by Shakti are a manifestation of energy. In other words, it is Shakti that "energizes" Consciousness, thus giving rise to the vast vibratory panorama that we call the universe.

Within this vibratory panorama, the interial force acts to maintain the structural integrity of an object while the exterial force seeks to break it apart. In order for a solid object to achieve a stable state of structural solidarity, the interial force must predominate over the exterial force, thereby preventing the disintegration of that structure. As a result a center or nucleus is formed and a dynamic equilibrium is established. The law of elasticity (Hooke's law), which tries to restore a body to its original condition when it is distorted, is one expression of this dynamic equilibrium. If the exterial force wins out, however, then a nucleus will not be formed and the object will undergo disintegration or disassociation. This can also happen within certain portions of an otherwise stable structure, such as with the biological wear and tear that was mentioned in the previous sutra. Even if the interial force succeeds in establishing a state of relative equilibrium, a solid object cannot maintain its structural solidarity without a proper balance between the five fundamental factors, which in turn necessitates a congenial environment where the five factors are present in requisite proportion. Thus there are two principle prerequisites for the creation of stable structures: the predominance of the interial force, which allows for the formation of a nucleus, and the presence of a congenial environment. This creation of stable structures within the context of a congenial environment, primarily with respect to planetary bodies, then sets the stage for the appearance of life and the beginning of the *pratisaiṇcara* phase of creation, the gradual expression of consciousness from the womb of previously inanimate matter.

देहकेन्द्रिकाणि परिणामभूतानि बलानि प्राणाः ॥ ११ ॥

I.11 *dehakendrikāṅi pariṅāmabhūtāṅi balāni prāṅāh*

deha, body, physical structure; *kendrikāṅi*, center-seeking; *pariṅāmabhūtāṅi*, resultant, transformed; *balāni*, energies; *prāṅāh*, vital airs, vital energy

"The resultant forces centered in the body are called *prāṅāh*."

The *pratisaiṇcara* phase of the creation begins with the appearance of living organisms, which in turn depends on the presence of two factors that will be treated in separate sutras: vital energy and mind. These two key factors—*the* two key factors—are conspicuously absent in the Life Sciences. Contemporary biologists recognize that metabolic processes are common to all living creatures, along with various other properties such as cellular organization, growth, reproduction, homeostasis, evolution, and so forth, but they fail to distinguish between energy processing and vital energy. Energy, as we have seen, is present everywhere in the manifest universe, but in *saiṇcara* energy is a blind force. It follows the laws of *saiṇcara*, what we commonly call the laws of physics, and those laws are a clear expression of macrocosmic intelligence, but energy in the inanimate world is not organized in a way that allows inanimate objects to perform functions over and above those dictated by the laws of *saiṇcara*. A rock responds to atmospheric conditions, it reacts in specific ways when it comes in contact with certain substances or stimuli, its constituent atoms maintain their bonds and exchange electrons, but if it is set in motion, rolling down a hill, for instance, it cannot decide to go left or right or take measures to avoid an obstacle looming in its path. In the absence of a localized intelligence to direct its actions, the energy on display in that rock is in effect blind.

That is no longer the case, however, with the expression of energy in a living organism, even in the most primitive unicellular life-forms. All living organisms absorb nutrients, expel waste material and toxins, avoid threats from their environment, and perpetuate their species. Even the simplest prokaryotes, the most primitive recognized form of life on our planet, perform a myriad of functions that display a level of localized control that goes far beyond the "mechanical" manifestations of *práńa* in the respective elements that make up that cell. How does this happen? How does the manifestation of energy in inanimate structures, following certain strict laws from which it never deviates, become transformed into the vital energy of a living organism possessing a functional intelligence all its own and with it the moment-to-moment unpredictability that is seen in all living beings, even the most primitive?

There are numerous theories about the origin of life, from different iterations of panspermia, the contention that life arrived on Earth in one form or another from a distant planet (which does not answer the question of how life arose but merely relegates it to a different ecosystem), to Intelligent Design, a vaguely scientific reformulation of creationism. The great majority of scientists, however, favor some form of biochemical evolution, and it is generally accepted in the scientific community that life on our planet began in the primeval oceans nearly four billion years ago with the appearance of the first-known anaerobic microorganisms. Prior to this, conditions were too hot to allow for the presence of amino acids and nucleotide bases. But as soon as conditions cooled enough for rocks to solidify and the first oceans to appear—approximately 3.9 billion years ago—life appeared.[36] As we can readily surmise, this was not a coincidence. These ancient oceans were full of the building blocks of life as we know it—hydrogen, oxygen, nitrogen, phosphorus, and carbon, mostly in compounds such as ammonia, methane, and water, and the basic tenet of biochemical evolution is that with the input of an energy source (solar radiation, lightning, the outflow of hydrothermal vents from the Earth's core) those building blocks gradually combined into more complex molecules such as amino acids, nucleotides, and lipids, which then banded together to form a protocellular membrane, and eventually the complex molecules within that protomembrane assembled themselves into self-replicating DNA, the genome that is the basis of life as we know it.

In 1953, operating on the assumption that those first oceans served as a huge natural cauldron whose primal soup eventually yielded the highly organized building blocks of life when subjected to repeated lightning strikes, a graduate student at the University of Chicago, Stanley Miller, and his supervisor, Harold Urey, succeeded in synthesizing amino acids, fatty acids, and sugars from a mixture of methane, ammonia, hydrogen, and water vapor by zapping the solution with sparks of electricity. Their experiment created a huge stir in the scientific community, but that was as close as anyone has gotten since to synthesizing life—which is to say, not very close at all. Their contention was that this reducing atmosphere reproduced primeval conditions, but recent research has suggested that the early atmosphere contained much higher amounts of nitrogen and carbon dioxide than previously believed, and subsequent experiments since then under more rigorous conditions have only been able to synthesize a single amino acid or two. At present, the gap between a few amino acids and a living cell with self-replicating DNA seems impossible to bridge, both experimentally and theoretically, and the contention that these simpler compounds "somehow" combined through chemical selection (in effect, chance) to form DNA and the complex proteins that are necessary for organic life is, as astronomer Fred Hoyle puts it, as improbable as a whirlwind passing through a junkyard and leaving behind a fully assembled 747, ready to fly. It is even more improbable when we consider that life arose virtually as soon as conditions permitted its emergence, which effectively takes pure chance out of the equation. There must have been a reason, a specific traceable cause. Not only have scientists been unable to trace this cause, however, they have yet to even propose a truly plausible theory,[37] much less create a living organism with vital energy, and thus the answer to the question of how life evolved continues to elude the scientific community.

The Sanskrit word for "vital energy," the "nonmechanical" energy we see manifest in a living organism, is *práńáh*. *Práńáh* is a plural word for the ten *váyus* or "vital airs," which according to yoga and Tantra are what animate a living body.[38] All animate bodies contain the five fundamental factors, and within each of these factors we see the expression of *prána* (the singular form), the multiplicity of energetic expressions that we see in those same factors when they are part of inanimate structures. Electrons spin in their orbits, liquid flows, heat is generated when larger molecules break down into smaller ones. But what orchestrates the functionality of cytoplasm, the absorption of nutrients, the various activities in the furnace of the mitochondria, the elimination of wastes? In short, all the functions we associate with life and only with life? This is the role of the ten vital airs, the ten currents of the aerial factor as it manifests within a living structure, the aerial factor being the subtlest fundamental factor to come within the scope of perception, as we will explore in detail in Chapter Two. *Prána* continues to operate in living structures just as it does in inanimate structures, such as in the myriad of chemical processes on display in a living cell, but the *práńáh*, the collection of ten *váyus*, functions like the different sections of an orchestra to turn those chemical processes into the music of life—playing certain notes at a certain time in a certain rhythm at a certain volume at the prompting of the conductor.

It is no surprise, then, that in many cultures the word for "breath" also means "life," as is the case in Sanskrit and the modern Indian languages derived from Sanskrit in which the word *práṇa* is now used in the sense of *práṇáḥ*,[39] and it is in that sense that the word has come into English—"prana," the vital principle. Similarly, the English word "spirit," the animating principle of life, comes from an Indo-European root that means "breath," and the same is true in Arabic and other Semitic languages. Without breath there is no life, no animation.[40] All living creatures must breathe in one form or another in order to absorb the aerial factor they need to sustain their life processes, ie., they must be able to exchange gases with their environment, whether it be through lungs or gills or tracheae or through simple diffusion, as in the case of plants and microorganisms; and all living cells depend upon different forms of cellular respiration to generate energy, whether that respiration be aerobic or anaerobic. Virtually all multicellular organisms breathe in oxygen,[41] which is then used at the cellular level to generate energy through cellular respiration (although certain cells can switch over to anaerobic respiration, if necessary), but even anaerobic bacteria and archaea, which in some cases are able to survive and even thrive under extreme conditions that were once thought to be prohibitive to the existence of life, depend on the intake of aerial factor in one form or another, whether it be diatomic hydrogen, methane, carbon dioxide, etc.[42] In such cases the critical element is generally hydrogen, and hydrogen transfer has been found to be the one common feature of all metabolic processes (fortunately, there is no dearth of hydrogen in our universe—it comprises 90% of the universe's atoms and three-quarters of its mass).[43] In short, *práṇáḥ* is indeed the breath of life, even if our means of absorbing the aerial factor from our environment is so radically different from that of a hyperthermophile archaea living on the walls of a deep-sea hydrothermal vent at 100°C.

There are five internal and five external *váyus*. In other words, the aerial factor, when it manifests as vital energy, is divided into ten categories or types according to the nature of the functions it performs. Their names and functions are as follows:

The five internal *váyus*:

1. *Práńa*: respiration and the circulation of vital energy.
2. *Apána*: excretion.
3. *Samána*: maintaining equilibrium between the *práńa* and *apána váyus*.
4. *Udána*: vocalization and expression of thought.
5. *Vyána*: circulation of vital fluids, and the perception and nonperception of experience.

The five external *váyus*:

1. *Nága*: extension.
2. *Kúrma*: contraction.
3. *Krkara*: the increase or decrease of air pressure, including yawning and stretching in developed creatures.
4. *Devadatta*: thirst and hunger.
5. *Dhanaińjaya*: sleep and drowsiness.

The study of *how* vital energy or *práńáh* functions within the physical body of a living being, however, does not explain *why* it functions, which brings us back to the same question: how does the blind expression of energy in an inanimate structure become transformed into the intricately orchestrated expression of energy in an animate or organic structure? What is the cause behind the effect, the catalytic agent, the touchstone that turns the iron of matter into the gold of life? What is it that directs the ten *váyus*, which after all belong to aerial factor and thus to *saincara*?

According to Anandamurti, the appearance of life requires a congenial environment that contains the five fundamental factors in requisite proportions. The present environment on the moon, for example, or on most asteroids,[44] does not have the requisite proportion of water or a viable atmosphere that a living being requires. If those requisite conditions are met, however, then it is inevitable that life will manifest through the emergence of individual physical structures in which the interial force is able to establish a dynamic equilibrium and thus a nucleus. Why is this inevitable, whether on this planet or on any other in which a congenial environment is present?

The answer to both questions is mind.

तीव्रसङ्घर्षेण चूर्णीभूतानि जडानि चित्ताणु मानसधातुर्वा ॥ १२ ॥

I.12 *tiivrasauṅgharśeṇa cúrṇiibhútáni jaḍáni cittáṇu mánasadhátur vá*

tiivra, excessive; *sauṅgharśeṇa*, by means of friction; *cúrṇiibhútáni*, pulverized; *jaḍáni*, matter; *citta*, mind, ectoplasm; *aṇu*, particle; *mánasa*, mind; *dhátuh*, substance, element; *vá*, or

"Due to excessive friction, matter is pulverized and ectoplasmic particles or mind-stuff emerges."

There are different theories in both science and philosophy to account for the origin of mind, which, as we know, is commonly confused with consciousness. Most scientific theories rest on the reductionist assumption that consciousness is a byproduct of certain chemical reactions or combinations, an assumption that often goes unquestioned but which on closer examination seems entirely implausible. As we have seen, scientists have created primordial soups, similar in theory to Earth's primitive oceans, and have been able to synthesize simple amino acids by running electricity at high voltages through those chemical soups, but they have come no closer to changing inanimate matter into animate life than they were before they entered the laboratory; and thus they walk out of the laboratory with a vague theory that the highly sophisticated human beings that performed that experiment somehow arose from a chance association of random molecules. On the other end of this philosophical divide, various theist doctrines talk of Intelligent Design and a divine infusion of the spirit of life into matter, an unexplained intervention that does not offer any logical explanation of how that happens. It remains an abstraction, untethered to the law of cause and effect.

The answer is simple. Mind arises out of matter because mind is inherent in matter, just as consciousness is inherent in mind, both mind and matter having been formed out of Consciousness through the gradual process of involution known as *saiṋcara*. In Anandamurti's view, the only real difference between the inanimate and animate worlds is that mind is dormant in inanimate matter and manifest in living beings. What is dormant can be awakened under the right conditions, and that is precisely what happens. Mind appears out of matter because it is already there, just as the nascent tree is present in the seed, needing only the proper conditions for it to sprout.

Those proper conditions have already been described in the previous sutra, where the contention was made that if a congenial environment is present then the appearance of life is inevitable, a conclusion many scientists have come to based purely on an observation of the biological record, prompting the Belgian biochemist and Nobel laureate Christian de Duve to call life "an obligatory manifestation of matter, bound to arise wherever conditions are appropriate."[45] The reason life is inevitable given the appropriate conditions is because the appearance of *citta* or mind-stuff is the logical conclusion of *saiṋcara*. In *saiṋcara*, Consciousness is suppressed, so to speak, by the qualifying action of *prakrti*. As logic and experience dictate, this suppression cannot last forever. A suppressed desire or impulse, being an expression of momentum, can remain suppressed for a time (although it never fails to leave traces in our behavior and thoughts, just as we see traces of intelligence in matter), but it cannot be suppressed forever — no momentum can be checked forever — and under the right conditions it resurfaces.

As mentioned in earlier sutras, the clash of forces produced by the binding pressure of *prakrti* continues to increase as matter contracts, reaching its zenith in the solid factor. There comes a point in this process where matter in a stable structure cannot be compressed any further. This state is called *svayambhú* in Sanskrit. Because the friction generated by the clash between those internal forces reaches its zenith as the densification of the solid factor reaches its terminus, and because the impact of the three relative factors of time, space, and person continues unabated, the jolt provided by these constantly changing factors of relativity, unable to crudify the solid factor any further, then acts to reverse the flow of creation.[46] Some minute portions of the solid factor get pulverized or powdered down and thereby

CHAPTER ONE

revert to *citta* or mind-stuff, what Anandamurti calls *cittáńu*, "ectoplasmic particles."

Think of rocks being hurled against each other in a small enclosure. The clash between those rocks gives off sparks—luminous factor—and this is possible because the luminous factor is already present in those rocks, all five factors being present in every solid structure. Another useful analogy is that of ice. Apply heat and a portion of that ice is transformed into water, which can only happen because ice is itself a condensed or congealed form of water. Or to use one of Anandamurti's analogies for the genesis of this transformation, imagine five hundred people bound together tightly. They will naturally struggle against their bonds, and due to their struggle they eventually snap those ropes and overcome their bondage. Here the bondage is the bondage of the binding principles of *prakrti*, specifically *tamoguńa*, which has bound Consciousness into its crudest form, solid matter. With the snapping of those bonds, some of that matter is transformed into *cittáńu* or ectoplasm—mind in its most rudimentary form.

With its release from the bondage of matter, the dormant *citta* reappears, this time on the microcosmic scale, thus signaling the beginning of *pratisaiṋcara*. The presence of mind acts as a catalytic agent, effecting the transformation of "mechanical" energy into vital energy, *práńa* into *práńáh*, and thus giving rise to the visible activities of life. What was blind energy is now directed by mind, which assumes control over what is henceforth a living structure through the agency of *práńáh*.

The transformation of *práńa* into vital energy or *práńáh* is concomitant with the appearance of mind or *cittáńu*, but what we generally call life is actually the sum total of the orchestrated animate activities resulting from the agency of *práńáh*. Thus the order of these two sutras. Mind is the hidden factor, the unseen and invisible controller, the catalytic agent that steadfastly avoids our sight. The visible signs of life are seen in the activities of *práńáh*, but the invisible ingredient that conjures *práńáh* out of the thin air of *práńa* is mind.

If *saiṋcara* is the involution of Consciousness into matter, passing through the intermediary stages of the Cosmic Mind, *pratisaiṋcara* is the evolution of consciousness out of matter, passing once again through the intermediary stages of mind but this time in the opposite direction and at the microcosmic level. *Saiṇcara* is the world of the Macrocosm and *pratisaiṇcara* is the world of microcosms. It can and should be called "evolution," but evolution as understood in the spiritual sense, not in the biological sense as it is commonly thought of today. *Pratisaiṇcara* refers to the evolution or expansion of the individual mind and the concomitant expansion of consciousness that is revealed through the medium of that individual mind — the more evolved the mind, the greater its reflection of consciousness. Evolution in this sense does not refer to the body, which is composed of matter and thus belongs to *saiṇcara*. The body is a vehicle, a material structure that grows increasingly complex in order to keep pace with psychic evolution. It is the mind that controls that structure and it is the mind that evolves.[47]

This is one of the fundamental failings of evolutionary biology: a failure to grasp the role of mind — and ultimately, of consciousness — in the journey of evolution. We look at the development of the central nervous system, the appearance of the prehensile thumb, the ability to walk upright, and so on, as being integral to the development of human intelligence, enabling our species and those of our ancestors to make their rapid climb up the ladder of evolution. And the mechanism for this evolutionary process, as proposed by Darwin, is commonly accepted to be natural selection. This mechanistic view of evolution, however, is not supported by *Ananda Sutram*, for it fails to identify the underlying cause. It is not that the evolution of a central nervous system allowed living organisms to become more intelligent and thus to better adapt to their environment. It is because their minds evolved that they required a more complex nervous system to express the necessities and potentialities of that developing mind. In other words, modern science sees the external effect but not the underlying cause. It is the developing mind that promotes the development of the body, not vice versa, and hence it is the mind that evolves while the body remains in *saiṇcara*, becoming more complex in order to keep pace with the needs of psychic development.

Organic evolution in the West was first proposed by the Greeks and rejected by and large by early Christian thinkers because it conflicted with the Bible. It has also been rejected by many present-day Christian nonthinkers. According to a 2014 Gallup poll, 45% of Americans believe that God created humans in their present form within the last ten thousand years, highlighting the role that religious belief has played in the evolutionary debate. Anandamurti, however, looks at evolution in a way that is markedly different from both science and religion. He does talk in general terms about apes and early hominids as our immediate ancestors, since our human bodies evolved from those of early primates in a biological chain of common ancestry that goes all the way back to the first unicellular life-forms in the primeval oceans. But from the more expansive viewpoint of *pratisaiṇcara*, the entire parade of living beings can be rightly seen as our ancestral tree because our individual minds had to pass through so many different life-forms before acquiring a human body. The physical evolution of our species and others remains an important field of study, but from the standpoint of philosophy, the body is only a vehicle subject to *saiṇcara* and animated by *prāṅāh*. It is the mind that evolves, and with psychic evolution comes the expansion of consciousness as reflected in those individual minds, the true raison d'être behind the evolutionary flow of *pratisaiṇcara*—the liberation of consciousness from its self-imposed bondage.

व्यष्टिदेहे चित्ताणुसमवायेन चित्तबोधः ॥ १३ ॥

I.13 *vyaśtidehe cittāṅusamavāyena cittabodhah*

vyaśti, individual; *dehe*, in the body; *cittāṅu*, ectoplasmic particles; *samavāyena*, by means of combination; *citta*, objectivated mind; *bodhah*, sense, feeling

"The sense of *citta* arises in the individual body through the combination of ectoplasmic particles."

The word *citta* has been used in different senses in the various schools of Indian philosophy dating back several millennia. In Yoga, for example, it refers to the mind as a whole, the composite of *buddhi*, *ahaṁkāra*, and *manas*, while in Advaita Vedanta it refers to one of four functional parts of the mind. Thus the meaning of the word depends on the context. In Anandamurti's lexicon, *citta* refers to the objectivated portion of the mind, the third of the mind's three functional layers, ie., that portion of the mind that assumes the form of the object of thought, whether that object be a perception, an emotion, or an abstract thought. Whatever content arises in the mind arises in the *citta*. If we use the traditional analogy, comparing the mind to a body of water, then the water itself, the material—or in this case, nonmaterial—substance is the *citta*, which by virtue of always being in motion is forever assuming an endless variety of different forms, the waves on its surface, the currents in its depths. Thus, *citta* as the nonmaterial mental substance and *citta* as the "objectivated portion of the mind" are essentially synonymous.

In the previous sutra, we saw how extreme friction or clash within the solid factor can, under the right conditions, produce *cittáńu* or ectoplasmic particles from minute portions of solid matter, like sparks flying from the colliding surfaces of two rocks. These ectoplasmic particles group together due to their natural affinity, similar to the way H_2O molecules attract each other through hydrogen bonds to form a cohesive substance that maintains its volume under different conditions. When sufficient water molecules group together, they form a whole that is more than the sum of its parts—that is, they show the emergent properties that we associate with water, such as its cohesive behavior, its liquidity or fluid nature, its versatility as a solvent, its surface tension. By contrast, the viscosity of an isolated H_2O molecule is nonexistent. A similar thing happens when *cittáńu* group together. Their conjunction gives rise to the sense of *citta*, its characteristic nature, including its ability to reflect the waves of matter, ie., to assume the form of those incoming waves, as in the example of the photographic plate that was used in sutra I.7. This potential is present in each ectoplasmic particle but it only manifests in conjunction with other *cittáńu*, just as a single H_2O molecule doesn't begin to flow until it joins with its fellow molecules through hydrogen bonds to form a drop of water, liquidity being an emergent property of the interaction between H_2O molecules.

What then is the nature of *citta*, its observable properties, as expressed in an undeveloped life-form such as a unicellular organism? In the context of a developed mind with all three functional layers, *mahat*, *aham*, and *citta*, the objectivated portion's inherent characteristics are easily distinguished from those of its subjective counterparts. This is not the case, however, in an emerging organism that has no manifestation of *aham* or *mahat*. How can there be perception without a perceiver? How do you construct a sentence with only an object, no verb or subject?

A primitive protist, akin to the early prokaryotes in the primeval soup of Earth's first seas, does not have organs in the sense that developed creatures do, but it does have sensory capacity, an emergent property of *citta*. It senses its environment and reacts on the basis of those sensations, another emergent property. In the biological sciences, this level of intelligence is called "instinct," an innate fixed pattern of behavior in response to certain stimuli. In Sanskrit it is known as *sahaj buddhi*, "simple intellect" or "native intelligence."

There is no question that even the simplest unicellular life-form displays a rudimentary level of intelligence. It ingests the nutrients it needs and rejects those it doesn't. It uses its vital energy to expel its wastes, avoid dangers, and gravitate toward favorable environments, performing the hundreds of functions that are necessary to guarantee its survival. It has no sense of authorship, no center of conscious control, much less any awareness of self, but it does have awareness, the rudimentary awareness we call "instinct." When nutrients reach the borders of its plasma membrane it recognizes their presence and welcomes them. When undesirable foreign matter approaches, it recognizes the difference and rejects them. This is a clear indication of awareness, regardless of the chemical mechanisms that underpin such behaviors. Earlier in this chapter we pointed out that there can be no perception unless *citta* identifies with the incoming wave emanated by the object. In the case of primitive life-forms, bereft of *aham* and *mahat*, there can be no perception as such, because perception implies a perceiver, which implies *aham*. Nevertheless, the incoming wave is reflected in the *citta* and the organism reacts accordingly in what we call instinctive fashion—that is, according to the native intelligence that is inherent to this rudimentary manifestation of mind. If that wave, whether internal or external, were not reflected in the *citta*, there would be no reaction, as is the case when a cell dies. But a living unicellular organism does react, and it does so on the basis of its recognition of the nature of the object or conditions. In other words, it has identified the object or conditions by faithfully reflecting those inferential waves. And the nature of its reaction is inevitably to safeguard its survival. This urge for self-preservation, which we see on display in even the most primitive life-forms, is, in and of itself, a clear sign of intelligence — the sign of a primitive mind acting in its own best interests — and this manifestation of intelligence will continue to grow as the *citta* expands, leading to the eventual development of metazoan structures to accommodate that evolving mind.

At this stage of the evolutionary process, in which *tamoguṅa* is predominant, the mind is purely reactive. The possibility for independent action (or choice) has not yet begun to manifest. This will come at a later stage, when *aham* begins to emerge in the consciousness-ward flow of *pratisaiṅcara*.

चित्ताद्गुणावक्षये रजोगुणप्राबल्ये ऽहम् ॥ १४ ॥

I.14 *cittád guṅávakṣaye rajoguṅaprábalye 'ham*

cittát, from *citta*; *guṅa*, binding principle; *avakṣaye*, in the waning; *rajoguṅa*, mutative principle; *prábalye*, in the dominance; *aham*, doer I, ego

"Due to the waning of the *guṅas* and the dominance of *rajoguṅa*, *aham* arises out of *citta*."

Pratisaiṅcara is characterized by the gradual waning of the *guṅas* and a corresponding unfolding of consciousness, which attains its release from the dominion of *prakṛti* through the medium of individual minds. While *saiṅcara* is centrifugal in nature, dominated by the *avidyámáyá* force of *prakṛti*, *pratisaiṅcara* is dominated by *vidyámáyá*, the centripetal force, which carries living beings toward the cosmic nucleus through the attractive power of *puruṣottama*, as if *puruṣottama* were a magnet, drawing those individual minds toward itself through the force field of *vidyámáyá*. The closer they get, the stronger that force is felt.

While the ultimate cause behind this expansion of consciousness is the macrocosmic desire to return to its original unbound state, at the microcosmic level Anandamurti identifies three causes that engender mental evolution: physical clash, psychic clash, and spiritual clash, which he also calls "the attraction of the Great." In undeveloped organisms, possessing only *citta*, there is no thought as we know it and thus no psychic clash. At this stage, evolution proceeds solely due to physical clash and is thus exceedingly slow, physical clash being by far the slowest of the three mediums of psychic evolution. To get an idea of just how slow, we can look at the evolutionary timeline for the development of metazoan structures, a prerequisite for the emergence of *aham*. The first unicellular life-forms appeared on this planet nearly four billion years ago, but the first metazoans—most likely sponges and bivalves—didn't appear until approximately nine hundred million years ago. In other words, it took nearly three billion years for protists to develop into metazoans, and even those first metazoan creatures had yet to manifest *aham* and thus pave the way for the accelerated progress afforded by psychic clash. But those primitive life-forms did evolve—the appearance of the early metazoans and the more developed life-forms that followed is proof of that. The struggle for survival at this primitive stage of evolution is the primary source of physical clash, and it is that physical clash or physical struggle that enables these primitive creatures to undertake their long and painstaking march up the evolutionary ladder as their rudimentary minds pass from one unicellular structure to another, gradually expanding along the way, albeit almost imperceptibly.

In one sense Darwin was right. Natural selection does promote those traits that allow the physical structures of different species to better adapt to their environment and thus become more complex and hence more capable hosts. But it is the struggle for self-preservation, "the battle for life," as Darwin called it, that promotes the evolution of the individual mind, at least until the later stages of the journey. All unicellular organisms face obstacles that threaten their existence, such as fluctuations in the temperature of their environment or a shortage of available nutrients, and they are thereby forced to adapt in order to survive. This purely reactive struggle is the medium for the gradual expansion of *citta*. From the macrocosmic perspective, the true impetus behind this evolutionary movement is the waning of the *guñas* as directed by the Macrocosmic Mind, the centripetal flow of the *vidyámáyá* force of *prakrti*, but the immediate cause of their psychic development is this physical clash, the struggle they are forced to undergo in the interest of self-preservation.

As the influence of *tamoguña* wanes, *rajoguña* begins to assert itself, and as it does, the faculty of *ahaṁtattva*, which is inherent or dormant in *citta*, begins to manifest. *Aham* is the subjective counterpart of *citta*, that portion of the mind that thinks, perceives, feels, and acts, while *citta* is the objective counterpart, whether it be a perception, a sensation, or a desire. With the manifestation of *aham* comes the beginning of individuation. In the absence of *mahat* there is no true self-awareness, but such creatures do have existential awareness, the existential awareness of the "doer-I," that of the actor who cannot see himself as the actor.[48] If we return to our analogy, comparing *citta* to an ocean, the waters of that ocean now become infused with a sense of authorship, the defining characteristic of individuality. The waves are still the waves of *citta*, the movement of the water, but a sense of "I" has begun to coalesce, a psychic self that is aware of those waves and acts accordingly.

We can gain some understanding of this level of awareness through a close examination of our own experience. There are times when we get so caught up in what we are doing that we lose sight of ourselves. We may be so focused on getting a stain out of a pot that for a few moments there is nothing else in our mind but that stain and our concerted efforts to get it out. We scrub a little harder, a little to the left, a little to the right, watching the stain gradually fade, our mind totally intent on the task at hand. Our *aham* is at work, making choices based on the feedback it gets from its environment. There is a strong sense of individuality, but for those few moments there is no reflective awareness of that sense of individuality. The moment *mahat* resurfaces, however, we are once again aware that we are doing what we are doing. It is a subtle difference but we can duplicate it in our mental laboratory by purposely suspending *mahat* in *aham*, even if we are only able to achieve that suspension for a few moments. To be aware of the ego at work, rather than being simply caught up in the work of the ego, requires *mahat*, which is the substantiation of our sense of individuality. This is habitual for human beings, but in creatures where *mahat* has yet to manifest, there is no reflective awareness of the mind at work. They lack the mirror of *mahat* to recognize *aham* as *aham*. Such creatures are not purely reactive, however, as is the case with those that possess only *citta*. They function on instinct but they are self-acting. They do not merely react to their environment but interact with it—that is, they are capable of initiating action and are thus capable of rudimentary learning. Something in their environment causes pain and they learn to avoid it. It is an instinctive reaction but it is also a form of conditioned learning. Something else causes pleasure and they learn to consciously seek it out. And this ability in turn greatly accelerates the speed of mental evolution.

Hence it is with the appearance of *aham* that we see the first expression of psychic clash. The mind is at work, reacting to its environment and making choices: fleeing from dangers, searching for food and comfortable surroundings, propagating its species. While it continues to reap the evolutionary benefits of physical clash through the experiences of pain and pleasure as it wages the battle for life, the actions of that primitive mind as it seeks to avoid pain and realize pleasure become key to its survival. This is indicative of mental struggle or mental clash, which greatly accelerates the evolutionary movement of that primitive mind. Even more importantly, that developing creature comes in contact with other minds, not only those of its own species but those of all the other species that share its habitat, more or less developed than itself. It must contend with these other living, thinking beings, and this clash of minds accelerates its progress even further. As the capabilities of *aham* grow, the mental aspects of the struggle for survival come increasingly to the forefront, propelling the living being forward faster and faster along the path of *pratisaiṇcara*.

सूक्ष्माभिमुखिनीगतेरुदये ऽहंतत्त्वान् महत् ॥ १५ ॥

I.15 *sūkṣmābhimukhiniigater udaye 'haṁtattvān mahat*

sūkṣma, subtle; *abhimukhinii*, toward; *gateh*, of the movement; *udaye*, in the emergence; *ahaṁtattvāt*, from *ahaṁtattva*; *mahat*, the pure I, the sense of existence

"With further movement toward subtlety,
mahat evolves from *aham*."

As the centripetal force of *vidyāmāyā* increases, the dominance of *rajoguña* gradually wanes and the *sattvaguña* force of *prakrti* becomes increasingly pronounced. Due to the influence of *sattvaguña*, the third functional layer of mind, *mahat*, begins to manifest, being latent in *aham*, as *aham* was latent in *citta*. *Mahat* is the pure I-feeling, the pure feeling of existence. With its initial expression comes the first glimmers of self-awareness. All creatures who possess *mahat* exhibit self-awareness, even if that self-awareness is exceedingly dim due to *mahat's* limited expression in that individual mind. If we go back to our example from the previous sutra, the moment we become aware of ourselves cleaning the pot, rather than being fixated solely on what we are doing, our *mahat* has made its presence felt. In human beings, the sense of self-awareness is highly developed, but all creatures with *mahat* are aware of themselves as individual beings, even if that awareness of selfhood is very faint. In more developed creatures, the sense of selfhood becomes unmistakable, as in the great apes, for example, who after learning some form of sign language or symbolic language are able to identify themselves and express their preoccupations and desires. What started out as pure reaction in *citta* and developed into interaction with *aham*, now reaches the stage of reflection or self-awareness under the growing influence of the sentient force.

As *mahat* expands due to the waning of the *guñas* and increased psychic clash, the body also keeps pace in order to allow that developing mind to express its increased complexity and depth. This is especially evident in the development of the nervous and glandular systems, which allows for the expression of more complex thought and emotion. At the same time, the interaction between minds, a potent source of psychic clash, also becomes increasingly significant, which in turn hastens the rate of evolution. Take the example of a hungry cheetah stalking an antelope. When the antelope becomes aware of the encroaching predator, she flees for her life. Her racing emotions send her adrenal glands into overdrive, a physiological indication of extreme mental agitation. She takes evasive measures, looking frantically for a means of escape. This is noted by the feverish cheetah, who increases his speed and adjusts his trajectory, simultaneously becoming uncomfortably aware that his limited stamina is waning. While their bodies are pitted against each other and against the elements, the principle struggle is between the two minds animating those bodies. Both minds are fully engaged in the struggle for survival, and their life-and-death encounter makes them contestants on the savanna. If the antelope survives she will have gained from the experience, and the same for the frustrated cheetah. If she doesn't survive, then her mind will migrate to a new body in which it will continue to evolve in the ongoing theater of incarnate life.

Physical and psychic clash, however, are not the only causes behind the evolution of mind at the microcosmic level. The third of the three causes of evolution is spiritual clash or attraction of the Great, a direct consequence of the attractive power of the cosmic nucleus. In a wider sense, this attractive power is present throughout the march of *pratisaiṅcara*. Consciousness is attracting all life-forms toward itself through the *vidyámáyá* force of *prakrti*, but its attractive power is not consciously felt by living beings until *mahat* becomes fully expressed, that is to say, in human beings. Unlike animals, even developed animals, human beings are never fully satisfied with their lot. Consciously or subconsciously, we are always seeking for something more out of life, whether it be more wealth, more power, more knowledge, or more love, and this endemic dissatisfaction is accompanied by a sense of separateness that can only be overcome when our spiritual journey brings us into contact with the source of our being. This constant longing for something more is a direct expression of spiritual clash, an initially unconscious or subconscious urge that eventually matures into the conscious recognition that we will never be able to achieve lasting peace or happiness until we achieve liberation from the dominion of *prakrti*. This enduring dissatisfaction is our greatest burden but it is also our greatest blessing, for this spiritual clash drives us forward on the path toward enlightenment.

As with the development of *aham*, the emergence of *mahat* further accelerates the journey of evolution. Not only does psychic clash increase in proportion to the development of *mahat*, the propulsive force of spiritual clash is much greater than that of psychic clash, and this in turn further accelerates our evolution. If we return to our evolutionary timeline, we can see that while it took nearly three billion years for the first metazoan life-forms to appear, and sometime thereafter before the first expression of *aham*, it took less than four hundred million years after that until the first vertebrates appeared, another three hundred million more till the first mammals, and less than two hundred million years after that until the first humans. Human beings have only been around approximately one million years,[49] and yet over the last seven thousand years we have numerous recorded instances of human beings who have achieved spiritual enlightenment and thus completed the evolutionary journey of consciousness. What was an exceedingly slow journey through the early stages of the developing individual mind has become a galloping movement due to the human mind's clearly reflected *mahat* and the concomitant expression of spiritual clash or spiritual attraction.

The word *mahat* means "great" or "high," and it was used interchangeably with the word *buddhi* in Kapil's Samkhya philosophy to refer to the first evolute of *prakrti*. In his elaboration of concepts that had long been part of the Indian spiritual tradition,[50] Kapil divided the Cosmic Mind into *mahat* or *buddhi, ahaṁkára*, and *manas*. The word *buddhi* in this context means "supreme intelligence," though it is more commonly translated as "intellect," and the Samkhya philosophers attributed to this initial qualification of Consciousness the faculty of discrimination, ie., the knowledge of differentiation without attachment or identification, while the *ahaṁkára* was seen as the ego principle, whether cosmic or individual, and *manas* the process of thinking. This tripartite division of the mind was accepted by subsequent schools of Indian philosophy, at times with some alteration, especially in the last of the six orthodox systems, Vedanta, which further divided the third evolute, *manas*, into *manas* and *citta*, with *manas* seen as being the process of thinking and *citta* the impressions left by those thoughts, analogous to *manas* being the waves on the surface and *citta* the depths.[51]

The founders of these different schools of philosophy by and large accepted Kapil's enumeration of the evolutes of *prakrti*, including the five fundamental factors (*mahábhúta*), the five inferences (*tanmátra*), and the ten organs, but each interpreted Kapil's teachings, beginning with the nature of *prakrti*, in different ways, in effect entering into a dialogue with Kapil and with each other. Their followers and commentators continued to develop those teachings and at times altered them to fit their respective visions of reality, and it was generally understood that they were participating in an ongoing discussion or debate about the nature of reality. Thus, later teachings purposely and perhaps inevitably carried echoes of earlier teachings. In *Ananda Sutram*, Anandamurti does the same, entering into a dialogue with earlier philosophers and philosophical systems through his reformulation of various aspects of these traditional teachings, while at the same time introducing new ideas and concepts. While his explanation of *mahat*, for example, overlaps with Kapil's (as we will explore in a later sutra), he emphasizes that the defining quality of *mahat* is the sense of existence, something Kapil and subsequent philosophers failed to do. And thus while Indian philosophers since Kapil continue to look at *mahat* or *buddhi* as the fundamental intellect, the power of discrimination untouched by attachment or identification (and thus by individuality or *aham*), Anandamurti has a very different explanation of intellect that appears for the first time in the Indian philosophical tradition.

चित्तादहंप्राबल्ये बुद्धिः ॥ १६ ॥

I.16 *cittád ahamprábalye buddhih*

cittát, over *citta*; *ahaṁ*, doer I or ego; *prábalye*, in the predominance of; *buddhih*, intellect

"The predominance of *aham* over *citta* gives rise to intellect."

There are three distinct expressions of intelligence, corresponding to the three functional layers of mind, *citta*, *aham*, and *mahat*. The native intelligence that we see expressed in organisms dominated by *citta* is what we commonly refer to as "instinct." In organisms that possess only *citta*, unicellular and primitive metazoan life-forms, this inborn intelligence functions exclusively as unconditioned response—that is, such organisms respond to a particular external stimulus in a fixed way every time. Creatures in which *aham* has begun to manifest, however, are capable of modifying their behavior through experience due to the sense of authorship that arises with *aham*. In other words, they are able to learn, the type of learning biologists refer to as "habituation" or "conditioned response." Wasps that are given food each time they detect a certain smell will learn to associate food with that smell and thereafter seek it out; honeybees recognize landmarks, which enables them to return to the colony; and cockroaches show the same classical conditioned salivation response that Pavlov showed in dogs at the end of the nineteenth century.[52] This kind of learning becomes even more pronounced and complex in more developed creatures, playing a pivotal role in the behavioral development of fish, birds, and of course mammals.[53] A bird in the wild, for instance, will flee when it sees a man approaching, but with repeated observation it learns to recognize that the man doesn't pose a threat. We have all seen birds gathering in a park, approaching human beings for food. They have learned not to be afraid in that situation, overcoming their instinctual fear response. Behind such behavior we see the *aham* navigating the terrain in front of it, gaining experience and acquiring useful knowledge from that experience—where to get food, what particular creatures do or do not pose a threat, and so on. This is still *sahaj buddhi*, simple intelligence, but it is *sahaj buddhi* in its apexed form. True intellect, however, only begins to manifest when the individual mind becomes capable of sorting through the contents of *citta*—its perceptions and previous experience—and analyzing that content independently of its desires. And this in turn only becomes possible when *aham* expands to the point that its periphery becomes greater than that of *citta*.

If, by way of analogy, we visualize *citta* and *aham* as concentric circles, with the circle of *aham* within the confines of the circle of *citta*, then the entire periphery of *aham* is subsumed within *citta*. In this case, the *aham* has no choice but to remain fully identified with the waves that *citta* presents to it and is thus in effect unable to see the forest for the trees. But when the bounds of *aham* oversteps that of *citta*, a part of *aham* remains free, so to speak, to analyze what it sees. Instead of being fully occupied with the immediate waves of *citta*, it is free to act on its own, to sort through its memories, compare them to the evidence of its senses, and base its subsequent action on that analysis, rather than being a slave to its conditioning. It can then experiment to see what works and what doesn't—not mere trial and error, but the testing of a simple hypothesis as suggested by the *aham* based on its comparison of the elements of the present situation with its previous experience.

Buddhi or intellect has two principal functions, thinking and memory, and it is characterized by the process of analysis, which is defined as the detailed examination of the elements or structure of something, or alternatively as the process of separating something into its constituent elements. In other words, it is the understanding of the relationship of the parts to the whole or to each other. This capacity emerges when an animal becomes capable of analyzing a situation through observation rather than simply reacting according to its inborn instincts, whether or not that instinctual response has been modified or refined due to experience. Wolves, for example, have shown under controlled conditions the ability to follow a logical sequence of cause and effect. They have significant problem-solving skills and are able to share the knowledge they gain across generations. Experienced hunters and trappers often talk of how intelligent they are, and there are numerous instances of wolves outsmarting their human adversaries. In one such account, a lone timber wolf continued to evade a group of homesteaders on the Little Sioux River for nearly two years, periodically making off with their livestock despite their best efforts to the contrary. It would even be seen watching them for hours, just out of the range of their bullets, sitting unconcerned when they fired. Finally they offered an accomplished trapper a tidy sum of money to track down the wolf. When he heard about its exploits, he declined. "When a buffalo wolf gets really cunnin'," he told them, "the wiles o' man is useless."

Examples of the ability to reason abound among developed animals: the wolf's close cousin, the domestic dog, can be trained to be the eyes of its blind master, learning to analyze the flow of traffic in order to know when and when not to cross; and chimpanzees use a variety of simple tools to unearth unseen food and they pass that knowledge on to their offspring. Through the use of this free *aham* they have the ability to direct matter according to their desires, that is, to manipulate the outside world so as to materialize their desires.[54] This is a great leap over conditioned learning. The minds of creatures whose *citta* is greater than *aham* are wholly dominated by matter. Their *aham* is identified with their desires and the objects of perception and is confined to establishing a link between the two. But once intellect begins to develop, they gain the ability to control their desires and apply their thinking capacity before acting—the greater the dominance of *aham* over *citta*, the greater this intellectual capacity.

Human beings, of course, are defined by their developed intellect, and it is commonly accepted that it is our intellect that sets us apart from the animals. We construct cities, study history, write philosophy, invent imaginary worlds, build atomic bombs, and threaten the safety of the entire planet. When our intellect contemplates the material world it gives rise to the material sciences, and when it contemplates the psychic world we get philosophy and the higher arts.[55] The human intellect has grown so great through these pursuits that it has become our dominant feature. Animal intellect is infinitely more limited by comparison, but it does have one advantage: animals cannot regress in the path of *pratisaiṇcara*. They are not mentally developed enough to go against what is in their best interests, the preservation of their existence. They don't eat when they are not hungry or when they are sick, as human beings sometimes do to the detriment of their health. Nor do they commit suicide to avoid the ignominy of public disgrace. Human beings, on the other hand, have the ability to go against the natural flow of evolution. Anandamurti refers to this as "negative *pratisaiṇcara*" and it is exclusive to the world of human beings with our developed intellect and the growing divide between our material and spiritual natures, a product of our clearly reflected *mahat*, which allows us to act independently from the flow of the Cosmic Mind.[56]

In principle, the cultivation of intellect increases the periphery of *aham* and thus accelerates a living being's movement along the path of *pratisaiṇcara*. This is easy to see in animals such as dogs and monkeys who undergo training. They quickly become more mentally advanced than wild dogs and monkeys, and that accelerated evolution may be sufficient for them to acquire a human body in the next life. The principle cause for this accelerated evolution is the psychic clash generated by their interaction with human beings, an opportunity wild animals by and large do not have. The more developed the minds they come in contact with, the greater the psychic clash they undergo and thus the faster their mental growth. This cultivation of intellect also speeds the evolution of human beings by gradually freeing them from their preoccupation with matter and thus decreasing the dominance of the static principle. Of course, the periphery of *aham*, as well as that of *mahat*, is to a certain extent fluid. There are times when our *citta* overpowers us and our *aham* fails to properly analyze the situation. Our intellect in those moments may become sluggish or even paralyzed. There are other times when we are more thoughtful and thus more prudent. But in general we all have a certain level of active intellect. In some it is greater, in others less so, and in all cases it can grow with effort, through clash and cohesion. We are all capable of developing our intellect through individual effort and contact with more advanced minds (hence the desire among students to gain admittance to better institutions of learning), just as animals can develop their intellect through training and association with human beings, and in most cases that development of intellect furthers the evolution of the individual mind. But in the case of human beings, the cultivation of intellect can become an obstacle to further development if it leads to increased vanity or ego, for it may block a human being from going beyond the intellect to reach the next stage of mental development, the flowering of intuition.

अहंतत्त्वान्महत्प्राबल्ये बोधिः ॥ १७ ॥

I.17 *ahaṁtattvān mahatprābalye bodhiḥ*

ahaṁtattvāt, over *ahaṁtattva*; *mahat*; pure I, sense of existence; *prābalye*, in the dominance of; *bodhiḥ*, intuition

"The predominance of *mahat* over *aham*
gives rise to intuition."

If we return to the analogy of concentric circles, intuition arises when the sphere of *mahat* becomes larger than the sphere of *aham*. As long as *mahat* is less pronounced than *aham*, it remains confined to its substantiation of the activities of *aham*. But once it exceeds the bounds of *aham*, that free portion is no longer tied to the ego and thus regains its identity with the cosmic *mahat*, which is the direct witness of the thought waves of the Macrocosmic Mind. *Mahat*, as we have seen earlier, is the pure feeling of existence, the pure I, unqualified by the sense of authorship, and there can be no differentiation in the sense of existence, no division between "my" sense of existence and "your" sense of existence. The feeling of existence is one and indivisible, whether we look at it from the macrocosmic or the microcosmic perspective. As long as *mahat* is tied to the individual ego, we experience it as our individual sense of self, but once *mahat* is freed from *aham* it immediately recovers its universal nature and thus becomes privy to the workings of the universe.

For this reason, Samkhya used the word *buddhi* interchangeably with *mahat* when referring to the first evolute of *prakrti*. The Samkhya philosophers thought of *mahat* as the supreme intelligence, often erroneously translated as "intellect." Consciousness is infinite intelligence in the highest sense of the word, and *buddhi* or *mahat*, which confers the sense of existence, is that intelligence manifest as the purest or subtlest form of mind.[57] In other words, the knowledge of existence is the zenith point of intelligence within the confines of the mind, which is why

Anandamurti also refers to *mahat* as the "knower-I," and thus the direct synthetic knowledge of the functioning of *aham* and *citta* is indeed the supreme intelligence. However, there are some functions of intelligence that the principal Samkhya commentators attribute to *buddhitattva* that rightly belong to *ahaṁtattva* or *ahaṁkára* due to the sense of authorship they imply.[58] *Mahat* does not act, per se, except in an indirect sense; rather, it is the knower of the actions of *aham*, the true actor.

Under normal conditions and in normal human beings, *mahat* is subsumed within *aham* and is thus confined to its substantiation of the thought processes of the individual ego-self. The *aham* typically remains in constant motion, flitting from one thought or sensation to another, and intuition cannot function if the waters of the mind are agitated. A faithful reflection can only be seen in calm water; otherwise it is inevitably distorted or cloudy. But if a person is able to still the activity of *aham*—whether through meditative practice, through prolonged intellectual activity leading to acute concentration, or simply due to an inborn mental tendency or *saṁskára*—then the waters of the mind turn crystalline and the consequent freeing of *mahat* gives rise to intuitive experience.

All the higher faculties that we commonly associate with intuition, including what is commonly known as ESP, are made possible by this connection to the cosmic *mahat*, which is in turn made possible when some portion of the individual's *mahat* is freed from its bondage to *aham*. Take clairvoyance, for example. A clear image comes into a person's mind of an explosion in a distant country and they know for certain, beyond the slightest shadow of a doubt, that what they have just witnessed is real, and a few hours later the news media confirms it. Psychics have been known to demonstrate this ability on occasion, and many people have had similar experiences at some point in their life—perhaps a sudden premonition that a family member has suffered a grievous injury, followed sometime later by the unwelcome news that their loved one had indeed suffered a serious accident at the very moment they had their premonition. Such extrasensory perceptions are due to a temporary freeing of *mahat* and only later are processed by the *aham*. This is an ability that can be cultivated. By practicing certain concentration techniques a person may be able to induce a momentary quieting of *aham* that allows the reflection of a clairaudient or clairvoyant perception to appear in the mirror of the knower-I. Such abilities, if they are not supported by an ethical consciousness, can also be put to dubious uses, as we learned in the 1990s when the US military declassified its experiments with remote viewing in which the government had employed a team of psychics for two decades to see if they could find a military application for their psychic abilities.

In order to illustrate this connection to the cosmic *mahat*, Anandamurti gives the example of a Hindu boy who is deathly ill and whose illness the doctors are unable to successfully diagnose or treat. The boy's distraught father goes to a nearby temple and prays all night to the goddess to save his dying son. In the early morning hours he falls into a trance-like state while kneeling in front of the idol, upon which the goddess appears to him and shows him a plant that will provide him with the remedy he needs. Overjoyed, he rushes home, procures the plant, prepares the remedy as the goddess instructed, and his son recovers. He attributes it to the grace and mercy of Mother Kali, but the true savior is the all-knowing Macrocosmic Mind. Due to his acute fear, the strength of his desire, and the long hours of anguished concentration, a portion of his *mahat* was liberated in that dreamlike trance to connect with the infinite storehouse of knowledge. This direct reflection of universal knowledge in the mirror of *mahat* then had to be processed by the *aham*. Once it came within the purview of his subconscious mind, it was interpreted according to the latent tendencies present there—that is, according to his psychic makeup and enculturation. Being a Hindu and a devotee of the goddess Kali, he had a vision of the goddess that his *aham* created out of the stored-up impressions in his mind. Had he been a Christian it might have been a vision of the Madonna. In this way, knowledge that was beyond the reach of his individual mind irrupted into his subconscious and thereafter crossed the border into his conscious mind.

Whereas the analytic mind is always subject to doubt, true intuitive experience is synthetic in nature and is characterized by the absence of doubt, an immediate awareness of the incontrovertible nature of the experience. Doubt is unavoidable in the realm of the intellect because analytic knowledge is, in the final analysis, a play of thoughts, the thoughts of the limited ego-self. It is thinking about reality rather than the direct experience of reality, what Anandamurti calls "the shadow of knowledge."[59] Thus the intellect has been compared in the Indian spiritual tradition to a blind man who thought an elephant was like a tree after he felt its leg. True intuition, however, is infallible.

In our current age there is a prevailing misconception that rational thought is the highest expression of the human mind. It is not. Rational thought is a function of the individual *aham* and is thereby subject to the limitations of analytic understanding. It is widely considered to be the pinnacle of human thinking simply because intuitive experience is so rare—indeed, so rare that many people have no experience of it, or if they do, they have no reliable context in which to interpret their experience. Intuition, on the other hand, is the direct perception of reality beyond the limitations of the senses and beyond the bounds of discursive thought. While rational thinking is capable of achieving a certain level of meaning by recognizing the relationship between discrete elements, the deepest level of meaning remains forever hidden from the rational mind, unless it is aided and supported by intuition, for it fails to see the true picture in which those elements appear. It is only *bodhi*, intuition, that can see reality as it is, rather than the shadow reality of those discrete elements, for it is unmediated knowledge as captured by the knower-I, the subtlest functional layer of mind.

In truth, the pinnacle of human understanding is attainable *only* through intuition, something our greatest thinkers throughout the ages have always understood, even those who made little or no effort to cultivate their intuitive powers. Time and again we find that their greatest discoveries came not through their intellect but through intuition. Albert Einstein, who arrived at his understanding of relativity in a flash of intuitive insight while gazing up at Bern's clock tower, put it most eloquently when he called the intuitive mind a "sacred gift" and the rational mind a "faithful servant."

Scientists like Einstein and thinkers like Nietzsche were able to achieve moments of intuitive insight through the cultivation of their intellect. Long periods of concentrated rational thought can lead to a profound state of concentration that calms the *aham* and thereby opens the door for *mahat* to shine its light upon the mind, giving rise to those flashes of intuitive wisdom that have long served as beacons for the forward progress of the human race. This is, in fact, a natural outcome of singleminded intellectual effort. But no one has contributed more to human understanding and human progress than those great sages who were able to gain unrestricted access to the universal wisdom of the cosmic *mahat* through the pursuit of meditation and other spiritual practices. While we periodically come across individuals with certain psychic abilities who are able at times to free a portion of their *mahat*, they normally have little control over their powers and only a limited understanding of the nature of their experience, often interpreting it in wildly different ways according to their enculturation. Highly developed yogis and saints, however, have direct access to this higher level of mental functioning, as has been attested to in the voluminous accounts of their psychic and spiritual powers. Such highly developed human beings have reached the point where they fully understand the purpose of the human journey, and nowhere is this more in evidence than when they turn the mirror of *mahat* toward Consciousness.

Mahat lies at the border between the individuality of *aham* and the universal singularity of the Supreme Self. In the previous examples, *mahat* served as a mirror for the workings of creation, the ever-changing heteromorphic waves generated by the cosmic *aham* and *citta*. But that mirror can also be turned in the opposite direction, toward Consciousness, toward the Supreme Subject whence the feeling of existence arises. This is the real thrust of the evolutionary journey and the culminating phase of human existence, when the mind seeks the Supreme Self, which is at once its origin and its destiny. When the mirror of intuition becomes spotless through spiritual practice, it becomes able to fully reflect the effulgence of that Supreme Consciousness, thus reaching the penultimate stage of spiritual enlightenment and paving the way for the final realization. "The Supreme is beyond the range of your *buddhi*. It is within the range of your *bodhi*."[60]

It is when the human being transcends the barriers of the intellect that they realize that supreme realization cannot be attained through science or philosophy, but only through intuition.[61]

महदहंवर्जिते ऽनग्रसरे जीवदेहे लतागुल्मे केवलं चित्तम् ॥ १८ ॥

I.18 *mahadahamvarjite 'nagrasare jiivadehe
latágulme kevalam cittam*

mahat, pure I; *aham*, doer-I; *varjite*, without; *anagrasare*, undeveloped; *jiiva*, living being; *dehe*, in a body or structure; *latágulme*, plants; *kevalam*, only; *citta*, objectivated mind

"In undeveloped living organisms and plants devoid of *aham* and *mahat*, there is only *citta*."

Sutras I.13 through I.15 traced the evolution of mind in the flow of *pratisaiṇcara*, beginning with the appearance of *citta*, followed by the emergence of *aham* out of *citta* and eventually *mahat* out of *aham*. In these next three sutras we turn our attention to that same evolutionary process as it pertains to the living structures that serve as a vehicle for the microcosmic mind as it makes its way up the evolutionary ladder in the progressive expansion of consciousness. Life as we know it is a combination of the microcosmic mind and the living body that allows that mind to function; for this reason, the biology of living beings parallels the development of the mind, growing in complexity in order to accommodate the burgeoning requirements of the psychic body. Thus we can to a great extent judge the development of the mind by studying the development of the body—for life to exist, one cannot be divorced from the other—and it is to this symbiosis or parallel development that we now turn our attention.

As we saw in sutra I.13, the first life-forms to appear on this planet were prokaryotes, which lack a nucleus, mitochondria, or any other membrane-bound organelle. Their DNA, proteins, and metabolites float directly in the cellular cytoplasm. Over time these microorganisms became increasingly more varied and more complex, developing into eukaryotes with membrane-bound nuclei, mitochondria, and other organelles—the beginning of the process of specialization that we see all the way up the evolutionary ladder—and from there into multicellular colonies and eventually into true metazoan life-forms. Throughout the nearly three billion years that it took those early prokaryotes to develop into metazoans with cellular differentiation, their simple *citta* mind was undergoing a process of gradual dilation or evolution that was paralleled in the increasingly complex bodies they inhabited.

Organisms that are still in the *citta* stage do not have differentiated sensory organs or anything analogous to a nervous system. They sense their environment with their entire bodies through the identification of *citta* with the incoming inferential waves, and due to the absence of *aham* there is no differentiation between perception and perceiver. This is the case with all unicellular life, whether it be the prokaryote bacteria and archaea, or the unicellular eukaryotes, such as protozoa, algae, and fungi. The same is true with multicellular colonies, such as volvox algae, and the simplest metazoans—sponges and bivalves, which lack true tissues or organs, regardless of whether we classify them as animals or plants. In this sutra, the word *latágulme* refers to the plant kingdom. The evolution of photosynthesis goes back almost to the beginning of life on Earth and eventually led to the oxygenation of the atmosphere, thanks to the early cyanobacteria, which in turn allowed for the development of more advanced forms of life. The lower plants, principally nonvascular plants such as algae and mosses, are still in the *citta* stage, albeit further along in that stage than unicellular organisms, but as we shall see in the next sutra, the higher plants or vascular plants all have some expression of *aham*.

Thus the expression of mind in these lower life-forms exists along a continuum, from the simplest prokaryotes with their fledgling *citta* to those simple metazoans in which the *citta* mind has evolved to the point that *aham* begins to emerge from its dormancy due to the struggle for survival and the concomitant waning of the *guńas*. And with *aham* comes the differentiation between perceiver and perceived, between *aham* and *citta*.

Chapter One

महद्वर्जिते ऽनग्रसरे जीवदेहे लतागुल्मे चित्तयुक्ताहम् ॥ १९ ॥

I.19 *mahadvarjite 'nagrasare jiivadehe latágulme cittayuktáham*

mahadvarjite, lacking *mahat*; *anagrasare*, undeveloped; *jiivadehe*, in the living body; *latágulme*, plants; *yuktá*, joined to, combined

"In underdeveloped organisms and plants devoid of *mahat*, there is *aham* and *citta*."

How do we know if a living creature possesses *aham* as well as *citta*? An easy first step is to look at the sensory apparatus of that living organism to see how it processes sensory information. Take a tiny fruit fly, for example. A fruit fly has a pair of composite eyes and a rudimentary brain and nervous system that processes visual information. An image appears in its eyes and is communicated to the brain with its 150,000 neurons, and on the basis of that perception the fruit fly acts or reacts. In other words, fruit flies can see. Perception demands a perceiver, which is a function of *aham*, and hence a fruit fly clearly has a functional *aham*, as do all insects. Moreover, it is capable of a host of "nonreactive" behaviors, that is, behavior that is initiated by the fruit fly rather than being a direct response to an external stimulus, a textbook example of a well-differentiated and fully functional *aham*. In the same vein, if a cockroach gets flipped on its back it will struggle to get upright. How does it know that it is upside down? Because it has sensors on its feet that enable it to be aware of its predicament and take measures to right itself. Cockroaches are arthropods, which comprise 80% of Earth's species, and all members of the insect class, even far less-developed insects than the highly able and much-maligned cockroach, possess a central nervous system, all five senses, and consequently a fully functional *aham*. The most primitive of known insects is considered to be the extinct Monura order from the Carboniferous-Permian period, and the members of this order had all five sense organs, as well as digestive, respiratory, endocrine, and nervous systems.

Since *aham* is clearly present in all insects, we know that the same is true of more developed animals and of the animal kingdom in general.[62] But what about the plant kingdom? This sutra states that some plants have *aham* as well as *citta*. Can we also see signs of *aham* in plants? The unequivocal answer is yes. While the higher plants, especially the angiosperms, which make up 80% of the plant kingdom, do not have a central nervous system like the arthropods and are thus lower in general on the evolutionary ladder, they do have internal systems that are analogous to an animal's nervous system and which enable them to perceive and interact with their environment. Moreover they do so by perceiving the same five sensory inferences that animals do—sight, sound, taste, touch, and smell—albeit without possessing specialized sense organs. Human beings have long believed that plants feel and perceive and react to their environment—lore about the inner life of plants goes back millennia—but it was only at the beginning of the twentieth century that scientific experiments began to demonstrate the truth of those ancient beliefs. In the early twentieth century, Jagadish Chandra Bose was able to measure how plants respond to various stimuli. Through the sensitive instruments he developed, he was able to show a clear parallelism between plant and animal tissue, including the transmission of electrical impulses in plants that parallels the role of the nervous system in animals (so similar in fact that in 2005 a group of plant biologists coined the somewhat controversial term "plant neurobiology" to refer to this field of study).

Through advances in contemporary biology, we now know quite a lot about the sensory capabilities of plants.[63] Plants turn toward light (phototropism) and alter their internal rhythms according to the diurnal movements of the sun (photoperiodism) because they have multiple photoreceptors, just as human beings and other members of the animal kingdom do. Similarly, plants not only emit but also perceive odors, both their own and those of their neighbors, and respond accordingly. They are likewise sensitive to touch. In our case, tactile impressions are transmitted by nerve cells through a combination of electrical and chemical signals,[64] and similar is the case with plants, who also transmit these impressions through electrical and chemical signals, only at a much slower rate. While we can transmit a nerve signal from the tip of our fingers to our brain in a matter of milliseconds, the electrical signals in tree tissue move at approximately one centimeter per second. It may take a adult redwood as much as half an hour to communicate information from its root system to its crown. And yet the fundamental mechanism of that transmission is eerily similar.[65] These same forest trees can differentiate between the saliva of different insects attacking their leaves, an indication that they can perceive the inference of taste, and while there are no scientific studies as yet to conclusively demonstrate perception of the sound inference in plants (though there is much anecdotal lore on the subject), there have been some studies that suggest that trees respond to certain sonic frequencies.[66] Plants also have a keen sense of up and down, that is, spacial orientation or proprioception (what some biologists call the "sixth sense"), which they gain in the same way we do—by detecting gravity, along with other signals from the environment.[67]

In addition to their sensory capacity, we now know that plants exhibit many of the same behaviors that animals do: they compete for territory and resources, repel predators, communicate with each other, and have visceral responses that are consistent with basic emotions, such as agitation and relaxation, pain and pleasure. Yellow jewelweed, for example, when faced with competitors for sunlight, put resources into their leaves to block the competitors' light, but they don't do this for relatives of their own species. Instead they alter their morphology through stem elongation and branching to acquire resources without shading their relatives, an example of both kin recognition and cooperation among members of the same species.[68] Plants have even been shown to have strong reactions to the death or mutilation of their neighbors. When grass is cut, for example, it emits greenleaf volatiles that act both as a defense mechanism and a distress signal that produces an agitated reaction in its neighbors. Plants have also been shown to retain the impressions of past stimuli, a rudimentary form of both short-term and long-term memory, and recent studies have shown that in some cases they are able to pass down memories of past traumas to future generations through epigenetic changes, just as animals do.[69] Because plants lack a developed nervous system, their mental activity is much slower than that of animals, but it is far from nonexistent. In a certain sense, "plants are just very slow animals," to borrow the title of Professor Jack Schultz's study on the shared biological systems of plants and animals.[70]

Given the parallelism between biological development and mental evolution, some elementary study of biology and a little reflection is enough to show the clear workings of *aham* in all but the simplest metazoan life-forms. It took approximately three billion years for the biological record to show evidence of metazoan creatures whose physical structures were consistent with the appearance of *aham*,[71] but once *aham* made its appearance, the rate of evolution dramatically increased (notwithstanding the several cataclysms during the last billion years that wiped out huge swaths of the earth's species), and it wasn't long, relatively speaking, before the earth began to be populated with cognitively sophisticated creatures: vertebrates, mammals, and eventually the first human beings, courtesy of the increasing psychic clash generated by the ever-active *aham*.

During this nearly one billion years of the development of *aham* and the concomitant expansion of consciousness through a myriad of different plant and animal forms, the groundwork was being laid for the emergence of *mahat* and the dawn of metacognition in living beings. To return to the insects for a moment, the largest class within the arthropod phylum, studies have shown that a wide array of insects, from fruit flies to the highly sophisticated honey bee, show responses to changing circumstances that are consistent with simple emotions. Fruit flies in the laboratory show a state of heightened agitation analogous to fear when menaced with what appears to be a predator, while honeybees and bumblebees show a pleasurable response when they encounter an unexpected source of sucrose and the opposite response when an expected source of sucrose doesn't materialize.[72] These are emotional responses at the simplest level, one of the many ways in which they display sophisticated cognitive capabilities, but while a honeybee's *aham* is highly capable, the honeybee shows no signs of metacognition, ie., the awareness that it is undergoing these mental or emotional states. A honeybee thinks, emotes, and acts on its own accord in order to successfully navigate its environment and fulfill its need for food, safety, sleep, and procreation—that is, to ensure its survival in a challenging and often dangerous world—but it does not have the ability to be aware that it is doing these things. For this it needs the mirror of *mahat*. Without *mahat*, it remains fully and irremediably identified with its thoughts and actions. In other words, it lacks the spark of self-awareness that is sleeping within its marvelously capable *aham*.

प्राग्रसरे जीवे लतागुल्मे मानुषे महदहंचित्तानि ॥ २० ॥

I.20 *prágrasare jiive latágulme mánuśe mahadahaṁcittáni*

prágrasare, developed; *jiive*, in living beings; *latágulme*, in plants; *mánuśe*, in human beings; *mahat*, I-feeling; *aham*, doer-I; *citta*, objectivated mind

"In developed animals, plants, and humans, there is *mahat*, *aham*, and *citta*."

Mahat, as we have seen, is the pure sense of existence, which functions as the substantiation of *aham*. In simple terms it can be defined as "self-awareness." *Mahat* is far more subtle than *aham*, just as *aham* is far more subtle than *citta*, and thus it is much more difficult to detect the signs of an emerging *mahat* when we reach this stage in the evolutionary ladder. Its presence is obvious in human beings, and it is relatively easy to see in the most highly developed animals, the great apes, who can identify themselves and communicate this sense of identity through different forms of symbolic language.[73] But how can we tell if a mouse has *mahat*—not the qualified existential awareness of *aham* but true self-awareness?[74] Or more difficult still, a towering redwood? This sutra states that there are plants who have *mahat*, and trees, particularly forest trees, are the most evolved members of the plant kingdom. But if some trees truly do have self-awareness, however dim it may be, how can we tell? The signs must be there—there is nothing truly hidden in the book of nature—but they are far more difficult to read.

We can start by looking from the outside, as we did with *aham*. In the animal kingdom we can study the brain, the nervous system, and the endocrine system, which helps to transmit and govern our emotional responses, and we can study the behaviors of developed animals. The more developed the nervous and endocrine systems, the more complex the behaviors an animal exhibits and the more evolved we can assume its mind to be. Nowadays there is a wealth of information available on animal physiology and behavior, but most of those studies focus on functions associated with *aham*. Communication, for example, is one of the most sophisticated expressions of *aham*, and we now know that virtually all members of the animal kingdom communicate with members of their own species by one means or another, whether it be through excretions, movement, or visual cues, as insects do, or through vocalization as well, as we see in birds and mammals. There is sufficient evidence to show that many plants do the same through chemical emanations such as pheromones. However, it is only when the use of language (in the sense of a structural system of communication), or its recognition, indicates a sense of self-identity that we can be sure of the presence of *mahat*. The great apes clearly have a developed sense of self-awareness that they are able to demonstrate through language, but they are not alone among the developed mammals. Dolphins identify themselves by signature whistles and can remember and identify the whistles of companions they haven't seen for as much as twenty years. Many dogs recognize their names and are able to differentiate their names from other similar sounds. Studies have shown that their brains respond to the sound of their name in much the same way as ours do. In addition, a number of animals, including the great apes, dolphins, orcas, horses, the Asian elephant, and the Eurasian magpie, have passed the mirror test, developed in 1970 by the American psychologist Gordon Gallup Jr. to determine visual self-recognition in animals.

We can also see evidence of *mahat* when we look at the complex emotions displayed in developed mammals. Emotions such as sadness, happiness, affection, hope, anxiety, and despair all require an awareness of individuality, ie., a sense of self. The ego of developed animals can be wounded or buoyed, and that can only happen due to the presence of *mahat*. A bee or a fly, for example, can experience fear or pleasure, but that fear or pleasure disappears in the absence of the external stimulus that brought it on and its absence leaves no lingering effect. A bee cannot become sad or traumatized due to a painful experience or feel content after a run of good fortune. Developed animals, however, can and do, and this is an unequivocal expression of self-awareness.

In her essay "Am I Blue?" Alice Walker describes the time she befriended a stallion named Blue who lived alone in a five-acre meadow next to the twenty she was renting. Soon after they met, she looked into his eyes and realized that the horse was lonely. "I was shocked" she wrote, "that I had forgotten that human animals and nonhuman animals can communicate quite well; if we are brought up around animals as children we take this for granted. By the time we are adults we no longer remember."[75] One day another horse appeared in the same paddock, this time a mare. Almost instantly Blue's behavior and mood changed. He started spending all his time with the mare, and when he did come to the fence for one of the apples Alice would bring him, she could not mistake the look of contentment in his eyes. Suddenly one day the mare was gone—as it turned out, she had been put there to breed—and Blue's behavior completely changed. He tore the ground with his hooves and repeatedly butted his head against a tree, not much different than what a human being might do in the same situation. When Blue did accept an apple from her, the look she saw in his eyes was one she was quite familiar with: sadness and despair.

This is something most pet owners and almost all children are aware of. They know their pets have complex emotions, that they feel contentment and sadness, and that their ego can be wounded. In some cases they can even become neurotic, which has spawned the profession of pet psychologist. These complex emotions are related to the sense of self and require a clearly differentiated *mahat*, as we can understand by examining our own experience. And there is evidence to indicate that this sense of self is present to varying degrees even in less-developed mammals. For example, recent studies have shown signs of metacognition in rats as well as empathic behavior, both of which point to the presence of *mahat*.[76]

Is there any evidence then to suggest that some members of the plant kingdom may have *mahat*, at least to some small degree? Again the answer is yes. The ancient Indian sages considered plants to be sentient beings with a dim expression of consciousness whose minds would eventually migrate into animal bodies as they climbed the ladder of evolution (a belief that is paralleled in their lack of a brain or central nervous system),[77] but in the *Yogavasistha*, a seminal yogic text that is thought to date back to the early centuries of the common era, some degree of self-awareness was attributed to trees. As this sutra demonstrates, Anandamurti concurs.[78] He has stated that the evolution of the animal mind picks up more or less where the evolution of the plant mind leaves off,[79] but there is some overlap, and that overlap is seen in the most advanced members of the plant kingdom, trees, specifically modern hardwood trees. There is convincing evidence to show that trees live in families, support their offspring and sick neighbors, communicate with each other in various ways, cooperate to fight off predators, and extend that cooperation to trees of other species in order to preserve the health of the forest, prompting the coining of the phrase "wood wide web." Individual trees have unique behavioral traits that differentiate one from another, including those who sprouted at the same time and who have grown up side by side under identical conditions. There is even evidence to show that trees form friendships and treat some trees differently than they treat others, of and by itself a clear indication of *mahat*, for it takes some sense of self to be able to differentiate between unique individuals. Although trees process information far more slowly than animals, they also have the capacity for memory and make decisions based on past experience. For example, trees that have suffered through a drought consume less water in the spring so they can have more available for the hot summer months. And injured trees are able to pass on the legacy of their struggles to their neighbors. Scientists are still discovering the physiological mechanisms behind these behaviors, but taken in toto it is abundantly clear that modern hardwood trees have at least a faint sense of self-awareness.[80]

There is another way to detect the presence of self-awareness in other living creatures that does not depend on the analytic powers of the intellect. We can also look from the inside, by applying our intuitive perception, provided it is sufficiently developed. Our intellect can understand *aham* with relative ease, but it is our intuition that truly understands *mahat*, which is, after all, beyond the bounds of analytical thought. This ability is well documented in the yogic world. *Aṅimá*, one of the eight occult powers (*aeshvarya*), allows an accomplished yogi to enter the minds of others, including those of nonhuman creatures. In the Yoga Sutras, Patanjali talks about the power of entering another's body in sutra III.38. Nor is this knowledge limited to the world of yoga. Shamans of different traditions have practiced this art for millennia, entering the minds of birds and animals and perceiving their subjective experience through the meta-empathic capability of intuition, and mystics throughout the ages have been able to communicate with both animals and plants and understand their experience. This is actually the more reliable method — the more scientific method, in fact — since the mind is the subtlest and most powerful instrument available to us. Our observation of other creatures coupled with the subtlety that comes from meditative practice allows us to intuitively perceive the inner experience of other living beings, not only their emotions but also their sense of self-awareness, to whatever extent it has developed. And unlike with the intellect, true intuitive perception is infallible. As discussed in sutra I.17, it is the direct perception of reality rather than the mediated perception of reality that is proper to the intellect. This is something many, if not most scientists balk at, or even dismiss out of hand, but there is an inner science as well as an outer science and the two cannot be divorced, just as Shiva and Shakti, awareness and the object of awareness, cannot be divorced if we wish to arrive at a true understanding of existence. That inner science concerns the knowledge of the mind and consciousness, and those scientists who do not strive to become adepts at the inner science as well as the outer science are poor scientists in the truest sense of the word, which comes from the Latin word for "knowledge." The pursuit of knowledge or the pursuit of truth demands that we give both the inner and the outer science their due importance.

Our intuitive capacity to resonate with the subjective experience of other living beings also helps us to understand and appreciate them. As I look out my window, I am surrounded by countless living beings with individual minds, all moving on the path of spiritual evolution. We share this path with them, and in a certain sense those nonhuman beings who share our environment are our ancestors, because each of us has had to pass through a myriad of lower life-forms to arrive where we are today. We are patient with children because we were once children ourselves. We know their limitations, empathize with their struggles, and hope that they will grow to be as good or better than we are. In the same way, we were once ants or trees and thus it behooves us to develop our empathy for less developed forms of life, as well as our understanding of their experience. When we see an ant, we know that in the absence of *mahat* it has yet to develop a sense of self-awareness, and it may be a very long time before that particular mind does, but we should remember that it will also be a human being one day, and thus we should not take its life intentionally if we can help it. "Compassion for living creatures is the highest dharma,"[81] says Anandamurti, and as our awareness grows of the web of life inching its way forward on the path of evolution, our compassion grows as well.

In this sutra, human beings are mentioned separately from plants and animals for a reason. When we look at the evolution of incarnate life in the path of *pratisaiñcara*, we human beings belong to a separate category all our own, a distinction that is determined not by our bodies but by our minds. Human beings have been called rational animals, but in Anandamurti's view, a human being is no more a rational animal than an animal is a moving plant. What is it then that sets us apart? We know that we humans have a highly developed *aham* that far exceeds the periphery of our *citta* and which has given birth to the enormous accomplishments of the human intellect, but there are animals who also have some degree of intellect. We also know that human beings have a keen sense of self-awareness, the ability to step back and be aware of our thoughts and feelings, the product of a highly developed *mahat*, but many other living creatures also have *mahat*, even if it be to a far lesser degree. They care for their children as we do, feel affection for them, and grieve when they lose them, all expressions of self-awareness. These are differences of degree, not of substance. So wherein lies the substantive difference?

It was mentioned in sutra I.16 that animals cannot go against the evolutionary flow of *pratisaiṇcara*, while human beings can and sometimes do. Therein lies the fundamental difference. In human beings *mahat* has reached the threshold where the individual mind achieves relative independence from the evolutionary flow of *pratisaiṇcara*. *Pratisaiṇcara* is like a river and we are subject to its impetus, as are all creatures, but unlike other living beings we can either accelerate our movement or degrade it by the conscious choices we make. An animal, even a highly developed animal, will always make the choices that are in its best interests, the choices that promote its ultimate welfare. It can neither accelerate its evolutionary movement nor impede it. Not so a human being. Some of us make choices that are clearly to our detriment, choices that degrade our minds and send us careening backward against the flow of *pratisaiṇcara*, while others take the opposite course and consciously accelerate their forward movement for the express purpose of completing their evolutionary journey, displaying a potential that is only seen in human beings. In other words, human beings are capable of apprehending the goal of incarnate life—spiritual perfection—and of making efforts to reach that goal. In short, we are capable of doing spiritual practice, of meditating on Consciousness and attaining enlightenment, while animals are not.

Thus human beings represent the final stage in the evolutionary journey of *pratisaiṇcara*. The individual mind, right from the most primitive unicellular microorganism with its emergent *citta*, is the vehicle for the expansion or unfolding of consciousness, which had hitherto been imprisoned in matter through the binding influence of the *guṇas* in the involutionary phase of *saiṇcara*. And the human mind is the last step in that expansion in which we bear witness to the full flowering of consciousness, its final release from the bondage imposed by *prakṛti* and its subsequent return to its original unbound state.

भूमव्याप्ते महति अहंचित्तयोः प्रणाशे सगुणा
स्थितिः सविकल्पसमाधिर्वा ॥ २१ ॥

I.21 *bhúmavyápte mahati ahaṁcittayoh praṅáshe saguṅá sthitih
savikalpasamádhir vá*

bhúmá, macrocosm; *vyápte,* pervaded; *mahati,* into *mahat;*
ahaṁ-cittayoh, of *aham* and *citta; praṅáshe,* in dissolution,
merger of effect into cause; *saguṅa,* qualified, with *guṅa;*
sthitih, state; *savikalpa,* with thought, determinate; *samádhih,*
complete concentration or absorption, ecstatic trance; *vá,* or

"When *aham* and *citta* merge into the all-pervasive macrocosmic *mahat,* it is the *saguṅa* state or *savikalpa* samadhi."

Human beings are the only creatures who can consciously direct their minds toward Consciousness. They are the only creatures who ask the questions "Who am I?" "Where have I come from?" and "Where am I going?" And they are the only creatures who have the capacity to find the answer to those questions through direct experience. Ordinarily the human mind, like the animal mind, remains absorbed in the dance of maya. Due to the attractive power of Consciousness, however, human beings cannot remain satisfied with the objects of this world, be they physical or psychic. Eventually they turn their minds within in a quest for fulfillment, and this quest ultimately leads them to the goal of their evolutionary journey, the merger of the mind into Consciousness. This merger is accomplished in two distinct stages: *savikalpa* and *nirvikalpa.* The first of these, also known as the *saguṅa* state, is the merger of the microcosmic *mahat* into the macrocosmic *mahat.* In this penultimate stage of spiritual evolution, the *guṅas* are still expressed and thus Consciousness is qualified; it is *saguṅa,* "with *guṅa.*" Consciousness has an object, and that object is the macrocosmic *mahat,* the universal or cosmic I.

In order to understand this state and the means of achieving it, we can examine once again the three functional layers of the mind. *Citta,* whose function is to take the form of the object of thought, be that object physical or psychic, is the crudest functional layer. *Aham*, the next layer in subtlety, is the thinker or doer-I and the direct substantiation of *citta*. And *mahat*, the pure I, the pure sense of existence, is the substantiation of *aham*. Beyond *mahat* lies consciousness, the final frontier—in this case, the individual consciousness or *jiivátmá*, which is witness to the play of the microcosmic mind. As long as the mind remains absorbed in the waves of *citta* it cannot look beyond itself, toward the source from which it has come. Thus the *citta* must be brought to a standstill if our attention is to proceed inward, toward Consciousness. When the *citta* ceases its activity—ie., when there are no thought waves in the mind—then the *citta* temporarily ceases to exist. This is called *prańásha*, the merger of the effect into its cause, since *citta* emerged out of *aham* in the *saiṉcara* phase of creation. *Aham*, however, is still active. The sense of individuality remains, and as long as it persists, Consciousness remains forever out of reach. Thus the *aham* must also be merged into its cause, *mahat*, from which it emerged in the flow of *saiṉcara*. In other words, the sense of individuality must be transcended. When this is accomplished, the aspirant reaches the border of consciousness, the hinterland between mind and spirit.

This sutra tells us, however, that *citta* and *aham* must be dissolved into the macrocosmic *mahat*, not the individual *mahat*. I experience my individual *mahat* as my personal sense of existence, my fundamental sense of self. In the language of philosophy it is the substantiation of my individual ego, the "I" of "I am Devashish." My thoughts are changing from one moment to the next, as they have all my life—I may not have a single thought or feeling at sixty-five that I had when I was two—but my sense of existence remains the same, continuous and unchanging. That is my individual *mahat*. The cosmic *mahat*, on the other hand, is the unchanging sense of self behind the ever-changing drama of the cosmos, the "I" of "I am Brahma." The thoughts it witnesses are planets and living beings and the stars that illumine them both. Thus it is *bhúmávyápta*, all-pervading. But while the difference seems enormous—and it is, as long as we remain confined within the limits of our individual mind—that difference disappears the moment we are freed from those confines. Some of the early astronauts wrote accounts describing their first experience of space, how overwhelmed they were by a sense of awe at the grandeur of the creation and how it radically changed their outlook on life. Edgar Mitchell, who went on to found the Institute of Noetic Science to conduct research into meditation and consciousness, had this to say about his experience: "And that was accompanied by a sense of joy and ecstasy, which caused me to say, 'What is this?' It was only after I came back that I did the research and found that the term in ancient Sanskrit was *samadhi*."[82] It wasn't the *savikalpa* samadhi of this sutra—his *aham* was still active, perceiving the cosmos through the window of his eyes—but the object of his attention was so vast that his mind underwent a corresponding expansion that gave rise to a sense of ecstasy. What happens then if we take it once step further and remove the object altogether, along with the intermediary presence of *aham*, leaving only the conscious awareness of the self? In this case, the *mahat* also becomes infinite; that is, the individual *mahat* is automatically converted into the macrocosmic *mahat*. What limits or circumscribes our individual I-feeling is *aham* and *citta*—the presence of our ego and the contents of our mind. That same feeling of existence, when it is freed from its substantiation of individuality, automatically rediscovers its unity with the cosmic *mahat*, for there is no essential difference between the two. The only difference lies in the object, in the boundaries imposed by the contents of the mind and the actions of the individual ego-self. Remove the object and the actor, and *mahat* stands alone as the cosmic I.

It was explained in an earlier sutra that the cosmic *mahat* is the first modification of Consciousness when Shakti awakens from its dormancy, the first qualification of the previously unbound, unqualified *puruśa*. Consciousness becomes aware of itself only when *mahat* emerges from the womb of creation under the binding power of *sattvaguńa*. The cosmic *mahat*, prior to the emergence of the cosmic *aham*, creates the sense of existence in the Universal Consciousness. When the cosmic *aham* and the cosmic *citta* emerge, the cosmic *mahat* then stands as the nominal witness of the cosmic thought waves. Thus there are two stages of *savikalpa*: the first, in which Consciousness is aware of its cosmic imagination, and the second and higher state, in which Consciousness is only aware of itself.[83] This is the zenith point of *savikalpa* samadhi, the trance of determinate absorption, which brings the human being to the verge of enlightenment, the complete liberation of Consciousness from the bondage of *prakrti*.

Thus the goal of yogic practice is to still the mind through concentration and direct that concentrated mind toward Consciousness by gradually merging *citta* into *aham* and *aham* into *mahat* until the *savikalpa* or *saguńa* state is reached. It is the most difficult of all mental achievements but it can be attained through constant practice. The mind must be weaned from its dependence on the world of forms through detachment or *vaerágya* and trained through constant practice to focus its entire attention on Consciousness.

The word *samádhi* refers to a state of absolute absorption in the object of concentration. Its etymological meaning is "joining" or "putting together." Here it refers to the joining of the diverse flows of the mind into a unitary flow that unites with its object of attention. It is used in yoga and Tantra to refer to states of trance where the mind attains complete identification with its object. Thus the type of samadhi depends on the object. If the object of ideation is a crude object, it is called *jadá* or crude samadhi; if the object is subtle then it is spiritual samadhi, of which there are different types and stages. In either case, it is a temporary achievement. *Savikalpa* samadhi is not liberation or enlightenment but a temporary casting off of the chains of *prakrti*, thereby ensconcing oneself for a time in the Supreme Self. When a person who has yet to achieve enlightenment enters samadhi they are still bound by their unrequited *saḿskáras* or mental tendencies, a concept that will be discussed in the following chapters. When those temporarily suspended *saḿskáras* again begin to vibrate, the sense of individuality returns and the person is evicted from paradise. If that state becomes permanent it is called *mukti* or liberation. But though it be temporary, with the attainment of the *saguńa* state the doors to the final triumph of Consciousness begin to swing open. Anandamurti talks of four direct consequences of the attainment of *savikalpa* samadhi. They are: 1) the realization of the Absolute, in which one perceives the Supreme Entity behind the apparent multiplicities of the world;

2) an acceleration in the requital of reactive momenta (*saṁskára*), by which all afflictions caused by defective cognition gradually disappear; 3) the loosening of the bondages of reactions, in which one continues to perform actions but does not acquire the reactions of those actions; and 4) movement towards the undifferentiated state of cognition, the *nirvikalpa* state.[84]

In other words, after achieving *savikalpa* samadhi one is no longer subject to spiritual ignorance.[85]

There are, it should be pointed out, many kinds of lesser samadhis that are precursors to the *savikalpa* or *saguńa* state. For example, a person may become absorbed in the contemplation of a realized master or an image of God and thereby experience indescribable bliss. This is known as *bháva* samadhi, absorption in an elevated idea. In a general sense, these lesser samadhis can be divided into four stages that correspond to the ascent of the kundalini through the lower chakras.[86] As the kundalini ascends, the sense of identification with Consciousness grows progressively stronger. Almost all of us have experienced watching a movie and identifying with a character to the point that we forget that we are watching a movie and become absorbed in the emotions and experiences of that character. This sense of identification is a natural result of concentration, and the depth of the identification depends on how deeply we are absorbed in what we are watching. Similarly, our identification with Consciousness grows as our concentration deepens, and this is accompanied by the upward movement of the kundalini, until we lose our sense of individuality altogether and completely identify with Consciousness. This complete identification with Consciousness is *savikalpa* samadhi and it is attained when the kundalini reaches the sixth chakra.

This is an extremely high state of realization, the penultimate rung on the ladder of evolution, and it is as far as the mind can go. There is still one more leg of the journey, however, one final achievement before Consciousness can regain its perfect freedom. But to reach that supreme state the mind will have to remain behind.

आत्मनि महत्प्रणाशे निर्गुणा स्थितिर्निर्विकल्पसमाधिर्वा ॥ २२ ॥

I.22 *átmani mahatprańáshe nirguńá sthitir nirvikalpasamádhir vá átmani,* into atman; *mahat,* I-feeling; *pranáshe,* in the dissolution; *nirguńa,* without *guńa,* unqualified, objectless; *sthitih,* state; *nirvikalpa,* undifferentiated, objectless, transconceptual; *samádhih,* trance; *vá,* or

"When the *mahat* merges into the atman, it is the *nirguńá* state or *nirvikalpa* samadhi."

Consciousness in its unbound, unqualified state is *nirguńa,* "without *guńa.*" It is undifferentiated and objectless. It is from this objectless, undifferentiated Consciousness that the creation arises under the binding power of *prakrti,* and it is into this objectless Consciousness that the individual mind must merge in order to complete the evolutionary journey of *pratisaiṉcara,* being the final stage in the conversion of mind into Consciousness. The merger of the mind into its source is equivalent to its dissolution. In *savikalpa* samadhi the mind achieves its ultimate expansion, its merger into the cosmic I, but in order to enter the *nirvikalpa* or *nirguńa* state the *mahat* must undergo its own *pranásha.* It must disappear into its source so that Consciousness can regain its absolute freedom.

In the *saguńa* state, Consciousness has as its object the universal sense of existence, the cosmic I. This is the pinnacle of mental experience. But in *nirvikalpa,* which is attained when the kundalini reaches the seventh chakra, the I is transcended and thus Consciousness is no longer aware of itself. It has reached the stage of pure awareness. Consciousness is cognition, that which allows us to be aware that we exist, the mirror upon which the sense of existence is reflected. When that sense of existence is transcended, when the image in the mirror disappears, there is no reflection, only an empty mirror. Without the I, there is no longer any mind to be aware of its experience.

To many this can seem not only perplexing but undesirable. There is a saying in the devotional literature of the Vaishnavas: "I don't want to be sugar, I want to eat sugar." The *savikalpa* state is a state of infinite, unfading bliss. It seems only natural that the mind would be content to remain forever in that lofty state of realization, rather than leave it behind for what might appear to be nothing. But the *savikalpa* state is not the ultimate achievement, since even this state is perceptible by consciousness. Eventually the spiritual aspirant wants to go beyond that awareness of the ocean to become one with the ocean itself. And while it might appear to the mind to be nothing, it is not. Consciousness in its pure unqualified state is the ultimate something, though that something is forever beyond the mind's comprehension. And even if it seems undesirable at first, we have no choice but to seek it out, for it is the final destination of incarnate life and it pulls at us like a magnet that cannot be resisted. As with *savikalpa* samadhi, *nirvikalpa* samadhi is temporary, but once it is achieved the urge to return is irresistible. When it becomes permanent it is called *mokṣa* in Tantra and *nirvana* in Buddhism. The most common English equivalent is "enlightenment," and it is the final culmination of the evolutionary journey, the final destiny for each and every one of us, for we are the vehicles of evolution.

This state, however, cannot be described because ...

तस्य स्थितिरमानसिकेषु ॥ २३ ॥

I.23 *tasya sthitir amánasikeśu*

tasya, of it, of that; *sthitih*, state; *amánasikeśu*, beyond the mind

"This state is beyond the mind."

In Buddhism, the *nirvikalpa* or *nirguña* state is called *shunya*, the void. In English we say "nothing"—no thing. In other words, there is no object. But it is not a void in the true sense of the word. What *shunya* really means is that the state of unqualified Consciousness cannot be described since there is no object (no thing) to apprehend and no mind to apprehend it. The void is in fact full—full of consciousness—but consciousness cannot be known or apprehended or described without mind, since it is the mind that knows, apprehends, and describes. Consciousness is a priori, that is, it exists before mind, and thus mind cannot know consciousness, any more than a pair of eyeglasses can know the eye.

There is a famous story related by the disciples of Sri Ramakrishna, a nineteenth-century Bengali saint and an important figure in the history of yoga. Once a group of disciples asked him to describe *nirvikalpa* samadhi. "That is not possible," he said. "It cannot be described." They begged him and finally he said, "Okay, let me go into *nirvikalpa* and when I come out I'll tell you what I can." When he came out of samadhi, he said, "No, it is not possible because there is no one there to describe it. A salt doll went to measure the depth of the ocean, but before it had gone far into the water it melted away. It became entirely one with the water of the ocean. Then who was to come back and tell the ocean's depth?"[87]

But ...

अभावोत्तरानन्दप्रत्ययालम्बनी वृत्तिस्तस्याः प्रमाणम् ॥ २४ ॥

I.24 *abhávottaránandapratyayálambanii vrttis tasyáh pramáńam*

abháva, vacuity, void; literally, "no-thought"; *uttara*, after; *ánanda*, bliss; *pratyaya*, conviction, firm belief, trust; *álambanii*, shelter, support; *vrttih*, mental propensity; *tasya*, of that; *pramáńam*, proof

"The experience of bliss that follows this state of vacuity is its proof, the basis for firm conviction."

Samadhi is a temporary state of transcendental bliss, whether it be *savikalpa* or *nirvikalpa*. When the suspended *samskáras* begin to vibrate again, the mind is drawn back into the world of phenomenal experience. In *savikalpa* the mind is present in its most exalted or expanded form, and thus one is fully aware of one's experience, but in *nirvikalpa* the mind undergoes temporary dissolution and thus there is no such awareness. When the mind returns, however, and with it the awareness of experience, one knows where one has been from the trailing waves of bliss that inundate the mind.

Deep sleep is generally considered to be a state of vacuity. While this is not actually the case—during deep sleep the causal mind remains active, even though the conscious and subconscious minds do not—we can draw on the analogy. When we feel the onset of sleep, we know where we are headed, and when we wake out of a deep slumber, we know where we have been, even though we weren't aware of it at the time. We say, "Oh, I was asleep." And if it was deep sleep from which we wake, rather than a dream, then we experience a pleasant feeling of restfulness—the natural tranquil pleasure that immediately follows a period of nonthinking.

If deep sleep is a state of relative unconsciousness, *nirvikalpa* samadhi is very near its opposite. The bliss one feels upon returning from *nirvikalpa* is the greatest that the mind can experience. It serves not only as the basis for the mind's firm conviction of where it has been but also as proof that the mindless state was one of absolute bliss. And as with sleep, the mind not only knows where it has been but also where it is going. Before reaching *nirvikalpa* the mind must pass through *savikalpa*, even if its stay there be brief—for the kundalini to reach the seventh chakra it must pass through the sixth—and thus the feeling of bliss that the aspirant feels grows until it reaches the zenith point of *savikalpa*, whereupon the all-attractive force of Consciousness becomes so powerful that it pulls the mind in like a moth to a flame or an iron filing to a magnet, causing it to lose its existence in the ocean of absolute bliss. When the mind returns, its first experience is the mirror of its last, passing through *savikalpa*, if only momentarily, on its way back into normal consciousness, but though the sense of self returns, the *nirvikalpa* state is so powerful that the waves of bliss trail on for long afterward, reminding the yogi of where they have been, like a powerful wake that can be seen from a great distance well after the ship that left it has disappeared from sight.

> In the stage immediately after this state, that is, after the break of that samadhi, when the faculty of understanding returns, then one realizes that some unknown current of bliss from some unknown region has flooded one's entire entity, carrying it away to some ultra-sensual celestial realm vibrating with consciousness ... After the break of that self-lost state of fathomless fulfillment, when one feels the return of their hazy ego carried along in a current of bliss, they realize that their preceding state was without question a state of the loftiest ecstasy, which is called *nirvikalpa* samadhi.[88]

Chapter One

भावभावातीतयोः सेतुस्तारकब्रह्म ॥ २५ ॥

I.25 *bhávabhávátiitayoh setus tárakabrahma*

bháva, idea, the manifest universe, Saguńa Brahma;
bhávátiitayoh, beyond *bháva*, the unmanifest Nirguńa Brahma;
tayoh, of the two; *setuh*, bridge; *táraka*, liberating

"The bridge between Saguńa and Nirguńa Brahma
is Táraka Brahma."

The word *bháva* means "idea" or "ideation." Here it refers to Saguńa Brahma, in the sense that the creation is an internal thought projection of the Macrocosmic Mind. That which is beyond *bháva*, beyond thought, is *bhávátiitayoh*, ie., *nirguńa*. Because Nirguńa Brahma is beyond the mind, beyond thought, beyond all attribution, it is not possible for the mind to meditate on Nirguńa Brahma.[89] This is a dilemma that is recognized in Tantra in both practice and philosophy. Ideation or meditation can only occur when both subject and object are present; thus the mind can only ideate on Saguńa Brahma, the Cosmic Consciousness as the witness of its creation, for by definition there is neither subject nor object in *nirguńa*. Nor can Nirguńa Brahma liberate the living being from bondage, since *nirguńa*, being objectless, has no contact with the manifest world, the world of *saguńa*.[90] Meditation on *saguńa* can lead the aspirant to the *saguńa* state, that is, to *savikalpa* samadhi or *mukti*, but not to *nirvikalpa* or *mokśa*. We meditate with the mind, so how can we possibly attain that which is beyond the mind, beyond conception?

The answer to this dilemma is what Anandamurti calls Táraka Brahma, the tangential point between *saguńa* and *nirguńa*, a concept unique to Tantra. Being tangential, it is that aspect of Brahma that remains in contact with both *saguńa* and *nirguńa*, thus serving as a bridge between the two. And since it exists for the sole purpose of effecting the liberation of living beings, he calls it Táraka Brahma, "Liberating" Brahma.

This is philosophy, but how does philosophy translate into practice? How does this tangential point manifest in the visible world and how can it be accessed? While this will be discussed in greater detail in sutras III.8 and III.9, the simple answer is that the liberating function of Brahma is effected through enlightened beings, through those who are themselves permanently liberated from bondage and are thus established in the *nirvikalpa* state. Only a liberated soul can liberate a soul in bondage, just as it takes a free man in possession of the key to free a prisoner from his cell. Such beings remain in *saguña*, in the manifest world, but they have free access to the unmanifest world as well, keeping one foot, as it were, in *nirguña* and the other in *saguña*. Thus they can act as a bridge by which the soul in bondage can cross from one to the other.[91]

In India one comes across images of Shiva with his eyes half closed in contemplation. This is symbolic of the *táraka* state. When his eyes are open he is in *saguña*, the witness of his creation; when his eyes are closed, he is immersed in *nirguña*, oblivious to the manifest world; but when his eyes are half closed he maintains contact with both the manifest and unmanifest worlds, with both *saguña* and *nirguña*. In the Tantric tradition, the meditation of Táraka Brahma is considered to be unique from other forms of meditation. Spiritual aspirants and yogis practice other forms of meditation to expand their minds and undertake the journey to *savikalpa*, but in order to make the final crossing from *saguña* to *nirguña* the Tantric yogi meditates on a specific form of the enlightened being. That form remains in the manifest world and is thus visible to our inner eye, but the mind of the enlightened being remains in the *nirguña* state. Perfect concentration in meditation, *dhyána*, brings identity between subject and object, between the meditator and the object of meditation, the *dheya*. When the *dheya*, the object of *dhyána*, is in the *nirvikalpa* state, though their body or image remains perceptible and thus within *saguña*, the meditator, upon fusing their mind with their object of ideation, achieves oneness with the *dheya* and thus effects the crossing from *savikalpa* to *nirvikalpa*.

This is the philosophy behind the practice. Anandamurti tells us, however, that "Táraka Brahma is not a figure of philosophy—it is a creation of devotional sentiment."[92] In other words, in order to reach this fusion, Táraka Brahma must come alive within the aspirant's mind, and this is only possible through intense devotion. The Supreme Consciousness is the witness of our existence, and in the meditation of Táraka Brahma the *dheya* is the personification of that witnessing Consciousness. With other human beings we will always experience some separation, but there is no separation between our innermost Self and the human figure of the *dheya*, once it becomes fully "alive" within our minds, for the *dheya* is the visible form of our innermost Self. And it is our devotion that makes the *dheya's* presence more real, more alive, more strongly felt, than any other presence. When Naren, the future Vivekananda, asked Ramakrishna if he had seen God, the master replied that he saw God more clearly than he saw Naren, and this is the experience of all devotees and yogis when the *dheya* becomes fully alive within their minds through the alchemy of devotional sentiment. When devotion for the *dheya* reaches its zenith point, the point of maximum attraction, the mind becomes ripe for the fusion that leads the aspirant across the bridge from *saguńa* into *nirguńa*.

In his short explanation of this sutra, Anandamurti introduces the concept of *mahásambhúti*. *Mahá* means "great" and *sambhúti* means "creation" or "created being."[93] Everything in this universe is the *sambhúti* of Supreme Consciousness, the manifest form of the Divine, but the *mahásambhúti* is a special form, a special creation that functions as a conduit for Táraka Brahma in order to bring liberation to human beings in all spheres of life, not only the spiritual sphere. Such great souls have been celebrated in India and in yogic literature for millennia, and their importance is personified in the famous couplet from the Bhagavad Gita: *paritráńáya sádhunáḿ vináshaya ca duśkritham; dharma saḿsthápanártháya saḿbhavámi yuge yuge*. "To save the righteous, destroy evil, and reestablish dharma, I manifest myself age after age." *Mahásambhúti* and Táraka Brahma, however, are separate concepts. The first is a unique physical form through which Táraka Brahma acts in the world to assure the spiritual elevation of living beings, while Táraka Brahma is that aspect of the Divine that maintains a link between *saguńa* and *nirguńa* and thus serves to bring the individual living being's journey to its culminating point, liberating consciousness from the last vestiges of its bondage through the focalized nexus of each newly enlightened soul. Táraka Brahma cannot be limited to the *mahásambhúti* but rather can act through any suitable form in order to take the aspirant from *saguńa* to *nirguńa*.

Chapter Two

In Chapter One we looked at the universe through the widest possible lens, tracing the cycle of creation through its two complimentary phases: the formation of the Macrocosm through the involution of Consciousness into matter, and the evolution of consciousness out of matter through the plurality of microcosms. In Chapter Two we narrow our focus to the fundamental nature of living beings within the context of the cosmos, with a particular emphasis on the human being, since it is to the human being that philosophy is addressed, the same human being that is reading this book in an effort to understand their own nature. We begin the chapter with the fundamental impulse of not only human beings but of all living beings, the desire for happiness, and the role this fundamental urge plays in spiritual evolution.

अनुकूलवेदनीयं सुखम् ॥ १ ॥

II.1 *anukúlavedaniiyaṁ sukham*

anukúla, congenial; *vedaniiyaṁ*, feeling, sensation; *sukham*, pleasure, happiness

"Happiness is a congenial mental feeling."

The word *sukha* means both "pleasure" and "happiness," while its antonym, *duhkha*, means both "pain" and "suffering." That is, both pleasure and pain, *sukha* and *duhkha*, exist on a continuum of congenial or uncongenial mental feeling, being varying expressions of the same phenomenon. In essence, all incarnate experience falls into one of these two categories, pleasant or painful, regardless of degree, being the two poles of a fundamental polarity. This is easy enough to understand, for it accords with our everyday experience, but the actual nature of pleasure and pain, happiness and suffering, and the role they play in incarnate life presents a far greater challenge, both for psychology and philosophy.

Aristotle defined happiness as a life well-lived, a free interpretation of the Greek term *eudaimonia*, which literally translates as "good spirit" and which carries with it an implicit sense of virtue, and the work of modern psychologists who have developed influential theories of happiness, such as Abraham Maslow's hierarchy of needs and Victor Frankl's exploration of man's search for meaning, can be seen as an extension of ideas advanced by Socrates, Plato, and Aristotle twenty-five centuries earlier. One thing they all have in common is that their understanding of happiness remains entirely and perhaps unavoidably subjective, for it seems that a subjective description may be as close as we can come to understanding what appears to be an abstract and often ineffable experience.

In recent decades, neuroscientists have endeavored to add to our understanding of this crucial but elusive aspect of human experience by studying what happens in our brain when we feel pleasure or happiness, a reflection of the reductionist paradigm that dominates contemporary scientific thought. Aided by advances in neural imaging, they have discovered that certain brain centers are associated with physical pleasure and others with the more abstract feelings of happiness, especially the nucleus accumbens, the most studied pleasure center in the brain in contemporary neuroscience. The activity of these pleasure centers depends on the secretion of certain neurotransmitters, most prominently dopamine, which is associated with the nucleus accumbens, but also endorphines, endocannibinoids, oxcytoxin, gaba (the anti-anxiety molecule), and serotonin, although little is really known about how they work. While this research has helped us to understand the physiological basis of our experience, it has not brought us any closer to understanding what happiness actually is. Neuroscience can help us to know what kinds of activities increase the secretion of these neurochemicals, thus stimulating those brain centers — social bonding, physical exercise, and meditation are examples of such activities, and studies have even shown that eating more fruits and vegetables increases happiness, irrespective of country or culture—but that doesn't further our understanding of the experience itself. The chemical changes in the brain are related to the experience but cannot be equated to the experience. The one is a chemical reaction and the other remains purely subjective. In the words of Richard Davidson, a prominent neuroscientist, "of all the emotions, happiness is the one scientists least understand."

In Indian philosophy, the different varieties of subjective experience have been meticulously cataloged according to what senses are involved, the nature of the external object, its presence or absence, and so on, perhaps nowhere more so than in Buddhist philosophy, but again all subjective experience is ultimately divided into *sukha* and *duhkha,* with the exception of some systems that classify certain experiences as neutral in character. Rather than make any effort to explain the actual nature of pleasant or painful experiences, however, the focus of Indian philosophy has always been the attainment of the enlightened state, and thus all subjective experience, whether pleasant or painful, has by and large been seen as an obstacle to the final attainment, even experiences of profound happiness or joy, for reasons we will explore later in this sequence of sutras. In this sutra and its accompanying commentary, the first of seven on the subject of dharma, the fundamental nature of the living being, Anandamurti takes a different approach, one that appears for the first time in the Indian philosophical tradition. He defines the experience of pleasure and pain, *sukha* and *duhkha,* in terms of the interaction between one's mental waves and the waves one encounters in the manifest world, whether those waves be material or psychic. This implies, of course, that every expression in this universe has a wave nature, something that will be explored later in this chapter and again in Chapter Four. For now, let it suffice to say that in Tantra, as in quantum mechanics, all expression is considered to be vibrational in nature; that is, everything is composed of waves of one order or another. Energy flows in waves, and matter, which Anandamurti has variously described as bottled-up energy or a container for energy,[1] is also a collection of waves. Nor is this wave nature confined to the material universe of *saiṇcara*. Thoughts are also vibrational patterns, ie., waves—psychic waves—and each individual mind has its own characteristic wavelength, which is a function of all the mental propensities active or dormant in that mind. Which propensities become active in which situations depends on the latent *saṁskáras* or tendencies of the individual mind, just as the ocean currents depend on wind, water density, tides, and the features of the ocean floor. In other words, it depends on a person's mental makeup, their tendency to react in certain ways under certain conditions.

Thus when the mind encounters an incoming vibration, whether it be from an object or another mind, that incoming vibration will be experienced as pleasant or unpleasant depending on the amount of harmony or discord between the vibrational character of one's mind, as determined by one's *saṁskáras*, and that of the incoming wave. The greater the harmony, the easier it is for the mind to assimilate that wave and thus the greater the pleasure or happiness one feels; the greater the discord, the more difficult it is to assimilate and the greater the displeasure or unhappiness. Whether the experience is pleasant or painful depends on both the nature of the mind and the nature of the vibration one encounters.

Take for example a rose. A person walking in a park sees a rose and their sense of aesthetic beauty is aroused, which is in turn a product of the impressions left in their mind from previous experience, be it from this life or from previous lives—for example, pleasant experiences associated with roses or with flowers in general. The flower's form, color, and fragrance induces a relaxed sensation in the body and a pleasant feeling in the mind. Later on their walk, the same person comes across a decomposing body and feels an instant sense of revulsion accompanied by a twinge or two of fear. The smell of putrefaction, the flies crawling on the decaying flesh, the specter of death and mortality that surges in their mind, the fear that they might be in danger—all combine to create tension in their nerves and a corresponding sense of discomfort in their mind. A different person, however—thankfully rare in human society—might have quite the opposite reaction were they to happen by. They might hate flowers, especially red roses, and feel a kind of morbid fascination with dead and decaying bodies, even a kind of aesthetic pleasure. For such a person the sight of a rose gives rise to disharmony and discord in their mind, whereas the dead body elicits a harmonious or pleasurable reaction.

To choose a more commonplace example, suppose a person arrives at a park with a boombox and starts playing a heavy metal song at a loud volume. One passerby loves the music and feels an immediate sense of euphoria, while another passerby hears the same song and is so bothered by the music, she thinks about lodging a complaint with the owner of the boombox. The same music, the same vibration, the same environment, but an entirely different reaction due to the difference in the mental makeup of the two individuals. This is not only true of human beings but also of less developed beings. Through experience they discover those objects that create pleasurable feelings in their minds and bodies and those that create unpleasant feelings, and thus they learn to run after those objects that give them pleasure and avoid those that give them pain.

The experience of pleasure and pain, happiness and suffering, thus depends on the relative parallelism or lack thereof in the mind, or more specifically in the *citta*, when it comes in contact with its environment, and that mental experience is reflected in the body—in the brain and nerves and glands. The nature of the ensuing mental experience, the intensity and emotional shading of the congenial mental feeling (*anukúla vedaniiya*) or uncongenial mental feeling (*pratikúla vedaniiya*), in turn depends on two factors: the individual's *saṁskáras*, or mental predispositions, which give rise to certain propensities, and the nature of the vibrations the mind encounters. If the incoming vibration corresponds to those predispositions then it will be easy to assimilate and will be experienced as pleasant; if not, then it will be difficult to assimilate and will be experienced as unpleasant.[2]

A key point to keep in mind here is that pleasure and pain, *sukha* and *duhkha*, *anukúla vedaniiya* and *pratikúla vedaniiya*, are constantly changing states. We are all in a state of constant flux, fleeing *duhkha* and running after *sukha*. These are relative states and will always be so because the mind is a relative entity and moves relative to its environment. We may sometimes experience feelings of happiness or sadness that do not appear to be related to our environment or to be the result of any external contact, which seem to be solely the result of internal predisposition.

But the mind always moves relative to the world and those predispositions or *saṁskāras* only become active under certain conditions, as we will explore in greater detail later in this chapter. The role of these external conditions may not be readily apparent, especially if it is a very strong and persistent *saṁskāra*, a tendency toward depression, for example, or a persistently cheerful nature, but a deeper examination will show that mental tendencies are brought out by the environment or the general circumstances of one's life. They are a reaction to the world we find ourselves in, albeit an often deeply programmed reaction.

Aristotle thought the pursuit of pleasure to be a frivolous and almost contemptible pursuit for a mature human being, and many Indian philosophers have said very nearly the same thing in even more emphatic terms, but in neither do we see a thorough exploration of the role that *sukha*, in all its varied expressions, plays in the evolution of incarnate life.

सुखानुरक्तिः परमा जैवी वृत्तिः ॥ २ ॥

II.2 *sukhánuraktih paramá jaevii vrttih*

sukha, happiness, pleasure; *anuraktih*, yearning, attraction, attachment, passion; *paramá*, supreme; *jaevii*, of living beings; *vrttih*, propensity

"The desire for happiness is the
primary propensity of living beings."

The idea that what we desire above all is happiness has had its adherents among philosophers throughout the ages. Arguably the two most important Christian philosophers, for example, Aquinas and Augustine, agreed that the supreme goal of human life is happiness. The majority of philosophers, however, both Western and Indian, contemporary and ancient, have relegated the emotions to an inferior plane of human experience, giving more importance to cognition and reason. Nietzsche famously said that mere happiness is a contemptible goal, whereas suffering and struggle play the critical roles in achieving something great in human culture, and Aristotle's views have already been mentioned. Nietzsche and Aristotle notwithstanding, this idea is so pervasive that it has found its way into political doctrine, as in the US Declaration of Independence: "We hold these truths to be self-evident, that all men are created equal, that they are endowed by their Creator with certain unalienable Rights, that among these are Life, Liberty and the pursuit of Happiness."

In this sutra, Anandamurti extends this principle to all living beings. The literal meaning of the word *vrtti* is "occupation" or "livelihood." The occupation of the mind is to think, and thus the word *vrtti* is used in yoga and Tantra to refer to mental propensities or tendencies. These propensities are what give propulsive force to the mind. In other words, it is the *vrttis* that stir up the ocean of *citta* into waves. There are different systems of classification for the *vrttis*. Patanjali, for example, divides human *vrttis* into five categories, each of which can be either painful or pleasant depending on the circumstances. While this is a valid system—Anandamurti has given a detailed analysis of Patanjali's classification of the *vrttis* in his discourses[3]—Tantra identifies fifty primary mental propensities that can be expressed in an infinite variety of ways and gradations.[4] In the Tantric system, each of these fifty *vrttis* is controlled by a particular chakra, more specifically, by one particular "petal" in that chakra.[5] The first chakra, located at the base of the spinal column, has four petals that serve as the controlling points for the four core desires of living beings: physical desire, psychic desire, psycho-spiritual desire, and spiritual desire—*káma*, *artha*, dharma, and *mokśa* in Sanskrit. As this sutra implies, these four desires, which supply the primary propulsive force to the individual mind, are different expressions of the one fundamental drive that motivates all incarnate life: the desire for happiness, which is innate to all mental expression, being a function of the evolutionary pull of Consciousness. That fundamental drive can be expressed in four different arenas, which correspond to the four levels of psychic expression. In the spiritual literature of India, *káma*, *artha*, dharma, and *mokśa* are known as the *caturvarga*, the four phases of spiritual development.

Káma, the desire for physical well-being or physical pleasure, is common to all living beings, from the simplest unicellular organism to the most elevated human being. In undeveloped organisms, in which there is no expression of *aham*, *káma* is synonymous with what the biological sciences call the "instinct for self-preservation."[6] The *sukha* they seek is purely physical, and the instinct for self-preservation is a function of this instinctive desire for physical well-being, for the loss of one's physical existence becomes an insuperable barrier to the pursuit of *káma*, the pursuit of physical well-being.

With the growth of *aham*, this same fundamental urge begins to express itself in the psychic arena, where it is known as *artha*. This is especially evident in developed animals where both *aham* and *mahat* are present—in a pet dog, for instance, for whom the affection and attention of its caretaker becomes as much or more a source of pleasure than food or shelter, even though that affection has little or nothing to do with its physical survival. All developed mammals show affection for their offspring and enjoy many of the same psychic satisfactions that human beings enjoy, albeit to a far lesser degree. While *káma* continues to be the primary driving force in plants and animals, the role of *artha* continues to grow as the mind develops.

The role of *artha* becomes even more predominant in human beings, for whom psychic satisfaction is much more important than physical satisfaction. This is reflected in the Sanskrit word for "human being," *manuśa*, which means "mind-preponderant being." For human beings the physical pleasures of life pale in comparison with the psychic pleasures, whether these be found in familial bonds, worldly success, or pure artistic and intellectual pleasure. So much so that a human being may even go to the extreme of sacrificing their life for the highest or noblest of psychic satisfactions—for love, for honor, for glory, for the preservation of their integrity, for the promise of paradise—something no animal would ever do, except perhaps in the rarest of instances.[7] The instinct for self-preservation continues to be as strongly felt in us as it is in the lower life-forms, but in such cases it is trumped by a greater motivation, and when we examine the landscape of human motivation it soon becomes clear that the instinct for self-preservation is itself a consequence of the desire for happiness. As with all living beings, there is nothing more dear to us than our own existence, which is why we run toward that which guarantees our existence and away from that which threatens it — unless the preservation of our existence in some way threatens our happiness, as for example when a person feels that they cannot live with cowardliness or ignobility or their own selfishness were they not to risk their life to save their companions or to save a loved one.

The same principle is at work when a person's unhappiness grows to the point that their continued existence becomes a barrier to any possible future happiness. The more one is threatened by unhappiness, the closer one's unhappiness brings them to the brink of seeming destruction, the more they run in the opposite direction. But if that supreme refuge, the holy grail of happiness, appears forever out of reach, if one's life becomes so burdensome and the prospect of happiness so remote as to seem unattainable, then a human being may even go to the extreme measure of committing suicide, putting an end to their physical existence rather than bear that unhappiness any longer. Buried behind the thought that this desperate act will bring them a welcome relief from their burden is the unconscious feeling that if happiness is unattainable in this present form, then it is only by doing away with this present form that there might be some possibility of happiness in the future.[8] For without happiness, or at least the prospect of happiness, life is not worth living.

It is only in human beings that the two highest expressions of the desire for happiness, dharma and *mokṣa*, psycho-spiritual desire and pure spiritual desire, find expression. In these two propensities the source of the living being's desire for happiness — the pull of Consciousness as it seeks to throw off its chains and return to its original state of unbounded bliss — steps out of the shadows and into the light.

सुखमनन्तमानन्दम् ॥ ३ ॥

II.3 *sukham anantam ānandam*

sukham, happiness; *anantam*, endless; *ānandam*, bliss

"Infinite happiness is *ānanda*."

Many influential Western philosophers, beginning with Plato and Aristotle, have argued that the highest expression of human life rests in purely cognitive pursuits. For that reason they considered the emotions to be an obstacle to rational thought, in effect divorcing these "higher" pursuits from human affect or human emotion. Many if not most schools of Indian philosophy are similar in this respect, considering the pursuit of happiness to be, in the final analysis, an impediment to the attainment of spiritual enlightenment.[9] Some have gone so far as to contend that all *sukha* is ultimately *duhkha*, since all pleasure inevitably involves pain. In Vatsyayana's *Nyāya Bhāṣya*, for example, a commentary on the Nyāya Sutras, we find the following passage:

> Pain is a necessary factor in pleasure; without suffering some pain no pleasure can be obtained; hence as leading to pleasure, this pain is regarded by the man as pleasure; and such a man, having his mind obsessed by this notion of 'pleasure,' never escapes from metempsychosis, which consists of a running series of births and deaths. And it is as an antidote of this notion of pleasure that we have the teaching that all this should be looked upon as 'pain.'[10]

Buddha's Four Noble Truths, centered around *duhkha*, present a similar picture: everything is suffering (*sarvaṁ duhkham*); this is the origin of suffering (*duhkha samudāya*); this is the cessation of suffering (*duhkha nirodha*); this is the path that leads to the cessation of suffering (*duhkha nirodha gamini pratipada*). For this reason, Buddhism has often been portrayed as a negative or even pessimistic philosophy, where embodied existence is characterized by suffering and the spiritual path by the effort to put an end to suffering. Patanjali, who was born some five centuries or so after the Buddha by most reliable accounts, advances a similar argument in his Yoga Sutras (II.15): "For one who has discrimination, everything is suffering on account of the suffering produced by the consequences [of action], by pain [itself], and by the *saṁskāras*, as well as on account of the suffering ensuing from the turmoil of the *vṛttis* due to the *guṇas*."[11] And other yogic schools emphasize the unconscious fear of the loss of *sukha* as an unavoidable component of every pleasurable experience. Ultimately in Yoga, as in Buddhism and Nyaya, *sukha* is seen as an obstacle to enlightenment, a chain of gold that must be cast off if the mind is to reach the undifferentiated state of pure Consciousness, for chains of gold bind just as tightly as chains of iron.

Anandamurti's approach is radically different. Rather than seeing the pursuit of *sukha* as an obstacle to be overcome, he recognizes that the desire for happiness is a direct expression of the living being's innate urge for spiritual expansion, that it is in fact the propulsive force that leads the living being to liberation. What begins as *káma* ultimately matures into *mokśa*, the final attainment, as we can deduce from a careful examination of our own lives. Behind everything we do lies the desire for happiness. It may sometimes seem otherwise, but if we can successfully trace the chain of motivation behind our actions we inevitably find a conscious or unconscious desire for happiness propelling us forward. Even that most desperate of acts, the taking of one's own life, has at its root the longing for happiness. And the same is true for all living beings, even the least developed organisms in which the desire for happiness in its inchoate form masquerades as the instinct for self-preservation. It follows therefore as a natural consequence that no living being can remain satisfied if its needs or desires are not met. Even the most undeveloped creatures cannot be satisfied with an insufficient supply of nutrients. If they do not get enough for their sustenance, thus putting their existence in jeopardy, they are propelled forward by their own internal urge until they either satisfy their physical needs or die trying. And even when they do get enough to fulfill their needs, that state of satiation is temporary. They soon require more and thus their inborn instinct once again propels them forward, resulting in a constant effort to maintain what is ultimately a fragile homeostasis.

This attraction toward an ever-evolving happiness becomes more and more evident the more the mind develops. The distress of developed animals when their basic desires are not met, whether it be the desire for food or safety or procreation, is patently evident. Even more telling is the fact that they do not remain content with a little mental pleasure. If you caress a pet dog for a moment or two or give it a little attention, it inevitably wants more. But it is in human beings that the desire for a deeper, more lasting satisfaction reaches its apex. Unlike less developed creatures who remain temporarily satisfied when their basic needs are met, no human being is ever fully satisfied in their pursuit of fulfillment. We always want something more. In the initial stage of human development we try to satisfy that inner urge with physical objects and physical pleasures. We want a house of our own for the security and comfort it affords, but the satisfaction we feel after acquiring a "starter" home doesn't last. Once it fades, we inevitably look for something else to fill that void. It may be a bigger, more comfortable house in a better neighborhood with a nicer car in the garage, or it may be something else, but that void does not leave us in peace. If we hunger after wealth, driven by the unconscious assumption that it will bring us greater happiness, we will not be satisfied with our first million. We want a second million and then a third in an ongoing quest for a greater sense of fulfillment. Inevitably, however, a sense of disillusionment with material achievements sets in, for no matter how often we attain our dreams, they never bring the fulfillment we hoped they would, and each new achievement in the physical realm brings with it a diminishing return.

Eventually we begin to realize that material pleasures cannot bring us lasting satisfaction. As this realization grows, the mind naturally turns more and more toward the psychic world for fulfillment. Relationships become more central to our sense of well-being. The esteem of our peers, a sense of accomplishment in our chosen profession, the expansion of our intellectual horizons, the aesthetic pleasures of nature and the arts, all serve to enrich our sense of well-being, and that psychic wealth becomes the hallmark of our humanity. But even then we inevitably find ourselves wanting more. No matter how deeply satisfying these purely mental pleasures may be, they cannot fully satisfy our thirst for happiness, for while it is an axiom in the mental arena that the more subtle the experience, the deeper and longer lasting the pleasure it affords, such pleasures still belong to the world of relativity and are thus subject to impermanence. Their vibrations create a harmonious feeling in the mind but that harmonious feeling cannot last, and when it fades it leaves us searching for something to take its place. The life of the mind is far richer than the life of the body, but eventually the realization dawns that the happiness we are searching for cannot be fully satisfied within the precincts of the mind.

All the satisfactions and joys of the manifest world, be they physical or psychic, belong to the world of *sukha* and *duhkha*, the world of weal and woe. They are limited in nature and cannot be otherwise, for that is the nature of the manifest world. But our desire for happiness, by contrast, is unlimited, and an unlimited desire cannot be satisfied by something limited. Every happiness we find in the world is destined to wane, whether it is because that particular object disappears or because we get used to the experience and once again find ourselves wanting something more, and it is through this repeated disillusionment that we gradually learn that no relative object can satisfy the unlimited hunger we feel. This insatiable desire to want more out of life is what Anandamurti calls "spiritual clash," and it is fueled by the irresistible attraction of Consciousness, which pulls at us like a magnet. When the mind starts to intuit that the objects of this manifest world, no matter how subtle, cannot satisfy its limitless desire, it starts seeking a source of happiness that lies beyond the sphere of pleasure and pain. A source that never fades and never fails. And that source is and can only be Consciousness. This inward turning of the mind toward the source of its being is the dawn of psycho-spiritual desire, otherwise known as *dharma* in the yogic lexicon. In philosophical terms, dharma is the effort to convert the waves of the mind into pure cognition. It is still the same fundamental urge, the desire for happiness, but it has now matured into the desire to attain the Infinite. Infinite happiness is called *ánanda* in Sanskrit, and it refers to the state of absolute bliss and absolute peace that is beyond both *sukha* and *duhkha*.[12] Once the waves of happiness become infinite they can no longer be called *sukha* because they are no longer waves at all. The ocean has reached the state of perfect tranquility, the sea of pure cognition.

आनन्दं ब्रह्म इत्याहुः ॥ ४ ॥

II.4 *ánandaṁ brahma ityáhuh*

ánandam, absolute bliss; *brahma*, Supreme Consciousness; *ityáhuh*, this they call

"This *ánanda* is called Brahma."

The use of the phrase *ityáhuh* grounds this sutra in the Indian philosophical tradition and brings us back to Brahma, the Supreme Being, with whose definition Ananda Sutram began. Brahma is often described in yogic literature as *satcidánanda*. *Sat* means "immutable," *cit* means "consciousness," and *ánanda* means "bliss." The immutable blissful Consciousness that is the source of the creation. Thus the nature of Consciousness is absolute bliss, just as it is absolute peace, being different descriptions of the same state. The opposite of peace is turbulence. As the turbulence in our mind calms, we feel an increasing sense of peace. When that turbulence disappears entirely, when there is no agitation whatsoever to ruffle the waters of our being, that immutable state of perfect quiescence can rightfully be called a state of absolute peace. In the same way, when the waves of happiness grow to the point that they become infinite, then that immutable state of perfect, unfailing happiness can rightfully be called a state of absolute bliss. It is not the awareness of bliss but bliss itself, the state in which there is no modification of mind to attenuate the pure, unconditioned, blissful nature of the Self.

By definition the Infinite can only be one. It cannot be two, otherwise it would not be infinite, and that singular entity, which is synonymous with the state of absolute bliss, the state of perfect happiness, is Brahma, the One without a second. Thus the fundamental propensity of living beings to seek an ever-greater happiness, their *paramá jaevii vrtti*, is in fact a search for Brahma, the Supreme Consciousness, for infinite happiness and Brahma are synonymous.

तस्मिन्नुपलब्धे परमा तृष्णानिवृत्तिः ॥ ५ ॥

II.5 *tasminn upalabdhe paramá trśńánivrttih*

tasmin, that; *upalabdhe*, in the attainment; *paramá*, supreme, absolute; *trśńá*, thirst, desire, craving; *nivrttih*, cessation

"When that is attained, desire comes to an end."

Our desires appear to be endless. Whether those desires are bound up with physical satisfaction or psychic fulfillment, one desire inevitably follows another in what appears to be an endlessly revolving wheel, and thus the very nature of desire appears to be one of infinite variation. But as we have seen, a close examination reveals the truth to be otherwise. All desire stems from the four core propensities, the *caturvarga*, and these in turn are different expressions of the same fundamental urge for fulfillment, an urge that respects no limits, that cannot be held in check, no matter what barriers seek to bar its path.

"There is in the living being a thirst for limitlessness," Anandamurti tells us in the short commentary that accompanies this sutra,[13] and yet the fundamental nature of incarnate life is that of limitation. We are limited by our bodies, which are confined within the physical world, and by the tendencies or momentum of our minds, which are likewise confined within the psychic world. The role of *saiṅcara* is to delimit or subjugate Consciousness, and thus the living being, the focal nexus of *pratisaiṅcara*, finds itself on a course in which it has to struggle against the physical and mental limitations imposed by *prakrti*. This is the natural outcome of the demarcation of Consciousness. Once imprisoned within the boundary walls of matter, Consciousness begins its struggle to free itself and return to the unbound state, for the impetus or momentum behind this return movement is an inevitable legacy from the process of qualification that defines *saiṅcara*. If we press a rubber ball, thus creating an impression, the energy that creates that impression is the same energy, in the form of its opposing or rebounding force, that returns the ball to its original state once the finger is removed, ie., once the appropriate conditions are met. With the appearance of organic life, Shakti, which was responsible in its centrifugal movement for the creation of matter, automatically assumes its centripetal form, which is expressed within the individual mind as the urge to expand its horizons in search of an ever-deeper, longer-lasting fulfillment. This inherent urge is what is referred to as *tṛṣṇā*, thirst, the innate desire for mental expansion that assumes an endless variety of different forms, beginning with physical desire and the instinct for self-preservation, which matures into the desire for happiness and eventually culminates in the effort to attain the Infinite by merging the mind into Consciousness. This *tṛṣṇā* is the source of the underlying dissatisfaction of the human condition, the sense of incompleteness that no physical or psychic experience can satisfy. That desire is limitless, and only an unlimited entity can satisfy an unlimited desire; hence it will not cease to drive human beings along the path of mental expansion until they achieve their goal, the merger of the mind into Brahma.

While the individual is the means through which consciousness approaches that ultimate liberation, it can only be attained by surrendering that individuality to Brahma. The progressive spiritual expansion of the mind is dharma, the effort to comprehend and attain the Infinite, but the highest expression of *tṛṣṇā* is the desire to transcend individuality and dissolve the mind into Consciousness—otherwise known as *mokṣa* or pure spiritual desire, the last of the four stages of spiritual evolution. Dharma or psycho-spiritual desire can take the mind to the *savikalpa* or *saguṇa* state, the point of ultimate mental expansion, but the finality of *pratisaiṇcara* can only be reached through the dissolution of the mind that is achieved in the *nirvikalpa* or *nirguṇa* state. Only then can that unquenchable thirst for happiness be quenched and all suffering come to an end.[14]

बृहदेषणा प्रणिधानं च धर्मः ॥ ६ ॥

II.6 *bṛhadeṣaṇā praṇidhānaṁ ca dharmaḥ*

bṛhad, the Great; *eṣaṇā*, longing; *praṇidhānaṁ*, to take shelter in, to bring the mind to a point; *ca*, and; *dharmaḥ*, property, nature, psycho-spiritual desire, spirituality

"To long for and make efforts to attain the Great is dharma."

Consciously or unconsciously, all living beings are searching for the Supreme (here the word *bṛhad*, "the Great," is synonymous with Brahma).[15] This is the motive force behind all incarnate life, the raison d'être that sets in motion the river of evolution.

In undeveloped beings this longing for the Great is expressed in a rudimentary form through physical desire and the instinct for self-preservation. As the river of evolution progresses, it finds further expression in the desire for mental satisfaction and contentment. But it is only in the human kingdom that this fundamental longing, the source of life's momentum, becomes fully conscious;[16] and thus only human beings can make conscious efforts to accelerate their movement toward Brahma. This is dharma, one of the most important words in the Sanskrit lexicon, the psycho-spiritual longing that culminates in *dharma sádhaná*, the effort to attain the Supreme.[17]

The word *dharma* is derived from the verbal root *dhr*, "to hold" or "uphold." That which sustains an entity or maintains their existence is their dharma in the etymological sense of the word, and thus dharma in a more general sense refers to the essential or defining properties of any particular entity—that which makes it what it is. The one essential property that is common to all beings is their movement toward Brahma, however unconscious that movement may be, but all beings also have certain properties that differentiate them from other beings, and thus every entity has its own unique dharma. Water has its own dharma, as does fire, and it is due to these intrinsic properties that we can distinguish one from the other. Dharma in this sense has been divided into three broad categories according to certain shared properties: *vastu* dharma, *jaeva* dharma, and *manava* dharma—the dharma of inanimate matter, the dharma of living beings, and the dharma of human beings.

The shared properties of inanimate beings needs no elaboration. They react to their environment in specific predictable ways, and they are inanimate or non-living, ie., they have no expression of mind. While they belong to the phase of *saiṇcara* and thus betray the least manifestation of consciousness, the destiny of matter is also to one day enter the phase of *pratisaiṇcara* and make its way back to Consciousness.

Living beings also share a common dharma, certain properties that are common to all, foremost among them sleep, fear, the need for food, and procreation. Food, sleep, and fear are all integral to survival and thus to the pursuit of physical well-being, since the lack thereof puts one's existence in jeopardy.

Procreation ensures the survival of the species, the continuation of life, for death is also common to all living beings.

While we human beings share this *jaeva* dharma with other living creatures, we are a class apart from the standpoint of evolution. We have a dharma all our own that we do not share with animals or plants. Less developed living beings are content with the life of the senses, with the satisfaction of their physical and emotional needs and desires. Human beings are not. We often use the expression "human nature" when we talk about our species, and it is this human nature that we mean when we say *manava* dharma, human dharma. But here the phrase has an implicit spiritual sense, which is why it is commonly referred to in yoga and Tantra as *bhagavad* or *bhágavata* dharma, "divine nature," since the defining characteristic of our human nature, what separates us from other living beings, is our conscious longing for transcendence together with our capacity to make conscious efforts to attain that transcendental state. This is the defining feature that makes us human.

If we look again at this sutra, it becomes patently obvious that Anandamurti is referring here to human dharma or *bhagavad* dharma. The word *eśaná* means "longing," but unlike the more common Sanskrit word for "desire," *iccha*, *eśaná* implies the effort to fulfill that longing, an implication that is reinforced by the word *praṅidhána*, which refers to the act of directing the apexed mind toward the Supreme.[18] The intrinsic nature of human beings is to long for and run after Brahma, and thus we can never be truly happy or satisfied until we fulfill that infinite longing through the attainment of self-realization — or at least until we are well established in the path that leads us there. Not all human beings are conscious of their divine nature; nevertheless it is what makes us human. It is what drives us from one limited pleasure to another, none of these pleasures ever being enough, until we realize that neither material objects nor the products of our intellect can bring us lasting happiness; and thus we begin making efforts to seek the one undying source of limitless fulfillment, the Supreme Consciousness.

According to Anandamurti, *bhagavad* dharma, our real human nature, has three distinct aspects or characteristics: *vistára, rasa,* and *sevá* — expansion, flow, and service:[19]

Vistára. To realize the Infinite, one must expand the mind. Self-realization is a gradual process of mental expansion from finite to infinite, until the mind loses itself in the ocean of Consciousness. In the natural course of evolution the mind undergoes gradual dilation, and this is even more in evidence in human life with the human being's highly developed intellect. The increased psychic clash generated through education, social interaction, and the assimilation of new ideas accelerates the process of mental growth or mental expansion, although it is also true that human beings are the only living creatures capable of contracting their minds—that is, of going against the natural evolutionary flow—by limiting themselves to material pursuits and dogmatic or restrictive ideas. Fortunately this is comparatively rare, since the human mind harbors an innate urge to grow in scope and knowledge and wisdom, and that urge cannot be permanently dammed. By and large, concern with oneself and one's family gradually expands to include one's community, the greater society-at-large, and eventually the entire world, moving gradually from egoism to altruism, from selfishness to selflessness, even if this process requires lifetimes. But to fully expand the mind and unlock its full potential, one must take the Infinite as one's object of ideation. As long as one's thought remains confined to the material and psychic worlds, the mind will inevitably feel the bondage of limitation. And thus this innate urge eventually leads human beings to ideate on Consciousness, which in turn results in an ever-accelerating expansion of mind and the gradual dropping away of all limitations. Whatever isms might have affected the mind become dissolved in the waters of universalism, and compassion for all beings, both animate and inanimate, becomes the hallmark of one's dealings with the world. In the commentary to this sutra, Anandamurti refers to ideation on Consciousness, or spiritual meditation, as *iishvara prańidhána*, to accept the Supreme as the only ideal of one's life.[20]

Rasa: As the mind expands, it must align itself with the cosmic will if it is to reach its goal. If it fails to do so, then that expansion will be impeded or distorted. The infinite Cosmic Consciousness is an unending, unbroken flow of cognition, comparable in wavelength to a straight line. But when the manifest world emerges from the womb of the unmanifest, that unbroken flow becomes filled with curvature, like waves dancing on the surface of the ocean. If the mind cannot tune itself to those waves then it finds itself at cross-purposes with the flow of evolution. Due to the lack of a fully developed *mahat*, animals and plants are not capable of truly independent action. Without the capacity for self-reflection, they are guided by the Cosmic Mind and thus follow unerringly their *jaeva* dharma as they climb the ladder of evolution. But human beings are blessed with the capacity for independent action, a blessing that is also a curse. When the human ego feels that it is in control—the fundamental illusion that perpetuates the prison of separateness—then its egocentric desires inevitably clash with the cosmic flow, thus generating the tension or discord that is felt as suffering. But when one is able to surrender their individual desires to the flow of the divine will, then that tension and discord disappears and is replaced by an awareness of the harmony that reigns at the heart of the creation.[21] Knowingly or unknowingly, all created beings dance to the music of the cosmic flute, but when a human being consciously tunes their footsteps to the rhythm of the dance, then the ego's self-created obstacles no longer stand in the way of the mind's expansion.

Sevá: Not only is the spirit of service intrinsic to human nature, it is a necessary prerequisite to the full flowering of consciousness that is the goal of human evolution. *Sevá* loosens the bonds of the ego and thus paves the way for spiritual elevation. While self-interest or egoism is part of our *jaeva* dharma, the dharma we share with animals and plants, altruism is an expression of our divine nature or *bhagavad* dharma. The pursuit of self-interest without regard to the welfare of others may bring crude pleasure in the short run, but in the long run it generates suffering because it tightens the bonds of the ego. This is something we all understand instinctively, even if we have not yet become conscious of the fact and thus blindly pursue our egocentric desires (to our detriment). When people are asked why they do altruistic acts, by far the most common answer is some variation of "Because I feel happy when I help others; it makes me feel fulfilled." Deep inside we know that altruistic action brings out the best of our humanity, while selfish action takes us down the opposite path.

Nevertheless, there is a prevailing assumption in the social sciences that self-interest is the principal motivation of human beings. "It is not from the benevolence of the butcher, the brewer, or the baker," wrote Adam Smith, the father of capitalism, "that we can expect our dinner, but from their regard to their own interest." Altruistic behavior tends to be explained away as self-interest in disguise. According to the biologist Edward Wilson, who won a Pulitzer Prize in 1979 for *On Human Nature*, "Altruism is ultimately selfish. The altruist expects reciprocation for himself or his closest relatives. His good behavior is calculating ... and its principal vehicles are lying, pretense, and deceit, including self-deceit, because the actor is more convincing who believes his performance is real."[22] He even goes so far as to call altruism "the enemy of modern civilization."

This misguided reasoning, which is central to the functioning of modern-day capitalism, is antithetical to the best interests of human beings, which lies in the expansion of their minds and the concomitant expansion of their consciousness, and has had a disastrous effect on human society. Without developing a spirit of selfless service toward the creation along with the recognition that all created beings are different expressions of one Divine Consciousness, the evolutionary journey cannot attain fruition.

Since the innate nature or fundamental characteristic of human beings is to consciously seek the Supreme, the word *dharma* is commonly used as a synonym for spirituality or the spiritual path. In Buddhism, for example, it is the second of the three jewels: the Buddha, the dharma, and the sangha. In India, however, as in other places, spirituality is often confused with religion, and hence the word *dharma* is used in many Indian languages to mean "religion"—Hindu dharma, Christian dharma, Muslim dharma. This is an incorrect use of the word. There is only one dharma for human beings, *bhagavad* dharma, regardless of creed or race or culture or any other differentiating factor. While religion has a tendency to divide human beings, as history attests, dharma is universal in character and only serves to unite. It is not based on belief but on experience, being the practical expression of the human urge to attain the Infinite. Thus there can only be one dharma. When asked about different spiritual paths, Anandamurti is reputed to have replied, "There is only one spiritual path—the path that the kundalini takes from the *muládhára* chakra to the *sahasrára* chakra."[23]

तस्माद्धर्मः सदा कार्यः ॥ ७ ॥

II.7 *tasmád dharmah sadá káryah*

tasmát, therefore; *dharma*, spirituality, spiritual practice; *sadá*, always; *káryah*, to be practiced

"Therefore dharma should always be practiced."

Here the word *dharma* refers to the practice of spirituality, the effort to establish oneself in the Infinite. The attainment of limitlessness is the goal of human life, and since limitlessness can only be attained through spiritual practice, it becomes incumbent upon us as human beings to practice dharma and thus fulfill the purpose of our lives. We need no particular effort to follow *vastu* dharma or *jaeva* dharma. When we feel hungry we eat; when we feel thirsty we drink. We don't need to be reminded that we are hungry or thirsty. But it requires a special effort to follow *bhagavad* dharma,[24] and if we fail to make that effort then we are not fulfilling the purpose of our human incarnation. The failure to practice dharma prevents us from attaining the unfailing happiness we all long for and in effect consigns us to a life of pleasure and pain in which suffering is inescapable, thus binding us to the wheel of birth and death.

Anandamurti takes this reasoning one step further by contending that human beings who do not practice spirituality are human in name only, since what separates us from other creatures is precisely our capacity for the practice of dharma, which less developed living beings do not possess. In his view, human beings who do not practice dharma are no better than animals, a jarring contention that echoes similar statements in the Indian spiritual tradition.[25] It is important to point out, however, that he is not using the word "animals" in a pejorative sense, as we sometimes do. Developed animals have familial bonds; they feel affection for their children and in some cases go to great pains to ensure their survival. They feel happy and sad, as we do, and use their limited intellect as best they can to solve the challenges that life presents them with. They are not nearly as sophisticated in any of these areas as we are, but the basic tenor of their lives is similar to ours—with the exception of our sense of *bhagavad* dharma. Developed animals follow their *jaeva* dharma, and if we don't follow our human dharma then our lives are essentially like theirs—the same basic concerns, the same physical and emotional needs and comforts, albeit far more developed. Thus, from the spiritual or Tantric point of view, if we are to truly manifest our humanity, it is not enough to simply inhabit a human body and make use of our marvelous intellect. We must express our human nature, and the defining characteristic of our human nature is dharma. The most precious body in the universe is the human body, for without it a living being cannot do spiritual practice, and if we fail to do so, then we are not only wasting this precious opportunity, we are neglecting the true purpose of our lives.

विषये पुरुषावभासो जीवात्मा ॥ ८ ॥

II.8 *viśaye puruśávabháso jiivátmá*

viśaye, in the object; *puruśa*, consciousness; *avabhásah*, reflection; *jiivátmá*, individual consciousness, individual soul

"The reflection of consciousness in an object is the *jiivátmá*."

The word *jiivátmá* is commonly translated as "individual consciousness" or "soul," but as Anandamurti reminds us in the short commentary that follows this sutra, consciousness is one. Spiritually speaking, it cannot be divided into microcosmic consciousness or Macrocosmic Consciousness, except in the sense that the one singular *puruśa* is reflected in individual beings, be they animate or inanimate, and thus appears to be differentiated according to the nature of the receptacle that harbors that reflection, analogous to the moon's reflection in various pools of water.[26] The reflection in each of these pools varies according to the size of the pool and the clarity of the water, but the moon itself is one and indivisible. If the reflection is clear, then one can get a clear idea of the nature of the moon; if it is hazy, then less so.[27] In either case that singular moon remains unchanged. Another common analogy is that of a variety of mirrors. If a mirror is in pristine condition then the moon will be clearly reflected—the larger the mirror, the greater the reflection—but if the mirror is clouded then it will be hard to make out the moon at all, though in neither case is the moon affected.

This is increasingly evident as we go up the ladder of evolution. The more evolved the mind, the greater the reflection of consciousness in that mind. There is unquestionably a greater expression of consciousness in developed life-forms possessing a functional intellect, such as a dog or a monkey, than there is in undeveloped life-forms that display only instinctual intelligence, such as an earthworm. There is an even greater expression of consciousness in human beings, but even in the human kingdom the quality of the mirror varies markedly. Some individuals are so caught up in the world and in their egos that they barely pay any attention to their consciousness and entirely conflate it with mind, while there are others who are deeply aware of their spiritual nature and the evolutionary journey they are on. We commonly say that such individuals are more "conscious," since the expression of consciousness in them is more patently visible. Rather than being absorbed in the mundane world and thus metaphorically "asleep," they are "awake" to the spiritual reality of which the mundane world is a manifestation. This higher level of consciousness is equivalent in philosophical terms to a greater reflection of the atman in the mind of that particular individual. Consciousness is one—it cannot be greater or higher—but it can be more clearly reflected due to the relative purity of the mental mirror and the degree of mental expansion. In other words, the mind is capable of feeling the presence of Consciousness, and such individuals are more acutely aware of its presence as the substratum of their existence and the witness of their thoughts and experience.

From the standpoint of the microcosm, our individual consciousness appears to be confined to the witness-ship of our individual thoughts and actions. As a consequence, it becomes identified with the objects of enjoyment and is thus subject to the polarity of pleasure and pain, like the bird eating the fruits of existence in the analogy cited in sutra I.7.[28] But in reality our consciousness is not trapped by the mind's limited experience. It only appears that way as long as our attention remains tied to the contents of the mind. It can be compared to the addition of a coloring agent to water. As long as thoughts are present in the mind, consciousness apparently takes on their color. When we turn our attention toward Consciousness itself, however, that apparent limitation disappears. Is the water itself actually colored? No. Remove the coloring agent and the water appears once again in its true form, utterly transparent. Remove the mirror of the mind and there is only the one moon, shining in its unreflected glory.[29]

"In the Shruti it has been said:

"*yacched váuṇmanasi prajiṇastad yacchejjiṇána átmani;- jiṇánamátmani mahati niyacchet tadyacchecchánta átmani.*

"[Wise persons first merge their organs into their *citta*, then their *citta* into *aham*, then *aham* into *mahat*, then *mahat* into *jiivátmá*, and finally *jiivátmá* into *paramátmá*, Supreme Consciousness. — Katha Upanishad]

"The zealous and intelligent spiritual aspirant is to suspend his sensory feelings into the crude mind; those of the crude mind are to be guided, are to be diverted, unto the subtle mind, the working mind, the individual ego; those of the individual ego are to be guided, are to be diverted, towards the pure 'I' feeling; and the pure 'I' feeling should become one with the pure cognition."[30]

— Anandamurti

The word *jiiva* refers to living beings, and thus the word *jiivátmá* commonly denotes the reflection of Consciousness in the mind of any living being, whether developed or undeveloped, but in this sutra the word *viśaya*, "object," is used, rather than *deha* or body. Anandamurti makes the distinction between manifest mind, as seen in plants and animals and other living beings, and unmanifest mind, which is present in inanimate objects like earth or iron. Matter is a condensed or crudified form of mind, just as mind is a condensed or crudified form of Consciousness, and thus the only real difference between the animate and inanimate worlds is that mind is in an unmanifest or dormant state in the inanimate world.[31] In both cases, Consciousness is reflected in the object. In the case of matter, there is no visible reflection of Consciousness as we see in the mind of living beings, but the reflection is there nonetheless. The same moon shines equally on the pools and mirrors in which its reflection is visible as it does on the surrounding earth and hills in which its reflection is not. Thus in a certain sense one can equate the Macrocosm to the sum total of all microcosms. The Supreme Consciousness is the witness of every particle of the creation, and thus this collective witness-ship is, by the same logic, the sum total of all *jiivátmás*.

आत्मनि सत्तासंस्थितिः ॥ ९ ॥

II.9 *átmani sattásamsthitih*

átmani, in the atman, in consciousness; *sattá*, entity; *samsthitih*, residence, being together

"Every entity resides in the atman."

In his commentary on this sutra, Anandamurti reprises the process of perception from the standpoint of substantiation. As we have seen, matter is substantiated in the *citta*—that is, in order for mind to be aware of matter, matter must be reflected in the *citta*. Thus the *citta* is the container or substratum of matter. This reflection in the *citta* then finds its base in the *aham* when the thinking faculty recognizes the incoming wave. And the authorship of *aham* in turn has its foundation in the *mahat*, the pure sense of existence. But the recognition of *mahat* depends on consciousness, the cognitive faculty, the "I know I am." Without the awareness of existence provided by consciousness, *mahat* would have no support or base and thus could not perform its function. Hence every stage in the substantiation of thought or perception depends on the atman, the witnessing faculty of consciousness, from which stems our knowledge of existence.

This sutra, when properly understood, puts to bed the materialist or reductionist philosophies. Materialist thinkers, by and large, not only believe that consciousness is a random byproduct of matter, but that the material universe exists independent of consciousness. As we have seen, this is not only experientially untenable but philosophically unsound. The very idea that matter can exist independent of consciousness depends on consciousness for its existence. Without consciousness that thought cannot exist. Indeed, for matter to be substantiated at all, mind must be present to perceive it. Thus matter is dependent on mind for its substantiation, just as mind is dependent on consciousness. Consciousness is a priori. It exists before mind and before matter, both of which depend upon it for their existence, making consciousness the only independent entity and hence the first cause and the ground of being. Nothing in this universe can exist apart from consciousness and thus every entity, whether physical or psychic, mind or matter, is embedded in the atman, their one and only true abode.

ओतप्रोतयोगाभ्यां संयुक्तः पुरुषोत्तमः ॥ १० ॥

II.10 *otaprotayogābhyāṁ saṁyuktaḥ puruṣottamaḥ*

ota, individual association; *prota*, collective association; *yogābhyāṁ*, union; *saṁyuktaḥ*, connected; *puruṣa*, consciousness; *uttamaḥ*, supreme

"*Puruṣottama* is connected to all entities through both individual and collective association."

The witness-ship or substantiation of existence by Consciousness can be experienced in two different ways: individually and collectively. From the macrocosmic point of view, the manifest universe is an internal thought projection, and the nucleus of the universe, the Supreme Consciousness or *puruṣottama*, is the singular witness of that thought projection, as if it harbored within its vast body a theater of infinite proportions and was watching all of existence play itself out on its internal screen. The sun of Consciousness thus simultaneously illumines the entire *bhavaságar*, the ocean of existence. This is known as *prota* yoga, the collective conjunction of Consciousness with its creation, and it can be fully experienced when the microcosmic mind merges into the Macrocosmic Mind in the state of *savikalpa* samadhi and thus becomes witness to the vast panorama of the cosmic imagination, though we can also gain a partial awareness of this collective conjunction to the extent that we are able to transcend our ego and ideate on the Supreme as the witness of its creation. At the same time, however, that same sun illumines each and every drop in the ocean. That link is experienced as the individual relationship of the drop to the sun. The reflection of the sun in each particular drop is the *jiivátmá*, the individual witnessing consciousness, and the direct conjunction of Consciousness with each particle of creation, whether mind or matter, living or nonliving, is known as *ota* yoga. To use a more contemporary analogy, if we think of Consciousness as a screen of infinite size in which an image of the manifest universe appears, that screen illumines the entire image as well as each individual pixel. It is a matter of perspective, of which there are two, the part and the whole. Thus the association of Consciousness with the creation is both individual and collective.

This personal association, or *ota* yoga, takes on particular importance in devotional practice, and since the development of devotion is critical to the attainment of spiritual realization, the individual relationship with the Supreme has been particularly emphasized in the Tantric tradition, as in most other spiritual traditions. The Supreme Consciousness is not only the impersonal witness of the creation in its *prota* yoga association—it is also the personal source of inspiration and guidance for each and every created being as they wind their way along the pathways of spiritual evolution. It is through the direct link of *ota* yoga that we are able to feel the presence of our soul, the *jiivátmá*, and it is through the *jiivátmá* that we are able to know the *paramátmá*. In this sense, the *jiivátmá* is the Supreme Consciousness as it appears to us within the precincts of our mind. With the awakening of dharma comes a dawning sense that there is an unseen power that is guiding us in our life, the same force that guides the heavens through its *prota* yoga, watching over us and illuminating the path as it draws us irresistibly toward the fulfillment of our evolutionary journey. It is that way for those whose spiritual consciousness is just beginning to awaken, and it is even more so for elevated yogis and saints who feel their personal connection to the Supreme with every breath they take.

Regarding devotional practice, or bhakti yoga, Anandamurti divides devotees into three classes according to the nature of their personal relationship with Brahma. The relationship of the most advanced devotees with the Supreme is exclusive in nature. "No, no, I can share all my belongings with others, but not my *parama puruśa*. He is mine and mine alone; he belongs to no one else. I cannot even think of sharing him with anyone."[32] While this statement may give us pause, it is both devotionally and philosophically correct. It is philosophically correct because our direct relationship with Brahma—which is all we can truly know of the Supreme until we achieve the highest realization—is through the *jiivátmá*, and our *jiivátmá* is ours and ours alone, being the reflection of the *puruśottama* in our individual mind, witnessing our individual thoughts and feelings. And it is devotionally correct, because in order for love to reach its zenith it must become exclusive. We don't share our lover with the world; otherwise the relationship would be diminished. If devotion is to rise to the heights of one-pointed ideation, it must become exclusive and all-encompassing. There can be no third party. We must feel that the Supreme Consciousness is ours and ours alone. Only then can love reach its apogee and thus usher us through the gateway to spiritual union.

मानसातीते ऽनवस्थायां जगद्बीजम् ॥ ११ ॥

II.11 *mánasátiite 'navastháyám jagadbiijam*

mánasa, mind; *atiite*, beyond; *anavastháyám*, in a non-state, in the non-finality (of a proposition); *jagat*, universe, that which is always in motion; *biijam*, seed

"The seed of the universe lies beyond the mind, in a state that cannot be comprehended."

CHAPTER TWO

The law of cause and effect was first formulated in philosophical language by Maharishi Kanada more than two thousand years ago in his Vaisheshika Sutras: *káraṅábhávát karyábhávah,* "there is no effect without a cause."[33] Everything in this universe is in motion, and all motion requires a cause. If we use the simplistic example of one billiard ball striking another, the motion of the first billiard ball is the cause, and the motion of the second is the effect.[34] But the motion of the first billiard ball is also the effect of a previous cause, in this case, the motion of the cue stick. Likewise, the motion of the cue stick is also the effect of a previous cause, the physical movements of the person holding the cue stick, which are in turn the effect of the person's intention, and so on, ad infinitum. Every expression in the universe is the effect of a particular cause, and that cause is in turn the effect of a previous cause, successive links in a chain that inevitably disappears from sight when we try to trace its origin. This is not to say, however, that the cause and effect relationship is strictly linear.[35] Everything in the universe is linked together in one causal fabric so that the ripples of one event spread throughout that fabric. "Nothing is isolated, everything is interconnected," says Anandamurti.[36] In contemporary physics this is known as the "butterfly effect"—if a butterfly flaps its wings in San Juan it can lead to a rainstorm in Hawaii. The contention of some scientists that life arose from a fortuitous, ie., accidental, combination of elements is not an assertion of fact, as they sometimes make it out to be, but rather a failure to admit that they are unable to find the cause.[37]

The endeavor to trace the chain of cause and effect backward along the arrow of time is common to the human species. We try to figure out why the world is the way it is, or why we have landed in a particular predicament, or why we are struggling with certain thoughts or emotions, looking into our hidden motivations or the motivations of others (and in some cases to cosmic factors) in an effort to unwind the infinitely complex skein of karma, the play of action and reaction. In this effort to understand the causal sequence of our lives, whether individual or collective, we have no choice but to travel backward along the path of *pratisaiṇcara*. But however far back we are able to trace the chain of cause and effect, we eventually reach a point where the prior cause remains hidden from our eyes. Were we able to unwind the skein of karma without restriction, however, we would find the cause of our present life lying in a previous life, as it is with all beings in the complex web of interrelation to which we belong. And the cause of that life in a previous life, until we finally arrive at the beginning of our journey in the flow of *pratisaiñcara*—the inanimate particles from which the germ of our present mind first arose. But those inanimate particles also had a cause, and thus we would have to continue back even further, retracing the outgoing waves of *saiñcara*, from the denser elements to the subtler elements to the cosmic *citta*, continuing on until we arrive at the cosmic *mahat*, the first modification of Consciousness. But what caused that first modification, thus setting in motion the seemingly endless chain of cause and effect that has led to our present condition at this precise moment in time? What caused the seed of creation to sprout in the first place?

The phrase *anavasthá doṥa* in Sanskrit can be translated as "the fallacy of infinite regression." In ancient times it was commonly illustrated by using the analogy of looking into one of two facing mirrors and trying to find the original image. While tracing the chain of cause and effect we inevitably reach a point beyond which we cannot go, because beyond that point there is no existence as we know it. That point is the point from where the creation originates, the seed of creation. As with a sprout that emerges from the earth, we can see the effect but we cannot see the cause; we can only infer it. The unseen origin of the creation lies in *nirguña*, the objectless, unqualified Consciousness. It is a non-state, *anavasthá*, in the sense that existence is a quality, the quality of "I am," which in its pure state is known as *mahat*, whereas *nirguña* is beyond the mind and thus beyond all qualities, all description, beyond existence itself. The mind has emerged from *nirguña*, thus we can infer that the seed of creation lies in *nirguña*, but the mind cannot comprehend *nirguña*. It cannot comprehend or even conceive of a state that is prior to its own existence. Hence the search for the first cause, the primogenitor, a search that is initiated and carried out by the mind, ends in nothingness. We know the seed is there, somewhere, but it cannot be found, because in order to bring that search to fruition the mind must disappear into its source.[38]

The great questions of philosophy in the human quest for understanding begin with "Why?" "Why did God create the universe (if indeed he did so)?" "Why am I here?" "Why is there suffering?" The ultimate answer to these and all such fundamental questions, from a philosophical standpoint, is that there is no answer, because the first cause, the seed of creation, lies beyond the mind, and the mind cannot comprehend what lies beyond it—that is, it cannot comprehend the state in which it does not exist. In our search for the ultimate answers to existence we can go to the very edge of *nirguña*, but we cannot cross over without leaving the mind behind, without leaving behind the vessel that brought us there. So the answers to the when and why of creation are ultimately untenable, because these are questions put forth by the mind, and any answer would perforce be confined within the realm of the mind. The two facing mirrors will never yield to the onlooker the original image.[39]

Nevertheless, we still feel a need to know the why and wherefore of the creation. It is the nature of the mind to feel uneasy with the uncertainty of not knowing. This thirst for meaning is an expression of *artha*, psychic desire, one of the four core propensities controlled by the first chakra and a motivating force behind *vistára*, mental expansion. Philosophy, however, teaches us that the first cause cannot be known, and thus there is no answer to the question, "Why did God create the universe?" The most philosophy can say is that Brahma is the cause and the creation is the effect. According to Anandamurti, however, there is a higher logic than that of the philosopher, and that is the logic of the devotee. The devotee is more intelligent than the philosopher, because a devotee knows that the only truly meaningful answer is the answer that enables us to reach our goal. Our goal is not to answer the questions of philosophy. Our goal is to attain the *nirvikalpa* state, and any answer that remains confined to the realm of the intellect will not, of and by itself, help us to reach our goal, which is beyond the intellect, beyond the mind. *However,* we can train the intellect in such a way that it facilitates our spiritual realization, and therein lies the beauty of the devotional approach.

Anandamurti sums up the spirit of the devotional approach in the following way:

But these replies will not satisfy a spiritual aspirant. The spiritual aspirant, or the devotee, will say the reply is very simple—"Before the creation, my Supreme Father was alone in this universe. There was nothing, and for want of the quinquelemental factors,[40] there was nothing to see, nothing to do. He was alone. Suppose you are alone in a particular village or in a particular house. What will be your position? What will be your mental condition? You will be just like—what? An insane person, a madman. So in this vast cosmos my Father was alone. Just try to feel what his condition was, what his mental condition was. So just to save himself from the monotony of singularity, he created this universe. Just to play with his children. This is the only reason. I know no other philosophy." This will be the reply of the devotee.[41]

What makes this the more intelligent answer? Or rather, what makes it the more useful, more meaningful answer? The secret lies in the power of the devotional relationship. As we will examine more closely in Chapter Three, devotion—love for the Supreme—is the easiest and most effective means to achieve the pinnacle of spiritual realization. And the most effective way to develop devotion is to cultivate a personal relationship with the Supreme. Sri Ramakrishna used to say that trying to cross the ocean of existence without devotion is like trying to row across the ocean in a sailboat. It is theoretically possible but extremely taxing and ultimately unattainable in practice. But when devotion arises, it fills the sails and the passage becomes both easy and pleasurable. Love for the Supreme makes it easy to concentrate the mind on Consciousness. Not only easy but blissful. The devotee is in love with the Supreme and sees the world as its divine play, and play is blissful by nature. By entering into the spirit of the divine drama, urged on by the blissful power of attraction, the mind naturally becomes pinnacled and eventually brings us to the gate of *nirguṅa*.

सगुणात् सृष्टेरुत्पत्तिः ॥ १२ ॥

II.12 *saguṅāt srṣṭer utpattiḥ*

saguṅāt, from *saguṅa*; *sṛṣṭeḥ*, creation; *utpattiḥ*, origin, birth

"The creation originates from Saguṅa Brahma."

While the seed of creation, the first cause, lies in *nirguṅa* and is thus beyond the scope of comprehension, the creation itself originates in Saguṅa Brahma, since the creation is the result of the influence of the *guṅas* on Consciousness, and the *guṅas* are inactive in *nirguṅa*. Indeed the creation is defined by the action of the *guṅas*. The play of qualities is what differentiates one object from another, be that object physical or psychic, and it is also what differentiates *saguṅa* from *nirguṅa*. From the first sprout of *sattvaguṅa*, which gives birth to the subtlest of all expression, the sense of existence, to the zenith point of *tamoguṅa*, which is responsible for the densest manifestation of matter, all is the play of the *guṅas*, and hence the creation logically had to have evolved from *saguṅa*, not *nirguṅa*, which is devoid of qualities. There can be no creation without the *guṅas*, and hence Nirguṅa Brahma has no relationship with the creation.

This is not to imply, however, that *saguṅa* and *nirguṅa* are separate entities. They are different states of the same entity. The same person can be asleep or awake, at rest or in motion. The waking state is analogous to *saguṅa* and the quiescent state to *nirguṅa*. Where this analogy falls short, however, is that in Consciousness these two states are coexistent. Brahma is both *nirguṅa* and *saguṅa* at the same time, both qualified and nonqualified. They are simultaneous facets of one integral entity. This is something the mind is unable to comprehend, but such is the nature of the Infinite, as we are reminded in the famous verse from the beginning of the Upanishads of the Sukla Yajurveda:

Pūrṅamadaḥ pūrṅamidaṁ pūrṅād pūrṅamudacyate;
Pūrṅasya pūrṅamādāya pūrṅamevāvashisyate.

"*Nirguṅa* is infinite; *saguṅa* is also infinite.
When the infinite is taken away from the infinite, the remainder is also infinite."

The best the mind can do is to use an analogy. In the most common of these analogies, *saguńa* is compared to an iceberg of form within the formless ocean of *nirguńa*—in this case, an iceberg of infinite dimensions. Yet at no point does the ocean cease to remain a singular entity.

Thus the question of the creation arising or disappearing has no locus standi. The creation is an eternal flow of the Cosmic Mind. The beginning and end of the universe are mental concepts that only exist within the purview of the mind, which is unable to comprehend either beginninglessness or endlessness. The nuclear Consciousness is constantly emanating the thought waves of creation and yet it remains constantly absorbed in itself, being both *nirguńa* and *saguńa*. It is both quiescent and active, asleep and awake, something we have not yet learned to do. The world in which we live, however, is *saguńa*, and *saguńa* is all we can know of existence until the moment we merge into the *nirvikalpa* or *nirguńa* state through the gateway of Táraka Brahma. And even then we will have to leave our knowing behind.

पुरुषदेहे जगदाभास: ॥ १३ ॥

II.13 *puruśadehe jagad ábhásah*

puruśa, consciousness; *dehe*, in the body; *jagat*, universe; *ábhásah*, reflection, semblance, shining forth

"The universe is a reflection in the body of Consciousness."

In order for us to see a physical object, light must reflect off that object and make its way to our retina. What we see is thus a reflection, a semblance. Similarly, the existence of any object, be it physical or psychic, depends on its reflection in the mirror of Consciousness. The universe consists of the thought waves of Saguńa Brahma, and for those thought waves to exist they must be cognized—that is, they must be substantiated within the field of cognition. In this sense, *puruśa* acts as a mirror, the mirror of cognition, and the cosmic thought waves are reflected in that mirror. If Consciousness were not present, there would be no reflection and thus no universe. Hence the universe as we know it is a semblance or reflection in Consciousness. For the microcosm, the universe consists of both physical and psychic realities: matter, energy, and the minds of other microcosms with their respective microcosmic thought waves. At the macrocosmic level, however, matter, energy, and microcosmic minds are all internal thought forms reflected in the mirror of the Macrocosmic Consciousness.

In this sutra Anandamurti uses the word *deha*, "body," and in his commentary he makes the point that nothing can exist outside the body of Consciousness; everything is within.[42] *Deha* here implies that the creation is the vast body of a singular entity, seemingly broken up into an infinitude of disparate entities but never ceasing to be one, like a surging ocean of countless waves. This is true monism, the realization that all of existence is comprised of the thought waves of a singular divine mind reflected in the Universal Consciousness. All is contained within that vast cosmic body, and what appear to be physical realities are in truth psychic realities reflected in the Cosmic Consciousness, just as the images that arise within our individual minds are reflected in the mirror of our individual consciousness and thus remain entirely within us.

It is worth noting here that the word *ábhása* has been used in both Shaeva and Shakta Tantra to denote the entire system of cosmic manifestation, from the first expression of cosmic ideation to the formation of the *tattvas*, the fundamental factors.[43] It has sometimes been translated as "shining forth," in the sense that the waves of creation are a "shining forth" of Consciousness. The use of the word *ábhása* in this context thus carries echoes of these systems of thought.

Sir Arthur Eddington, the noted astronomer and physicist who was the first to successfully explain stellar processes, had this to say about the nature of the physical universe:

> The external world of physics has thus become a world of shadows. In removing our illusions we have removed the substance, for indeed we have seen that substance is one of the greatest of our illusions…In the world of physics we watch a shadowgraph performance of the

drama of familiar life. The shadow of my elbow rests on the shadow table as the shadow ink flows over the shadow paper. It is all symbolic, and as a symbol the physicist leaves it. Then comes the alchemist Mind who transmutes the symbols....To put the conclusion crudely, the stuff of the world is mind-stuff.[44]

ब्रह्म सत्यं जगदपि सत्यमापेक्षिकम् ॥ १४ ॥

II.14 *brahma satyaṁ jagad api satyam ápekṣikam*

brahma, Supreme Consciousness; *satyam*, truth, immutable; *jagat*, universe; *api*, also; *ápekṣikam*, relative

"Brahma is absolute truth;
the universe is also truth but relative truth."

In the previous two sutras Anandamurti addressed the origin and nature of the creation. In this sutra he continues his examination of the nature of the creation by taking on a contentious topic in philosophical discourse—the question of the reality or irreality of the manifest universe as reflected in the body of Consciousness.

While Anandamurti is clear about the creation being the internal thought projection of Saguṅa Brahma, the assumption of form by the infinite Supreme Consciousness, the reality of the manifest universe has long been a subject of debate. The realist or materialist philosophies consider matter to be the one undeniable truth. In their view, mind and consciousness, which they generally conflate, arise from matter as epiphenomena, and they tend to discount spiritual ideas as running contrary to logic (their logic) and to the evidence of the senses. The idealist philosophies, on the other hand, prioritize mind and spirit, which they generally do not conflate, and while they have different takes on matter, they all agree that matter is dependent on mind and/or spirit for its existence (to the extent that they allow for its existence at all). In the *Critique of Pure Reason*, for example, Immanuel Kant had this to say about the nature of reality: "If I remove the thinking subject, the whole material world must at once vanish because it is nothing but a phenomenal appearance in the sensibility of ourselves as a subject, and a manner or species of representation."

This debate on the nature of reality has been going on for millennia, and it has had a determining influence on how human beings see the world. Western education since the eighteenth century has been increasingly dominated by materialist thought—it is natural selection, rather than divine design, that determines the evolution of biological systems, and either class struggle or the market's invisible hand that propels the evolution of society. As a consequence, there is a rising wave of prominent intellectuals actively campaigning against the belief in God, which they see as primitive, debilitating, and unnecessary, if not dangerous (the titles alone of Richard Dawkins's books *The Blind Watchmaker* and *The God Delusion*, and his documentary *Enemies of Reason* are indicative of their thinking). In the East, on the other hand, especially in India, the spiritual or idealist philosophies still by and large hold sway over the collective psychology, although the materialist philosophies are gradually gaining ground. Of these spiritual philosophies, the one that has arguably exerted the greatest influence on the development of Indian thought over the last thirteen centuries, and consequently on yogic philosophy and teaching, is the Mayavada of Shankaracharya, otherwise known as Advaita Vedanta. Mayavada is the doctrine that only Consciousness exists; everything else is illusion. While Mayavada existed long before Shankaracarya, he became its greatest proponent,[45] and the essence of his teaching on the nature of reality can be summed up in what is perhaps the single most influential aphorism in all of Indian philosophy: *brahma satyaṁ jaganmithyá*; "Brahma is truth and the world is false."[46]

For Shankaracharya (whom Anandamurti has called "the greatest philosopher that India ever produced"),[47] there is no actual creation. The phenomenal world has the appearance of reality to the *jiiva* as long as the *jiiva* remains in its bound condition, but that semblance has no actual substratum. It is merely an appearance cast over the real through Brahma's association with maya. He explains this through a series of analogies, of which perhaps the most well known is that of a mirage. An expanse of water appears in the middle of the desert or on a stretch of asphalt but that water has no actual existence. It is merely an illusion that disappears the moment we cognize the truth. Likewise, when the *jiiva* attains true knowledge and thus no longer views Brahma through the veil of maya, it realizes that the world of phenomenal experience was an illusion, like a dream that the dreamer knows to be unreal upon awakening, another in this series of analogies.

Shankaracharya's modern descendants are still very influential in the realm of spiritual philosophy, and they are commonly grouped together as the "nondualist" schools, a modern rendering of Advaita Vedanta. Arguably the most influential nondualist master in the twentieth century was the Sage of Arunchala, Ramana Maharsi. The following passage from David Godman, the author of numerous books on Ramana's teachings, is a colorful and effective summary of Indian idealist thought:

> Everything you see is a creation of your own mind ... the Papaji you see on the bench who says "Welcome, David" is my projection. The guru is like a lion that appears in an elephant's dream. The lion roars and the elephant wakes up. The Bhagavan who sat on the sofa, the Papaji who sat on a bench and said "Welcome" is part of your projection. There aren't separate individual *jiivas* inhabiting a common universe. You create all the *jiivas* out there and you designate one of them to be enlightened and say, "Please help me." *Dršti sršti* (sight, creation) instead of *sršti dršti* (creation, sight). What Ramana would say is that once you know you are the Self, you know that birth and death never happened; you know there is no reincarnation, no creation. But if you think you are a *jiiva*, a whole set of apparent illusory rules come into effect that govern the functioning of that body. *Iishvara* is created. Samsara continues indefinitely because of your idea that you are a body. As soon as that idea ends, you know there is no reincarnation. The true experience of the *jiṇáni* (sage) is that nothing ever happened; no world ever came into existence.[48]

Another influential twentieth-century nondualist master was Sri Nisargadatta:

> What begins and ends is mere appearance. The world can be said to appear, but not to be. The appearance may last very long on some scale of time, and be very short on another, but ultimately it comes to the same. Whatever is time bound is momentary and has no reality. [49]

It is in this context that Anandamurti steps into the breach, aligning himself neither with the idealist philosophies, nor with the realist or materialist philosophies, but squarely in the middle, in a way that acknowledges the strengths of both and mitigates their weaknesses, and he does so by wording his sutra as a direct refutation of Advaita Vedanta's iconic *brahma satyaṁ jaganmithyá*.

The word *satyam* is commonly translated as "truth," but its etymological meaning is "immutable," that which undergoes no change. *Satyam* in this sense means "absolute truth." As opposed to all manifest realities, which are subject to relativity, *satyam* is beyond relativity and is thus absolute. There is only one absolute entity beyond the bounds of relativity and that is Brahma; hence Brahma is the one absolute truth. In this respect, Anandamurti agrees with Shankaracharya and other Indian idealist philosophers, but when it comes to the nature of the world, he disagrees. For Anandamurti the world or the creation is also truth. In other words, the world is real. In this he agrees with the materialist philosophers. It is not in any sense an illusion. *However*, it is a truth that is subject to relativity and thus to impermanence.

Relativity in Anandamurti's philosophy is defined by three factors: time, space, and person. These three factors are always changing; hence both mind and matter, being within the bounds of relativity, are constantly changing. The essence of relativity therefore is movement. Everything in the universe—every particle, every thought, every physical and mental expression—is in constant motion, and thus everything is relative because everything is moving in relation to everything else. The valley outside my window appears to be fixed in space, but the Earth which harbors us both is in fact spinning at a speed of one thousand miles per hour relative to the Sun while at the same time traveling around the Sun at twenty miles per second, fast enough to reach the Moon in four hours were it headed that way, while the Sun in turn drags the Earth through the Milky Way at a blazing 140 miles per second relative to other star systems. There is no fixed point in nature, since nature itself is not fixed. Nor is the mind that perceives the Earth, the Moon, and the Sun, itself a part of nature and thus equally subject to relativity, as we well know from our own experience. The only fixed point is Brahma. Only that which is immutable can be motionless and the only immutable entity is Consciousness, the ultimate backdrop against which everything appears. And since mind and matter are relative entities that are locked together in an inseparable relationship, that of perceiver and perceived, the world appears as an absolute truth to the mind. In other words, it is real, undeniably real. Two relative entities are not just passing phenomena to each other, and any effort to deny the other's reality is nothing more than an exercise of the imagination—the mind denying its own reality, which has traditionally been the most common charge leveled against Shankaracharya's Mayavada.[50] Thus both mind and matter have absolute existence relative to each other but not relative to consciousness. And this relationship will continue as long as mind and matter exist. They will remain absolute truths to each other but relative truths in relation to the one immutable entity, consciousness. A particular object may arise and disappear but the objective world as a whole, in its inseparable relative relationship, is eternal to the mind.

Thus the two modalities of the Supreme Spirit, Shiva and Shakti, the quiescent, unchanging state of pure Consciousness and the kinetic, constantly changing state of Consciousness in motion, are the twin aspects of reality. Both are true, both are indisputably real, one changeless Consciousness beyond the bounds of relativity that manifests as a changing, temporal reality subject to the bonds of relativity.

Anandamurti has made it clear in his writings that the extreme positions of both the materialist and idealist philosophies have had pernicious consequences for human society. The idealist teachings, represented here by the Advaita Vedanta of Shankaracharya with its denial of the reality of the world, have led to apathy and neglect in regard to our physical existence and a consequent lack of mundane progress;[51] while the materialist philosophies, by denying the primacy of Consciousness and spiritual evolution, have led to egocentricity, a degradation in ethical standards, and a lack of spiritual progress, the prime ingredient in the human quest for happiness and fulfillment. In the Isha Upanishad it is said that those who follow only the material fall into darkness and those who follow only the spiritual fall into even greater darkness.[52] Success in human life—the sole reason for the existence of philosophy—depends on both, and this in turn depends on the recognition that the material and the spiritual are twin facets of one integral existence.

पुरुषो ऽकर्ता फलसाक्षीभूतो भावकेन्द्रस्थितो गुणयन्त्रकश्च ॥ १५ ॥

II.15 *puruśo 'kartá phalasákśiibhúto bhávakendrasthito guñayantrakash ca*

puruśah, consciousness; *akartá*, non-doer; *phala*, fruit; *sákśii*, witness; *bhútah*, entity, fundamental factors; *bháva*, existence, Saguńa Brahma; *kendra*, center, nucleus; *sthitah*, situated; *guńa*, binding principles of *prakrti*; *yantrakah*, machinist, controller; *ca*, and

"Consciousness performs no action but is the witness of the fruits of action; situated at the center of the ideational cosmos, it is the controller of the *guñas*."

We know from the practice of introspection that our individual consciousness or *jiivátmá* performs no action. It is merely the witness or substantiation of the movements of our mind. Doership resides in the mind, originating from the sense of I. And yet we cannot do anything in the absence of our individual consciousness; thus everything we do is dependent on it. The same is true of the Cosmic Consciousness. It has no agency, no intention, no modification or quality of any kind. Being the screen upon which the universe is reflected, it witnesses or substantiates the motions of the Universal Mind without being affected by them. But something is being done, a universe has been set in motion, and where energy is manifest there must be a cause, a controlling faculty, a *kartá*. If *puruśa* is *akartá*, "non-doer," then where is the *kartá*? Logically, there must be some other principle that is responsible for the creation. This creative principle, as we have seen, is *prakrti*, the magic wand of maya through which the world comes into being. But *prakrti* cannot act in the absence of Consciousness, just as nothing can be seen in the absence of light, and thus it is Consciousness that is ultimately responsible for the creation and everything that happens within it. In this sense it can be compared to a catalytic agent. A catalytic agent is not directly involved in a chemical reaction and undergoes no change thereby, but its presence is not only indispensable to that reaction but determines its nature. Similarly, the ultimate governance of the universe lies in Consciousness but that governance is indirect.[53] All vibration, all manifestation of mind and matter, is a result of the interplay between the three *guńas* of *prakrti*, but *puruśa*, in whose absence nothing can take place and from whom the *guńas* have emanated, is the de facto controller of those *guńas*. Though actionless, *puruśa* is the ultimate controller of the universe, the supreme commander behind the forces of *prakrti*. There can be no *kartá* without the immanent presence of the *akartá*, the ultimate catalytic agent. Being the center of this ideational cosmos, the Cosmic Consciousness is perforce its supreme controller, the first and final cause. This is conceptualized as Consciousness being situated in the nucleus of Saguńa Brahma, controlling the *guńas* through which the creation comes into being.

We can compare this to a large company whose owner and founder is not involved in the daily running of the firm but who nevertheless remains aware of everything that is going on. The company has a board of directors to make its decisions, managers to implement those decisions, and workers to carry out the work. In addition, it has a set of guidelines and procedures that must be adhered to—if not, there are consequences built into the system—and all of this transpires without any direct input from the owner. The workers work, the managers direct, the board deliberates, issues its directives, and authorizes dividends and payments. But none of this could happen without the owner. Without her there is no bank account to pay the employees, no production, no company. And because the board knows she is there, knows that without her they have no standing, they make sure that the procedures and guidelines are followed. The company seemingly functions on its own, but in truth everything depends on the owner. Another useful analogy is that of the headman in a village function. The headman does not take part in the action—he simply observes—but due to the great respect he commands, the participants are careful to carry out their respective roles accordingly.

The word *citishakti*, the force of Consciousness, has sometimes been used for *puruśa* in this sense, since without the presence of *citishakti* nothing can happen.[54] In other words, cognition is a kind of *shakti*. *Prakrti* is a blind force. Without the guidance of Consciousness it cannot function. Everything in the expressed universe follows a certain set of laws, the laws of *prakrti*, and *prakrti* can only function according to this system because the force of Consciousness is behind it.[55] It is Consciousness that provides the inspiration for the living being's forward movement through its all-encompassing power of attraction; it is Consciousness that guides the living being down the pathways of spiritual evolution through the laws that govern the universe; and it is Consciousness that becomes a personal presence in the life of a spiritual aspirant as they near the culmination of their journey, the central figure in the devotional practice that ultimately opens the gates to enlightenment.

For Anandamurti, *parama puruśa* is not only the cognitive faculty; he is also *iishána* or *iishvara* (the controller), even if that control be indirect.[56] His conception of Consciousness as *akartá* thus differs significantly from that of both Advaita Vedanta and Samkhya. In Advaita Vedanta, Brahma has no real connection with maya, whose existence after all is merely illusory, and thus *iishvara* has no actual existence, being a creation of maya. In Samkhya, *puruśa* and *prakrti* are considered to be independent entities. While *prakrti* cannot act in the absence of *puruśa*, whose conjunction with the creative faculty gives the unconscious *prakrti* the appearance of consciousness, it is not seen as being subject to the control of *puruśa*, which would make *prakrti* a dependent entity.⁵⁷ Both points of view limit the role of Consciousness, which, being unlimited, is both the impersonal Brahma and the personal *iishvara* simultaneously, both *nirguńa* and *saguńa* at the same time.

It is the natural tendency of human beings to blame God for their ills, both individual and collective, but from a philosophical point of view this is an incorrect understanding. The universe follows certain laws that have come into being as a result of the functioning of *prakrti*. If we stick our hand in fire it is sure to get burnt. That is the nature of fire. Rather than blame God for our suffering, we would do better not to stick our hand in the fire. The universe supplies everything we need to live a peaceful and productive life as we scale the ladder of evolution toward our final liberation, but if we fail to create a just society that protects and promotes the welfare of all, we have only ourselves to blame. If we are to successfully navigate the pitfalls of incarnate life, then we must live in harmony with the laws of *prakrti*, beginning with the law of action and reaction. In the Bhagavad Gita, Krishna says, "Neither do I do anything, nor do I make anybody do anything; it is the law of nature that is taking its course."⁵⁸ That law is the law of action and reaction, which keeps the universe on track. But without the nucleus, the machine of the *guńas* cannot turn. Consciousness is apart and untouched by the universal drama set in motion by the *guńas*. And yet the drama goes on because of Consciousness, because the creative principle, *prakrti*, is an emanation of Consciousness. You can say that *puruśa* gave birth to the *guńas* but that would be misleading, since *puruśa* is *akartá*. We would do better to call it an immaculate conception.

अकर्त्री विषयसंयुक्ता बुद्धिर्महद्वा ॥ १६ ॥

II.16 *akartrii viśayasaṁyuktá buddhir mahad vá*

akartrii, non-doer; *viśaya*, object; *saṁyuktá*, joined to, associated with; *buddhih*, *mahat*, feeling of existence, I-feeling; *vá*, or

"The *buddhitattva*, or *mahattattva*, is not the agent but remains associated with objects."

We first looked at the three layers of mind—*mahat, aham,* and *citta*—early in Chapter One during their emergence out of the Macrocosmic Consciousness in the flow of *saiṇcara*. Later in that chapter we took a prolonged look at them at the microcosmic level by tracing their gradual manifestation in living beings during the phase of *pratisaiṇcara*. In these next three sutras we examine *mahat, aham,* and *citta* in the context of the dharma of living beings—more specifically, in the context of the human being and its divine dharma. Not from the cosmic lens of involution or evolution but from the localized lens of our experience of incarnate life, of which the human being is the highest expression. In other words, we now take a closer look at the nature of the individual mind and its concomitant sense of individuality.

These three sutras form a unit with the previous sutra. Taken together we thus have four levels to our cognitive existence: first our *jiivátmá*, or individual consciousness, the actionless witness of the mind's existence, followed by the three functional layers of mind. They are termed "functional" layers because the mind is one but that one mind can function in three different ways. Fundamentally, the mind is the sense of "I," but that "I" can perform three distinctly different functions. And because those functions are an expression of different levels of subtlety, we can think of them as layers arranged according to the subtlety of the function they perform.

Consciousness, being *akartá*, has no qualities and performs no function. It is pure cognition, the substantiation of all that is, but cognition is not a function. It is pure being, the field of cognition in which action arises and is substantiated, like a screen upon which the sounds and images of incarnate existence are projected. When Consciousness begins to undergo qualification, however, giving rise to functionality, we call it mind. If we take rice and process it by milling it into rice flour then it is no longer rice, in the sense that it has qualities that differentiate it from the original substance. Similarly, it is Consciousness that has become mind, and as a result of that transformation, qualities arise that differentiate mind from consciousness. The first and subtlest of these is the sense of existence. Through deep introspection, we discover that our sense of "I" is an abstract idea, ie., a thought, the primordial thought in the mind of human beings. Before other thoughts can arise, the sense of existence must first be present. Before there can be a "you" there must be an "I." This is called *mahat* or *buddhi* in Sanskrit and it is the subtlest of the three functional layers of mind. It arises due to the influence of *sattvaguña*, the sentient principle, which produces the knowledge of existence. Consciousness in its unqualified state is pure awareness; it is not aware *of* anything because it has no object. With the appearance of the sense of existence, however, it now has an object, the "I am," and thus consciousness becomes aware of itself.

Through that same act of profound introspection we discover that our sense of existence, the pure "I am," also performs no action. Nor can it be differentiated from that of any other living being. It can be strong or faint, depending on the level of evolution, but the feeling of existence is one and indivisible, just as distilled water in a thimble is essentially the same as distilled water in a reservoir, despite the difference in volume, and thus *mahat* is free from the sense of individuation. When the mind grows calm, whether in deep meditation or in some quiet moment, perhaps sitting alone on a beach at sunset, we begin to feel the pure joy of existence that was hitherto hidden beneath the turbulent waters of the mind. That is our *mahattattva*, the purest form of mental expression, and like consciousness it is *akartá*. And yet, when the mind becomes active again, when our sense of individuality reasserts itself and erupts into thought and action, that "I" goes with us, for it is the same I that has vaulted into action. It then becomes associated with our mental experience, and to the extent that our attention is absorbed by that mental experience, by our thoughts and actions, by the colors and forms of the world around us, we lose sight of that pure I. It is now inseparably associated with our thoughts and perceptions, with the objects that populate our mind, be they physical or psychic, as if the water of *mahat* were absorbed by the sponge of *aham* and *citta*. And because it remains associated with our mental experience, it indirectly imbibes the results of those actions, the "I" at the root of "I feel sad." Nevertheless, like the unseen water in the sponge, our sense of existence remains inescapably present, whether or not we pay it any mind. We cannot go anywhere without our I, and however hidden it may appear to be, however seemingly caught up with our thoughts and desires, the essential nature of our sense of existence remains unsullied. Whether we feel happy or sad, whether our mind is caught in a whirlpool of its own making or is sitting quietly by the beach, watching the sun setting over the horizon, the moment we set aside those thoughts and desires we find our *mahat* to be what it has always been—the pure, blissful feeling of existence, untouched by individuality.

अहं कर्ता प्रत्यक्षफलभोक्ता ॥ १७ ॥

II.17 *ahaṁ kartá pratyakṣaphalabhoktá*

ahaṁ, ego, doer-I; *kartá*, doer, agent, actor; *pratyakṣa*, direct; *phala*, fruit; *bhoktá*, enjoyer, eater, consumer

"The *aham* is the agent and
the direct experiencer of the fruits of action."

Aham is the Sanskrit first-person pronoun, the equivalent of the Latin *ego*. In philosophical terms, it refers to the mind in its role as the actor—or "doer-I," as Anandamurti sometimes calls it. When the pure I of *mahat*, due to the influence of *rajoguña*, undergoes metamorphosis and assumes the role of the I that perceives, feels, and acts, then a second layer of functionality has been added to the mind, and that further qualification gives rise to the sense of individuality. If the pure subject stands alone, manifesting only the sense of existence, there can be no action and thus no differentiation between the I of one living being and that of another. The sense of existence, as we have seen in the previous sutra, is one and indivisible. But the moment the pure subject takes on the quality of authorship, the moment the subject acquires a verb, then the sense of individuality arises, separating one subject from another. The "I see" or "I want" or "I feel" of one subject is necessarily different from that of a second subject, the difference lying in their respective *upadhis*, their respective qualifications or conditions. The "I see" or "I feel" of one microcosm will always be unique to that microcosm.

And due to the presence of a thinking, feeling, perceiving subject, the mind is bound to bear the consequences of its actions. The "I want" bears the consequences of that desire, the "I perceive" bears the impact of that perception, the "I act" bears the reaction of that action. Each of these acts distorts the previously undistorted mind, and the resultant momentum must be served in the form of the consequences of action, as we will explore more fully in sutra II.19.

Under normal conditions *aham* dominates our consciousness, and for that reason we generally remain only subliminally aware of *mahat*. For all intents and purposes, *aham* constitutes our sense of identity, and this continues to be our experience until we begin to transcend the bounds of individuality. This distinction becomes clear through meditative practice, but we can gain some understanding of it if we examine the experience of awakening directly from deep sleep. For a brief moment, the awakened mind has not yet begun to think (except in the sense that the feeling of existence is also a thought). In that moment, before the tumult of thought sets in, we are aware of our existence but we are not actually thinking, nor in that moment do we have any intention of doing so, for intention is a product of the thinking mind. And because we are not yet thinking, we have no sense of *who* we are, only *that* we are. But the moment our thinking mind becomes active, our sense of individuality kicks in. We become aware of our body, aware that we were sleeping, aware of our desire to begin the day, or conversely, to go back to sleep. This potential to think and act was there before our sense of individuality returned. It is inherent in our feeling of existence, even before that feeling of existence gives birth to the sense of individuality and to the energy of thought and action that inevitably follows in its wake. In other words, it is the same I, but our experience of that I is totally different as a result of its having taken on a new and entirely different function. We have changed our state, and that changed state is a world apart—the world of activity, the world of thought and feeling, the world of individuality. The I is now the actor, the ego, and sees itself as such. When I get up, I am aware that *I* am getting up; if I am engaged with my thoughts I know that they are mine; if I am beset by some emotion, I am the one who is affected and no one else. As long as I remain involved with my individual thoughts and feelings, my perceptions, desires, and actions, I remain identified with the thinker—unless and until I develop the ability to transcend that sense of identification with individuality.

Mahat in its pure state performs no action and thus cannot suffer the consequences of action, except indirectly, by association. It is indivisible and undifferentiated and hence has no peaks and valleys, no pleasure and pain, just the innate joy that is inherent to existence itself, being a reflection of the bliss that is the nature of Consciousness. Our *aham*, however, being identified with our thoughts and actions, is irrevocably fated to face the direct consequences of those thoughts and actions. If I feel sad, it is the ego, the actor, that is feeling sad. Sadness is a thought wave in the mind experienced by the thinker of that thought. If I am struck by an errant baseball, it is the *aham*, the perceiver, that feels the blow. If I receive an unexpected compliment and feel a surge of pride, it is my sense of individuality that revels in its inflated sense of self. My *mahat* is present, indirectly involved in each experience, and as long as it is associated with *aham* it appears to be affected by the actions of my ego, just as a mirror appears red when a red flower is placed in front of it. But take away that flower, take away the functionality of *aham*, and in the absence of the ego there is no sadness, no pain, no inflated sense of self, just the pure mirror of the I, serene and unaffected. And thus we know that it is the *aham* and only the *aham* that suffers or enjoys the consequences of its actions.

कर्मफलं चित्तम् ॥ १८ ॥

II.18 *karmaphalaṁ cittam*

karma, action; *phalaṁ*, fruit; *cittam*, mind-stuff, the objectivated I

"The results of action are *citta*."

The third functional layer of mind is known as *citta* or mind-stuff in Anandamurti's lexicon. He also refers to it as the "objectivated

I," because it denotes the mind's ability to adopt the form of its mental object. *Karma* means "action" and *phala* means "fruit"; hence *karmaphala* refers to the fruits or results of action. In this context, *karma* denotes mental action and the result of the act of thinking is a thought. To put it more succinctly, *citta* is the content of the mind, whether that content be a perception, a memory, or an abstract thought or emotion. This is equally true for physical actions, since whatever action we perform originates in our mind. Even an apparently "unconscious" action, such as adjusting our posture while looking at a computer screen or shifting gears while keeping our eyes on the road, begins with a thought, whether we are aware of that thought or not, and only then does it get translated into action.[59] Whatever the nature of that thought, it takes shape in the *citta* like a wave rising from the surface of the ocean, where it then becomes the object of *aham*; and since the mind is fundamentally the "I," it is thus our own "I" that has become the object of our thinking self.

Let us return for a moment to the process of perception, so fundamental to our understanding of the mind. When I look at a flower, the light waves reflected from that flower strike my retina and give rise to a corresponding image that is then transmitted to the brain via the optic nerve, whereupon the visual cortex registers that transmitted impression. In order for me to see the flower, however, that impression has to register in my mind. If my mind is in a suspended state—due to anesthesia, for example—then I will not see the flower even though the image reaches my brain intact.[60] In other words, what I see is not the external object or even the impression in the visual cortex but an image in my mind, and in order for that to happen, the mind must have the ability to form that image, as if it were a photographic plate registering the impact of the incoming light waves. The same is true for any type of thought, be it an emotion, a bodily sensation, a memory, or an abstract rumination. If I feel pain, I experience it in my mind, even though that experience is triggered by signals sent to my brain via the afferent nerves. I will not experience any pain if I am under anesthesia because the activity of my mind has been forcibly suspended by the drugs. The same is true for emotions, memories, and abstract thought, whether waking or dreaming. All human experience is experienced in the mind as waves in the *citta*, with the exception of the direct experience of the Self in *savikalpa samadhi*. For this reason, some idealist philosophers contend that the world only exists within our minds. Anandamurti does not accept this—the world exists as thought waves within the Cosmic Mind and is then apprehended by the individual mind, one relative entity to another—but it is true that our experience of the world takes place entirely within our mind. And since it is within my mind that each thought arises—each sensation, perception, desire, feeling, or abstract formulation—those thoughts are thus aspects or facets of my mind; that is, they are my "I" in the form of the object of thought, in this case the "objectivated I," or *citta*, rather than the pure I or the individual doer I. As Anandamurti puts it, "To hear a sound, one has to become the sound itself. Thus human beings themselves become the result of their actions, and whatever one sees, feels, hears, touches or smells is their own feeling of "I" or their own transformed self."[61]

This is the third of the three functions of the mind, which correspond to the three basic parts of a sentence: subject, verb, and object. The I of *mahat* springs into action and becomes the thinker, the *aham*, which witnesses its thought waves as they arise in the *citta*. One mind, one I, playing three different roles, all of which are reflected in the mirror of consciousness. This understanding of the tripartite nature of the mind is especially emphasized in Anandamurti's teachings because it is by unraveling the threads of the mind and tracing them back to their source that we can realize our identity with Consciousness and thus achieve the goal of our human journey.

विकृतचित्तस्य पूर्वावस्थाप्राप्तिः फलभोगः ॥ १९ ॥

II.19 *vikrtacittasya púrvávasthápráptih phalabhogah*

vikrta, distorted, deformed, altered; *cittasya*, of the *citta*; *púrva*, previous; *avasthá*, condition, state; *práptih*, gaining, acquisition; *phala*, fruit; *bhogah*, experience of enjoyment or suffering

"The distorted *citta* regains its prior state through the experience of the fruits of action."

Having looked at the functional layers of the mind in the previous sutras, the stage is now set to examine the effect of mental action on the mind. It is an axiom of both science and philosophy that every action presupposes a reaction coexistent with the original action.[62] Newton's third law of motion states that every action has an equal and opposite reaction. This is a law of classical mechanics. When one object exerts force on another object, the second object will react with equal and opposite force. Newton came to this conclusion through his observation of the physical universe, but the law he discovered governing the application of force between objects in the material plane is but one aspect of a fundamental law of the universe that applies as much to the psychic plane as it does to the physical plane—the law of action and reaction, sometimes referred to as the "law of karma." In this sutra we examine the mechanics of this law as it applies within the mental arena, especially in the context of the human mind. This is the first of three sutras dedicated to this subject, one in this chapter and two in the next, an indication of the central role that action and reaction plays in the lives of human beings, and indeed, of all beings.

Mind in its original state is quiescent. The unmodified *mahat* performs no action and suffers no affliction. Being quiescent, undistorted by the sense of individuality, it imbibes or reflects the unlimited blissful nature of Consciousness. But when *aham* becomes active, whipping up the waves of *citta*, that pure sense of existence becomes subject to the storms of the individual mind. No matter how distorted it becomes, however, the mind's natural tendency is to return to its original quiescent state, and the means by which it does so, in accordance with the laws of *prakrti*, is through the reactions to the actions engendered by *aham*.

Anandamurti illustrates this by using the analogy of a rubber ball. In its original state a rubber ball shows no deformation and experiences no tension. It is round and at rest. But if we press our finger into the ball, creating an indentation or impression, it is no longer round nor at rest. The ball has been deformed and a state of tension has arisen. That tension exists because the force that created the indentation gives rise to its opposing force, which seeks to return the ball to its original, undistorted state. Once our finger is removed, the ball springs back, releasing that tension. The mind acts in much the same fashion. In its original, undistorted state *citta* is quiescent. There are no waves to disturb the surface of the mind, no currents to disturb its depths. But when *aham* acts in pursuance of its desires, an impression is formed in the mind, the result of the action of thought, and with that impression comes a concomitant tension, an inherent momentum that seeks to return the mind to its original state of equilibrium. The release of that tension is effected by the enjoyment or suffering of the reaction to that mental action, something that can only occur when the appropriate conditions are met, analogous to the removal of one's finger from the rubber ball. Until that tension or momentum is released, the mind cannot be free.

It is easy enough to recognize this state of tension in the restless nature of the conditioned mind. The *aham* is forever running after some objects and away from others, thereby constantly distorting the *citta*. Depending on the nature of its actions and the nature of the objects it pursues or shuns, it experiences either pleasure or pain upon facing the consequences of those actions. Suppose an otherwise ethical person commits a reprehensible act under the momentary influence of a crude propensity, say an act of theft committed out of greed when no one is looking. They know that their action will be a source of suffering to the owner, and though they escape without having to face any apparent consequence, they cannot escape the impression that the action has left in their mind. The memory is lodged in their *citta* along with a certain sense of unease or guilt or agitation. Even if they feel safe from discovery, they instinctively fear that one day they might have to suffer the consequences of what they have done, and even if they are not consciously aware of that internal turbulence, that tension will remain in their *citta* until the time comes when they face the consequences and are relieved of that karmic debt. This is what leads some people to confess to a crime for which they would have never been caught. Being conscious of that tension, they attempt to alleviate it by seeking out their own punishment rather than letting nature make the arrangements.

Unlike in the physical plane, the opposite reaction that enables the mind to regain its lost equilibrium is not always immediate.

In fact, it rarely is, due to the nature of psychic actions where the expenditure of psychic force in most cases does not immediately affect its object. Even a mental theft, one that is never carried out, leaves an impression in the mind, a sense of unease or mental distortion that will have to be counteracted by some form of equivalent suffering when the appropriate conditions have been met. Those appropriate conditions, however, may take years to materialize and may even be postponed to a future life, as we will discuss in Chapter Three.[63] However long it takes, those consequences will eventually have to be undergone, for without the *phalabhoga*, the coexistent reaction that inevitably accompanies the impression left in the *citta*, the mind cannot regain its equilibrium, and thus this tension, which is the source of the mind's inherent momentum, continues to drive it forward in a never-ending quest for freedom.

Every human being, to a lesser or greater degree, has a general sense that their mind has been distorted in various ways by a lifetime of thought and action that has given rise to the complexes, compulsions, and unresolved needs and desires that condition our behavior and determine our ever-fluctuating sense of well-being. And every human being has at least a vague understanding that some of these psychic tendencies have been with them since their earliest memories, whether or not they have any inkling that these tendencies may have been carried over from a previous life. Due to the nature of psychic action, however, where the gap between cause and effect can be a canyon that spans not just years but lifetimes, it is very difficult, and often nigh on impossible, to see the link between our sufferings and enjoyments and the original actions that begot them. Nevertheless, without a clear understanding of the nature of *karmaphalabhoga*, of the fact that our fate is determined by our thoughts and actions, both past and present, our spiritual evolution becomes immeasurably more difficult, as we shall see in the two sutras of Chapter Three dedicated to the subject of *saṁskára*, the requital of past actions that we have yet to face.

न स्वर्गो न रसातलः ॥ २० ॥

II.20 *na svargo na rasátalah*

na, no; *svargah*, heaven; *rasátalah*, hell

"There is neither heaven nor hell."

As long as unserved reactions continue to condition the mind, leaving it in a deformed or distorted state, the human being cannot attain freedom. In this sense, spiritual liberation or salvation is equivalent to freedom from these unserved reactions, which are experienced as mental conditioning that leads to experiences of pleasure and pain. These stored-up impressions, the resultant of previous actions, are thus the source of the mind's bondage. Only when the mind is completely free from *karmaphalabhoga*, from mental conditioning or mental distortion, can consciousness return to its original, unqualified state. As long as these impressions remain, their inherent momentum will drive the mind forward in an effort to free itself from its accumulated reactions, and this necessitates that the mind inhabit a body that provides the opportunity to undergo those unrequited reactions. The idea that an individual who has yet to achieve liberation from their accumulated reactions could merit ascension to heaven—according to popular belief, a terminal state or realm of spiritual perfection and a permanent end to suffering—is both illogical and contrary to the laws that govern the creation. Unserved reactions cannot simply disappear without having been expressed—they are a form of psychic energy or momentum, and energy in whatever form it appears can be transmuted or transformed but it cannot simply vanish. The ordered nature of the universe dictates that this momentum be expressed, and expression can only take place within the expressed universe. By the same token, the idea of hell, which is popularly understood to be a terminal state or realm of constant suffering, is equally illogical. Were those unserved reactions to be served through the mind's suffering in the underworld (assuming for a moment that such a thing could be possible in a bodiless state, itself a fundamentally illogical proposition), then that suffering would pave the way for the mind's liberation by exhausting those reactions, rendering hell null and void.

Hence the idea of heaven and hell as realms or states that exist outside or beyond the law of cause and effect, action and reaction, runs contrary to both logic and experience, since there is nothing in this manifest universe that is not subject to the law of action and reaction. Rather, as Anandamurti points out, they should be understood to be states of mind.[64] When the mind enjoys the fruits of its positive actions, that state of happiness or well-being is indeed heavenly, and when the mind is forced to undergo the consequences of its evil or misguided thoughts and deeds, then that atmosphere is indeed hellish. We have all met people whose lives are a living hell and others whose lives are quite the opposite. In both cases, they are undergoing the fruits of their previous actions, and in neither case is this a permanent condition. Their lives are what they are due to their past thoughts and actions, and it is their present thoughts and actions that will determine their future. This idea is echoed in the famous opening verses of the Dhammapada:

> All experience is preceded by mind,
> Led by mind,
> Made by mind.
> Speak or act with a corrupted mind,
> And suffering follows
> As the wagon wheel follows the hoof of the ox.
>
> All experience is preceded by mind,
> Led by mind,
> Made by mind.
> Speak or act with a peaceful mind,
> And happiness follows,
> Like a never-departing shadow.[65]

The belief in heaven and hell is one of the main differences between traditional dualistic religious thought and that of Tantra and other monistic spiritual ideologies for which there is no world other than the one we inhabit—"no hell below us, above us only sky," as John Lennon famously said in "Imagine"—bearing in mind that our knowledge of the universe is limited to what we can capture with our minds. It is within this universe that the drama of spiritual evolution plays out as we pass from one body to another until we finally merge back into pure

Consciousness. The question then naturally arises, "Why, if the founders of the world's major religions were highly evolved souls, did they allow the belief in heaven and hell to persist?"

A case can be made that the founders of these religions were speaking in metaphors, ie., using a highly symbolic language that was later misinterpreted by their less enlightened followers. In July and August of 1999, during a series of general audiences, Pope John Paul II issued four catecheses revising the Catholic Church's stand on heaven and hell.[66] The new eschatology stated that "hell is not a place but the state of being separated from God" and that "heaven is not a physical place among the clouds; it is the state of being close to God." Similarly, purgatory was downgraded to a provisional state of purification that had nothing to do with any particular location. As with earlier interpretations of Church dogma, the law of cause and effect continued to play a key role, good actions bringing one closer to the Divine and evil actions leading to a painful state of separation. For most Christians, however, this revision of heaven and hell barely registered. A great many otherwise rationally minded people belonging to widely different cultures and religious traditions continue to believe in a literal heaven and hell, a collective fantasy or mythic tradition that hearkens back to prehistoric times.

The American philosopher Ken Wilbur, in his analysis of psychological development, talks about the mythic-literal stage, an undeveloped stage of psychological growth that is alluded to in the work of different developmental psychologists.[67] In this stage, people believe in fantasy and myth, which supply simple, comforting answers to the difficult and challenging questions of existence. Like most fantasy, it is not how things are but how we wish they could be: to be absolved from the consequences of our misdeeds and to enjoy eternal bliss without having to work particularly hard for it, but simply by following some basic ethical principles. While this mentality may have served a useful purpose in the past for certain segments of the population by motivating people to lead ethical lives, thus ensuring them some modicum of progress on the path of evolution, it is a stage, as Wilbur and others point out, that people must eventually outgrow if they are to continue the journey toward psychological self-actualization and spiritual realization.

This literal understanding of heaven and hell, however, has had negative consequences as well, due in great measure to the use of fear as a motivating factor for good behavior. Over time, and perhaps even from the very beginning of the human search for meaning, it became a tool of exploitation in the hands of the clergy to gain control over the masses, something that Anandamurti has emphasized in his social teachings:

> Just as intellectuals have exploited the common people by filling their heads with imaginary ideas about heaven and hell, they have also been harmed under the impact of this same psychology by ignoring the past and the present. A doctrine that emphasizes an imaginary heaven and hell and considers the traditions of the past and the solid earth of the present as false and illusory, is particularly deadly to society.[68]

Even today, in the twenty-first century, we can still see the effects of such superstitions rending the fabric of human society. Suicide bombers who are lured into mass murder through the promise of heaven, and other religious dogmas, such as the virtue of killing infidels or the persecution of homosexuals, are extreme examples of this, but the anxiety and guilt that the belief in heaven and hell has sowed in the minds of the faithful is a far more pervasive though often unnoticed consequence.

भूमाचित्ते सञ्चरधारायां जडाभासः ॥ २१ ॥

II.21 *bhúmacitte saiṇcaradháráyáṁ jaḍábhásah*

"*bhúmá*, cosmic; *citte*, in the *citta*; *saiṇcara*, involution, centrifugal phase of creation; *dhárayáṁ*, in the flow; *jaḍa*, matter; *ábhásah*, reflection, semblance

"In the flow of *saiṇcara*, the semblance of matter takes form in the cosmic *citta*."

Having established that this expressed universe is the stage on which the mind enacts the drama of spiritual evolution,

CHAPTER TWO 167

Anandamurti now takes a closer look at the material universe and the mind's interaction with that universe through the process of perception before shifting his focus to the completion of the human being's spiritual journey in Chapter Three. Perception requires the existence of matter—it is through perception that we gain knowledge of the world—and while modern science has yet to venture an explanation for the existence of matter, Anandamurti's Tantric cosmology not only explains both the genesis and gradual formation of matter but does so in such a way as to shed light on some of the seemingly insoluble problems facing modern physics, where the search for answers to questions such as the origin of the universe has forced some of our most accomplished scientists to expand the scope of physics into the realm of metaphysics.

At the outset of *Ananda Sutram* we saw how Consciousness comes under the progressive influence of the *guńas* in the flow of *saiṋcara*, giving rise to the cosmic *mahat*, *aham*, and *citta*. With the emergence of the cosmic *citta* due to the influence of *tamoguńa*, Consciousness becomes demarcated or objectified. With this demarcation of Consciousness, the material universe comes into existence as a reflection or semblance within the Macrocosmic Mind. As Anandamurti details in his commentary to this sutra, this material manifestation occurs in stages—it is a gradual process, an unfolding or "going out" (the etymological meaning of *saiṋcara*)—and the first of the resulting five stages is known as *ákáshatattva* or *vyomatattva* in Sanskrit, "ethereal factor." *Ákásha* is roughly equivalent to what we know as "space." However, space is not what we commonly conceive it to be.

Until relatively recently, space was commonly conceived of as an infinite void containing the objects of existence, from the tiniest subatomic particles to the largest stars. This was Newton's view and it seems to tally with the evidence of our senses. According to Anandamurti, however, there is no such thing as a true void in the material universe, nor can there be. A true void would be synonymous with nonexistence, and that is an impossibility within the parameters of the expressed universe. Rather, what we think of as "empty" space is actually the subtlest of the five *mahábhútas*, which Anandamurti refers to as the five "fundamental factors": ethereal, aerial, luminous, liquid, and solid. It is the subtlest expression of matter, from which all subsequent forms of matter arise, and upon reflection we know this to be true because we are aware of space as the subtlest component of the material universe in which we find ourselves.[69] Space does indeed contain the objects of existence, but only in the sense that a body of water contains the currents and eddies that form within it. We can call space the backdrop of materiality but it remains a material reality in our perception of existence, despite the fact that we are conditioned to think of matter as something solid, even at the conceptual level of an imperceptible atom or subatomic particle. Space is just as much matter, just as much a material existence, as an atom or a stone. There is no space within the mind, only the perception or conception of space, for the mind, unlike space, is nonmaterial. And this is even more true of Consciousness.

The word *mahá* means "great" and the word *bhúta* means "created being." *Bhúta* is commonly translated as "element," thus the five *mahábhútas* are often referred to in popular literature as the five great cosmic elements, but that is a misnomer, since the *mahábhútas* are both conceptually and materially distinct from the elements of material science as found in the periodic table. There are many elements but only five *mahábhútas*, five fundamental factors or *tattvas*,[70] and they can best be thought of as the five perceptible forms of matter. They are called the *mahábhútas* because all created objects, *bhútas*, are evolved out of these five fundamental factors.

This division of matter, that is, of the material universe, into the five *mahábhútas*, or more simply, *bhútas*, has been a part of traditional cosmology for thousands of years in different parts of the globe—not only in India and China but also in the West, where it was taught by the ancient Greek philosophers and ascribed to by alchemists and medieval physicians. After the development of the modern atomic theory, however, the scientific community by and large dismissed the *bhútas* as a primitive classification of matter from the days before the discovery of the atom—the Merriam-Webster dictionary, for example, defines the *bhútas* as "formerly believed to compose the physical universe."[71] This dismissal, while understandable on one level given the dizzying advance of scientific knowledge in the last couple of centuries, nevertheless betrays a profound misunderstanding of an ancient wisdom that continues to be equally as true today as it was then. The five *bhūtas* are the five sensible forms of matter that emerge during the flow of creation. They are cosmological rather than elemental and are best understood in terms of perception. We have five senses—hearing, touch, sight, taste, and smell—as do all creatures possessing *aham*, because matter is perceptible in five different forms. How do we know that the world exists? Because we can see it, feel it, hear it, taste it, and smell it. In truth, we can only conceive of matter in these five distinct forms because our perception of matter depends on our senses, more specifically, on the five inferences emanated by the five *bhūtas*, each of which is perceived by a different sensory organ. The elements of contemporary science, being the building blocks of matter, may be found in any of these forms, excepting the ethereal factor which is subtler than the subtlest atom or element, but the forms themselves are independent of their constituent atoms or molecules.

Despite dismissing this ancient classification of matter, however, the idea of the existence of ether as a material substance persisted in the Western scientific community even after the ascendancy of the atomic theory, as a way to account for the propagation of different forces, such as gravity or magnetism, which were thought to require a medium through which they could act. In the seventeenth century Descartes advanced the idea that the ether of the Greeks was indeed this medium, a motionless, frictionless, imperceptible material substance that pervaded space and allowed objects to act upon one another at a distance, such as the moon on the tides, and this idea eventually gained wide acceptance, so much so that the concept became central to nineteenth-century physics, since it offered the only plausible (up until then) explanation for the wave nature of light and electromagnetism in general. But when the Michelson-Morley experiments demonstrated that the speed of light was constant under all conditions, later paving the way for Albert Einstein's special theory of relativity, the Western concept of ether was discarded as unfounded. For decades afterward, space was once again considered to be a void, until Einstein again changed the course of modern physics with his general theory of relativity. After spending the previous decade trying to reconcile Newton's theories of gravity—and by implication, his idea of space as a void—with his own special theory of relativity, which fused space and time into a single concept of space-time, Einstein had the groundbreaking insight that the gravitational field, as it was then known, *was* space. In other words, space was not a void. It was a material entity that bent and fluctuated. This led to a number of predictions that seemed fantastical at the time. If space was curved, then time, being an aspect of space, must also be curved. If large masses, due to greater gravity, increased that curvature, then large masses must cause light to bend. The theory also predicted the existence of black holes, gravitational waves, and an expanding universe. It would be decades before physicists would have the means of testing the predictions generated by Einstein's theory, but one by one they were all proved to be true. Light does indeed bend as it passes close to a star; time does pass more quickly at higher altitudes, where there is less gravity; black holes have been discovered and become a subject of intense study; and the visible universe is indeed expanding.

Einstein was reluctant to accept the findings of quantum mechanics, but for the generations of physicists that came after him, both relativity theory and quantum theory had become the cornerstones of contemporary physics, and as efforts intensified to find a common ground for these two seemingly incompatible theories, it became even more evident that space was material. The latest research into quantum gravity, for example, describes space as constituted of grains or quanta of a finite minimum magnitude, the Planck length.[72] "The quanta of gravity, that is, are not *in* space; *they are themselves space.*"[73] It is now accepted among physicists that space is material rather than nonmaterial, a mysterious field that ripples and bends. Exactly what it is—the Higgs ocean, rippling waves of gravitons, infinitesimal vibrating strings—is still under debate in the scientific community and promises to be for the foreseeable future, but modern physics finds itself once again drawing nearer to a Tantric vision of the universe in which *ákásha* is the subtlest form of matter, too subtle to be perceived even with the most powerful instruments.

From the standpoint of philosophy, Consciousness in its unqualified state is infinite and nonmaterial, but once it gets demarcated under the influence of *tamoguña* it becomes finite and assumes a particular shape or form, while still remaining infinite. While this apparent paradox is beyond the mind's capacity to comprehend, we can make a reasonable approximation if we visualize the universe as a finite iceberg within an infinite ocean of Consciousness—one ocean encompassing two different states. The expressed universe is immeasurably vast, far beyond our powers of imagination—the visible universe contains an estimated 140 billion galaxies, each containing an average of 100 billion suns, and each galaxy separated from its nearest neighbor by an average of millions of light years (and that is just the visible universe)—but it is nevertheless finite. Anything that is demarcated is necessarily finite and thus has a particular form. There is an ongoing debate among contemporary physicists as to the shape of the universe, and there are numerous proposals, but according to Anandamurti the universe is elliptical or oval-shaped. For this reason, it is sometimes referred to in Indian philosophical texts as *brahmáńd́a*, the cosmic egg.[74] And because the universe is finite, because it is delimited, space can only be a material substance. Whether we think of that substance as energy or matter makes little difference. It is Consciousness in various states of vibration, such that the vibration obscures or transmutes the essential nature of Consciousness.

Shakti, the creative principle, is often translated as "energy," the potential or kinetic energy of Consciousness. In the philosophical sense, Shakti is not energy as we know it—rather it is the creative principle that whips Consciousness into motion, thus giving rise to the various manifestations of energy that we experience in the manifest universe—but it essentially amounts to the same thing, since the energy or vibrational expression that we encounter in the expressed universe is the result of Shakti's binding influence on Consciousness. Hence every material expression, from a seemingly motionless stone to the nuclear fusion in a distant star, is a manifestation of Shakti, a vibrational expression of Consciousness, one of the infinite variety of constantly changing poses of Shakti as she dances on the quiescent body of Shiva. Dive into any atom, the elemental building block of nature, and you will find protons, neutrons, and electrons. Dive into the proton and you will find still smaller particles. Dive into those and you will find yet smaller particles. Dive even deeper and what appears to be solid matter devolves into patterns of energy (the fundamental proposition of both superstring theory and Tantra). Every expression in this universe can ultimately be reduced to energy or vibration, no matter how solid it appears from a distance, matter being in essence a container formed out of patterns of energy. All form is Shakti creating the appearance of form through its vibratory power, and that manifestation of energy is itself the kinetic manifestation of Consciousness.

To borrow an analogy from a technology that is yet to exist, imagine a holographic image that is not only visible but which we can touch, taste, smell, and hear, a holographic image that can be perceived with all five senses and each of those inferences so distinct and so clear that the image is indistinguishable from the original, say a speaking, smiling, gesticulating image of our philosophy professor sitting in front of us that we cannot tell apart from our actual professor sitting in his office hundreds of miles away. We know that it is "merely" an image generated by a confluence of inferential waves, but the evidence of our senses tells us that the image is real, as real as we are. Similarly, Consciousness in motion—Shakti—creates patterns that take on the appearance of form, and those forms are perceptible through five different types of inferential waves, as we shall take up in the next sutra. The container of matter that is formed from these energy patterns in the dance of Shakti can be as solid as a stone, as tiny as a subatomic particle, or as subtle as the fabric of space, but the fundamental principle remains the same.

If we look at the so-called "vacuum" of space through the lens of twenty-first century physics we find that it is teeming with vibratory expressions, whether we think of them as particular or energetic in nature: cosmic background radiation, electromagnetic radiation, dark energy, dark matter, baryonic matter, including a plethora of different subatomic particles (all told, less than 5% of the known universe), perhaps even the theoretical Higgs field, referred to by some as the "ocean of

Chapter Two 173

space-time." Space is matter and matter is energy, and thus our perception of space as a void rests on our inability to perceive the true nature of *ákásha* due to its extreme subtlety. For the same reason the thermal death of the universe, the attainment of absolute zero or absolute pause, is both a philosophical and material impossibility (heat being one measure of the motion of matter). A universe without energy, a universe without motion, is a nonexistent universe.

Continuing with the *bhútas*, each of the five perceptible forms of matter gives rise to a particular inference, and it is these inferences that make possible the process of perception. *Ákáshatattva* carries the subtlest of the five inferences, the inference of sound. According to Tantra, all vibration, no matter how subtle, emits sound, that is, all vibration is sonic in nature, and the sum total of all sonic vibration, the hum of the universe, is known as the *oṁkára*, symbolized in the Indian spiritual tradition by the sound Om. The sound inference is thus indicative of the existence of the ethereal factor, the means by which it can be known.[75] While we cannot perceive the sound inference directly—our ear can only hear sound through the medium of the aerial factor and the inference of touch—we can capture those waves with certain instruments. The audio signal in a radio wave, for example, travels through the ethereal factor, but it is only when those radio waves are transformed into aerial sound waves with the help of a receiver and a speaker that our ears can hear that transmitted sound. It is possible for a highly developed mind to perceive the sound carried by those radio waves without the aid of physical organs or a receiver, but in the absence of advanced psychic capability, *ákáshatattva* is too subtle to be perceived unaided.[76]

As we learned in Chapter One, the binding influence of *tamoguńa* becomes increasingly dominant in the flow of *saiṇcara*, and as a result, the interparticular spaces in the ethereal factor gradually decrease until it is eventually metamorphosed into the aerial factor or *váyutattva*, which transmits the inference of touch. This is a gradual process, a continuum rather than an abrupt transition. Just as the subtlest stage of ether is essentially indistinguishable from the crudest stage of the Cosmic Mind, the crudest stage of ether is for all intents and purposes equivalent to the subtlest stage of the aerial factor.[77] The defining difference is that the aerial factor begins to become perceptible through touch while the ethereal factor is not. For a human being to hear sound, a wave pattern in the air (what we commonly call a sonic wave) must vibrate the tympani, which causes the tympani to reproduce that vibration and retransmit it to the cochlea, which then sends an electrical signal through the auditory nerve to the brain, where it is captured by the mind. The reception of that wave by the tympani and its subsequent transmission to the mind is effected through the inference of touch. We both feel the changing air pressure due to the compression of the molecules and hear the sound. Thus the aerial factor carries both the touch and sound inferences. In the absence of the inference of sight the aerial factor is invisible to the eye but we can feel it on our skin. If we analyze the composition of air we can see that though invisible it is far denser than the imperceptible ethereal factor. A cubic centimeter of the air we breathe typically contains some twenty-five quintillion molecules while a cubic centimeter of interstellar space has on average a single atom of interstellar gas, either hydrogen or helium.

As the influence of *tamoguńa* grows, it compresses or constricts the aerial factor until it is eventually transformed into *tejastattva*, luminous factor. The resultant friction generated by this increasing constriction and the corresponding decrease in interatomic and intermolecular space gives rise to the inference of sight. It is at this point that matter becomes visible. The luminous factor thus carries three inferences: sound, touch, and sight. In the same way, *tejastattva* is eventually transformed into *apatattva*, liquid factor, which carries the additional inference of taste, and finally *apatattva* is transformed into *kśititattva*, solid factor, which adds the fifth and final inference of smell. *Tamoguńa* does not stop increasing its pressure after the formation of the solid factor but no further sensible forms of matter are created. From there either life arises through the pulverization of the solid factor described in sutra I.12, or else *jad́asphot́a* occurs, the explosion or disintegration of an unstable object that transforms the dense solid factor into the four subtler factors, which subsequently retrace the path of positive *saiṋcara*.

This then is the cosmological understanding of the formation of the material universe according to *Ananda Sutram*. If we turn now to the contemporary scientific understanding of the creation of the known universe, we can see some clear parallels that, depending on your point of view, can serve, at least to some degree, to validate either the philosophical understanding of Anandamurti's Tantra or the findings of modern science. According to contemporary Western cosmology, the visible universe appears to have begun with a bang, a Big Bang, to be precise—a hypothetical explosion of the universe's entire store of matter in a state so highly compressed it would be invisible to the naked eye. This hypothetical explosion is thought to have then generated almost instantaneously a vast expanse of rapidly expanding space (ethereal factor), followed by the first atoms—hydrogen and helium (aerial factor)—formed from subatomic particles. Thereafter followed a gradual process of contraction and cooling (a decrease in intermolecular and interatomic spaces) in which gas clouds coalesced to the point they began giving off sparks of light, luminous factor, and eventually clumped together to form stars, consisting principally of aerial factor and luminous factor in a process of combustion, referred to in physics as a plasma state. From a distance a star appears solid but we know that it is not—it is a burning mass of combusting atoms, like the interior of a furnace, which becomes in time a forge for the production of heavier elements, which are then ejected into the interstellar medium. Planets eventually formed around these nascent stars, gradually cooling until the point where they developed solid crusts from a mixture of elements in liquid form, and on our particular planet the presence of all five *bhútas* in requisite proportions created conditions congenial to the appearance of life.[78]

While there are significant similarities between contemporary Western cosmology and Anandamurti's Tantric cosmology, there are significant conceptual differences as well, beginning with Anandamurti's explanation of the genesis of matter from Consciousness. The Big Bang (or Big Crunch or Big Bounce, depending on which theory one supports) was advanced to account for Hubble's law, the discovery of cosmic background radiation, entropy, and other observable phenomena, and it traces the origin of the universe to a specific point in time, approximately 13.8 billion years ago, in a state of near-infinite density and maximum temperature. According to Anandamurti, however, time is entirely dependent on the observer—that is, it only exists within the purview of the microcosmic mind. There are three relative factors—the spatial, temporal, and personal factors (space, time, and the observer, in the language of contemporary physics)—and the temporal factor, being the mind's measurement of motion, is a function of the individual observer.[79] From the macrocosmic perspective, the universe is atemporal. It has no beginning or end, no arrow of time. Rather, it is a constant flow of creation existing outside of time in which there is both contraction and expansion.[80] While we talk about the process of *saiṇcara* as if it were bound by the relativity of time—the ethereal factor being gradually transformed into the aerial factor, and so on—we have no choice but to do so because any philosophical or scientific description of the genesis of the cosmos can only be explained and understood within the ambit of the individual mind, and that understanding is thus bound by the relative factor of time, the individual mind being unable to comprehend atemporality. Nevertheless the Macrocosm is atemporal, and thus it is a fallacy to talk of the beginning of the universe. We can talk about our observation of certain processes within the universe from our standpoint as the observer, and those observations will be subject to the time factor—the relative nature of time and its relationship to space, as delineated by Einstein in his special theory of relativity, is valid from the standpoint of the individual observer—but we cannot project time onto the universe as a macrocosmic whole. The universe has no age. Only the universe *as we see it* can have an age.

Similarly, entropy is an observable phenomenon, but it cannot be applied to the ultimate destiny of the universe. New matter is constantly being created through the influence of *tamoguńa* over Consciousness, and thus there is a constant infusion of new energy into the creation, in addition to the periodic stirring up of cosmic thought waves known as *jaḋasphoṭa*. The universe undergoes contraction and expansion, as well as movement between higher and lower states of entropy, but it is an eternal atemporal expression of the kinetic energy of Consciousness.

It bears mentioning here that the five *bhūtas* also play an important role in our understanding of the body, especially in the context of certain traditional systems of medicine, including Chinese medicine, Ayurveda, and ancient Greek and medieval European medical practices. All living bodies are composed of the five fundamental factors, which need to be in requisite proportion in order to sustain life. Our bodies depend on the ethereal factor for their existence in the material world, on the aerial factor for their vital energy, on luminous factor for the combustion of nutrients and the generation of heat and energy, on liquid factor for the protoplasm of our cells and the circulation of blood and lymph, and on solid factor for the various solid tissues, such as bone and muscle. Any of these factors can go out of balance in relation to the other factors, and this lack of balance among the *bhūtas* along with the resulting accumulation of toxins (a product of inefficient combustion) leads to a loss of health, which these systems of medicine then try to correct.

We will return to the five *mahābhūtas* in sutra II.23, where we will examine them from the microcosmic perspective and further explore the relationship between our modern understanding of the material elements and the ancient conception of the five sensible forms of matter.

भूतलक्षणात्मकं भूतवाहितं भूतसङ्घर्षस्पन्दनं तन्मात्रम् ॥ २२ ॥

II.22 *bhūtalakṣaṇātmakaṁ bhūtavāhitaṁ*
bhūtasauṅgharśaspandanaṁ tanmātram

bhūta, fundamental factor; *lakṣaṇa*, sign, indication; *ātmakaṁ*, composed of; *vāhitaṁ*, carry; *sauṅgharśa*, friction, clash; *spandanaṁ*, vibration; *tanmātram*, inferential wave, microscopic fraction of the fundamental factors; literally, minutest quantity or fraction

"*Tanmātras* are indicative of the *bhūtas*, are carried by the *bhūtas*, and are created by vibrations from friction within the *bhūtas*."

As with the five *mahábhútas*, the concept of *tanmátras* has been integral to Indian thought for thousands of years. Even more so than with the *bhútas*, however, Anandamurti redefines this ancient concept in a way that brings it closer to our modern understanding of the physical universe, a reformulation that is less overtly esoteric and more in keeping with our actual experience. In Kapil's Samkhya philosophy, *tanmátras* were conceived of as the five supersensible elements, the underlying essences corresponding to sound, touch, sight, taste, and smell, a subtle substratum that subsequently gave rise to the five gross elements, the five *bhútas*. In Samkhya the *tanmátras* are considered evolutes of *prakrti* that arise from *ahamkára* under the influence of *tamoguńa*, being prior to the *bhútas* in terms of the genesis of the creation, and subsequent systems of Indian philosophy, up to and including Vedanta, adopted this aspect of traditional Indian cosmology without modification. In Anandamurti's Tantric philosophy, however, the *bhútas* are the direct evolutes of *citta* under the influence of *tamoguńa*, and the *tanmátras*, rather than being evolutes in their own right, are the minutest fractions of those *bhútas* that make possible the process of perception.

Modern physics and Tantra are in agreement that the universe is, in the most fundamental sense, entirely vibrational. While we perceive the universe with our senses as being composed of objects, "objectivity," as Anandamurti puts it, "is nothing but a wave motion within the body of the cosmos."[81] The five *bhútas* that make up the expressed universe are essentially heterogeneous wave patterns in a constant flow that partake of certain shared characteristics, whether we conceive of them as matter or energy, making the manifest universe a mesh of innumerable waves of different wavelengths. These innumerable heterogeneous waves are forever striking each other, undergoing reflection and refraction, or in some cases passing through each other relatively unimpeded, depending on the subtlety of the waves and the degree of harmony between their crests and troughs. As a result of this constant vibrational interaction, all objects emanate inferential waves. Think of a pond and the waves that radiate out after a pebble or a drop of rainwater strikes its surface. Imagine numerous drops or pebbles falling intermittently at different points of the pond. The result is a mesh of waves of different sizes, velocities, and trajectories crisscrossing the pond, and as they meet each other one wave influences another, which influences another, seemingly ad infinitum. What are those waves but motion within a medium, patterns of energy that travel through that medium and interact with other patterns of energy or motion? Similarly, the universe consists of five *bhūtas*, like five interpenetrating ponds, or rather, like a single pond composed of five intermingled but distinct liquids of different densities in which an infinite variety of wavelike patterns of energy propagate, influencing each other to a greater or lesser extent as they come in contact.

The word *mātra* means "minutest quantity," and the word *tat*, "that," refers to the particular *bhūta* in question. Here the word *tanmātra* does not refer to a particle, however (except in the sense that waves can also be perceived as particles, the basic postulation of quantum physics), but rather to the minutest fraction of the inferential waves emanated by an object, waves that are heterogeneous in nature but which are of five different types or categories: sound, touch, sight, taste, and smell—*shabda, sparsha, rūpa, rasa,* and *gandha tanmātras*.[82] Thus a solid object will emanate five different types of waves: a collection of different olfactory waves, each with its own frequency, that combine to convey the characteristic smell (or smells) of that object; another bundle of gustatory waves that combine to convey the object's taste; and so on. We can recognize a book, for example, by sight and differentiate it from a similar book in the same way, taking advantage of the light waves reflected from its surface, but we can also recognize it by its sound if someone drops it, by its feel if we touch it, by its smell, and even by taste, were we so inclined. These inferential waves are a result of the vibrations arising from friction or clash within their respective *bhūtas* (which are in turn a product of the interplay between the interial and exterial forces); they are conveyed to the sensory organs through the medium of other *bhūtas*, whereupon they undergo reflection, refraction, or diffraction, or else pass through unimpeded (in which case they remain outside the scope of perception); and it is through the waves generated by the reflection of subtler *bhūtas* on cruder ones that we are able to perceive the *bhūtas* that form a particular object (such as light reflecting off water or solid objects but not off air)—that is, they are indicative of the nature of the object.

We are constantly being bombarded by a seemingly infinite influx of inferential waves, and it is through these waves that the mind comes in contact with the external world. When these inferential waves, flowing through the media of subtler *bhútas*, pass through the gates of the sensory organs, they are assimilated by the *citta*, giving rise to simulative waves in the *citta* that constitute our perception of the external world, whether that perception be auditory, tactile, visual, gustatory, or olfactory. Similarly, it is the function of the motor organs to generate outgoing inferential waves, through which the mind interacts with the external world.

It is an inescapable fact of our existence that our perception of the world is mediated through our senses, and thus the idea of "direct perception" is a misnomer. What we actually perceive is "the shadow of a shadow."

> The unit mind does not enjoy objects in their physical form. Through the sensory organs, the mind enjoys the *tanmátras* emanated by the physical world composed of the five fundamental factors. So here the mind does not enjoy the original object, but rather its shadow, i.e. the *tanmátras* of the object. But this physical world itself is a shadow of the Cosmic Mind. So it can be said that the unit mind does not enjoy the original object, the Supreme Consciousness, or its shadow, the physical world, but the shadow of the shadow, i.e. the *tanmátras* emanated by the physical world.[83]

This then is the mechanism behind the process of perception that is so integral to our understanding of the mind. Because this process of perception governs our interaction with the world—the world that is the stage upon which we enact our pursuit of dharma, our evolutionary march toward perfection—it logically forms the nexus of the concluding sutras of Chapter Two, which began with the elaboration of dharma and concludes with the nature of the universe in which the pursuit of dharma takes place.

भूतं तन्मात्रेण परिचीयते ॥ २३ ॥

II.23 *bhútaṁ tanmátreña pariciiyate*

bhútaṁ, fundamental factor; *tanmátreña*, by the *tanmátras*; *pariciiyate*, known, recognized

"The *bhútas* are known through the *tanmátras*."

It is through the *tanmátras* that we recognize the *bhútas*, from which the objects of perception are formed. Since the ethereal factor carries one *tanmátra*, aerial factor two, luminous three, liquid four, and solid five, we can determine the *bhúta* of an object or substance according to the *tanmátras* it emanates—as long as we bear in mind that we are only capable of perceiving a tiny fraction of the waves that reach our senses. If the frequency of a sound is too high or too low, for example, we will be unable to perceive it without the help of a special instrument that amplifies our receptive capacity, such as a hearing aid, and even such instruments are subject to their own limitations. The same is true if a sound is too loud or too soft. Likewise, our eyes can only apprehend a minute portion of the electromagnetic spectrum. The fact that something appears invisible, a protist, for example, doesn't mean that it is invisible per se, only that our naked eyes cannot perceive the form *tanmátra* emanated by that protist without the aid of a microscope. When those light waves are magnified then we can indeed see that protist with our eyes. Be that as it may, we can apply our knowledge of *tanmátras* to that portion of the world that we are able to perceive, either with or without the help of scientific instruments.

Since the determination of which *bhúta* a particular object or material substance belongs to depends on the *tanmátras* produced by that object or substance, the easiest way to make this determination is to ascertain the crudest *tanmátra* emanated by that particular substance. Solid factor, for example, being the result of the progressive transformation or contraction of the previous four *bhútas*, carries all five *tanmátras,* and hence we can smell, taste, see, touch, and hear solid objects—or if we can't, then other living creatures can. The crudest of the five *tanmátras* is the smell *tanmátra*. Thus any substance with an odor is either solid factor or contains solid factor (air, for example, is odorless but is abundantly capable of carrying fragrances, to the delight or dismay of our noses). By the same token, liquid factor, the next *bhúta* in ascending order of subtlety, does not carry the smell *tanmátra,* and hence any object that does not emit the smell *tanmátra* but possesses the other four *tanmátras* belongs to liquid factor. Neither water nor ethyl alcohol, for example, the two most abundant pure liquids in the universe, have any odor of their own, but they can be heard, felt, seen, and tasted. Again, the determining factor is the presence or absence of the respective *tanmátras*. For this reason, the *bhútas* cannot be directly equated with the four states of matter in contemporary physics—solid, liquid, plasma, and gas. These two systems of classifying matter are based on different criteria, although there is considerable concordance between them.

The four states of matter are determined principally by the relationship of the molecules that constitute a particular substance. When the molecules remain in a more or less fixed position relative to each other then that substance is considered to be in a solid state; when the attraction between the atoms or molecules is strong enough to keep them relatively close together but not strong enough to prevent them from moving past one another, then it is in a liquid state; and when the attraction between the atoms or molecules is not strong enough to hold them together then it is in a gaseous state. This in turn depends on the amount of kinetic energy present, and thus a particular substance can pass from a solid state to a liquid state to a gaseous state and vice versa depending on the thermodynamic conditions (the plasma state is a case apart when it comes to phase change). This is something we learn in our grade-school science classes, where we were taught that even metals have a melting point and boiling point as well as a freezing or congealing point, and we have a more or less daily experience with this state change in regard to water, the only common substance that occurs naturally in three different states. While most commonly found in the liquid state, it is always present in the air we breathe in the form of water vapor, the gaseous state of water, and in the ice we use to cool our drinks or the snow we shovel from our driveways in the winter in colder climates, the solid state of water. With the *bhūtas*, however, the determining factor is not the behavior of the constituent molecules but the *tanmātras*. If ice were solid factor, *kṣititattva*, it would have to carry the smell *tanmātra*. If it does not—and it does not appear to as long as it is free of any admixture—then it remains liquid factor in a congealed or solid state, *apatattva*, one instance where the two systems differ. For water vapor to be aerial factor rather than liquid factor, it would have to be invisible and tasteless, and so it seems to be. We can feel the humidity in the air but we cannot see it or taste it, and so in this case the two systems agree, although it is possible that scientific research could one day prove otherwise.

Based on our perception of the individual *tanmātras*, that is, of the five sensible forms of matter, we can now make the correlation between the five *mahābhūtas* and the elements of material science. The elements of the periodic table provide the building blocks of matter, and like any fundamental building block they can be combined and recombined into a nearly infinite array of different forms, each of which comes within the purview of a particular *bhūta*. The hydrogen atom, for example, the smallest reducible unit of matter from the standpoint of the periodic table, representing 90% of the universe's atoms and three-quarters of its mass, is created during the process of *saiñcara* with the formation of aerial factor, being colorless, odorless, and tasteless on its own. The same hydrogen atom, however, provides fuel for the burning furnace of a star, in which case it functions as a building block of luminous factor. When it combines with oxygen to form water it is a building block of liquid factor, and when it combines with carbon to form aromatic hydrocarbons it becomes a building block of solid factor.

It is rare that we encounter pure elements in nature. Through human intervention we can separate molecular oxygen, for example, and use it for a variety of purposes, but the oxygen we encounter in the natural world belongs to different substances, such as the air we breathe (aerial factor), the water we drink and use to bathe (liquid factor), and the food that fuels our bodies, whose key ingredients—proteins, fats, sugars, and so on (solid factor)—all contain oxygen. Similarly, the *bhūtas* as they appear in the natural world are experienced as diverse substances formed out of the different elements of material science. However, this system of classification is equally valid for pure elements as well, whether naturally occurring, or, as is usually the case, extracted by different processes. A case in point is the element mercury. It is classified as a metal due to a certain configuration of free electrons, but it almost never appears on this planet as an isolated element. Rather, it is found as a component of certain ores, most commonly the mineral cinnabar (mercury sulfide), in which case it functions as a building block of solid factor and has a distinct smell. When cinnabar is heated in a furnace, however, mercury escapes as an invisible vapor and subsequently cools into a visible liquid. Mercury is a metal but appears as a vapor when heated past a certain point and as a liquid at standard temperature and pressure. From the standpoint of the *bhūtas*, however, the behavior of its electrons and its physical state are incidental to its classification. If it has no odor at standard temperature—and distilled mercury is believed to have none, although its smell may be beyond our perceptive capacity—then it belongs to liquid factor. If it did have an odor then it would be solid factor in a liquid state. If mercury vapor were truly invisible and tasteless, as it appears, then it would belong to aerial factor for the time it remained a vapor. Similarly, the Earth's molten outer core appears to be liquid factor, assuming the absence of the smell *tanmātra*.[84] Incidentally, the apparently solid inner core is thought by some geophysicists to be a plasma behaving as a solid due to a combination of intense pressure and extreme heat, with a composition similar to that of a star, ie., principally luminous factor, which accords with Anandamurti's assessment.[85]

Another useful example to demonstrate the difference between the two systems, an instance where there is an obvious lack of concordance, is that of chlorine gas, Cl_2. At room temperature and normal pressure it appears in a gaseous state due to its weak covalent bonds, despite being much heavier than air. Chlorine gas is neither colorless nor odorless, however, and hence belongs to solid factor despite being in a gaseous state in an aerial-factor medium. Chlorine and the other halogens, the salt-producing elements, do not occur in nature in their free state. They are found as solid compounds formed in the process of *saiñcara*. Chlorine, for example, can be found in naturally occurring compounds such as sodium chloride (table salt), halite (NaCl), carnallite ($Cl_3H_{12}KMgO_6$), and sylvite (KCl), all of which belong to solid factor. Chlorine gas can be liberated from these compounds through chemical techniques but it remains solid factor.

It is also worth pointing out that there is an inverse relationship between the number of *tanmátras* that a substance emanates and its subtlety relative to other *bhútas*, an understanding that is absent from modern physics's conception of the states of matter. In the Tantric system, the more *tanmátras* a substance carries, the cruder the factor it belongs to, and as a result the less expansive it is and the easier it is to divide. Solid objects are easily divisible and less expansive in relation to subtler *bhútas*. If we make a division in water it disappears within moments, which is not the case with a solid object, and water is less condensed, less demarcated, than solid matter. This is a reflection of its being less removed from its original source, Consciousness, which is infinite and indivisible. The next factor in order of subtlety, luminous factor, is even less subject to division. It can be heard, felt, and seen, but it cannot be tasted or smelled (fire has no smell though the substances it burns do), and it is amorphous, apparently taking on the form of that which it burns. Aerial factor, the next level of material subtlety, is devoid of the form *tanmátra* and is hence invisible. Air is mostly nitrogen and oxygen with trace amounts of other gases that on their own belong to aerial factor. It can be felt and heard, but it cannot be seen, tasted, or smelled, although it does serve as a medium for the luminous, liquid, and solid factors. Its expansiveness and seeming indivisibility bring it even closer to the nature of Consciousness. And in ethereal factor, the most expansive and subtlest of the five *mahábhútas*, we find the closest approximation of matter to Consciousness. We experience it as space, the apparently boundless vastness that surrounds us—or rather, we conceive of it as space, since it is the mind's apprehension of ethereal factor that we call "space," not any physical perception per se. For all intents and purposes, *ákásha* is imperceptible, since the sound *tanmátra* cannot be perceived unaided, placing *ákásha* beyond the scope of human perception but not beyond the scope of human apperception.[86]

It is through our sensory organs' apprehension of the five inferential waves that we are able to gain a sense of material objects. We do not directly perceive those objects but instead form images of them within our *citta* through our reception of the different *tanmátras* they emanate. Likewise, our motor organs transmit our internal or inherent *tanmátras* to the outside world. For example, we can generate sound by clapping, talking, walking, and so on. But our organs' ability to receive and transmit *tanmátras* is not the sole factor in determining our perception of and interaction with the external world. The *práńendriya*, as Anandamurti explains in his commentary to this sutra, also plays a vital role.

The word *indriya* means "organ," and *práńáh* refers to the vital energy of a living organism, which is a product of aerial factor, as we explored in sutra I.11. Together the two words form the compound *práńendriya*, which refers to the vital airs functioning as a unified whole to help the *citta* in the assimilation of *tanmátras*. In other words, it acts as a kind of additional sensory organ. For this reason, the *práńendriya* is sometimes referred to as a sixth sense. Its principle role is to conjoin the *tanmátras* and the *citta*, but it also facilitates subtler perceptions that the five sensory organs are unable to assimilate, such as the sensation of lightness or heaviness, hardness or softness, smallness or vastness.[87]

In order for a visual image to make its way from the retina to the *citta* via the optic nerve and the brain, vital energy is required. Without that vital energy the visual *tanmátras* cannot be relayed to the *citta*. The same is true for all the afferent organs and likewise for the efferent organs. In order for a human being to utter a sound as conceived in their mind, that is, to externalize their inherent sound *tanmátras*, vital energy is again required. Thus the vital energy, or *práńendriya*, acts to conjoin the *tanmátras* with the *citta*, whether those inferential waves are incoming or outgoing.

Inevitably then, the quality of the reception or transmission of *tanmátras* depends on the state of the *práńendriya* at any particular moment in time. We have all had the experience of trying to concentrate on something when we are breathing very heavily or very rapidly, immediately after strenuous aerobic exercise, for example. If someone asks us to taste something or read a text at that moment we are likely to ask them to give us a few moments to catch our breath. The flow of vital energy in our body is inextricably linked to our breathing, since it is principally through our breathing that the aerial factor enters our organism. Our breathing thus regulates the vibrational flow of our *práñáh*, which is pulsative by nature, as is all manifestation of energy.[88] When our breathing is slow and steady, the flow of *práñáh* is slow and steady. When it is agitated, the flow of *práñáh* becomes agitated. And when the *práñáh* is agitated it becomes difficult for the *práñendriya* to properly assimilate the incoming *tanmátras*, to conjoin them with the *citta*, which is why we need a pause to catch our breath. If we eat something when we are breathing heavily, it is much more difficult to appreciate its flavor than when our breathing and vital energy are calm and steady. The same goes for any of the *tanmátras*. Since the *práñáh* facilitates the transmission of the *tanmátras*, that transmission is compromised when the *práñáh* is agitated. A simple analogy is that of the reflection of an image in a pool of water. If the water is still, the image is clearly reflected; if the water is agitated, it will be difficult to make out. For this reason, pranayama, yogic breath control, plays an important role in yogic practice. Calming the respiration calms the mind and not only facilitates the assimilation of *tanmátras* but aids in concentration as well, thus making it easier to meditate.

The other function of the *práñendriya* is to facilitate subtler perceptions that are beyond the capacity of the sensory organs to assimilate—for example, the sense of hardness and softness, melodiousness and harshness. If we touch a piece of metal and a piece of cotton, our organ of touch will differentiate between the two textures but it is the *práñendriya* that transmits the sense of hardness and softness.[89] These are subtler aspects of the touch *tanmátra* that are present in those inferential waves and which are subsequently conveyed to the *citta* by the *práñendriya*. The same is true for a piece of music where the organ of hearing assimilates the amplitude and frequency of the sound waves but the *prāṇendriya* is responsible for the perception of their melodiousness or harshness. Similarly, when we meet certain people, we sometimes get a sense of one person being hard and another being soft. This is also a function of the *prāṇendriya*, caused by the similarity between the psychic waves of that person, as expressed through their speech or behavior, and the waves of soft or hard objects previously reflected in the *citta*.⁹⁰ Even when their speech or behavior appears otherwise—a cynic pretending to be solicitous, for example—our *prāṇendriya*, if it is sufficiently calm and composed, allows us to perceive the vibration masked by their behavior.

द्वारनाडीरसपीठात्मकानीन्द्रियाणि ॥ २४ ॥

II.24 *dvāranāḍiirasapiithātmakāniindriyāṅi*

dvāra, gate, door; *nāḍii*, nerve; *rasa*, fluid; *piitha*, seat; *ātmakāni*, composed of; *indriyāṅi*, organs

"The organs consist of the gateways, the nerves and nerve fluid, and the sensory centers in the brain."

Normally we are conditioned to think of the sensory organs as the nose, tongue, eyes, skin, and ears. But this is belied by a closer look at the process of perception. Upon examination, we find that our external sense organs function as gateways to initiate the transmission of the respective *tanmātras* to the *citta*. Our physical eyes, for example, act as points of entry for the form *tanmātra*. In order for the image on our retina to make its way to the mind, however, it must be picked up by the optic nerve, which in turn transmits that vibration to the appropriate visual centers in the brain. Only then can the *citta*, with the help of the *prāṇendriya*, reproduce that image in the form of psychic waves, which must be attended to by the *aham* for that image to register in our consciousness. If there is any defect at any point in the path of *tanmātric* transmission then the image will be compromised, as with certain types of glaucoma and other eye conditions. Thus the actual organ consists of the gateways of the organ—in this case, the physical eyes—the nerves, and the visual centers in the brain.

In Tantra the organs are classified according to the nature of the *tanmátras* they assimilate or transmit. Sound is the subtlest of the *tanmátras*, followed by touch, and thus the organs of hearing, touch, and speech (ear, skin, and vocal cords) are dominated by *sattvaguña*. Next in order of subtlety comes the form *tanmátra*, and thus the eyes, along with the hands and feet, are dominated by *rajoguña*, the mutative principle. The tongue, nose, anus, and genitals are dominated by *tamoguña*, the static principle. An understanding of the nature of the different organs and how they function plays an important role in spiritual evolution, since our interaction with the manifest world is dependent upon our organs, and the manifest world is the platform upon which the drama of spiritual evolution is enacted. If the organs are allowed to run after cruder vibrations then the mind will be negatively affected; if they are directed toward subtler vibrations or *tanmátras* then the mind will be elevated. Thus control over the organs and the ability to direct them toward subtler pabula is essential for spiritual evolution and is hence a key element in yogic practice. Without this control it is impossible for the mind to merge into Consciousness.

Finally, it should be pointed out once again that the process of perception plays a key role in spiritual meditation, since in order to complete the journey of spiritual evolution, the aspirant must develop the ability to merge the *indriyas* in the *citta*, the *citta* in the *aham*, the *aham* in the *mahat*, and the *mahat* in the atman. The process of perception begins in the world of matter and terminates in the witnessing consciousness, which is the goal of all spiritual practice.

> When *indriyas* are engaged with an external object, they lose their own identity. For instance, when our eyes see an elephant in the external world, the *tanmátras* from the physical elephant strike the optical nerves, and as soon as the optical nerves become vibrated in this way, their original nature becomes lost to some extent. The vibrations of the optical nerves become nothing but the reflected inferential vibrations coming from the elephant in the outer world. Likewise, when the *indriyas* are engaged with the objects of one's internal world, they become

vibrated with the vibrations of the internal objects. It can be compared to a railway engine being placed in the rear instead of in front. So the *indriyas* get merged in the *citta*, and at the next step the *citta* becomes merged in the *ahaṁtattva*, the "I do" feeling. Thereafter the *ahaṁtattva* will become merged in the *mahattattva*, or existential "I" feeling, and the *mahattattva*, the existential "I", will merge in the *átmá*. This is *átmajiṇána* [self-knowledge]. In order to attain this self-knowledge, one is to divert the extroversial movement of the *indriyas* toward the inner world.[91]

Chapter Three

WHILE THE FIRST CHAPTER dealt with the cycle of creation and the second chapter with dharma and the nature of the world in the context of the pursuit of dharma, Chapter Three focuses on the completion of the human being's spiritual journey, beginning with one's ascension through the five stages of mind and culminating with the appearance of the guru and the attainment of devotion, singleminded love for the Supreme.

पञ्चकोषात्मिका जैवी सत्ता कदलीपुष्पवत् ॥ १ ॥

III.1 *paiṇcakośátmiká jaevii sattá kadaliipuśpavat*

paiṇca, five; *kośa*, layer, sheath, body; *átmiká*, composed of; *jaevii*, living; *sattá*, entity; *kaladii*, banana; *puśpavat*, like a flower

"The living being is composed of five sheaths,
like a banana flower."

The ancient Indian conception that the living being is composed of five sheaths or bodies dates back at least three thousand years. The earliest commonly cited reference to *kośas* is found in the Taittiriya Upanishad of the Krishna Yajurveda, which divided the human being into the *annamaya, práṅamaya, manomaya, vijiṅánamaya,* and *ánandamaya kośas*, and they have since been variously interpreted by a wide variety of sages and commentators, most famously Shankaracharya in his *Atmabodha* (Self-Knowledge) and *Vivekachudamani* (Crest Jewel of Discrimination).[1] In this sutra, Anandamurti redefines the *kośas* in a way that is consistent with his modern-day elaboration of yoga psychology. Just as in Chapter One, Anandamurti redefined the functional layers of the mind that were originally expounded in Samkhya, he opens this chapter with his redefinition or reformulation of the Vedantic conception of the *kośas*.

He begins by combining the first two *kośas* of traditional Vedanta, the *annamaya* and *práńamaya kośas*, and placing them in a separate category. The word *anna* means "food"; hence the *annamaya kośa* refers to the physical body, being formed from food. The *práńamaya kośa* refers to the vital energy or vital airs (*práńáh*), which cannot be divorced from the physical body without it ceasing to be a living structure. For that reason, the *práńáh* or *práńamaya kośa* is more rightly seen as an integral aspect of the physical body or *annamaya kośa*, and since the physical body is a material expression within the flow of *saiṇcara*, it is, from the spiritual point of view, external to the living being, just as a car is external to its driver. The *jaeviisattá* or living being is synonymous with the individual mind, which belongs to *pratisaiṇcara*. We inhabit bodies, which serve as vehicles for our minds, and our minds are illumined by the light of consciousness, but the essence of our individual existence resides in the mind. The *annamaya kośa* with its vital energy or *práńamaya kośa* is intimately linked to the evolving mind for the time that it inhabits a particular body, but we are not the body, any more than a driver is the car. When we talk of the *kośas* of the living being, we are rightly talking about the sheaths or layers of the individual mind.

The *kośas* are the expressional layers of the mind, as opposed to the functional layers. The mind realizes three different functions—the "I am," or sense of existence (*mahat*), the "I do," or sense of authorship (*aham*), and the "objectivated-I" or mental content (*citta*), corresponding to the subject, verb, and object of linguistic science. All three are necessary for the realization of a thought—in order to think, one must think something, ie., thought requires an object—but the nature of that object or mental content varies widely, and in yoga the nature of thought is classified according to its degree of subtlety. When we savor the taste of a mango, our object of thought is a physical sensation, and thus our mind remains engaged with the physical world. When we endeavor to understand the logic of spiritual philosophy, our mind is occupied with an abstract idea and thus ascends to a subtler ideational plane that is disconnected from the senses. And when we free ourselves from discursive thought and become absorbed in deep meditation, drawn by the pure bliss of the Self, our mind enters yet another, even subtler realm. In all three cases, the degree of elevation depends on the nature of the content of the mind. In the first example, the object of *aham* is a sensory perception; in the second, it is an abstract thought; and in the third, the mind experiences the pure glow of being. The mind continues to perform the same three functions, but the nature of the mental experience or mental expression is radically different. Thus the *kośas* are the layers of the *citta*, the mind-stuff or objectivated portion of the mind, and they are arranged like the petals of a banana flower, where the outer layers hide the inner layers. It is a characteristic of the mind that it can only think one thought at a time, although it generally appears otherwise due to the astonishing rapidity with which it can move from one thought to another. If we are savoring the taste of a mango, our mind will automatically disengage from any philosophical rumination it might be entertaining, and vice versa, and thus when our mind is active in one particular *kośa*, the deeper *kośas* remain either partially or entirely hidden. It is only by removing or suspending the outer *kośa* that one can properly understand what lies beneath it. If we compare the *citta* to an ocean, then the outermost *kośa* is analogous to the surface of the ocean, with its constant motion, and the innermost or subtlest to its tranquil depths. The deeper we go, the subtler the *kośa*.

While the mind has been divided into three *kośas* in Vedanta—*manomaya, vijñānamaya,* and *ānandamaya*—Anandamurti recognizes five distinct *kośas* for reasons that should be clear from a close examination of our own experience. The first of these in order of ascending subtlety is called the *kāmamaya kośa*. It is absent in the Vedanta system, which fails to differentiate between the *kāmamaya* and *manomaya kośas*. The *kāmamaya* is that part of the mind that interacts with the physical world through the gateways of the senses, the part of the mind that registers the incoming *tanmātras* and reacts to those inferences through the motor organs in order to materialize its desires. It is called *kāmamaya* because our interaction with the physical world is inextricably linked to *káma*, physical desire, the first of the four fundamental urges that are common to all living beings (*maya* means "embodiment" or "made of"), and it is the first of the *kośas* to be evolved in the *citta* during the initial phase of evolution.[2] When life first manifests, the mental activity of those primitive organisms is solely dedicated to the preservation of life through their dealings with their environment and the maintenance of their bodies. They seek out nutrients and recoil from environmental threats in order to survive and procreate, and they have no capacity for thought as we know it. Thus their mental experience is limited to *kámamaya kośa*.

In developed animals and in human beings, where the mind's horizons are far wider, the *kámamaya kośa* is our link to the world of phenomenal experience. Whenever I am aware of what I am hearing, seeing, smelling, tasting, or feeling—in other words, whenever I am aware of the outside world, which includes my body—my mind is actively engaged in *kámamaya kośa*. Whenever I direct my motor organs to interact with my environment—walking, talking, eating, and so on—I am likewise immersed in *kámamaya kośa*. Implicit in these activities is the propulsive energy of *káma*, the attraction to physical well-being or physical pleasure and the aversion to pain that is fundamental to our desire for self-preservation. When I feel cold, that sensation is assimilated in *kámamaya kośa*. It feels unpleasant and so I reach for a sweater or get up to turn on the heat. *Kámamaya*. A sound is pleasant, I pay attention; it's harsh and I wince. *Kámamaya*. I feel hunger pangs and get up to make some lunch, propelled by both my desire to satisfy the unpleasant rumblings of my stomach and my desire to enjoy the pleasure of a good meal. *Kámamaya*. As long as I am engaged with my environment or my body, I am in the world of *kámamaya kośa*, and that world revolves around the play of *káma*, the initial and most primitive manifestation of the search for happiness. The *kámamaya kośa* is sometimes referred to as the "conscious mind," and the term can be useful in certain contexts, but it is by and large an inaccurate appellation. Anandamurti refers to it instead as the "crude mind," being that part of the mind that deals with the material world, and its witnessing consciousness is called *prájiṇa*.[3]

The next *kośa*, ascending the ladder of subtlety, is the *manomaya kośa* and its witnessing consciousness is called *taejasa*.[4] *Mana* means "mind," and thus *manomaya kośa* can be translated as the "mental layer," ie., the thinking mind. Its principle activities are thinking and memory, and it is characterized by mental content that is not directly dependent on the senses or *tanmátras*. It is the domain of intellection and imagination and it draws its propulsive force from *artha* and *dharma*, psychic desire and psycho-spiritual desire. Anandamurti calls it the "subtle mind," to differentiate it from the crude mind, but it is also sometimes translated as the "subconscious" mind, and while this is not entirely accurate, it is useful in certain contexts, especially as regards its relationship with *kámamaya kośa*. The *manomaya kośa* develops from the *kámamaya kośa* in the process of evolution and it can be seen to some degree in the higher animals who are able to think thoughts that are not directly dependent on their senses. The most obvious example of this is dreaming, which can be seen in dogs, primates, and the higher marine mammals—dolphins, porpoises, and whales—but it is also evidenced by the presence of memory in developed animals and the rudiments of intellectual processes.

It is in human beings, however, that the *manomaya kośa* becomes fully expressed, to the point that it dominates our experience. The Sanskrit word for "human being" is *mánuśa*, which means "mind-preponderant being," again from the root *mana*, "mind." While the *kámamaya kośa* is our gateway to the world, the greater part of our experience, unlike in the animal kingdom, lies in the *manomaya kośa*. By way of illustration, imagine that we are in a small club listening to a jazz ensemble. As long as we are immersed in that sensory experience, rather than escaping into our thoughts, we are in the domain of *kámamaya kośa*, which in this instance we can call the "conscious mind." We are conscious of the music, the excitement we feel, the captivating image of the musicians playing their instruments, the charming jazz-club ambiance, the kaleidoscopic panorama of sights and sounds and smells. Our ears are engaged, our eyes are engaged, we may be subliminally aware of certain smells—or not so subliminally. When we sip our drink or munch on a snack our taste buds get involved; we savor the flavors and feel a certain added satisfaction. The room may be a tad bit too warm for our taste, so we take off our sweater to feel more comfortable. The other patrons may be talking too much or too loudly, making it difficult for us to appreciate the music as much as we would like to, and someone at a nearby table may have just received a foul-smelling order of nonvegan food, making us recoil in disgust, but all things considered we are really enjoying ourselves. Yet, even though our attention is engaged by the music and the all-around sensory experience, our thoughts continue to meander behind the curtain of our attention. Our mind is constantly commenting on what is going on, constantly narrating our experience, even when we are only subliminally aware of it: "Oh, what a great solo!" "How cool is that!" "Can they not be quiet over there? I'm trying to listen to the music." "God, I wish they would outlaw nonvegetarian food in public!" Images float through our mind that vie for our attention—for a few brief moments we see ourselves onstage blowing a saxophone and wowing the audience; maybe we remember a similar experience, a concert we attended, or an old jazz recording the music reminds us of—snatches of reverie that we barely notice. Because we are not paying attention to these thoughts, being caught up in the experience mediated by our senses, they can justifiably be called "subconscious," since they lie beneath the surface of our conscious attention—the word *sub* means "beneath"—and thus in this case the *manomaya kośa* can be referred to as the "subconscious mind." But the moment we pay attention to those thoughts they become conscious, and once we do, our attention is diverted from the sensory world of *kámamaya kośa*. We have all had the experience of listening to music or watching a play or a movie and getting so caught up in our thoughts that for a few moments or a few minutes we are no longer aware of the music or the actors or our environment. We have all been in a conversation and found ourselves paying more attention to what we want to say, rehearsing it in our mind, than to what our interlocutor is actually saying. And because the mind can only pay attention to one thing at a time, we lose contact with the outside world in those instances, if only for a few moments, and at times it is almost as if we were dreaming with our eyes open. If it goes on for more than a few moments the people we are with are likely to notice, and thereupon ensues the famous repartee: "Where were you just now?" "Sorry, I was a million miles away." Our friends certainly know the feeling, since studies have shown that the average person spends up to half their waking hours in such daydreams, mostly of very short duration, their mind wandering in and out of contact with the outside world.[5]

In the waking state both our *manomaya* and *kámamaya kośas* remain active, and we tend to shuttle back and forth between them, between the inaptly named conscious and subconscious minds. At one moment we may be absorbed in what we are doing and what we are experiencing through our senses and thus be unaware, or only subliminally aware, of our underlying thoughts and feelings (though they are still there, just below the surface). A minute later we may be so absorbed in our thoughts that we barely notice the outside world. In the former, *kámamaya* is dominant and in the latter *manomaya*. While we can only pay attention to one thing at a time, the mind is able to move between disparate thoughts and perceptions with unfathomable speed, and so our normal waking experience is a composite of *kámamaya* and *manomaya kośas*, an interplay between these two distinct levels of experience. Either, however, can be suspended through the act of concentration. If we concentrate fully on a task or on a certain perception, say a candle flame in the yogic practice of *tratak*, then *manomaya kośa* can be temporarily suspended. Likewise, if we concentrate fully on our thoughts, then *kámamaya kośa* can be suspended. This plays a fundamental role in yogic meditation, where the meditator purposely suspends *kámamaya kośa* through the practice of sensory withdrawal in order to redirect the mind toward the deeper *kośas* and eventually toward consciousness itself. This suspension also happens quite naturally to a lesser or greater extent when we focus on our thoughts — for example, when we are solving a problem or otherwise engaging our intellect. When we read a book, for instance, our mind easily becomes absorbed in *manomaya kośa*, with only a tenuous awareness of our environment or of the visual or tactile experience of the book itself or the act of turning the pages.

This suspension of *kámamaya kośa* also occurs naturally during the dream state, where the stored impressions in our mind recombine to form imaginary sequential narratives according to the prompting of our *saṁskáras* or mental tendencies. When we fall asleep, our *citta* is automatically disconnected from our senses—if someone enters the room we won't see them or hear them or smell them—and this disconnection is equivalent to the suspension of *kámamaya kośa*, which is why a daytime reverie where we temporarily lose contact with our immediate sensory experience is commonly called a "daydream." The content of our dreams is drawn primarily from memory, one of the two principle functions of *manomaya kośa*, and these memories can be of two kinds: cerebral or extracerebral. Cerebral memories are those impressions accumulated in the current life and stored in the brain, and the vast majority of our dreams are composed exclusively from these cerebral memories. Extracerebral memory refers to the storehouse of memories from previous lives that have no corresponding impressions in the brain. These memories remain active in very young children and naturally surface in their dreams, though they have no context in which to understand the significance of such dreams, and thus they normally go unnoticed. Such memories generally cease to appear in the *manomaya kośa* during the dream state by the age of five, due to the overlay of new memories from the current life, the current memories being much more vivid and impactful as a result of recency bias and the physical presence of those impressions in the brain. The one exception to the memory-based content of our dreams occurs in what are sometimes called "prophetic" dreams, where material from the higher *kośas* enters into the *manomaya kośa* during the dream state. These kinds of dreams often contain premonitions of future events that subsequently prove true. They may also contain deep insights into the nature of existence or they may manifest as spiritual experiences. As might be imagined, such dreams are very rare. For the vast majority of human beings, our experience remains almost exclusively confined to the *kámamaya* and *manomaya kośas*, whether in the waking state or the dream state.

But our mind and its potential does not end here. We have three more *kośas*, which, taken together, are commonly referred to as the "unconscious" or "superconscious" mind. Anandamurti refers to them collectively as the "causal mind" and their witnessing consciousness is called *vishva*.⁶ Most people will have occasional glimpses into these higher *kośas*, but for the most part their access is barred to us unless we develop the higher potential of our minds through spiritual practice, since the incessant activity of the *kámamaya* and *manomaya kośas* conceals the presence of those deeper recesses. For this reason, the analogy of the banana flower is particularly apt. To gain access to the higher *kośas*, the lower *kośas* must be "peeled away." In other words, we must develop the ability to still the *kámamaya* and *manomaya kośas* in order to reveal those hidden depths and tap their unlimited potential.

The first of the three layers of the causal or superconscious mind is called the *atimánasa kośa*, which translates literally as the "supramental" mind. It is absent in the Vedanta system. *Ati* means "beyond" and *mánasa* means "mind," referring specifically to the *manomaya kośa*, the thinking mind. Discursive thought or intellection is a function of *manomaya kośa* and is analytic in nature. When we go beyond analytic thought, however, we enter into the realm of *atimánasa kośa* in which mental functioning becomes synthetic in nature. This is the end of intellect and the beginning of intuition, the layer of the mind in which true insight as well as true creativity is born. Mozart famously commented that he didn't "compose" his definitive works. They appeared fully formed in his mind; all he did was transcribe them. Antonio Carlos Jobim, the great Brazilian composer, had a similar experience when he wrote "Wave." He was sitting at his piano one day when his mind went quiet and the melody to "Wave" suddenly "dropped" into his consciousness, whole and complete. He didn't improvise his way to "Wave." He didn't experiment with different combinations of notes, gradually refining the melody. It was, as he called it, a "gift from the muse," a small instance of what Mozart experienced on a nearly daily basis when he was at the height of his creative powers. The melodies they heard didn't come from their limited individual minds, but from "beyond," that is, from the *atimánasa kośa*. Many creative geniuses over the centuries have had the same experience, including many scientists and philosophers. Einstein came up with his special theory of relativity in a flash of intuitive insight, and the great mathematician,

Henri Poincaré, discovered the complex Fuchsian functions in a similar flash of intuition, accompanied in his words by "brief, sudden, and immediate certainty." Nietzsche wrote eloquently of similar experiences he had when he was writing *Thus Spoke Zarathustra*,[7] and all three experienced sudden transports of joy along with these insights or bursts of creativity. Even far lesser creative artists, scientists, and thinkers are well aware of this phenomenon. The mind grows quiet, usually as a result of a prolonged period of concentration, and suddenly, like a flash from beyond, the insight or creative fire bursts into the mind, accompanied by feelings of intense joy. True creativity doesn't come from discursive thought, or even from the imagination, and it is accompanied by ecstatic feelings because that is the nature of the causal mind.

From the standpoint of Tantra, there is essentially no difference between the individual causal mind and the cosmic causal mind.[8] The only thing that separates them is the seeds of the *saṁskāras*, which are stored in the *vijiṇānamaya kośa* and first sprout in the *atimānasa kośa* before finding their full expression in the *manomaya kośa*. Otherwise the causal mind is one. Thus, if the *kāmamaya* and *manomaya kośas* can be stilled, the individual automatically gains access to the vast cosmic storehouse of knowledge and creativity that is the cosmic causal mind. In the case of these creative and scientific giants, their concentrated pursuit of artistic perfection or solutions to the problems of science or philosophy led them to a kind of partial or momentary trance, temporarily stilling the *kāmamaya* and *manomaya kośas* enough to allow these bursts of insight and creative genius to transit the border between the superconscious and subconscious minds. Dmitri Mendeleev, for example, had been trying for years without success to classify the elements when he had a dream in which the periodic table appeared to him in the pattern that had hitherto escaped him and which is now familiar to us all. That long period of concentrated intellectual effort opened the door for that knowledge to pass from the *atimānasa kośa* to the *manomaya* through the medium of an oneiric vision.

The *atimānasa kośa* is also the source of the phenomena known as ESP, such as clairvoyance, clairaudience, telepathy, and so on. The principle is the same. The cosmic causal mind is the storehouse of universal knowledge, whether past, present, or future. For the Cosmic Mind everything is internal and thus nothing is hidden; nor is it bound by the time factor, being beyond relativity. Thus when a psychic sees a future event or is able to visualize what is going on in a distant place, or when an ordinary person gets a premonition of something that is soon to happen, say to a loved one, a premonition that subsequently proves true, they have gained some temporary access to that infinite storehouse of timeless knowledge. Such perceptions are beyond the scope of our individual thinking mind, our *manomaya kośa*. They are not arrived at through analytic thought, and for that reason science has been slow to accept such phenomena, since science operates almost entirely within the bounds of the intellect and its observation of the visible world.

In most cases, such abilities are beyond the individual's control. They may use certain aids to facilitate their concentration, such as crystals, hypnosis, or a Ouija board, but they are not able to control when or in what form such knowledge comes—or if it will come at all. And when it does, it is invariably filtered through the lens of their individual *saṁskáras*, which often distorts the form this knowledge takes and colors their understanding of their experience. This is not true of great saints and yogis, however, who have developed the ability through yogic practice to still the *kámamaya* and *manomaya kośas* at will. For them, the doorway to this infinite storehouse of universal wisdom and knowledge stands forever open, anytime they choose to step through it. They need only concentrate their minds to enter the higher *kośas*. This is the mechanism at work behind the stories of omniscience and other psychic abilities demonstrated by realized spiritual masters: the ability to enter the superconscious mind at will.

The second layer of the superconscious or causal mind is the *vijiṇánamaya kośa*, which Anandamurti also calls the "subliminal mind." *Vijiṇána* means "knowledge," but here "knowledge" does not refer to the knowledge of coming events or what medicine can cure what disease or in fact anything that belongs to the phenomenal world. Here knowledge refers to *viveka* and *vaeragya*, discrimination and nonattachment. These are the highest faculties of the mind and they constitute real knowledge, without which the goal of spiritual evolution cannot be reached. *Viveka*, discernment or discrimination, is the ability to discern between what is real in the absolute sense and what is relative, that is, between consciousness and phenomenality, whether that be the objects of perception or the manifestations of mind. True discrimination is the ability to see beyond the veil of appearances to the true nature of manifest existence. In this elevated arena of mental experience, one sees things as they really are—waves of Consciousness in an ocean of Consciousness, the constantly changing forms of the formless. Consequently, *viveka* manifests as the voice of our conscience, the voice that knows in every situation what is the correct choice or correct action, that which speeds our evolution and renders maximum service to the world and that which doesn't. V*aeragya*, nonattachment or dispassion, is a corollary of *viveka*. When one perceives each and every expression of existence as a manifestation of Consciousness, then one automatically transcends the attraction to any one particular form, since it is the same blissful Consciousness that one experiences, no matter what the form. The word *rága* means "the act of coloring or dyeing," and by extension, "passion," while the prefix *vi* means "without." Thus *vaeragya* literally refers to the ability to keep the mind from being colored or influenced or impassioned by the phenomenal waves of the manifest world, the ability to keep from being pulled or pushed by the twin forces of attraction and repulsion, thus freeing the mind from the slavery of its egocentric desires. The *vijiṅánamaya kośa* is also where one feels the sense of bliss that comes from the contemplation of the fine arts, a prelude to the pure spiritual ecstacy that is experienced in the last and subtlest of the five *kośas*, the *hirañyamaya kośa*.

Anandamurti calls the *hirañyamaya kośa* the "subtle causal mind." In Vedanta it is known as the *ánandamaya kośa*. *Hirañya* means "gold," and it is the last and most diaphanous of the veils that cover the pure light of Consciousness. It is here that the mind experiences the effulgence of Consciousness in its purest perceptible form, the direct reflection of Consciousness in the mind, which can only be experienced when the mind becomes perfectly calm and one pointed. The only desire here is the desire to merge in the Supreme Self, *mokśa* or spiritual desire, the pure attraction toward the Infinite, and the only feeling is that of bliss. It is the realm of the most elevated mystical or spiritual experience and is called the "golden" layer because Consciousness is experienced by the mind as an infinite ocean of effulgence. After describing his first experience of samadhi, Paramahansa Yogananda had this to say:

> The breath and the restless mind, I saw, were like storms which lashed the ocean of light into waves of material forms — earth, sky, human beings, animals, birds, trees. No perception of the Infinite as One Light could be had except by calming those storms. As often as I silenced the two natural tumults, I beheld the multitudinous waves of creation melt into one lucent sea, even as the waves of the ocean, their tempests subsiding, serenely dissolve into unity.[9]

In this *kośa* lie the seeds of objective and subjective manifestation, which begin to be expressed in the *vijiṅánamaya kośa* and then become manifest in the *atimánasa kośa*. Establishment in this layer is equivalent to *savikalpa* samadhi.

In summary, there are seven levels to the microcosmic existence, of which all seven levels become fully manifest in the highest form of incarnate life, the human being. These seven levels are the physical body, or *annamaya kośa*, which Anandamurti calls the crude body; the five *kośas* of the *citta*, which Anandamurti calls the subtle body and which he divides into the crude, subtle, and causal minds; and the *aham* and *mahat*, which he calls the *samanya deha* or supracausal body, that which lies between the *kośas* and pure Consciousness. Because the subtler layers are hidden by the previous layers, it is necessary to perfect each *kośa* in order to elevate the mind. Each *kośa* must be rendered tranquil and crystalline before the spiritual aspirant can rise to the next stage and eventually aspire to the highest realization by transforming his mind into a pure mirror of Consciousness.[10] In the practice of ashtanga yoga, different techniques are instrumental in perfecting the different *kośas*. The body or *annamaya kośa* is perfected through diet and the practice of asanas. The practice of *yama* and *niyama*, the yogic code of ethics, perfects the *kámamaya kośa*; the *manomaya kośa* is perfected through pranayama, breath control; the *atimánasa* through *pratyahara*, sensory withdrawal; the *vijinánamaya* through *dharana*, concentration; and the *hiranyamaya kośa* through *dhyána*, meditation. These five *kośas* also control the first five chakras and hence the five fundamental factors, with *kámamaya* controlling the first chakra along with the solid factor, and so forth. The sixth chakra, the *ájiná* chakra, is the seat of the mind and is thus the indirect controller of the five lower chakras and the five *kośas*. The seventh or *sahasrára* chakra is the seat of consciousness.

	Microcosm			
	Kośa	Mind	Witnessing Entity	Body
	Annamaya			Crude
Citta	Kámamaya	Crude	Prájina	Subtle
	Manomaya	Subtle	Taejasa	
	Atimánasa	Causal	Vishva	
	Vijinánamaya			
	Hiranmaya			
Ahamtattva	above Hiranmaya Kośa		Puruśottama	Sámánya Deha
Mahattattva				

सप्तलोकात्मकं ब्रह्ममनः ॥ २ ॥

III.2 *saptalokátmakam brahmamanah*

sapta, seven; *loka*, plane, sphere, world; *átmakam*, composed of; *brahma*, Supreme Consciousness; *manah*, mind

"The Cosmic Mind comprises seven *lokas*."

It is an axiom in spiritual science that the microcosm is a reflection of the Macrocosm—thus the famous Hermetic saying, "As above, so below." The same idea appears in the Vishvasara Tantra: "What is here is there; what is not here is nowhere." It is no surprise then that in Anandamurti's Tantra, the Macrocosmic Mind is divided into seven *lokas*, seven planes or spheres that correspond to the seven layers of the microcosm that have just been enumerated in the previous sutra—the physical body, the five *kośas*, and the supracausal mind. The names of the three lower *lokas* are familiar to anyone who has recited the Gayatri Mantra. The first line of the Gayatri—*oṁm bhúr bhuvah svah oṁm*, commonly translated as, "O Lord of the seven worlds"—names the first three *lokas*; the remaining four are understood. As with the *kośas*, the idea that the creation consists of seven planes of existence is an ancient concept in the Indian spiritual tradition, so ancient in fact that it hearkens back to the Rigveda,[11] far predating both Samkhya and the Bhagavad Gita. In this sutra, Anandamurti redefines this ancient concept for our contemporary understanding, divesting it of its mythic or fanciful overlay.

In traditional Hinduism the *lokas* are worlds or dimensions inhabited by different classes of beings, and descriptions of the *lokas* can be found in different texts, especially in the Puranas, most notably in the Bhagavata Purana. According to the Bhagavata and similar texts, *satyaloka* is the realm of Brahma, the Supreme Being. Below *satyaloka* comes the *taparloka*, inhabited by immortal beings that are the personification of knowledge. Next comes the *janarloka*, home to the fully enlightened souls. Just below that is the *maharloka*, the abode of great sages and saints. Below that is the *svarloka*, the heavenly skies above the Sun where the various deities of Hindu mythology dwell. Next is the *bhuvarloka*, the realm between the Sun and the Earth, inhabited by semi-divine beings. And finally there is the *bhúrloka*, the Earth and other inhabited planets, home to human beings, plants, and animals. There are also seven underworlds, bringing the total to fourteen in traditional Hinduism. A modern rendering of this traditional conception can be found in Paramahansa Yogananda's *Autobiography of a Yogi*, where the *lokas* above *bhúrloka* are conceived of as different astral worlds,[12] and the appeal of his account is easy to appreciate, for who wouldn't want these astral planes and planets to exist, dimensions in which there is no death, just a fully conscious transformation to a higher form. Some modern yogis, most notably Sri Aurobindo, have equated the *lokas* to specific states of consciousness;[13] however, there is no textual evidence to support this idea in the Indian philosophical tradition.

In the Tantra of Anandamurti, *bhúrloka* is the first of the seven *lokas* that make up the Macrocosmic Mind. Just as the physical body or *annamaya kośa* is the first layer of the microcosmic existence, the physical universe of the five fundamental factors is the first layer of the Macrocosmic Existence—in effect, the physical body of the Macrocosm. Unlike the microcosm, however, where the physical body is external to the mind and serves as its vehicle, *bhúrloka* is internal to the Macrocosmic Mind, since there is nothing outside the Macrocosm. *Bhúrloka* is the crudest manifestation of the waves of the Cosmic Mind, the culminating stage in the process of *saiṇcara*.

The next *loka* is the *bhuvarloka*, the crude mental world. It corresponds to the *kámamaya kośa* of the microcosm. It is through the *bhuvarloka* that the Cosmic Mind directly enjoys the material universe, just as it is through the *kámamaya kośa* that the living being directly enjoys the external world. All sensory experience occurs in this *loka*, as well as the accompanying mental tendencies—hunger, sleepiness, avarice, indolence, and so on. In effect, the *bhuvarloka* is the collectivity of all the innumerable individual *kámamaya kośas*. Each living being, from the most primitive unicellular organism to the most elevated yogi, serves as an individual focal point through which Brahma enjoys his mentally begotten creation. At the microcosmic level, the living being is confined to its individual sensory experience of the world, to its individual attractions and aversions, but at the macrocosmic level these innumerable expressions meld into a singular psychic experience witnessed by the Macrocosmic Consciousness. The *bhúr* and *bhuvar lokas* together are known as the crude body of the Macrocosm in Anandamurti's system, since together they constitute the Macrocosm's direct experience of the material universe. The witnessing Consciousness at this level is called *iishvara*, the controller.[14]

The next *loka* is the *svarloka* or subtle mental world, equivalent to the *manomaya kośa* of the microcosm. This is the pure mental sphere of discursive thought and imagination that is principally seen in human beings and developed animals. It is also the sphere in which pleasure and pain are felt, and as with *bhuvarloka*, *svarloka* is equivalent to the collectivity of all the innumerable individual *manomaya kośas* in the flow of *pratisaińcara*—all the thoughts and dreams and memories of so many different beings, the psychic apprehension of pleasure and pain, the play of imagination, all melding together into one universal psychic experience whose witnessing Consciousness is called *hirańyagarbha*, the golden womb.[15] It is in the *svarloka* or *manomaya kośa* that the living being reaps the consequences or fruits of their actions, and thus the popular religious conception of heaven, where one enjoys the results of one's virtuous deeds, is synonymous with *svarloka*. The Sanskrit word for "heaven" is *svarga*, a synonym for *svarloka*.

After *svarloka* comes the three layers of the cosmic causal mind, the *mahar*, *janar*, and *tapar lokas*, which are the cosmic equivalents of the *atimánas*, *vijińánamaya*, and *hirańyamaya kośas*. Along with the *svarloka* they constitute the subtle body of the Macrocosm. Consciousness in its role as the witnessing counterpart of these three *lokas* is called *viráta*, the Great, or *vaeshvánara*, the Cosmic Self.[16] The *maharloka*, or supramental sphere, is the repository of cosmic knowledge. The knowledge of how to cure a seemingly incurable disease, the knowledge of past and future events, including all the past and future lives of all beings, the various psychic powers, are all found in the *maharloka*. It is the *loka* of omniscience. It is also the sphere in which the *saḿskáras* first begin to vibrate and in which the inspiration to do spiritual sadhana arises. When an individual has deep intuitive insights, extrasensory perceptions, and other such experiences, their mind has risen to this plane of existence. The *janarloka*, or subliminal sphere, is where the I-feeling, the knowledge of existence, is experienced, along with *viveka* and *vaeragya*, discrimination and nonattachment. The pure aesthetic pleasure that comes from the subtle appreciation of the fine arts is also experienced here, and as a result people who are able to access this *loka* sometimes have a tendency to become self-forgetful[17] In *taparloka*, the subtlest of the three *lokas* of the cosmic causal mind, the sense of individuality becomes indistinct, and even this is only a reflection due to its proximity to the *janarloka*. When the mind rises to the level of *savikalpa samadhi* it enters the *taparloka*.

The final *loka* is the *satyaloka*, and as with the supracausal body of the microcosm, the *satyaloka* consists of *aham* and *mahat*, in this case the cosmic *aham* and *mahat*. This is the causal body of the Macrocosm from which the creation, beginning with *taparloka*, blossoms forth, and its witnessing Consciousness is *puruśottama*. As was noted in Chapter One, the transformation of pure Consciousness into *aham* and *mahat* is purely theoretical, for in this *loka* there is the complete absence of cosmic thought waves, and thus it is coexistent with the *nirguńa* state. "Since the causal body is conceived to be in existence from a philosophical point of view, it is termed *satyaloka*."[18] *Satya*, derived from *sat* (immutable), refers to the infinite immutable Supreme Consciousness. *Satyaloka* then is the realm of pure Consciousness as the witness of the macrocosmic causal body.

Macrocosm					
	Kośa	Mind	Witnessing Entity	Deha (Body)	Loka (World)
Mahattattva			Puruśottama	Causal	Satya
Ahaṁtattva					
Citta	Hirańmaya	Causal	Virāta or Vaeshvánara	Subtle	Tapah
	Vijińánamaya				Janah
	Atimánasa				Mahah
	Manomaya	Subtle	Hirańyagarbha		Svah
	Kámamaya	Crude	Iishvara	Crude	Bhuvah
					Bhuh

कारणमनसि दीर्घनिद्रा मरणम् ॥ ३ ॥

III.3 *kárańamanasi diirghanidrá marańam*

kárańa, causal; *manasi,* in the mind; *diirgha,* long; *nidrá,* sleep; *marańam,* death

"Death is a long sleep in the causal mind."

No spiritual philosophy can be complete without explaining the phenomenon of death—what it is and why it is. Life and death are the two states that define our microcosmic existence, and thus it is not enough to explain life without also explaining death. Implicit in this is the role it plays in the spiritual journey. In his short explanation of this sutra, Anandamurti references the three principal mental states of incarnate life—the waking state, the dream state, and deep sleep—in terms of the five *kośas,* which, as we have seen, constitute the essence of the living being. In the waking state, all five *kośas* are active. In the dream state, the *kámamaya kośa* is inactive or suspended, while the other four *kośas* remain active. In deep sleep both the *kámamaya* and *manomaya kośas* are suspended but the causal mind remains awake. There is also a fourth state that is extremely rare, the *turiiya* or nondual state in which the causal mind is suspended in Supreme Consciousness, also known as *nirvikalpa* samadhi, but this state is attained only by the most elevated souls as they near the end of their spiritual journey. Otherwise, the one state we all experience in which the causal mind ceases to function is the state of death.

Anandamurti attributes death to a loss of psycho-physical parallelism, which is in turn a corollary to his definition of life. Life, as he defines it, depends on parallelism between the psychic and physical bodies,[19] and it arises when this psycho-physical parallelism is established between a bodiless mind and a suitable physical body, such as an embryo or fertilized ovum. That embryonic physical structure has its own characteristic wavelength, as does the bodiless mind, being a product of the mind's latent *saḿskáras,* or accumulated mental tendencies, which are the source of the mind's inherent momentum. The coupling is effected by *prakrti,* which propels the bodiless mind in search of an appropriate vehicle for expressing that inherent momentum. Once they come in contact, their affinity enables the coupling. A human mind not only requires a human body, it requires a human body that fulfills certain conditions: a physical structure and a familial and societal environment that will allow for the expression of its inherent *saṁskáras*. As long as that body and mind remain healthy, they will remain together. But if the body loses its vibrational vitality due to disease or accident or old age, that is, if the physical waves degrade to the point that they can no longer maintain adjustment with the mental waves, or in special cases, if the mind's wavelength degrades to the point that it can no longer maintain adjustment with the physical waves, then that parallelism is lost and the mind separates from the body.[20] The direct physical cause of this separation is the loss of integrity of the ten *váyus*, which gradually merge with each other, causing a loss of functionality, until they finally leave the body.[21] Once the mind disassociates from the body, the causal mind becomes inactive because it is no longer associated with a brain and is bereft of the support of vital energy. It then becomes a bodiless mind, the subject of sutra III.5. It is this condition that Anandamurti defines in psychological terms as a "long sleep in the causal mind."

Sleep is an appropriate word for several reasons. After death the causal mind becomes dormant, and with its inactivity our individual self also enters a state of dormancy. What defines our existence as individual beings at this point is the *karmáshaya*, the bundle of *saṁskáras* in seed form harbored in the dormant causal mind, as witnessed by the *jiivátmá*. The *kámamaya* and *manomaya kośas* have dissolved — they will have to be formed anew in the next life — but the causal mind, whose differentiation from the cosmic causal mind is due to the presence of the *karmáshaya*, remains intact though inactive (in the absence of *saṁskáras* it would automatically merge into the cosmic causal mind). It is a long sleep because anything over eight hours is a long sleep, and it can take days, weeks, months, or years before that bodiless mind encounters an appropriate physical structure that will allow it to express its *saṁskáras*. It is said that the more evolved the individual, the more difficult it is to find an appropriate body due to the subtle nature of spiritual *saṁskáras* and the scarcity of suitable parents. So this long sleep can in some cases last a very long time.

The concept of death as a long sleep in the causal mind presupposes transmigration. Sleep implies awakening. It is a long sleep, not a permanent or eternal sleep, as death is sometimes referred to. Thus the purview of this sutra, by implication, not only includes the nature of death but also the culmination of that long sleep, ie., the reawakening to a new life. Upon death, or dissociation between the mind and body, the mind ceases to function. The bodiless mind, however, still has its inherent momentum, supplied by its latent *samskáras*. That momentum must be satisfied, and thus it propels the mind forward until it can find a vehicle for expression. The ovum and spermatozoa are created within the bodies of the mother and father in developed beings (in less developed beings, procreation uses other, simpler methods), and as living cells they each have a certain wavelength, derived from the mother and father respectively. When they combine, they create a new cell, the fertilized ovum, that combines the characteristic wavelengths inherited from the mother and father. All that remains is for the bodiless mind to establish parallelism with that nascent physical structure,[22] which will depend upon there being a preexisting affinity or parallelism between the latent *samskáras* of the bodiless mind and the vibration of the fertilized ovum. At a certain point thereafter, the causal mind will reawaken and a new *kámamaya* and *manomaya kośa* will begin to form.[23] But instead of waking up at the start of a new day, the newly reincarnated mind wakes up in a new body, in a new place, in a new time. Due to the suspension of the activity of the causal mind during the bodiless state and the dissolution of the *kámamaya* and *manomaya kośas*, there is no feeling of continuity between the new life and the previous life, as there is when the mind awakens from deep sleep, although that sense of continuity can be recovered through spiritual practices if one gains access to the causal mind and with it the memories of past lives.

While it is natural for living beings to fear death—fear plays an essential role in the pursuit of self-preservation, which is itself a motive force in the process of spiritual evolution—Anandamurti contends that death is in fact a benevolent system.[24] First of all, death is the most efficient and most logical mechanism to sustain spiritual evolution, a case of perfect design. The mind, from its initial manifestation in the flow of *pratisaiṋcara*, has to pass through an exceedingly long process before it can evolve enough to achieve spiritual liberation. How long? Many millions of years at the very least, which we can easily understand through a close examination of incarnate life. As we saw in Chapter One, it took nearly three billion years for unicellular life-forms on this planet to evolve into metazoan life-forms with the capacity to accommodate the expression of *aham*, and another seven hundred million years until the first expression of *mahat* in the early mammals and hardwood trees. If we study the life of any primitive organism, we can get an idea of how little its mind evolves between birth and death. All living beings experience mental growth—such is the inevitable nature of incarnate existence—but in undeveloped life-forms that growth is so slow as to be imperceptible. The behavior of ciliates, such as the *Stentor roeselii*, arguably among the most advanced forms of protists, shows no appreciable change between birth and death. Thus the simple *citta* mind of a unicellular organism has no choice but to pass through an untold multitude of unicellular lives before it can evolve enough to attain a multicellular body in which *aham* can begin to emerge out of *citta*. Once *aham* manifests in metazoan life-forms, evolution undergoes a process of rapid acceleration, but how much does a mosquito actually evolve between its birth and death? Far more than a ciliate, without question, but nevertheless a long journey lies ahead of that individual mind before its *aham* can evolve to the point that it begins to manifest *mahat*, an evolutionary attainment that requires a body far more complex than that of a mosquito. How many insect lives and thereafter how many reptilian lives will it need before it attains such a body? And how many plant lives did it pass through before attaining the body of a mosquito?

When seen in this light it quickly becomes evident that it would be impossible for a living being to achieve realization if it had to retain the same undeveloped or underdeveloped body for an indefinite period of time. A unicellular organism would never be able to evolve to the point that it could develop *aham*, and a mosquito would never be able to evolve to the point that it would be able to manifest *mahat*. In neither case would their bodies allow them to gather the requisite experiences or face the requisite challenges, an evolutionary necessity that can only be obtained by exchanging bodies. Thus when the mind outstrips the expressional capacity of one body, it migrates to a structure with a higher level of complexity, which then facilitates further growth. This is a concept that applies not only to biological structures but to the inanimate world as well. In 1977 Ilya Prigogine won the Nobel Prize for his work on dissipative structures, demonstrating the tendency of inanimate structures to break down and then reemerge at a higher level of complexity, a concept that he and other scientists later applied to biological structures. When considered from this perspective, it becomes patently obvious that death is indeed a necessary and extraordinarily efficient system. We outgrow one body and graduate to another, like a child outgrowing a set of clothes that have become constraining, and in the process we get a newer, better, more up-to-date physical structure, which allows us to have a new and more varied set of experiences and challenges that in turn stimulate further growth. To use an analogy from the world of technology, we upgrade our hardware to be able to take advantage of our advancing software.

Secondly — and this applies especially to human beings — *saṁskáras* undergo a process of ripening during that long sleep due to the disassociation of the mind from the body. *Saṁskáras* ripen whenever the mind becomes detached from the body and the *práṅendriya*. It happens in samadhi and in other circumstances when the mind becomes suspended, for example, during a prolonged coma, which is why people coming out of a prolonged coma exhibit marked changes in their thinking and behavior. But for most of us, it happens primarily during the bodiless state. It is during this period that the *saṁskáras* become prepared for expression in the coming life.[25] When the mind becomes active again in the new life, it starts reaping the consequences of those *saṁskáras* that have ripened during death. Thus death not only allows us to upgrade our body, providing the mind's software with more advanced hardware, it also expedites the future expression of latent *saṁskáras*, which facilitates further development in the next life.

Finally, there is a further boon built into this particular element of cosmic design: Providence has arranged the mechanics of transmigration so that we forget our past lives due to the absence of past impressions in the newly acquired brain.[26] This enables us to make a fresh start, rather than being weighed down by the memories of the people we lost in previous lives, the mistakes we made, the traumas we suffered. Even in this life, we often get a jolt of new energy, hope, and inspiration when we get a chance to leave our problems behind and start afresh, a fruitful experience that has been the subject of countless stories since the earliest days of mankind's literary efforts—the chance to start a new life, as we like to call it. We can see this principle at work in the eyes of young children. They are not weighed down by their past lives. They arrive on this planet full of energy, eager and ready to go. Of course, we don't really leave it all behind, because we carry our *saṁskáras* with us, but it feels that way because we've forgotten the experiences that led to their formation. We've left behind the situations in which we had been entangled, and this in turn makes it easier to deal with those *saṁskáras* anew when they start showing up in the new life.

मनोविकृतिर्विपाकापेक्षिता संस्कारः ॥ ४ ॥

III.4 *manovikrtir vipákápekṣitá saṁskárah*

manah, mind; *vikrtih*, distortion; *vipáka*, fruition, ripening; *ápekṣitá*, expected, required, awaiting; *saṁskárah*, reactive momenta, reaction in potentiality

"A distortion of the mind awaiting expression is known as *saṁskára*."

As we saw in sutra II.19, every action, whether virtuous or vile (and this includes purely psychic actions), distorts the *citta* and leaves an impression that remains stored in the mind until it can be released through the process of *karmaphalabhoga*, the suffering or enjoyment of the reaction to that action. This release or compensative reaction, which is the mechanism by which the mind seeks to regain its original, undistorted state, can only occur when the appropriate conditions are met. If a finger is pressed into a rubber ball, those conditions are met when the finger is removed, thereby allowing the ball to regain its original shape. The impression or deformation left in the mind by the action is a source of tension, like the tension in the ball generated by the insertion of the finger. This tension constitutes the inherent momentum of the individual mind, the source of its incessant quest for liberation, and ultimately it is this inherent momentum that obligates the bodiless mind to seek a new physical structure after death.

These unrequited reactions, the consequences of our previous actions that we have yet to face, are known as *saṁskára* in Sanskrit, which Anandamurti translates into English as "reactive momentum," or more commonly, "reactive momenta," since our mind invariably contains untold numbers of *saṁskáras* acquired not only in this life but in previous lives as well. They are held in abeyance until the appropriate conditions arise that allow for their expression. This concept is popularly referred to as "karma." *Karma* means "action" in Sanskrit, but in this case the word is used to refer to the reactions generated by our actions, reactions that by and large determine the circumstances of our life, an implicit recognition that the challenges, both internal and external, that we are destined to face are a direct consequence of our own actions, our largely unseen and forgotten karma. However, the more precise term when referring specifically to those unserved reactions is *saṁskára*.

Under normal conditions, the reactions we reap in our present life consist principally of reactions accumulated in the previous life. Having ripened after death, those *saṁskáras* from the previous life determine the conditions of our birth—our family, our friends, the society we are born into, and so on—conditions that are propitious for their expression, while the *saṁskáras* we earn in this life are held in abeyance until our next incarnation, after they have had a chance to ripen during the bodiless state. There are exceptions, however.[27] If the *saṁskáras* generated in this life are similar to those from the previous life, for example, then both may be expressed concurrently. Spiritual aspirants may also exhaust *saṁskáras* from the same lifetime, since spiritual practices and association with a realized guru accelerate the ripening of *saṁskáras*.

In the case of human beings, *saṁskáras* are of three kinds—inborn, imposed, and acquired—whereas Anandamurti refers to those of plants and animals as "infused." Less developed beings are not capable of truly independent action—that is, they cannot go against the evolutionary flow of the Cosmic Mind. With the manifestation of *aham* in primitive life-forms comes the capacity for self-initiated action, but the decisions nonhuman creatures make invariably follow their inborn nature in strict accordance with the evolutionary design of the Cosmic Mind. Hence the term "infused." They cannot go against their nature and thus they cannot degenerate, while human beings can and sometimes do.

Inborn *saṁskáras* are those we carry with us from our previous lives. They are the ones that determine the conditions of our birth and why we react the way we do. They are why twins raised in the same environment react differently to the same conditions. Our inborn *saṁskáras* must also fit with the inborn *saṁskáras* of those around us. If we have a *saṁskára* to die at a young age, then our family members must have the *saṁskára* to lose a child or a sibling at that age. It all has to mesh, which makes the tapestry of action and reaction an unimaginably complex weave.

Imposed *saṁskáras* are those imposed upon us by our new environment. If we are born into a culture where people have a habit of daily tea drinking, we will tend to develop an affinity for tea at an early age due to the constant exposure. Things that are repeated to us frequently also create imposed *saṁskáras*. The brother of a young girl, influenced by cultural bias, repeatedly tells his young sister that the hair on her legs is ugly, and thus she gradually develops an aversion to having hairy legs, an aversion that is imposed rather than inborn. Many cultural values are imposed in this way. They are by and large less deeply rooted and thus easier to overcome than inborn *saṁskáras*.

Acquired *saṁskáras* are those we acquire in the current life once our ego develops enough to be capable of original actions. These will then be added to the inborn and imposed *saṁskáras* that are already stored in our mind. If these acquired *saṁskáras* are not expressed in this life, as is usually the case, they will be the primary factor that will determine the nature of the bundle of *saṁskáras* that will come due in the next life.

Original actions are called *pratyayamúlaka* in Sanskrit, while reactive actions are called *saṁskáramúlaka*.[28] In the case of reactive actions, it is as if our hands were tied, as if we had no say in the matter, and indeed we don't.²⁹ We are impelled by our *saṁskáras* to act in a certain way. Say, for example, that a person says something we don't like. A sudden surge of anger takes possession of us and we lash out, impelled by that reaction. For those few moments while we are under the sway of the reaction we are powerless to restrain ourselves. We may immediately regret our words and apologize for our behavior, but while we were in the grip of the reaction we had no real agency. Such actions do not generate new *saṁskáras*, since they are a reaction rather than an original action, a purging of that pent-up momentum.

Original actions are independent actions that proceed from our sense of volition, from our *aham* or feeling of authorship, our ego. We choose to act, whereas in the case of reactive actions we have no actual choice. Original actions are only possible in the waking state,³⁰ and the *saṁskáras* they generate will be either good or bad, in the sense that they will either promote the elevation or the degradation of the mind. That is not to say, however, that original actions are not influenced by our *saṁskáras*. They almost invariably are. To return to the previous example, once we recover our awareness of what we are doing we may feel remorse and apologize. But if we have a habit of angry or belligerent behavior, or if we get a kind of perverse pleasure from it, perhaps from the adrenalin rush it engenders, then we may continue speaking harsh or sarcastic words out of habit or for the pure pleasure of it, even though we have the conscious option of doing otherwise. The behavior that followed the initial reaction is now original action, but it is influenced by our previous *saṁskáras*, which then act to limit our freedom. Imagine a person trying to swim against a powerful undertow. If the swimmer wishes to hold fast to his course, he has to make a substantial effort to overcome the undertow that would otherwise push him off course. An underlying habit of angry speech—in most cases an inborn *saṁskára*—can be overcome, but only by concerted effort. If we relax our efforts then the undertow will take us.

As most of us are well aware, the waters of our mind are full of undertows. In fact, our mind sometimes seems to be nothing but a vast body of eddies and riptides. The most common colloquial meaning of the word *saṁskára* is "mental tendency."

Another less common meaning is "superstition." It is our latent mental tendencies that make us unique, and they are not always logical, often taking the form of superstitions or quirks or complexes. Never in the history of this planet have there been two people with the same identical personality or the same identical destiny, and never will there be, because each human being has a unique history composed of countless actions stretching back over a host of lifetimes. It is the sum total of our *samskáras* that has made us who we are today, determining both our character and the circumstances we are destined to face. The more accurate word for "mental tendency" in the yogic lexicon is *vrtti*. As we have seen, *vrtti* literally means "occupation"—a shoemaker's profession is his *vrtti* in colloquial parlance—but here *vrtti* refers to the occupation of the mind, which is to think. The most famous sutra in the yogic tradition is the second sutra from Patanjali's Philosophy of Yoga, better known as the Yoga Sutras—*yogashcittavrttinirodhah*, "yoga is the cessation of the modifications (*vrttis*) of the mind." As we saw in the previous chapter, Tantra divides these mental occupations or mental propensities into fifty principle *vrttis*, such as anger, hope, affection, spiritual longing, etc., each of which is controlled by a particular petal located at a specific chakra. These fifty *vrttis* combine together in different proportions to manifest the infinite complexity of human thought, much as the three color channels on a computer monitor combine together in different intensities to create millions of different colors. And it is our *samskáras* in conjunction with the external conditions that determine which *vrttis* will be active at any one particular moment.

We can compare the relationship between *vrtti* and *samskára* to seismic activity on the ocean floor. Underwater quakes are exceedingly common, and as with *samskáras* they are of three different types: strike-slip, dip-slip, and subduction. Moreover they can range from barely perceptible tremors to massive quakes measuring 9 or more on the Richter scale. The reverberations of these quakes pass through the ocean, altering the motion of its waters, and in the case of large quakes or underground volcanoes they can give rise to tidal waves and tsunamis thirty feet high that travel thousands of miles and devastate large land masses. When a latent *samskára* begins to vibrate, its effects are felt throughout the mind in the form of *vrttis*. The stronger the *saṁskára* the stronger the effect.

Each one of us then has a unique combination of latent *saṁskáras* that have determined the conditions of our birth. Mr. X has a tendency to get angry in certain situations, Ms. Y in others, while Ms. Z rarely gets angry at all but often feels shy or inhibited, and Mr. P has a tendency to get so lost in his mathematical musings that he frequently forgets to eat. We all have certain mental tendencies or patterns of thought that stand in the way of our happiness and impede our spiritual evolution. Suppose we have a fear of crowds that undermines our social life. It's not always active—we don't feel it when we're alone or with family and friends—but we know it's there, waiting to erupt under certain conditions. We do our best to avoid crowds but it's not always possible, and when we do have to face a crowd, our mind is inevitably thrown into turmoil. That's the way it is with *saṁskáras*. They don't simply go away on their own. We can try to avoid situations that set them off but that doesn't set us free. They just lie in wait until the right conditions arise, and in the meantime they continue to affect us at a subliminal level. We may have some idea how certain *saṁskáras* developed—a traumatic experience with crowds, for instance, when we were young—but that doesn't explain why we were traumatized in the first place while someone else in the same situation was not. Inevitably, the chain of cause and effect goes so far back as to disappear from sight, and all we can truly know is that we have these reactive patterns that we want to be free of. And there are so many more *saṁskáras* hidden deep below the surface that we are not even aware of but which condition how we feel and act.

Whether or not we are familiar with the theory of *saṁskára*, we all have an innate understanding that our mental conditioning stands between us and freedom, between the turmoil that periodically besets us and the abiding serenity and happiness we all long for. This turmoil has its roots in our accumulated *saṁskáras*, which find expression in our anxieties, prejudices, complexes, and other conditioned patterns of thought. Thus the process of spiritual practice is a process of clearing that mental debris from the mind, liberating it from those inborn, acquired, and imposed tendencies that keep us confined to the prison of individuality. It can be equated to clearing a minefield, a difficult task that is made even more difficult by the fact that we keep creating new *saṁskáras* in the process, and thus there can be no liberation from suffering, no attainment of spiritual enlightenment, unless we can learn to stop creating *saṁskáras*. This is compounded by the fact that purely psychic actions are also actions and thus earn *saṁskáras*, even if they are not expressed externally. If we think ill of someone, it will leave an undesirable impression in the mind.[31] The resultant *saṁskára* will not be nearly as strong as it would have been had we acted on that thought and followed it up with an unkind act, but it will nevertheless continue to condition our mind until it can be eliminated or exhausted.

Fortunately, there are certain actions that do not create *saṁskáras*, specifically those actions in which the agency of the actor-ego is absent. Unconscious actions do not involve volition and thus do not generate *saṁskáras*. If we scratch an itch automatically or step on an ant unknowingly we do not acquire any new *saṁskára*. On the opposite end of the spectrum, the conscious end, if we are able to transcend the ego and act while in a state of identification with the Universal Consciousness, then again the *aham* is absent and we do not generate any new *saṁskáras*. And in the meantime we continue to exhaust the old ones.

In the end, our character is mutable. By working with our *saṁskáras* we can not only change our character but our destiny. In the words of Ralph Waldo Emerson:

> Sow a thought and you reap an action;
> Sow an act and you reap a habit;
> Sow a habit and you reap a character;
> Sow a character and you reap a destiny.[32]

विदेहिमानसे न कर्तृत्वं न सुखानि न दुःखानि ॥ ५ ॥

III.5 *videhimánase na kartrtvaṁ na sukháni na duhkháni*

videhi, bodiless; *mánase*, in the mind; *na*, no; *kartrtvaṁ*, agency, doership; *sukháni*, pleasures; *duhkháni*, pains

"In the bodiless mind there is no agency, no pleasure or pain."

As we saw in sutra III.3, the causal mind enters a state of suspension the moment the mind disassociates from the body, and thus there is no mental activity during the bodiless state, no agency or experience of pleasure or pain. The question of the mind's experience between death and rebirth, or lack thereof, has been left unaddressed in classical Indian philosophy, which has led to a widespread belief in an afterlife among the followers of some Indian religious traditions—heaven and hell as way-stations between incarnations, the possibility of communication with the dead, and so on. Anandamurti, however, leaves no doubt about this point in his philosophy. The microcosmic mind requires a physical structure and vital energy in order to function, and thus there can be no sense of authorship or mental activity between incarnations. For minds that have evolved to the point where *aham* has begun to manifest, that physical structure either has a brain and a central nervous system, as we see in members of the animal kingdom, or else something analogous, such as we see in developed plants whose bodies support the functions of *aham* through electrical and chemical transmissions. The nervous system, or its equivalent in the plant kingdom, is required in order for the mind to think, that is, for *aham* to function. Even at the unicellular level, the instinctive mental activity that is proper to minds possessing only *citta* requires the support of the myriad forms of electrical and chemical transmission that are constantly taking place in a living cell.

This relationship between the mind and the nervous system, or its analogue in less developed life-forms, can be loosely compared to the relationship between a cellular phone and the signals it receives and transmits, waves that when decoded manifest a seemingly limitless variety of textual and audio-visual expression. The perception and transmission of those RF waves depends on the presence of a functional cell phone, with its brain-like motherboard, and a source of energy, in this case a battery with some amount of charge. In the absence of a motherboard or a charged battery the cell phone cannot function. It can neither receive nor generate text or images or sound. Likewise is the case with the microcosmic mind, which depends on a physical structure and vital energy for its operation.

After death the bodiless mind begins to circulate in search of a new body with which to continue its evolutionary journey. This is not a conscious process, however. That search is effected by *prakrti* in accordance with the *karmáshaya*, the bundle of *samskáras* that provides momentum to that bodiless mind. It is analogous to the attraction between a magnet and an iron filing. The inherent properties in each supply the motive power—in this case, those of the bodiless mind and the newly formed ovum or embryo. In the interim, the bodiless mind is incapable of thought and thus cannot experience pleasure or pain. For all intents and purposes, it has no experience until it establishes parallelism with a new physical structure. And even then, in the case of a more developed mind, there will be some lag time until that embryonic body develops to the point where it can support the activities of *aham*, ie., thought and perception.

This sutra runs contrary to popular beliefs throughout the world, beliefs that appear to have originated in ancient times to alleviate the fear of death and the unknown. The Japanese have traditionally offered prayers for their ancestors at periodic intervals so that they would not be displeased with them. The Hindu *shráddha* ceremony is meant to placate the departed soul and help it to reach heaven. The Egyptians buried utensils and personal items with their dead so they could take them with them to the afterlife, as did the Taino Indians that Columbus encountered when he first arrived in the New World. Many if not most devout Christians believe that their parents are looking down on them from heaven, and some claim to have received their help from beyond the grave, while Spiritists believe that the disincarnate mind goes to a spirit world where it keeps learning until it is ready to reincarnate. Even the Tibetan Buddhists, who belong to the Tantric tradition, have an elaborate system of rituals to help the disincarnate mind navigate the stages between death and rebirth.[33] Similarly, adherents of widely different religions believe in the possibility of communication with the dead, either on one's own or with the help of a medium.

In Anandamurti's view such ceremonies and rituals are for the living, not the dead. The beliefs on which they are based are either largely symbolic, as in the case of the Tibetan Book of the Dead and some of the Spiritist writings, or purely mythological, a comforting fantasy that can help the living cope with the challenging phenomenon of death but which has no basis in fact. Likewise, there are many phenomena associated with the dead that might lead one to believe that the bodiless mind can continue to communicate with the living or in some way make its presence felt, but such occurrences are more rightly attributed to the untapped potential of the individual causal mind.

It should be noted here, however, that not all bodies are created equal. The Tantric texts mention a rare type of being known as a *devayoni*, who upon the demise of their physical body retain the ethereal, aerial, and luminous factors, making it difficult to say whether they are alive or dead.[34] Anandamurti also refers to them as "luminous bodies." Having shed the solid and liquid factors, they are invisible to normal perception, although they can be seen under certain conditions by those with developed perceptual abilities. In the absence of solid factor they no longer have a nervous system or sensory apparatus, and thus their mental function is limited to certain psychic sensations. Nor do they have the ability to affect the world of matter. They inhabit these luminous bodies for a certain period of time in order to fulfill a particular *samskára* and then reincarnate in a physical body.

अभिभावनाच्चित्ताणुसृष्टं प्रेतदर्शनम् ॥ ६ ॥

III.6 *abhibhávanác cittáńusrśtaḿ pretadarshanam*

abhibhávanát, from concentrated thought; *cittáńu*, mind-stuff, ectoplasm; *srśtaḿ*, created; *preta*, ghost; *darshanam*, sight

"The sight of ghosts is created due to concentrated thought."

As with the afterlife and communication with the dead, the belief in ghosts is another popular transcultural belief with no objective basis in fact. If there is no mental function after death, then it naturally follows that there can be no such thing as ghosts. Nevertheless, the phenomena of ghostly apparitions has persisted since the dawn of recorded history, and in this sutra Anandamurti explains why. In short, they are figments of our imagination—which is not to dismiss them, however, since the imagination can be a very powerful instrument. Ghosts may not have any objective existence, but the experience of the person who sees one is very real.

The principal cause of such sightings is an unintended concentration of mind that lies outside the individual's control. The mind conjures the ghostly apparition out of the material of its own mental obsession, generally while under the sway of the fear *vrtti*, although other *vrttis*, such as anger, can be a contributing factor, as can hypnosis, both traditional hypnosis and self-hypnosis. It is in most cases an imposed *saḿskára* due to the influence of culture or religion, and it tends to affect weaker-minded or credulous individuals whose inborn *saḿskáras* make them particularly susceptible to the fear *vrtti*. This was especially common in medieval times when the clergy routinely planted such thoughts in the minds of the less educated populace. Such individuals become obsessed by the fear of ghosts, and due to their mental obsession they see what they are afraid of. When they say they have seen a ghost they are not lying, but what they don't realize is that their so-called ghost is a product of their own mind, what Anandamurti calls a "positive hallucination," as opposed to a negative hallucination, when we don't see something that is actually there. Strong-minded individuals who refuse to entertain such beliefs don't see ghosts, no matter how much their compatriots insist on their existence.

Anandamurti lists different grades of positive hallucination. The most common is to mistake an external object for the ghost that is hiding out in one's subconscious. In this respect he tells the following story:

> I had a certain acquaintance whose garden was quite large. One night his wife thought she saw a ghost in a corner of the garden. In Bihar, a female ghost is called *cureil* in Hindi. At the sight of the imagined ghost, she cried out in fear and fainted. She never regained consciousness and died some time later. The next night the same gentleman came out of his house at the same time.

He also thought he saw the ghost. "Why should people have to die one after the other in this way?" he thought. Stepping forward to strike at the imaginary ghost with a stick, he suddenly saw that it was nothing but a bush which, in the moonlight, looked just like a human being. His wife had died for nothing, terrified by the deceptive image of a bush. Most so-called ghosts are like this. Towards the end of the rainy season rotting vegetation often gives out a gas called marsh gas or will-o'-the-wisp, which bursts into flame when it comes in contact with oxygen. This burning gas may easily be taken to be a ghost. This is how a fear complex can develop.[35]

A less common form of positive hallucination is when the mind sees its own projection rather than mistaking a particular physical object for a ghost. Take, for example, a person spending a night alone in a house that is reputed to be haunted by the ghost of its former owner. If that person's fear propensity is strong enough, they may actually see the image that their own subconscious mind has created based on the ghost stories they have heard and a picture of the dead owner. When they tell someone the next day that they saw the ghost of the house's former occupant they are not lying, but what they saw was not an external phantom but a projection of their own thoughts that they were unable to recognize as such due to their fear. Almost invariably, such mental projections cannot be seen by others, but in certain rare cases, if the fear-born power of concentration is strong enough, that mental image may become visible to someone else.[36] Such is the power of the mind.

Anandamurti puts visions of gods and goddesses in this same category, as well as some visions of saints. The famous Marian apparitions at Lourdes and other places in the Christian world may have been of this type. Due to the power of a person's religious desire or devotional feeling and the resulting state of mental concentration, their mind outwardly projects the image and voice of the object of their devotion, even though they have no actual external or objective reality. Due to a temporary connection with the causal mind made possible by their mental elevation, such visions are often the source of clairvoyant knowledge or miraculous healings, which are then attributed to the agency of the imagined saint or god or goddess.[37]

These are all examples of external visions. Positive hallucinations can also be internal, in which case they are commonly referred to as "possession," either demonic or theophanic. It is a form of self-hypnosis in which the person becomes so absorbed in the imagined object that very little, if any, of their mind remains as the witnessing counterpart, and thus they tend to lose their sense of identity in the object of their imagination. In such types of possession or trance states, the person is generally not cognizant of their actual identity, or only vaguely so, as opposed to an external sighting where the person is aware of themselves and of the act of seeing. In such a self-hypnotic state, the person may display more knowledge and energy than their conscious mind and their body are ordinarily capable of, and they may act in ways that bear no resemblance to their normal behavior or personality.[38] They may even be capable of affecting nearby material objects with their mind, lending further credence to the supernatural cause of their possession or trance. In the case of "demonic" possession, the remedy is to try to bring the person's *kámamaya* and *manomaya kośas* back to normal functioning, which in such cases has been almost entirely lost. In such situations, both physicians and exorcists have the same goal, except that the exorcist either believes or feigns to believe that the person is possessed by some kind of spirit. The exorcist may use various techniques to try to shock the person back to their senses, filling the room with incense or the smoke of burning chilies and muttering mantras or prayers that have little or nothing to do with accomplishing their goal of "banishing" the spirit, and the physician uses other means toward the same end. In the case of theophanic trance, which is by and large viewed benignly by those present, the person naturally recovers their normal mental functioning after some time and in many cases has no recollection of what they said or did while they were in the hallucinatory trance state. The phenomenon of channeling or mediumship fits into this category.

According to Anandamurti, one of the reasons for the continued prevalence of the fear of ghosts—which arose in primitive times due to humanity's fear of death and the unknown—is that the clergy of different religions have purposely kept this belief alive, both in the West and the East. This has allowed them to play on people's fears and to earn money and prestige through the practice of exorcism.[39] Frightening children with ghost stories or letting them watch horror movies also helps to perpetuate this superstition. Children are more susceptible to the fear complex and hence this practice should be avoided. For the great majority of adults, however, who neither believe in ghosts nor will ever see one, ghost stories can be a harmless form of entertainment, and they can even be instructive for children if they are composed in a way that highlights their fanciful nature. Anandamurti composed a number of ghost stories for this purpose, both for children and for adults. The following is an excerpt from a story for older children:

Tarun Kumar said, "Who are you, brother?"
"I'm the chief ghost."
Tarun asked, "Is there anything I can do for you? You should know that I'm a medical student. Things like dead bodies and skeletons don't frighten me at all. And anyway, I don't believe in ghosts."
The ghost replied, "That may be, but you can see me, can't you?"
Tarun replied, "This is nothing but an optical illusion."
"Look here, Tarun," retorted the chief ghost, "it's no use arguing. I will do what I came to do. Other children would have fainted by now, but you are still conversing with me. I cannot but admire such strength of mind. However, I won't leave this place until I've frightened you."[40]

In India, *avidyá* Tantrics, practitioners of the lefthand path, have been know to use their occult powers to frighten people into thinking that a certain house or a certain place is haunted. They use their mental force to make objects move, seemingly on their own, thus scaring the inhabitants into thinking that a ghost is at work. In such cases Anandamurti recommends that we search the nearby area until we find the *avidyá* Tantric, who will normally be sitting in a trance state. Shake him out of his trance and the problem will vanish. Such powers do not work at a long distance, one or two hundred meters at most.

हितैषणाप्रेषितो ऽपवर्गः ॥ ७ ॥

III.7 *hitaeśaṅāpreśito 'pavargaḥ*

hita, welfare; *eśaṅā*, desire, longing; *preśitaḥ*, guided, sent; *apavargaḥ*, requital or completion of an action, emancipation

"The requital of action is guided by
the divine wish of welfare."

This is the third of three sutras on the subject of *saṁskāra*. Sutras II.19 and III.4 examined how *saṁskāra* works: the mechanism of *karmaphalabhoga* in sutra II.19, through which the *citta* regains its original, undistorted state; and the role that *saṁskāra* plays in determining our psychic makeup and the unfolding of our destiny in sutra III.4. This sutra examines the "why" of *saṁskāra*, and as with everything else in the universe, it is a case of perfect design.

There is within us a thirst for limitlessness, a longing that ultimately can only be satisfied by attaining Brahma. We all have many different desires, a seemingly endless stream of them, but these constantly changing desires are all subsumed in the conscious or unconscious quest for the Infinite. This is the view from the microcosm. The Macrocosm, by contrast, has only one desire: the liberation of all, the gradual release of consciousness from the bondage of *prakrti* through the locus of the individual living being. From the macrocosmic point of view, everything that happens in the universe is subservient to that divine wish of welfare. Every rising and falling wave in the flow of *pratisaiṇcara* is designed to bring that cosmic desire to fruition, and thus everything that befalls the individual living being follows the dictates of that unipurposive and supremely intelligent design. That includes, perforce, suffering and pain, no matter how cruel or unwarranted it may seem from where we are standing.

At the heart of this universal design is the law of action and reaction, which at the microcosmic level is expressed through the mechanism of *saṁskāra*, the requital of action, known as *aparvarga* in its completed form. Selfish or unjust actions generate painful reactions and benevolent actions generate pleasurable reactions, both of which teach us to act with benevolence and compassion. We all try to avoid suffering and we are all running after happiness. This is our dharma, our innate nature. And thus, in time, we learn to avoid those actions that cause us suffering and to cultivate those actions that increase our sense of happiness and well-being, and this aspect of the universal design leads us toward the Infinite.

While we all have an innate understanding of this, that understanding tends to remain largely unconscious during the initial stages of the journey, for the chain of cause and effect is so subtle and goes so far back that it is often nigh on impossible to see the cause behind the effect. We learn very quickly not to put our hand in fire because the pain is immediate, but it takes time to learn to avoid selfish or unjust thoughts and actions because we generally don't experience the backlash of the negative *saṁskāras* they leave in their wake until much later, and that "much later" may not be until the next life. In such cases, we have no way of seeing the link between the original action and its reaction. If the reaction were immediate, everyone would avoid selfish or unjust actions, and the drama of spiritual evolution would become simplistic. It would be a far easier road to liberation and thus far less entertaining—both for the Macrocosm and the microcosm. Instead, we have to slowly figure it out. It takes time—lifetimes, in fact—to see that actions that bring us egocentric pleasure in the short run lead to suffering in the long run, while altruistic actions, which may involve sacrifice or hardship in the short run, lead to happiness in the long run. But eventually we do figure it out. We may make the same mistake over and over again, but eventually we get the message, and as our compassion grows we begin to take great pains to avoid selfish actions and mean thoughts, recognizing the harm they may cause others and knowing that they will sabotage our spiritual progress. In the advanced stages of human growth, this knowledge illuminates everything we do.

Before we reach this point, however, the evolutionary journey can be compared to walking blindfold down a path bordered by stone walls on either side. Invariably we veer off course, slam into the wall on one side and then start heading in the other direction, until we collide with the other wall and once again have to correct our course. Gradually those deviations become smaller and smaller, until we learn to walk the time-honored straight and narrow. In the grand sweep of things, this understanding of *saṁskára* answers the age-old question of why there is suffering and pain in the world. The hardships and tragedies we face are the stone walls that serve to shunt us down the evolutionary path. Suffering has a divine purpose, just as everything has a divine purpose, and that purpose is to lead us to the path of welfare, the path of spiritual liberation.

This realization effectively eliminates the victim psychology from which so many people suffer and which only serves to debilitate the mind. "Why me? It's not fair. What did I do to deserve this?" The painful occurrences in our lives may very well be unjust from an external point of view—many things in life are—but they are not undeserved. If we understand the play of *saṁskára* then we know why they happen—they are payment for our past actions that has come due. This recognition allows us to take responsibility for our lives, not only for our actions but for our circumstances as well. I may not remember or quite understand how I got myself into this existential predicament, but I know that in a very real sense it is nobody's fault but my own. And if I got myself into this predicament then I can also get myself out, because just as I was the architect of my present, I am also the architect of my future. We cannot escape the consequences of our previous actions, but we can face them, and in the process we can use our present actions to build our future, one right action at a time.

As we learn this spiritual truth in our individual lives, we begin to see it playing out in the world around us. There is great tragedy and great suffering in the world, and as compassionate, spiritually aware beings, we must do everything we can to alleviate the suffering of others, be it physical, mental, or spiritual, knowing that compassionate action is a hallmark of the spiritual path, a magical talisman without which the doors to liberation cannot open, but at the same time we are also able to see the divine purpose behind the play of *saṁskára*. Death is not an end but a transition to the next stage of the journey. Suffering is often difficult to bear, but suffering is temporary while bliss is eternal. We may know this intellectually through the study of philosophy, but we can only assimilate this truth through experience, by gradually developing the capacity to recognize the divine hand at work in the greatest of tragedies—even as we fight to prevent them, knowing that we are instruments of Providence in the universal journey toward liberation.

The final liberation of consciousness, however, cannot be attained solely through benevolent actions and compassionate thoughts and feelings. Good actions also create *saṁskáras*, and while those *saṁskáras* generate good reactions, good reactions are also a form of bondage. By exhausting our negative *saṁskáras* and cultivating positive ones, we can greatly accelerate our spiritual progress, but in the final stages of the journey, chains of gold bind as tightly as chains of iron. The mind must be freed from all reactions and all conditioning in order to merge into Consciousness. In this sense, liberation is synonymous with the exhaustion of one's *saṁskáras*, which is why *apavarga* also means "emancipation." It is *saṁskára* that binds the mind, and thus freedom means freedom from *saṁskára*, good or bad.

How then can we learn to act without generating new *saṁskáras*, even as we burn the old ones? The secret lies in the sense of agency. If we can learn to act without involving our ego, then such actions do not generate *saṁskáras*, since only actions initiated by the *aham*, by our sense of individuality, generate *saṁskáras*. The principal means of doing this is by surrendering one's sense of authorship to the Divine, by cultivating the feeling that the Divine Consciousness is working through us, that we are instruments in its hands. When the sense of ego disappears through this increasing identification with the Supreme, no new *saṁskáras* are created and all such actions will be in perfect harmony with the divine will. This practice is called *madhuvidya* in Sanskrit, "honey knowledge."

> While doing one's duties properly with the application of *madhuvidya* one can achieve permanent cessation of afflictions from this relative world. Then all the entities of this world will be as sweet as honey for the spiritual aspirant.[41]
>
> — Anandamurti

This is an ancient practice in the yogic tradition whose spirit has been summed up in one of the most famous verses from the Bhagavad Gita:

> *brahmárpanaṁ brahmahavir brahmágnao brahmańáhutam;*
> *brahmaeva tena gantavyaṁ brahmakarma samádhiná.*[42]

> The act of offering is Brahma, the offering is Brahma, the one to whom the offering is made is Brahma, the one who offers is Brahma. One will merge in Brahma after completing the work of Brahma.

मुक्त्याकाङ्क्षया सद्गुरुप्राप्तिः ॥ ८ ॥

III.8 *muktyákáuṇkśayá sadgurupráptih*

mukti, liberation; *ákáuṇkśayá*, by longing or yearning; *sadguru*, perfect spiritual master; *práptih*, acquisition, attainment

"Due to the longing for liberation, one gets the *sadguru*."

"When the disciple is ready the master appears" is a venerable saying in the yogic tradition. Here Anandamurti rephrases this time-honored adage in order to articulate what it means to be ready, to underscore the motive force that signals the coming of the guru in the life of a spiritual seeker. That motive force is the desire for liberation. Once that longing becomes strong enough, it presages the coming of the spiritual master in one form or another, for this is part of the universal design.

> There is no need to search for a *sadguru* in the forest or jungle. How then can the *sadguru* be found? Since the purpose of Saguńa Brahma in manifesting the creation is to liberate each of its microcosms, if it truly wants to liberate them, will it not have to appear before them in the form of the *sadguru*? Another name for this true desire for liberation is "the time has come." One whose time has not come, or whose desire for liberation has not truly matured, will never encounter the *sadguru*. And

for one whose time has come, who has a true desire for
liberation, the *sadguru* will appear before them no matter
where they are. If this were not so then the purpose of
the creation would not be fulfilled and it would become
the source of the living being's bondage. Thus I say that
there is no need to waste one's time searching here and
there, in the forest or jungle; the only necessity is an
intense desire for liberation.[43]

—Anandamurti

The use of the word *ákáuṅkṣá*, rather than more common but less emphatic Sanskrit synonyms for "desire," lays the stress on the intensity of one's longing. The nineteenth-century sage Sri Ramakrishna used to tell a story about a disciple who asked his master how he could attain God. The master brought him to a pond and without any warning held his head under the water. When he finally released him, the terrified disciple was gasping for breath. "When you want God as much as you wanted that next breath," the master told him, "then you'll know that you are close to attaining him."

The following is a more contemporary rendering of the same idea from Sri Nisargadatta:

> The desire to find the Self will be surely fulfilled, provided you want nothing else. But you must be honest with yourself and really want nothing else. If in the meantime you want many other things and are engaged in their pursuit, your main purpose may be delayed until you grow wiser and cease being torn between contradictory urges.[44]

This is true in the beginning of the spiritual journey, it is true in the middle, and it is true in the end. The more one's spiritual desire grows, the less it is diluted by the presence of other, contradictory desires, the faster one progresses, which eventually leads to the appearance of the *sadguru* in the aspirant's life. When this desire becomes all consuming, it carries the spiritual aspirant to liberation under the guidance of the guru. Indeed, desire is the motive force behind all our actions. The four fundamental propensities of living beings are physical desire (*káma*), psychic desire (*artha*), psycho-spiritual desire (dharma), and spiritual desire (*mokśa*). When dharma awakens in the human being they begin their spiritual search, and when *mokśa* awakens they seek their final liberation in earnest. Desire is thus the barometer of our sincerity and the truest indication of our readiness. Hence, rather than go looking for a guru, a spiritual seeker would be better served to cultivate their desire for liberation, which can be done by developing a fondness for spiritual pursuits. While some people hesitate to adopt the spiritual path for fear of what they will have to give up, Anandamurti tells us that we need not abandon anything. If we consciously cultivate subtler pursuits, our cruder desires will naturally fall away because subtler pursuits are more fulfilling. They may be more difficult to appreciate at first, due to their subtlety, but once we develop a taste for spiritual pursuits we discover that the satisfaction they give us is deeper and longer lasting. Doing spiritual practices, listening to spiritual discourses and spiritual music, studying spiritual teachings—these all conspire to elevate the mind and deepen our desire for liberation.

The word *guru* means "dispeller of darkness" (*gu* means "darkness"; *ru* means "dispeller"), and the word *sat* means "true." Thus *sadguru* means "true guru," one who is fully established in Supreme Consciousness. Implicit in this sutra is the idea that in order to achieve liberation a *sadguru* is necessary. Not all spiritual traditions agree on this point, but the fundamental importance of the guru is a key component of Tantra. While it is considered possible in Tantra, at least in theory, to reach the stage of *savikalpa* samadhi through one's individual efforts, the final leap from *savikalpa* to *nirvikalpa*, from *saguńa* to *nirguńa*, can only be effected through the medium or intercession of a *sadguru*. Anandamurti compares the disciple's predicament to that of a prisoner in a cell. Only someone who is outside the cell and in possession of the key can liberate the disciple from their imprisonment.[45] That person must themselves be free, and it is in this sense that the word *sadguru* is used. A *sadguru* is one who has achieved emancipation or enlightenment but who has taken a human form again for a predetermined period of time in order to help those in bondage attain the liberated state.⁴⁶ Hence a *sadguru* is free from the bondage of *prakrti*, though their body remains subject to the influence of the *guñas* for as long as they maintain their physical form. When they leave their body they return to the supreme unqualified state. In effect, the *sadguru* is the mechanism through which the Cosmic Mind frees the microcosm from the final chains of *prakrti*, thereby enabling the spiritual aspirant to complete the journey of spiritual evolution.

> At the root of *dhyána* (meditation) is the form of the guru; at the root of *puja* (worship) is the feet of the guru; at the root of the *mantra* is the word of the guru; and at the root of all liberation is the grace of the guru.⁴⁷
>
> — Kularnava Tantra

ब्रह्मैव गुरुरेको नापरः ॥ ९ ॥

III.9 *brahmaeva gurur eko náparah*

brahma, Supreme Consciousness; *eva*, only; *guru*, preceptor; *ekah*, one; *na*, no; *aparah*, other

"Brahma alone is the guru, none other.

The form of the guru exists for a reason, a very important reason, and it is natural and even healthy to get attached to the guru's form, since it is with the help of that form that we are able to complete the spiritual journey. But we must not mistake the form for the guru. That is, we must not limit the guru to that form, even if only subconsciously. Saguña Brahma, the author and architect of the creation, has been leading each individual being down the pathways of spiritual evolution through different forms and different mediums, and it is Saguña Brahma that appears in the form of the guru when the disciple's desire for liberation becomes sufficiently intense. When the human being reaches the stage where they are ready to complete the spiritual journey, the Macrocosm uses a specific vehicle to guide them to their final liberation. It is through that vehicle or that form that Saguña Brahma communicates the all-important teachings that the disciple will need in order to circumvent the countless obstacles that lay ahead as they direct their mind toward Consciousness. It is through that form that the aspirant receives the inspiration and guidance required to continue moving forward. And it is through that form that the devotee develops devotion, the all-consuming love for the Supreme without which the journey cannot be completed. Thus the guru is in effect a channel, a pure, unobstructed channel through which Saguña Brahma operates in the world of form.

That form is necessary because Brahma in its unqualified, *nirguña* state is beyond the mind's capacity to comprehend. It is formless and infinite, and the mind can neither perceive nor conceive of the formless and the infinite. Nor can that infinite Consciousness in its *nirguña* state communicate with living beings trapped within the world of form. In order to teach, guide, and inspire spiritual aspirants as they reach the final stages of their evolutionary journey, that infinite Consciousness must manifest itself in the world of form, and the form it adopts is the boat that carries the spiritual aspirant across the ocean of becoming and into the formless.

Imagine being confined in a room with no windows or doors. No light can enter and there appears to be no escape. Such is the human condition when the soul cries out for freedom. Suddenly, when our longing becomes sufficiently intense, a window opens, illumining our hitherto darkened existence. The freedom that lies just beyond those walls is suddenly in sight, and it is through that window that we can reach it. The light of Consciousness is everywhere, shining on and within every particle of the creation, but we can't see it, we can't experience it, we can't comprehend it due to the walls of our ego-prison—until a window opens that allows that light to come streaming in. It is that hitherto unseen and unimagined light, the light of Consciousness, that illumines our minds and guides us along the path, but it needs a medium through which to reach us, a medium that our minds can apprehend, a window that opens into the world of form. That window is the guru. What is a window, after all, but a transparent space through which light can shine. And just as the windows in many buildings serve as emergency exits, it is also an exit from the world of form that enables us to enter the formless.

Once Ram Dass was seated across the temple courtyard from his master, Neem Karoli Baba, who was surrounded by disciples massaging his feet and laughing and talking with him. Suddenly it appeared to Ram Dass as if he were watching a tableau, and at that moment he realized that his relationship with his guru was beyond time and space. *I don't need to be with him physically,* he thought. *In fact, it wouldn't really matter if I never saw him again.* At that very instant he saw the master turn and whisper something to an old Indian disciple. That man then rushed across the courtyard, touched Ram Dass's feet, and said: "Maharajji told me to come over and touch your feet. Maharajji said, 'Ram Dass and I understand each other perfectly.'" At that very moment," Ram Dass writes, "I knew that Maharajji had freed me from attachment to his form."[48]

It is our sense of individuality that prevents the light of Consciousness from fully manifesting in our minds, but in a liberated master there is no individuality to block the light. It is like an empty shirt on a clothesline. When the wind blows, the shirt dances on the line and it looks like there is someone inside, but what makes the shirt move is the wind. In the case of a realized master, it is the wind of Brahma, acting directly in the world of form, that animates that living body. It is the breath of Krishna blowing through the flute of the guru that fills the world with music.

> Thus in the spiritual world *parama puruśa* will have to appear, through the medium of the name and form of the guru, before those individuals who desire liberation. And when human beings properly receive the secret hints of the path from *parama puruśa*, they permanently establish themselves in their supreme goal, immortality. This is the final chapter in their prolonged peregrination; they henceforth attain the transcendental state beyond pleasure and pain.[49]

When seen in this light, there is no difference between God and the guru, and it is for this reason that the guru is so revered in Tantra.

बाधा सा जुषमाणा शक्तिः सेव्यं स्थापयति लक्ष्ये ॥ १० ॥

III.10 *bádhá sá juśamáná shaktih sevyaṁ sthápayati lakśye*

bádhá, obstacle; *sá*, that, she; *juśamáná*, helping; *shaktih*, force; *sevyaṁ*, the one who is being helped; *sthápayati*, establishes; *lakśye*, in the goal

> "Obstacles are the helping force that establishes one in the goal."

Progress in the spiritual sphere, as in all spheres, is a product of effort, and because the obstacles that appear in our path force us to make efforts to overcome them, they are our friends, not our enemies. They stimulate our growth and enable us to advance step by step toward the goal of spiritual emancipation, and thus we owe them an enduring debt. It is due to the struggle for survival that we have been able to climb the ladder of evolution and attain a human body, and it is due to the myriad struggles of human life that our mind evolves to the point that we seek out the spiritual path and begin the practices that will enable us to complete the journey of incarnate existence. For this reason, obstacles are not only welcomed in the Tantric tradition but are sought after in order to accelerate our growth.

This is a principle we are accustomed to in our daily lives, even if we haven't thought about it in these terms. We know that if we want to get in shape, we have to take on the challenge of overcoming inertia. We have to exercise. And so we go into the gym and pit our muscles against the weights, or against themselves and against gravity. It isn't easy and it often isn't pleasant. It demands a lot of effort, a lot of sweat, and afterward our muscles ache. But we do it because we want to get stronger and more physically fit, and we know this won't happen unless we pit our muscles against sufficient resistance. The weights are an obstacle, gravity is an obstacle, our own internal inertia is an obstacle, and without those obstacles we won't reach our goal of building muscle mass and improving our fitness.

The same principle holds in the psycho-physical realm. It is a maxim in the martial arts that in order to become an adept we have to hone our skills under match conditions against a worthy adversary. The better our opponent, the better it forces us to become. Without that worthy adversary it is nigh on impossible to reach our full potential. This is well known to sports enthusiasts at all levels, both in team and individual sports, which is why those athletes and teams who are intent on improving try to schedule better competition.

We see the same dynamic at work in the psychic realm. If we want to become mentally stronger we have to exercise our minds and navigate the obstacles that invariably present themselves. If a student is placed in a scholastic environment with more accomplished students, it forces them to expand their intellectual horizons in order to keep up, which is why so many parents hope their children will gain admittance to the best schools, where they will be forced to work harder and thereby reach a higher intellectual standard. The same is true in the arts. The jazz tradition has long been famous for after-hours jam sessions where the musicians pit their creative talents against each other, struggling to out-improvise their opponent. As the art form developed, they began to purposely compose tunes with difficult chord changes and fast tempos to force themselves to think faster, to create more quickly, which in turn improved their capacity for invention. The challenge is what made so many of them virtuosos, and jazz musicians often talk about these jam-session competitions as the training ground that unlocked their inborn talents. Nor are such informal competitions unique to jazz improvisation. There are numerous stories of classical musicians doing the same. Johann Sebastian Bach, arguably the greatest composer of European classical music, used to travel incognito in eighteenth-century Germany to pit his improvisational skills against local church organists. Similarly, composers have always had to continually develop their compositional skills to beat out other composers for lucrative contracts or prestigious positions, and the same is true for artists working in other art forms. The challenge forces them to become better artists. For this same reason, artists in different mediums have recognized that restrictions of form, such as the difficult demands of the traditional sonnet, force the artist to summon greater creative power in order to overcome the challenges that the prescribed form presents.

Anybody who wants to achieve success in any field needs such challenges; otherwise, they will not be able to maximize their potential. Is it any wonder then that the same applies to the spiritual sphere? The three causes of spiritual evolution, as previously discussed, are physical, mental, and spiritual clash, and without an obstacle there can be no clash. Oftentimes people measure the quality of their meditation by the peaceful or ecstatic feelings they experience, but such experiences are generally the fruit of earlier efforts. From the standpoint of spiritual evolution, the best meditation is that meditation in which we put forth the most effort to control our unruly minds. And that is hard work, like lifting weights or struggling to overcome a literary or musical challenge. Even spiritual clash, the attraction of the Great, manifests as the distress that stems from our sense of separation from the Supreme, the disquieting sense that there must be more to life. It is that sense of disquiet that drives us to end that separation through the quest for spiritual liberation. In this case, the sense of separation or disquiet is the obstacle.

Fortunately the universe is designed so that there is no shortage of obstacles. They are provided for us every step of the way. Wherever we go we meet with resistance. If we want to move forward we have to overcome inertia, we have to overcome air resistance, we have to overcome gravity. And the faster we move, the greater the resistance we encounter. If we stick out our arm while walking, we barely feel the breeze; if we stick it out from a car moving at 100 kmh, however, the resistance causes our muscles to tense to keep our arm steady; and if we stick it out of a plane window at 1000 kmh (a hundred times the force, since wind resistance goes up by the square of velocity), we may break our arm. The *tamoguña* force of *prakrti* is constantly working to bind consciousness. If we are to expand our minds, then we have to expend effort to combat that force, and the faster we grow, the more effort is required due to the increased resistance, which in turn accelerates our progress even further. For this reason, it is commonly observed that when people take to spiritual practice in earnest, the challenges they face in their lives increase considerably. This is considered a good sign in Tantra, an indication that the aspirant is making significant progress.[50] Thus Tantra symbolizes the spiritual journey as a great battle, the *sádhaná samara*, an ongoing war against the most worthy of all adversaries: maya or *prakrti*.[51] And in this *sádhaná samara* the obstacles we face, which seem to be our opponents, are in fact our allies, for without them we could not reach the goal.

In his book *The Art of Happiness*, the Dalai Lama has this to say about those we commonly consider our enemies:

> "In fact, the enemy is the necessary condition for practicing patience. Without an enemy's action, there is no possibility for patience or tolerance to arise. Our friends do not ordinarily test us and provide the opportunity to cultivate patience; only our enemies do this. So, from this standpoint we can consider our enemy as a great teacher, and revere them for giving us this precious opportunity to practice patience."[52]

The word "sadhana," which is normally used as a synonym for "meditation" or "spiritual practice," literally means "the effort to complete." Regarding the spirit of sadhana in Tantra, Anandamurti has this to say:

> It is impossible to conquer crudeness and replace it with subtlety without a fight. Hence, Tantra is not only a fight, it is an all-around fight. It is not only an external or internal fight, it is simultaneously both, that is, in the same yoga one must fight both ways. The internal fight is Tantra's subtle portion and the external fight is its crude portion.[53]

This emphasis on strenuous effort is in stark contrast to some modern schools of spiritual practice or spiritual philosophy, which insist that higher spiritual attainment can only be reached by abandoning all effort. It is their contention that since effort is a product of the ego, it cannot lead to liberation, a teaching that has its roots in Advaita Vedanta. This approach to spiritual practice, however, is not accepted either by Tantra or by yoga, since one's accumulated *saṁskáras* must be exhausted before one can attain final liberation, and they cannot be exhausted without continuous, determined effort, the *abhyása* that is so emphasized in the Bhagavad Gita and Patanjali's Yoga Sutras.

प्रार्थनार्चनामात्रमेव भ्रममूलम् ॥ ११ ॥

III.11 *prárthanárcanámátram eva bhramamúlam*

prárthaná, prayer; *arcaná*, ritualistic worship; *mátram eva*, and such, each and every; *bhrama*, confusion; *múlam*, rooted

"Prayer and ritualistic worship are rooted in confusion."

As a lead-in to the sutra on what is ultimately the last word in spiritual practice—devotion—Anandamurti takes a look at what mistakingly passes for devotion: prayer and external or ritualistic worship. Rather than being practices that promote the expansion of consciousness, thus leading the aspirant toward the ultimate goal of union with the Supreme, they create confusion in the mind and serve no beneficial purpose, either spiritual or mundane.

The most common form of prayer, regardless of religion, involves asking God for something or else harbors some hidden expectation of divine favor. Consciously or subconsciously, the person wants something, and what they desire is not to transcend the ego but something that perpetuates its existence. Such a desire is an expression of ignorance or confusion. It does no good to ask God for something, Anandamurti tells us, because God already knows exactly what each and every living being needs and he is providing it at every moment. The Macrocosmic Mind, the architect of this creation, is guiding the microcosms along the path to their eventual liberation, providing the exact environment and experiences they need at each step along the way. How can an individual human being, with their limited microcosmic mind, truly know what is best for them or for anyone else? Whether we realize it or not, when we ask Providence to do something for us or for others, we are in effect telling the Divine Provider that we know better than him what he should do. If we find ourselves in dire financial straights and pray to the Lord to help us attain the prosperity we desire, we are, at least at a subconscious level, implying that he has unjustly deprived us of the finances we need. We are in effect accusing him of partiality, and in the process we are strengthening the ego.[54]

This is a common mentality in the religious traditions of our planet—rather, the predominant mentality, regardless of religion or culture. How often do people thank the Lord in their prayers for their poverty or their sickness or their suffering? How often do they thank Providence for giving them exactly what they need, when what they get is not what they desire? Consciously or subconsciously, the person who prays for something wants to escape the consequences of their actions, since it is their own actions that have placed them in that predicament. But since everything in this universe is bound to the law of cause and effect, there is no escape from one's *saṁskáras* and thus no real point to such prayers, which do little more than muddle the mind.

Anandamurti classifies the different grades of devotion according to the nature of the object of ideation. Prayers and ritualistic worship are examples of inferior devotion, because along with the thought of God the mind harbors other desires. Inferior devotion is further subdivided into *támasikii*, *rájasikii*, and *sáttvikii* bhakti.[55] If the nature of the desire is static, such as praying to God to harm one's enemies, then it is considered *támasikii* bhakti. If the desire is mutative, such as praying to God for prosperity or success, then it is *rájasikii* bhakti. And if the desire is sentient, such as praying for salvation, then it is *sáttvikii* bhakti. Asking for favors can be entirely altruistic, and thus an example of *sáttvikii* or sentient bhakti, and yet still generate confusion about the spiritual nature of existence. There are prayer circles, for instance, where people get together to pray for a sick parishioner or to avert an impending social calamity, and there are studies that attempt to show that such collective prayers have a demonstrable effect. Regardless of what we may think of the scientific validity of these studies, there is no question of God altering the laws of the universe on behalf of that person or persons—their fate is entirely dependent on their individual or collective *saṁskáras* (at best we can say that the mental energy directed toward them may be one element in the fruition of those *saṁskáras*)—and any appeal to God to alter the laws of *prakrti* betrays a certain ignorance or confusion about the nature of those laws, as well as a lack of faith in the designs of Providence.

Hymns of praise or otherwise eulogizing the Supreme are similar in that they generally reflect a hidden or subconscious desire to please God so that he might be merciful—if the Supreme Being is happy with our worship then he is bound to be kind to us. In essence, this is a kind of flattery and is equally ineffective.[56] Moreover, adulation implies a sense of separation and tends to reinforce a feeling of distance. We don't express adulation for those we feel closest to. Songs of praise or eulogy are markedly different from devotional songs and poems that express intimacy rather than adulation and which do not contain any hidden desire or expectation that the Lord will bestow his mercy on us. Rather than praise, they express devotional sentiment—one's love for the Supreme—and sometimes contain evocative descriptions of the qualities of the Divine, as we might admire or appreciate the qualities of a loved one. Even then, the great Indian poet Padmadanta lamented the impossibility of describing the Supreme in the following verse:

> If the ink tablet were as big as the Himalayas, and the ink pot as large as the oceans; and if one of the branches of the divine *párijáta* tree was used as a pen, and if the Earth's lithosphere were used as a sheet of paper; and if Sarada, the goddess of learning, agreed to write through all the ages, even then, O Lord, your qualities could never be described.

Real devotion, as we will examine in the next sutra, is rooted in surrender.

> At a time of great difficulty, when agony swells people's hearts and they are unable to restrain themselves, the

sufferers should say only one thing to Parama Puruśa: "O my Parama Puruśa, the life of my life, the pupil of my eyes—give me the strength to endure."[57]

— Anandamurti

There is, however, one caveat that bears mentioning. While philosophy teaches that there is no escape from the law of cause and effect, devotees throughout history have insisted that their Lord never fails them in times of need. Since time immemorial, they have made a practice of asking for the Lord's help. "If I don't ask for the Lord's help," they say, "whom am I going to ask?" This apparent contradiction is easily resolved, however. It is part of the devotional strategy, and while it may sometimes seem at loggerheads with philosophy, the devotee is wiser than the logician. The devotee purposely relies on the Supreme at every step because it deepens and enriches the intimacy of the devotional relationship, and nowhere is this more in evidence than in times of great need or great difficulty, when the soul grows acutely aware that its fate is in cosmic hands. It may be while entering labor, standing before a judge, being prepped for surgery, or waiting for the results of a biopsy—in times of crisis the devotee turns their mind toward the Lord with all the power of their heart. They ask him to watch over them as they enter the mouth of the dragon, placing their trust in him like a very young child places their trust in their mother, knowing that whatever happens, his sure and loving hand will guide them safely through—even if that means guiding them safely into the next life.

The real benefit of this kind of thinking is not that it may in some way influence the outcome—the devotee knows that the outcome depends on *samskára* and divine will. The real benefit is that it helps us to focus our mind on Brahma, and that speeds our spiritual progress. By means of this internal conversation, we cultivate our personal relationship with the Divine, and the development of that personal relationship is the key factor in developing devotion, the subject of the next sutra.

भक्तिर्भगवद्भावना न स्तुतिनार्चना ॥ १२ ॥

III.12 *bhaktir bhagavadbhávaná na stutir nárcaná*

bhakti, devotion; *bhagavat*, God; *bhávaná*, ideation, contemplation, thought, meditation; *na*, no, not; *stuti*, praise; *arcaná*, external worship

"Devotion is ideation on God, not praise or external worship."

Devotion is the subject of the final sutra in this chapter, and it is the final word in Anandamurti's spiritual teachings, for it is his contention that it is through devotion—and only through devotion—that a human being can complete their spiritual journey and attain the enlightened state. The primacy of devotion when it comes to the highest attainment of incarnate life may be called into question by the adherents of certain spiritual traditions, including some Indian traditions. The six classical Indian philosophies, for example, have little or nothing to say on the subject of devotion, and the same is true for the heterodox philosophies. Apart from the Tantras and the devotional literature of the Vaishnava tradition, nowhere in Indian philosophy has bhakti been given the primacy that Anandamurti gives it. But when the true import of devotion is understood as it is explained in this sutra, then the reason for his assertion becomes abundantly clear.

The word *bhakti* is derived from the verbal root *bhaj*, and its literal import is to withdraw the mind from the thought of the phenomenal world and direct it toward God.[58] Here Anandamurti defines devotion in the psychological language of spiritual practice: bhakti is ideation on Supreme Consciousness. When it is understood in this way, devotion does indeed become a prerequisite for the final attainment. As long as the mind remains connected with the phenomenal world, it cannot merge into Consciousness. In colloquial terms, attraction to God is bhakti, while attraction to finite objects is *asakti*. Ultimately the two are mutually exclusive. Although the mind possesses the ability to jump with astounding speed between objects of thought, giving the impression of simultaneity, it can only think of one object at a time, something that is easily demonstrated in our mental laboratory. When we are fully concentrated on one object we cannot be aware of anything else.[59] Thus any engagement of the mind with the phenomenal world without full awareness of its divine nature precludes ideation on Consciousness and hence perpetuates the bondage of *prakṛti*.[60] In order to achieve the supreme state, the mind must go beyond thought, and it can only do so by surrendering its existence to Consciousness, which in turn can only be achieved by ideating on Consciousness to the exclusion of all other thoughts. This undivided, uninterrupted ideation brings about a sense of identification with the Supreme, and it is this sense of identification that allows the last vestige of the mind, the pure I-feeling, to merge into Consciousness through the act of surrender, thereby enabling the aspirant to cross the bridge between *saguṅa* and *nirguṅa*. This is true regardless of what spiritual tradition one belongs to or what type of spiritual practice one performs. Total absorption in the thought of the Supreme is bhakti, and it is a necessary precursor to the *nirvikalpa* state.

In order to better understand the nature of this undivided and uninterrupted ideation on Supreme Consciousness, let us turn our attention to the word *bhāvanā*, translated here as "ideation." *Bhāvanā* comes from the noun *bhāva*, which means, among other things, "sentiment."[61] The relationship between the two words is not aleatory, and indeed the word *bhāvanā* has been used on occasion in Sanskrit literature to mean "devotional feeling."[62] It is for all intents and purposes impossible for the human mind to remain fixed on a single object of ideation for any sustained length of time without feeling a strong attraction to that object. If there is no sentimental force involved, the mind inevitably gravitates toward something for which it does feel a strong attraction. A mathematician can think about numbers for extended periods of time because he loves mathematics, but most of us will get bored within minutes. Before we know it, our mind will entertain images from our favorite TV series or the face of a certain someone, whatever or whomever we feel attracted to. Literally, *dhyāna*, meditation, means to direct the mind in an unbroken flow toward the *dheya*, the object of ideation, and that is impossible to sustain without the backing of sentiment or attraction. If the spiritual aspirant does not feel love for the Supreme, then the practice of meditation will not bear fruit—not the ultimate fruit, the uninterrupted, undivided bliss of the supreme state.[63]

This is something all spiritual practitioners have experienced. We try to fix our mind on Consciousness but the mind keeps running away, caught by the sentimental pull of those aspects of the phenomenal world that attract us, and thus we are unable to attain or sustain that undivided attention. Sri Ramakrishna used to say that doing spiritual practices without devotion is like trying to sail across the ocean without wind. Our only recourse is to row, and rowing for any extended period of time is incredibly hard work—we can only go so far before we tire of the effort. But when the winds of devotion rise, they fill the sails and our boat speeds across the water, seemingly without effort. Thus the Tantric teachings place paramount importance on the cultivation of devotion. Even Shankaracharya, the champion of Advaita Vedanta, admitted in his *Vivekachudamani* that devotion is the best path to *mokṣa,* supreme realization.[64] But then the great Vedantic philosopher was a practitioner of Tantra and is reputed to be the author of several Tantric texts, including the *Prapaiṇcasára Tantra, Saundarya Lahiri* (Waves of Beauty), and a commentary on the *Sri Lalita Trishati.*

The second part of this sutra, *na stutirnárcaná,* tells us what devotion is not. It is not any kind of external worship or praise of the Divine. Devotion is purely internal and it is rooted in one fundamental mental act—directing one's mind toward Supreme Consciousness—and any kind of external act is extraneous to that endeavor. A spiritual aspirant may or may not engage in external forms of worship, but in either case they cannot be equated with devotion. If an aspirant finds that they help her to concentrate her mind on the Supreme, then they can be beneficial for that aspirant, but it is that concentration of mind on the Supreme that is sought after, and ideally it should not be dependent on any external form of worship, for with the absence of the form comes the absence or weakening of the ideation. The telling of beads, the spinning of Tibetan prayer wheels, the colorful offerings of Hindu pujas, the Christian mass and other prayer services, such as matins or compline—these can all prove beneficial to the practitioners of those traditions, as long as they remember that it is not the ritual that brings them closer to the Divine but the strength of their ideation. Father Joseph de Beaufort, in a conversation with Brother Lawrence, the seventeenth-century Christian mystic and Carmelite friar, had this to say about the saint: "That with him the set times of prayer were not different from other times: that he retired to pray, according to the directions of his Superior, but that he did not want such retirement, nor ask for it, because his greatest business did not divert him from God."[65]

In a certain sense, it comes down to a simple formula: how often do we think of the Supreme, how undivided is our attention, and how strong is our attachment or attraction? From this point of view, the different practices of yoga and Tantra are all geared toward the development of devotion. And because all these practices take place within the precincts of the human mind, they are predicated on a proper understanding of the nature and limitations of human psychology. The formless *nirguńa puruśa* is beyond our powers of conceptualization and beyond the reach of our sentiment. It is beyond both the mind and the heart. Thus we have no recourse but to conceptualize that Infinite Entity in order to meditate on it, and we have no choice but to personalize that conception if we are to arouse our sentiment, to awaken the all-powerful force of love that will enable us to fix our mind with undivided attention on the *dheya*, the object of our *dhyána*.

It is an innate characteristic of the human mind that we are unable to arouse profound feelings of love for an impersonal entity or an abstract idea. If we examine our experience of worldly love, we will find that it is always tied to a personal presence, be it that of a partner, a friend, a child, a parent, or a pet. We may even have similar feelings for our native city or a work of art, but in both cases they are felt as personal presences within our mind, rather than abstract ideas, and rarely are such feelings as strong as those we have for other human beings. The same is true with bhakti. In order to think of the Infinite we must conceptualize it — the mind cannot grasp the Infinite any more than the hand can grasp air — and the act of conceptualization binds our experience of the Divine to the world of form. Whatever form we associate with the Supreme in our thoughts, it must be personalized if it is to arouse the power of love—be it the form of a spiritual master, a personal image of God the Father, or the Divine Mother in the form of Kali Ma, as was the case with Sri Ramakrishna and the great mystic poet Ram Prasad. Only then can we truly enter into an intimate relationship with the Divine and thereby plumb the depths of divine love. Love is personal—nothing can be more personal—and thus Tantra takes advantage of this facet of human psychology to direct the mind toward Brahma.

We have all experienced how easy, how natural, and how pleasurable it is to think about someone we truly love, someone to whom we are deeply attached. This is implied in the very meaning of the word "attached"—the mind remains attached or bound to the object of our affection—and the stronger that attachment or attraction, the more we think about them, drawn by the blissful experience that is love and by the sense of identification it engenders. This can even be seen in lesser attachments. A person who loves football may think about football all day long, reading the scores, watching the games, talking to their friends about it, and from this is born a sense of identification with the sport and especially with their team, with the players and their accomplishments. It is not "they" or "them" but "we" and "us." Depending on the nature of the person or object we fall in love with, that attachment or attraction may or may not be a good thing. But with bhakti, it can only end one way—in liberation.

Our personal conception of the Divine is known as *iṣṭa* in Tantra, and the practice of devotion thus depends on the flowering of the relationship between the devotee and their *iṣṭa*.[66] The closer one feels to one's *iṣṭa*, the more frequently and singlemindedly the mind dwells on its object of adoration, the closer the mind draws to its final merger. And this in turn depends on feeling the tangible personal presence of the *iṣṭa* within one's mind. This living presence of the *iṣṭa*, the personification of Consciousness within the mind of the devotee, has been fundamental to devotional practice for millennia, irrespective of spiritual or religious tradition. In Christianity, for example, the figure of Jesus Christ has been the principal *iṣṭa* of Christian devotees for the past two thousand years, and that relationship has been at the heart of the mystical experiences of a plethora of Christian saints.

In India, Krishna has been perhaps the most popular *iśt́a* over the past few millennia, and the story of Krishna's youth cited in Chapter One, when he would play his flute at night on the banks of the Yamuna River and the *gopiis* would gather around him and dance, exemplifies an important characteristic of the devotional relationship. In the heights of their ecstasy, each *gopii* would feel that they were alone with their beloved, and the next morning each of them would swear that Krishna had been dancing with them and them alone. They were not mistaken, because the relationship between a spiritual aspirant and their *iśt́a* is purely personal. Our *iśt́a* is our own personal conception of the Divine, the form that the Divine takes within our thoughts, and that presence in our mind is ours and ours alone. The Krishna that came alive in one *gopii's* mind was not the Krishna that came alive in another *gopii's* mind, for each was their own personal conception or experience of the Divine. In effect, the relationship is between the devotee and their own soul.

When our mind is focused with undivided attention on the Divine, without distractions or conflicting desires, it is known as *kevalá* bhakti in Tantra, pure devotion, or *nirguńa* bhakti, nonattributional devotion. Anandamurti divides this nonattributional devotion into two stages: *ráganugá* and *rágátmiká*. These two stages are mirrored in earthly love, where the deeper the love, the more selfless it becomes, paving the way for the total surrender of the ego. In *ráganugá* bhakti the devotee loves the Lord because it makes them happy. Their love brings them joy. In *rágátmiká* bhakti, the highest stage of devotion, the devotee loves the Lord because it makes *him* happy, because they want their love to give pleasure to their beloved. This is the apex of self-abnegation and the gateway to the merger of the aspirant's mind into Supreme Consciousness.

> For the sake of maintaining balance in the universe, there is a mutual attraction among all things; every microcosm attracts other microcosms. All of his finite expressions, the microcosms, are entitled by birth to that

universal love with which he has bound each microcosm to himself, to the wave of that universal love in which his divine ocean of bliss is perennially flowing. Attraction is the innate characteristic of living beings. When this attraction is limited to finite entities, we call it *kámá*, and when it rushes toward the Great, we call it *prema*. Of course, it must be acknowledged that *kámá* is nothing but a limited form of *prema*. When living beings, drawn by *prema*, rush towards Parama Puruśa, it is termed "devotion."[67]

— Anandamurti

Chapter Four

In Chapter One of *Ananda Sutram*, Anandamurti describes the cycle of creation. In this chapter he looks specifically at how the creation arises, an explanation that is by and large lacking in the philosophical tradition that predates *Ananda Sutram*. Samkhya, on which the other five classical systems of Indian philosophy base their cosmology, details the various phases of the creation, which it enumerates into different *tattvas*, and describes *prakrti* prior to the state of manifestation, but it does not specifically address the genesis of the creation. The extant Tantras go one step further in the doctrine of *ábhása*, dividing the stages of cosmic manifestation into *kalá, náda,* and *bindu* and laying emphasis on causal stress as the root cause,[1] but apart from this, the genesis of the creation is not directly addressed. In this chapter Anandamurti addresses these lacunas and follows through to their logical conclusion with two sutras on kundalini, concluding what is the most abstract of the five chapters of *Ananda Sutram*.

त्रिगुणात्मिका सृष्टिमातृकाशेषत्रिकोणधारा ॥ १ ॥

IV.1 *triguńátmiká srśtimátrkáshesátrikońadhárá*

triguńa, three *guńas*; *átmiká*, composed of; *srśti*, creation; *mátrká*, mother, matrix; *asheśa*, endless; *trikońa*, triangle; *dhárá*, flow

"The causal matrix, composed of the three *guńas*, is an endless flow of triangular forms."

The creative principle, *prakrti*, is active in both Saguńa and Nirguńa Brahma. The principal difference between the two is that in Nirguńa Brahma the three *guńas* of *prakrti* remain in a balanced state and are thus unable to bind or influence Consciousness. This balanced state is represented by the triangle, the most stable of all geometric forms. Nirguńa Brahma is beyond the mind, and the mind cannot have knowledge of a state in which it does not exist (though a glimpse of that reality can be intuited by the mind when it comes out of the *nirvikalpa* state). Hence this sutra and the two that follow are a psychic representation of a state that exists outside the purview of the mind. Being a psychic representation, it is subject to the limitations of language, and in this context, the language of mathematics is the language best suited to understanding the interaction between the three principles of *prakrti* prior to their manifestation, the closest approximation possible to what is ultimately beyond the mind's power of conception.

The power of the language of mathematics to describe the functioning of *prakrti* at the cosmic level—that is, to describe the fundamental laws that govern the functioning of the material universe—was intuited by the ancient Greek philosophers and scientists, such as Democritus and Pythagoras, as well as by their ancient Indian counterparts, such as Kanada, and those ancient intuitions have matured into the complex equations of contemporary physics by which our modern physicists seek to symbolize the universal laws that govern our material existence. Kepler's laws of planetary motion, which revolutionized the world of astronomy and which Newton built upon to derive his laws of motion; Maxwell's equations, which laid the foundation for classical electromagnetism and thus paved the way for our modern radio, electrical, and optical technologies; Einstein's equations, beginning with his iconic $E=MC^2$, which radically changed the way in which we understand the universe; the equations of quantum mechanics, which made possible our semiconductors and computers, our lasers and molecular chemistry and biology; the ever-evolving equations of quantum gravity with their promise of the future—the deepest intuitions of our modern physicists have crystallized in the one language that best describes how the universe of *saińcara* works: the language of mathematics.[2] And thus it is also the one language best suited to describe the genesis of the creation—specifically, that visual representation of universal law known as "geometry" — even though that genesis lies beyond the reach of any language.

The trivalent *prakrti* represents the kinetic potential of Consciousness and is thus the causal matrix, the mother of creation. That kinetic, self-creative power can be quiescent or manifest, latent or active, but in whichever condition it exists it is always present, the eternal power of an eternal infinite Consciousness. In the unmanifest state, the three *guṅas* flow haphazardly in an endless linear fashion that leads them, in the symbolic language used in this sutra, to combine and recombine into different geometric shapes with innumerable sides. In this state, *prakrti* is *anucchūnyā*, latent, while *puruṣa* is *nirguṅa*, objectless and subjectless. Imagine an ocean of Consciousness in which there are an infinite number of underwater currents. As they flow in different directions they are constantly intersecting each other, and as a consequence they form an endless variety of geometric shapes, all of which are momentary in character. The ocean is never static. Each polygon is constantly mutating into a different polygon, but the ocean remains the same, an endless flow of different currents of the same singular Consciousness. Because these flows are composed of three distinct principles, these innumerable polygons tend to resolve into triangles, comparable to the ocean currents showing a tendency to resolve into three distinct types of currents, and these triangles represent the balanced state of the unmanifest *prakrti*.

त्रिभुजे सा स्वरूपपरिणामात्मिका ॥ २ ॥

IV.2 *tribhuje sā svarūpapariṅāmātmikā*

tribhuje, in the triangle; *sā*, she; *svarūpa*, nature, one's own form; *pariṅāma*, transformation, transmutation, result; *svarūpa pariṅāma*, homomorphic transmutation; *ātmikā*, composed of

"In the triangle of forces, the causal matrix is in a state of *svarūpa pariṅāma*."

It is the nature of the *guṅas* to constantly mutate, and hence this triangle of forces witnesses a constant change of identity among these three principles: *sattva* mutating into *rajah*, *rajah* into *tamah*, *tamah* into *sattva*. This ongoing, belligerent mutation of one force into another is known as *svarúpa pariṅáma*, "homomorphic transmutation," since it is a fundamental characteristic of the *guṅas* that they maintain their individual integrity, their *svarúpa* or fundamental nature, even as one transforms into the other.

At this stage there is equilibrium or equipoise among the *guṅas* and thus *puruśa* remains unqualified. The surface of the ocean remains as still as ever. But with the formation of a balanced triangle comes the potential for the creation to sprout. In this stage the three *guṅas* are beating against each other, and the resulting mutual transformation or *svarúpa pariṅáma*, as one *guṅa* flows into another, is the precursor for the manifestation of Shakti that will give rise to the creation.[3]

Svarúpa pariṅáma is a term that originated with Samkhya. In the Samkhya philosophy, the different phases of evolution arise out of a process of *pariṅáma* or transformation. The first differentiation in this theory of successive transformations is between *svarúpa pariṅáma*, the balanced or homogeneous state of the *guṅas*, and *virúpa pariṅáma*, the altered or heterogeneous state of the *guṅas*, ie., between the unmanifest state and the manifest state, which is further divided into different stages or types of *pariṅáma*. In Samkhya the *guṅas* in the unmanifest state do not interact with each other. Any transformation they undergo is purely internal. Anandamurti, however, does not agree with Samkhya's description of *prakrti* during the unmanifest state,[4] since it does not properly reflect the inherent nature of the *guṅas*, the constantly mutating valences of the causal matrix.

> When three principles remain active in three directions in a triangle of forces, then it is only natural that one force encroaches on another at one of the vertices, and as a result, differences occur in their respective strengths and wavelengths. Moreover, when two forces remain active within the same boundary, it is natural for them to interchange their inherent characteristics. In this way, the triangle's *sattva* will be converted into *rajas*, *rajas* into *tamas*, and *tamas* into *sattva* in an ongoing mutual transformation. This transformation can be called *svarúpa*

pariñáma (homomorphic transmutation). Some people use the term *svarúpa pariñáma* in a different sense, but I am not in favor of that.⁵

प्रथमाव्यक्ते सा शिवानी केन्द्रे च परमशिवः ॥ ३ ॥

IV.3 *prathamávyakte sá shivánii kendre ca paramashivah*

prathamá, first; *avyakte*, in the unmanifested; *sá*, she; *shivánii*, wife of Shiva; *kendre*, in the nucleus; *ca*, and; *paramashivah*, Supreme Consciousness

"In the unmanifest stage, *prakrti* is first called Shivánii and the witnessing consciousness in the nucleus is called Paramashiva.

With the formation of the balanced triangle of forces, Consciousness is encircled by *prakrti*. *Puruśa* is now circumscribed by the three *guńas*, but as long as the *guńas* maintain their equipoise, that circumscription is purely theoretical, since the influence of the *guńas* has yet to manifest. *Prakrti* remains latent and *puruśa* remains *nirguńa*, objectless and subjectless. However, the potential for the creation has been actualized; thus the creation is imminent. There is the potential for many triangles in this stage, an infinite number of triangles, in fact, but they all share the same nucleus, as if they were all on different planes around the same center. At this stage that nuclear Consciousness is called Shiva and *prakrti* is called Shivánii or Kaośikii. She is called Shivánii because *prakrti* is still in a latent state and thus there is no differentiation between Shiva and Shivánii, between Consciousness and its power. She is also called Kaośikii, because the manifestation of the macrocosmic *kośas* is imminent.⁶ This is the first phase of the creation, the premanifestation phase in which the potential for the creation becomes actualized.

द्वितीया सकले प्रथमोद्गमे भैरवी भैरवाश्रिता ॥ ४ ॥

IV.4 *dvitiiyá sakale prathamodgame bhaeravii bhaeraváshritá dvitiiyá*, second; *sakale*, in the manifest; *prathama*, first; *udgame*, in the sprouting; *bhaeravii*, Shakti; *bhaerava*, Shiva; *áshritá*, sheltered

"In the second, manifest stage, when the seed of creation first sprouts, Bhaeravii is sheltered in Bhaerava."

The points where the *guńas* meet as they undergo continual transformation in the flow of *svarúpa parińáma* are conceptualized as the vertices of the balanced triangle. These vertices are necessarily static by nature, having no absolute movement in relation to the flow of the *guńas*, and hence they are the weakest points of the triangle. In each of the vertices two opposing *guńas* exert a separate and unequal influence. Due to that pressure an imbalance arises and a resultant force emerges. The sentient principle is the strongest of the three *guńas*, much stronger than the mutative principle, just as the mutative principle is much stronger than the static principle, and thus it is the sentient force of *prakrti* that emerges from one of the vertices of the now-unbalanced triangle. Under the impetus of that singular sentient force, the seed of the creation bursts forth in a straight line or *náda*.[7] The sentient force thereupon imposes the sense of existence on a portion of the cosmic body, creating the cosmic *mahattattva*, or cosmic I, thus marking the beginning of manifestation. The word *sakala* refers to that which is manifest or expressed, ie., Saguńa Brahma.[8] At this point, the tangential point between the unmanifest *nirguńa puruśa* and the manifest Saguńa Brahma, there is as yet no curvature in the Cosmic Mind, hence its representation as a straight line. The sense of "I" has awoken but there is no doer and nothing is being done; no waves have as yet arisen in the cosmic ocean, and only the lightest of veils is resting on its surface.

This is the second stage of the creation, the intermediate stage between the balanced triangle of forces, or premanifestative stage, and the subsequent introduction of curvature, which characterizes the expressed universe as we know it. Hence *puruśa* and *prakrti* receive new names to signify this change in quality or change of state. In this intermediate stage *puruśa* is known as Bhaerava and *prakrti* as Bhaeravii, which Anandamurti also refers to as the "primordial principle." In Tantra, Consciousness and its power are sometimes symbolized as a gram seed, which contains two unseen halves within its sheath. Before germination the seed is one, but once it sprouts the two halves separate. With the sprouting of the seed of creation, *prakrti* is no longer dormant or latent. The dance of creation has begun and the two halves are now separate, in the sense that *prakrti's* influence can be experienced as separate from the witnessing consciousness, though in truth Consciousness remains forever unperturbed by this apparent change. What appears to be a change in Consciousness is simply the changing wavelengths of the *guńas*.[9]

Accompanying the sprouting of the sentient force is the *omkára*, the sonic manifestation of the Macrocosmic Mind, represented by the sound *aum* (commonly written as Om). The three letters—*a*, *u*, and *ma*—are indicative respectively of creation, preservation, and destruction (the merger back into Consciousness), and thus the entire creation is inherent in this cosmic sound. It is this sound that the yogi hears with his inner ear as he approaches the *savikalpa* state, the sound that leads the meditator to the ocean of Consciousness.

> This *oṅmkára* is the first expression of the Brahmic glory; thus it is known as the *shabda-brahma* (Sound-Brahma). The position of this *oṅmkára* is above all, for the cause of creation, preservation, and destruction is hidden in its three letters. One who has known this *oṅmkára* sounding in the vastness of space or humming in the firmament of the microcosmic mind has caught the essence of all things in the palm of their hand. Here one should bear in mind that if *oṅmkára* is sound, then to know it is to hear it or pronounce it. When *oṅmkára* is pronounced in the mind of Brahma, then it is meaningless for the *sádhaka* to pronounce it during his meditation of *oṅmkára*. Thus I say that the sadhana of *oṅmkára* means the endeavor to hear that sound.[10]
>
> —Anandamurti

सदृशपरिणामेन भवानी सा भवदारा ॥ ५ ॥

IV.5 *sadrshapariṅámena bhavánii sá bhavadárá*

sadrsha, similar; *pariṅámena*, from the resultant or transformation; *bhavánii*, name of *prakrti*; *sá*, she; *bhava*, creation, the world of becoming; *dárá*, wife

"With the rise of *sadrsha pariṅáma*, *prakrti* is called Bhavanii, the consort of Bhava."

The mutative force is inherent in the sentient force, and thus as the sentient force gradually wanes, the mutative force begins to assert itself, giving rise to clash within what was hitherto the homomorphic sentient expression of *prakrti*. Due to this clash between the *guṅas*, curvature or *kalá* arises, a transformation of what was initially a straight line (*náda*). Prior to the manifestation of curvature, there is only the Kárana or Causal Brahma, but from this point forward the Kárya or Effect Brahma begins to manifest, Saguṅa Brahma being the composite of the two.[11] With the progressive manifestation of curvature—that is, of vibration—comes the gradual unfolding of the manifest universe and the rise of heterogeneity. This progressive manifestation of curvature is known as *sadrsha pariṅáma*, homogenesis, in *Ananda Sutram*, a sequential similarity in the waves that arise in the ocean of Consciousness due to internal clash among the *guṅas*. The first curvature or wave gives rise to a second curvature that is almost identical to the first but whose wavelength is slightly shorter due to the increasing influence of *prakrti*. That second wave gives rise to a third wave, again almost identical to the second wave and one step removed from the first. And on and on it goes, wave after wave, curvature after curvature, a succession of unique but intimately related vibrations proliferating endlessly in the cosmic body. Each wave is virtually identical to the preceding wave but increasingly dissimilar to the waves that came before it, a function of how far apart they are. This is the fountain from which flows the vast vibratory panorama of the cosmos. In this third stage, *puruśa* and *prakrti* are again given new names to signify their change of state. *Bhava*, "the world of becoming," refers to the creation, the product of the cosmic imagination, which is nothing but an orderly sequence of waves pouring out of the cosmic nave in a never-ending flow. Thus *puruśa* here is known as Bhava, for it is Consciousness that has *become* the creation, and *prakrti*, the creator of this sequential force, is known as Bhavanii, the goddess of the ocean of existence, who has fashioned the creation out of the substance of her consort.

The phenomenon of *sadrsha pariṅáma* is fundamental to our understanding of the nature of the creation. It is the essence of the relationship that exists between all manifest entities, to the similarities and dissimilarities we observe in the perceptible universe, all of which are due to the proximity or distance between the generation of one *kalá* and another in the cosmic imagination. It is due to *sadrsha pariṅáma* that the child of today is different from the child of yesterday, however imperceptible that difference may be, and it is due to *sadrsha pariṅáma* that the young man of twenty-five is so noticeably different from the child of five. It is why the son is different but similar to the father, the grandson even more different, and the great grandson even more so. It is why the human beings of a million years ago were so markedly different from the human beings of today but still recognizably human. And it is why we are so radically different from the first unicellular organisms on this planet, despite our common ancestry and the fact that we share the essential characteristics of life. The universe is a great interweaving of waves but it is not chaos. All these waves or curvatures are related through *sadrsha pariṅáma*, some more closely than others, such as the man and the monkey, others more distantly, such as the man and the amoeba. All are related through this sequential proliferation of waves in the cosmic ocean, and yet no two waves are ever identical—no two human beings, no two thoughts, no two snowflakes, no two carbon atoms, no two electrons. Each vibration emanating from the Cosmic Mind in this sequential flow is entirely unique, now and forever.

शम्भूलिङ्गात्तस्या व्यक्तिः ॥ ६ ॥

IV.6 *shambhúliuṇgát tasyá vyaktih*

shambhú, controller of everything; *liuṇgá*, sign, symbol; *tasyáh*, her; *vyaktih*, expression

"Her manifestation arises from *shambhúliuṇgá*."

A point has position but no magnitude; thus it has been traditionally used in Tantra to signify the tangential point between the manifest and unmanifest worlds. It is from this tangential point that the creation issues forth, and it is into this point that the creation dissolves. In this sense, it floats like a bubble on the surface of the ocean of Consciousness. From that tangential point the universe extends outward, and like a bubble it can equally subside into the waters of the deep. Anandamurti calls this tangential point "the point of fundamental positivity," because it is from this point that the positive, outgoing motion of *saiṇcara* emerges, a creative movement that begins with the imposition of the sense of existence upon Consciousness and culminates with the formation of solid matter. In Sanskrit it has been traditionally called the *shambhúliuṇgá*, since this point is the controller of the universe, and being the first cause, it is itself causeless. It is also referred to as the *kámabiija* or *icchábiija*. Biija means "seed," *káma* means "desire," and *icchá* in this context means "will." It is from this point that the cosmic will or the cosmic desire for self-creation expresses itself.[12] The *shambhúliuṇgá* is the seed of creation, and the germination of that seed represents the motive force of macrocosmic desire, just as the motive force for microcosmic movement is microcosmic desire, as represented by the four petals of the first chakra—*káma, artha, dharma,* and *mokśa.*

Being the starting point of the creation, the *shambhúliuṇgá* is also its terminus, for in *pratisaiṇcara* the microcosm, having emerged out of matter, in effect retraces the journey that resulted in the involution of Consciousness into matter. This is symbolized in Tantra by the phrase *kalá, náda, bindu. Kalá* or curvature represents the actional force; *náda,* the straight line, represents the cognitive force; and the point or *bindu* represents the cosmic will.[13] In the process of Tantra sadhana, the aspirant will have to straighten the curvatures of their mind, proceeding backward against the sequential flow of *sadrsha parińáma* until the mind's curvature becomes fully straightened, indicative of the *savikalpa* state. This straightened or curvature-less mind will then have to merge into the *shambhúliuṇgá* or *icchábiija* in order to complete the journey back to *nirguńa*, like a bubble subsiding into the infinite tranquility of the unqualified ocean of being. The point that corresponds to the *shambhúliuṇgá* in the microcosm is also called the *paramapada*, the supreme stance.

> *Kalánádabindute abhivyakta tumi*
> *Triloke sájáyecha ogo triloker svámii*
>
> — Prabhat Samgiita 4684
>
> "You are manifest in *kalá*, *náda*, and *bindu*; you have decorated the three worlds, O Lord of creation."[14]
>
> — Anandamurti

स्थूलीभवने निद्रिता सा कुण्डलिनी ॥ ७ ॥

IV.7 *sthúliibhavane nidritá sá kuńḋalinii*

sthúliibhavane, what has become crude; *nidritá*, dormant state, sleep; *sá*, she ; *kuńḋalinii*, coiled serpentine

> "At the endpoint of crudfication, the dormant *paráshakti* is called *kuńḋalinii*."

With the beginning of *kalá* or curvature, *prakrti* in the role of Bhavanii Shakti progressively binds Consciousness into denser and denser forms, effectively veiling it from sight, until she reaches the zenith point of her binding power with the formation of solid matter. This binding power is also known as the *avidyámáyá* force of *prakrti*. At first glance, solid matter appears inert to the human eye. For this reason it has sometimes been given the appellation "dead" matter. But that seemingly inert, "dead" matter is Consciousness in its most condensed, most tightly bound form, and conversely it is the fullest expression of Shakti's power. Consider a lump of plutonium, one of the densest naturally occurring metals. It appears to be a lump of inert matter, the most static existence in the universe, but split those plutonium atoms under controlled conditions and they release an immense amount of raw energy. And that is but a crude and inefficient manifestation of this principle within the purview of *saiṋcara*, a mere glimpse of the power of Shakti that is concealed within those atoms.

That same universal Shakti is equally present in *pratisaiṋcara*, where it finds expression as the psychic existence of the microcosm, the *jiivabháva*. In *pratisaiṋcara*, however, Shakti reverses its role, working to liberate Consciousness from its bondage, to gradually convert mind into cognition. In this role it is known as the *vidyámáyá* force of *prakrti*. The same universal Consciousness that is imprisoned inside matter is also imprisoned inside the microcosmic mind, waiting to be liberated through the impetus of this *vidyámáyá* force. The word *kula* means "the container of the physical structure." In Tantra it refers to the lowermost chakra at the base of the spine, the *múládhára* chakra, the controlling point of solid factor. This is the crudest point in the human structure, and it is here that the Shakti of the living being resides in the form of the *kulakuńḍalinii*, or more simply, kundalini, which is said to be coiled like a snake three and a half times around the base of this chakra. The word *kuńḍalinii* means "she who is lying in a coil," ie., a female snake, but it is more commonly translated as "sleeping divinity." It is called the sleeping divinity because it is Shiva, the Supreme Consciousness, which has taken the form of *paráshakti*, the Supreme Shakti. This *paráshakti* or kundalini represents the entire psychic force of the individual mind. Normally this psychic force is in a dormant state—it is a sleeping divinity, a dormant goddess. The vast psychic potential of the human being, its immense storehouse of cosmic energy, which even in small amounts can lead to prodigious feats, is sleeping in a state of unconsciousness harbored within the physical structure, waiting to be awakened, and when it is awakened, that infinite psychic potential begins to manifest.

> The final, or culminating, point of retardation contains within it the history of the full expression. In the crudest

point of the human mind, therefore, lies the history of its innumerable lives. Even a timorous stroke will rip open the burden a person is carrying and make one able to see oneself. The development from the nadir of Supreme Cognition is progress.[15]

— Anandamurti

कुण्डलिनी सा मूलीभूतर्णात्मिका ॥ ८ ॥

IV.8 *kuńḋalinii sá múliibhútarńátmiká*

kuńḋalinii, sleeping divinity; *sá*, she; *múliibhúta*, fundamental; *rńátmiká*, negativity

"This kundalini is the fundamental negativity."

At the opposite pole from the *shambhúliuṇgá*, from where the creation originates, lies the *svayambhúliuṇga*, the point in which the creation culminates, the nadir point of the descent of Consciousness. If the *shambhúliuṇgá* is the point of fundamental positivity, then the *svayambhúliuṇga* is the point of fundamental negativity. *Svayam* means "self" in Sanskrit; thus *svayambhú* is the "self-created." In the Indian spiritual tradition, it commonly refers to the earthly manifestation of the deity.

In the human microcosmic structure, the *svayambhúliuṇga* is located at the base of the spine, wherein resides the dormant microcosmic force known as *kundalini*, the Shakti deity that is sleeping within the human being. If the *shambhúliuṇgá* is the point from where the Cosmic Mind emerges out of pure unqualified Consciousness, the kundalini, being the force of fundamental negativity sheltered in the *svayambhúliuṇga*, is that same Consciousness in the form of the microcosmic mind at its nadir, bound to the nth degree by the power of *prakrti*. Consciousness has arrived at this point of maximum psychic latency through a process of gradual crudification, and implicit in its confinement at the point of fundamental negativity is the undertaking of the return journey, retracing its course back to its point of origin, back to the *shambhúliuṇgá*.

By way of analogy, let us imagine a rushing river flowing downward from a mountain peak and culminating in the river's mouth thousands of figurative miles away. That mountain peak is our goal, the seat of unqualified Consciousness, analogous to the seventh chakra at the crown of the head, and the mouth of the river is our starting point, analogous to the first chakra at the base of the spine, situated at the farthest possible distance from that peak experience. We have no choice then but to go against the current if we wish to reach our goal. We must travel upstream, against the full force of the river. Similarly, the creative flow of *prakrti* gradually binds or crudifies Consciousness, and if we are to return to the unbound state we must struggle against that binding force every step of the way. If we denote *prakrti's* outgoing, *saiṇcara* movement as positive in character, then the opposing movement must be negative in character. That microcosmic force that negates the qualifying pressure of *prakrti* in the pursuit of liberation from the incarceration imposed by *prakrti* is the kundalini of the microcosm. It starts from the crudest or furthest point possible, the first chakra, also known as the *kámapiitha*, the seat of microcosmic desire, being the mirror opposite of the *kámabiija* of the Macrocosm, and its goal is the *shambhúliuṇgá*, the point of origin, which in the microcosmic structure is situated at the seventh chakra. Thus there is only one path that the living being can take to achieve liberation, and that is the path that the kundalini takes, rising up from the first chakra and passing through each successive chakra until it reaches the summit at the crown of the head, a journey against the current that requires immense energy and effort.[16]

Wherever and whenever human beings have been able to achieve spiritual elevation—irrespective of culture, spiritual tradition, or era—at the root of their experience lies the upward journey of kundalini. In the Christian tradition, for example, where the existence of kundalini has not been openly recognized, Teresa of Avila, the fifteenth-century Spanish saint, wrote about the seven chakras in her classic work of Christian mysticism, *Interior Castle*, detailing her experience in an abstruse or veiled language that she resorted to in order to avoid any possible repercussions from the Inquisition.

The German Christian mystic Jacob Boehme, who was seven years old when Teresa died, described his experience of kundalini in his *Confessions*:

> For the Holy Ghost will not be held in the sinful flesh, but rises up like a lightning-flash, as fire sparkles and flashes out of a stone when a man strikes it. But when the flash is caught in the fountain of the heart, then the Holy Spirit rises up, in the seven unfolding fountain spirits, into the brain, like the dawning of the day, the morning redness.[17]

Similar descriptions of kundalini experiences can be found scattered throughout the world's spiritual or mystical literature, both East and West.

This awakening can be effected in various ways. Devotion is one means that is common to most spiritual traditions, and being in the company of an enlightened soul can often be enough to awaken the sleeping serpent, like a powerful magnet magnetizing a nearby piece of iron. In Tantra and yoga, the process known as *shaktipáta* is specifically designed to awaken the kundalini from her dormant condition. *Shaktipáta* literally means "striking the kundalini." This is accomplished by the use of a *siddha* mantra, a mantra that has been energized by a realized master. During initiation the mantra strikes the kundalini and this begins the process of awakening, releasing its dormant energy like the controlled detonation that sets off the nuclear reaction within an atom bomb. Anandamurti has this to say about the role that mantra plays in awakening the kundalini:

> So long as the fundamental negativity does not receive a stroke, there does not occur any progress, any development. A seed sprouts forth if struck by light, water, and soil. Similarly, when the fundamental negativity of a unit—that is, the *kulakuṅḍalinii*—receives the stroke of the mantra, it awakens.[18]

Kundalini experiences can be manifold and may be accompanied by powerful mystical sensations, such as those of Gopi Krishna, as detailed in his popular memoir *Kundalini: The Evolutionary Energy in Man*:

> "Suddenly, with a roar like that of a waterfall, I felt a stream of liquid light entering my brain through the spinal cord. ... The illumination grew brighter and brighter, the roaring louder, I experienced a rocking sensation and then felt myself slipping out of my body, entirely enveloped in a halo of light."[19]

However, spiritual aspirants may also pass through the different stages of spiritual elevation without experiencing such psycho-physical sensations or any of the varieties of samadhi experiences so frequently described in the yogic literature.[20] In all cases, however, the aspirant feels their proximity to Supreme Consciousness growing as the kundalini reaches the various chakras on its way back to the *shambhúliungá*: the *svádhiśthána* chakra, the controlling point of liquid factor, the *manipúra*, the controlling point of luminous factor, the *anáhata*, the controlling point of aerial factor, the *vishuddha*, the controlling point of ethereal factor, the *ájiná*, the seat of the mind, and finally the *sahasrára* chakra at the crown of the head, the seat of consciousness. Each of these stages betokens a higher grade of spiritual realization. When the kundalini reaches the sixth chakra, the microcosmic mind merges into the Macrocosmic Mind, and when it reaches the seventh chakra, it merges into pure Consciousness, thereby completing the journey of spiritual evolution. Thus, while there are many spiritual traditions, there is only one spiritual path: the path of the kundalini rising.

In each of these first six chakras the aspirant experiences different degrees of freedom. While the dormant kundalini remains confined to the first chakra, the bondage of *prakrti* over the microcosmic mind is at its zenith, and thus the spiritual ignorance of the microcosm is also at its zenith. As the kundalini awakens and begins its ascent, the microcosm experiences an ever-increasing spiritual freedom that culminates in the final liberation of Consciousness from the bondage of *prakrti* when the kundalini reaches the seventh chakra. One contemporary analogy is that of the United States federal prison system, which has six levels of incarceration, ranging from maximum security, where the prisoners are confined twenty-four hours a day to a solitary cell, to minimum security, where the fences are mostly symbolic and the liberties they enjoy make for a comfortable life, though ultimately they are still in prison.[21] As a prisoner rises through the different levels, based on good behavior and time served, they are granted more freedom and more facilities, but true freedom can only be had when they have served their time and are liberated from their imprisonment. Likewise, the spiritual aspirant enjoys greater and greater spiritual freedom as the kundalini reaches the higher chakras, eventually giving them access to the wonders of the superconscious mind, but true freedom can only be attained when the aspirant leaves the mind behind and becomes one with Supreme Consciousness. When that dormant force fully awakens, the kundalini or *paráshakti* merges into Shiva, reuniting with her eternal consort in the *sahasrára* chakra. With this merger, Consciousness is liberated from its bondage through the locus of the individual human being who has attained the enlightened state in the eternal dance of bondage and liberation. The Infinite, which was once bound, is now free.

Chapter Five

> Those who say that the practice of dharma is purely an individual affair are mistaken. Dharma is very much the concern of the entire society.[1]
>
> — Anandamurti

THE CONCLUDING CHAPTER OF *Ananda Sutram* is a radical departure from the first four chapters, at least prima facie. While the first four chapters dealt with spiritual philosophy, from the creation of the universe to the attainment of spiritual liberation as the pinnacle and purpose of human development, Chapter Five outlines the fundamental principles of Anandamurti's social philosophy, and it is this chapter, more than any other, that sets *Ananda Sutram* apart from the other seminal works of Indian spiritual thought. It is the first major system that lays the ideological groundwork for the construction of a spiritual society, one based on the universal spiritual principles elaborated in the preceding four chapters, a society that endeavors to provide the most propitious environment possible for the well-being and spiritual development of each of its members, ie., for the fulfillment of the journey of spiritual evolution that is at the heart of all spiritual philosophy. Apart from the Manusmriti or Manava Dharmashastra (The Laws of Manu), which is not a philosophy per se but a Hindu social code embedded within the framework of Hindu religious and spiritual principles, the architects of the other major systems of Indian philosophy did not directly set out to teach human beings how to structure their society so that it would ensure their welfare and spiritual progress. That was left to emperors, politicians, and social thinkers, with less than desirable results. The etymological meaning of the Sanskrit word for "society," *samája*, is "to move together toward a common goal." It is implicit in this definition that each member of society should feel a sense of responsibility for every other member, and that no one should be left behind. Taken in that sense, it is safe to say, as Anandamurti does, that we have yet to create a true *samája* on this planet, one that reflects the true spirit of society.² This chapter is an attempt to address that lacuna, to extend the spiritual principles of human dharma by applying them to the organization and administration of human affairs. Taken in toto they form the guiding principles for Anandamurti's social philosophy, which he calls the Progressive Utilization Theory—Prout for short—"propounded," as he tells us at the end of this chapter, "for the happiness and welfare of all."

वर्णप्रधानता चक्रधारायाम् ॥ १ ॥

V.1 *varṅapradhánatá cakradhárayám*

varṅa, mental color, social class; *pradhánatá*, dominance, supremacy; *cakra*, cycle, circle; *dhárayám*, flow

"In the movement of the social cycle, a social class predominates."

In the opening sutra of Chapter Five, Anandamurti introduces a concept that is unique to his philosophy, the idea of the Samaj Chakra, or social cycle. Just as he began his exposition of the spiritual philosophy in Chapter One with the *brahmacakra*, the cycle of creation, he begins his exposition of the social philosophy with the Samaj Chakra. According to Anandamurti, human society comprises four distinct classes, one of which is always dominant at any one time, and these four classes succeed each other in a natural order that has been in evidence since the beginning of recorded history. These four classes are the *shúdra*, or laboring class; the *kśatriya*, or warrior class; the *vipra*, or intellectual class; and the *vaeshya*, or mercantile class, our modern-day capitalists. They are divided not by occupation, as it might appear and as is common with other social philosophers, but according to their prevailing mentality, which then predisposes those individuals toward certain occupations, and the natural class-wise movement is for the reins of power to pass from the *shúdras* to the *kśatriyas* to the *vipras* to the *vaeshyas*, with a subsequent *shúdra* revolution ushering in a new rotation of the social cycle. The Samaj Chakra is thus based on both an understanding of human psychology and a close reading of history. In his analysis of the evolution of human society, Anandamurti examines the mentality of each of these classes, both individually and collectively, as they evolved over the course of time, and in the process he shows how the natural course of mental and social evolution gave rise to these four classes in this particular order.

He begins his analysis with the early days of human society, when human beings were engaged in a constant struggle with their environment in order to ensure their survival. Everyone was a laborer in those days, whether their labor involved hunting and gathering, raising children, making tools, or building shelters, and their minds were inevitably preoccupied with the material world. Thus the predominant mentality in those days was the *shúdra* mentality. It was that way throughout the globe in prehistoric times, from the advent of human beings on this earth some one million years ago until comparatively recently.[3] Because their minds were preoccupied with matter, those prehistoric human beings were largely materialistic by nature and were therefore dominated by *tamoguńa*. This age in human history is referred to by Anandamurti as the Shúdra Age.[4]

As human society evolved, internecine conflict between different tribes became increasingly frequent, eventually becoming more of a threat to human survival than the ongoing struggle with the environment. As a natural response to the threat posed by these conflicts, those individuals who possessed greater valor and greater strength developed a martial spirit and rose to positions of leadership in their respective societies. They became the clan leaders, those who governed by force of arms and the example of their courage, and as the different tribes and communities became bigger and better organized, these martially minded individuals evolved into the warrior or *kśatriya* class. With their ascendence in human society, mankind entered into the Kśatriya Age. While *shúdras* were content with physical well-being and enjoyment, *kśatriyas* set out to conquer nature, and in the process the acquisition of honor, prestige, and glory became more important to them than mere physical enjoyment.

> When the individual mind rushes toward pleasure with intense desire, but not wanting to be a slave of matter, instead controls the waves of matter with its mental waves in an effort to assimilate them, then matter becomes its servant. The individual mind that has the capacity to direct matter according to its wish is called *kśatriya*. Struggle is the dharma of *kśatriyas*. Imbued with indomitable vital force, *kśatriyas* are not symbolized by the black color of darkness. They represent spiritedness. Their color is blood-red.[5]
>
> — Anandamurti

As society continued to grow and become more complex, those endowed with greater intellect gradually started to occupy positions of greater and greater influence within the *kśatriya* society. The warrior class needed to learn the arts of warfare, both the use of weapons and battlefield strategy. Statecraft became essential, the medical arts rose in importance, and the bigger a community became, the more it had to rely on the administrative and organizational capacity of its more intelligent members. The members of this emerging intellectual class acquired positions as ministers, administrators, counselors, and teachers, and even though the *kśatriyas* continued to govern society, the real power gradually shifted to the intelligentsia. Thus the Vipra Age was born.

> When we read in history the accounts of the great kings, it appears as though all these events belonged to the Kśatriya Age. But was that really the situation? A somewhat deeper analysis shows that nearly all the kings were at the beck and call of their *vipra* ministers. In almost every country we observe the hard fact that even the most powerful and mighty kings were mere puppets in the hands of their *vipra* ministers.[6]
>
> — Anandamurti

Power in the Kśatriya Age was in large part hereditary. *Kśatriya* genes and *kśatriya* values were passed on from warrior fathers to warrior sons, and if their genes or enculturation failed them, then other *kśatriya* families would seize power. But the *vipras* had to resort to other stratagems to maintain their power, and their primary stratagem was religion. The *shúdra* laborers and *kśatriya* kings were easily controlled by their fear of the hereafter, and the rise of religious institutions gradually solidified *vipra* power over the nominal rulers through the imposition of dogmatic ideas and the control of education. During medieval times in Europe, education was geared almost exclusively toward the clergy through monastic and episcopal schools, and the production and housing of books was by and large confined to monasteries. In many places there were even laws banning serfs and peasants from becoming educated. The same was true for *shúdras* in India, who could have molten lead poured in their ears simply for hearing the Vedas. It was during this time that the Church in Europe and the Brahmin class in India assumed full control of their respective societies, though the governance remained ostensibly in the hands of kings.

> Even though the *vipras* came into the forefront by the use of their marked intellect, it is more difficult than in the case of the *kśatriyas* to maintain a hereditary superiority of intellect. In an effort to maintain power amongst the limited few, they actively tried and prevented others from acquiring the use of the intellect by imposing superstitions and rituals, faiths and beliefs, and even introducing irrational ideas (the caste system of Hindu society is an example) through an appeal to the sentiments of the mass (who collectively cannot be called intellectual). This was the phase of human society in the Middle Ages in the greater part of the world.[7]
>
> — Anandamurti

Finally, as society became more and more complex, the production and distribution of food, consumer goods, and important raw materials began to take center stage. Those who controlled the means of production and distribution, the burgeoning merchant class, gradually rose in influence until they eventually took over control of the society. This marked the beginning of the Vaeshya Age, roughly coinciding in the West with the Industrial Age and the rise of democratic government, the form of government favored by the *vaeshyas*. This is the age in which we now find ourselves in many parts of the world, the late stages of the capitalist era, which is destined through the laws of social dynamics to give way to a second rotation of the social cycle.

The idea that society is divided into different social classes has been around for millennia. The Manusmriti, for example, which outlines a similar class-wise division, is over two thousand years old and was itself based on earlier social codes. While the Manusmriti did not advance the idea that society is dominated by one or another of those social classes, this idea has become integral to modern social thinking. The most famous social philosophy of our times, Marxism, which emerged as a reaction to the exploitative nature of late-nineteenth-century capitalism, focuses on the struggle between the exploited proletariat and the bourgeoisie exploiters—the *shúdra* and *vaeshya* classes in the terminology of *Ananda Sutram*—with the aim of overthrowing the hegemony of the ruling bourgeoisie. The Marxist division of society into two distinct classes parallels Anandamurti's contention that during the late-capitalist era the *vipras* and *kśatriyas* for all intents and purposes become absorbed into the *shúdra* class due to their dependence on the ruling *vaeshyas* for their livelihood and the concomitant sense of powerlessness and disenfranchisement engendered by the tyranny of wealth in such societies. The dominance of the capitalist class—which controls not only the blue-collar masses through its economic power but also the military, the government, and educational and religious institutions—is painfully familiar to us in the early twenty-first century, and the rising clamor to bring an end to capitalism is becoming equally familiar in many circles. While societies dominated by the *kśatriya* class—those ruled by dictatorships and military juntas—have become much less common in our modern world, they are hardly nonexistent, and we are quite familiar with the generally regressive and exploitative nature of these societies. The same can be said about modern states ruled by the clergy, such as some of the Islamist states. Not all social thinkers refer to religious states as being dominated by a separate class, but historically the *vipra* class has dominated society through religion, and such states appear to be modern examples of *vipra* dominance.

Thus we have a natural understanding of the four social classes based on our experience of modern societies, which are controlled either by capitalist interests, military rulers, or religious institutions, all of whom rule over the laboring masses. Anandamurti's concept of social class, however, is not based on occupation but on mentality. The principal meaning of the word *varńa* is "color." In this case, it refers to mental color—in other words, one's characteristic or prevailing psychology. Thought forms are psychic vibrations, and all vibrations emit color.[8] Thus, depending on the characteristic flow of one's *vrttis* and the varying dominance of *sattvaguńa, rajoguńa,* and *tamoguńa,* the individual human mind emanates a certain color. These mental colors as they pertain to human psychology can be divided into four broad categories,[9] and thus human beings can be divided into four basic psychologies. It is due to their psychology that people gravitate toward certain occupations and activities, and conversely, the exercise of other activities and occupations can over time change a person's characteristic psychology.

People with a *shúdra* mentality, for example, tend to gravitate toward manual or blue-collar labor. *Shúdras* are strongly identified with their bodies and primarily seek pleasure through their senses. If their basic needs are satisfied through their labor, they tend to remain content with their lot in life. *Kśatriyas*, on the other hand, want to conquer the world. They value courage, honor, and glory and thus gravitate toward those occupations and activities that satisfy these mental tendencies: the military, law enforcement, competitive athletics, and so on. *Vipras* are satisfied neither with the pleasures of the senses nor with the thrill of conquest. They gravitate toward those occupations and activities that give them free scope to pursue their intellectual interests, such as education, science and engineering, the arts, politics, and religion and spirituality. It is the life of the mind that attracts their attention, rather than the opportunity to amass a fortune and gain influence through their economic weight, as is the case with *vaeshyas*, whose mentality we are all very familiar with, living, as most of us do, in capitalist-dominated societies, where we are taught to value the pursuit of economic prosperity and the accumulation of wealth as an end in itself, a sure conduit—or so we are told—to the attainment of happiness. People of *vaeshya* mentality can be found in all walks of life but tend to gravitate toward the business world, from small business owners to corporate CEOs, from bankers to speculators. They may also be attracted to the world of politics, since it is through politics, especially in democratic societies, that the capitalist agenda is promoted and protected. Though most of us have some qualities of all four *varṅas* and may feel a varying attraction to each of them, we all belong to one of the four and tend to gravitate toward professions that allow us to satisfy those *saṁskáras*—with the exception of those who have transcended *varṅa* consciousness, the subject of the next sutra. And because this is a mental predisposition, it is possible to change *varṅa* during a single lifetime, especially if a person spends a lot of time in activities belonging to a *varṅa* that is not initially natural to them. For example, a person who dreams of being a career soldier may be assigned to the signal corp and after twenty years his interest in communications and technology grows to the point that his *kṣatriya* tendencies are superseded by his *vipra* tendencies.

The division of human society into these four distinct *varṅas* is an ancient idea that eventually developed into the Indian caste system. The oldest reference to the *varṅas* can be found in the Rig Veda, mankind's oldest literature, whose composition began well over ten thousand years ago. Mandala ten, hymn ninety of the Rig Veda says that the gods created the caste separations by sacrificing the primal Puruśa, the Supreme Spirit. His feet became the *shúdras*, his thighs the *vaeshyas*, his arms the *kṣatriyas*, and his mouth the Brahmins or priestly class, ie., the *vipras*, since religious offices were the main occupation for intellectuals in ancient India. This division, which was essentially a division of labor, brought certain benefits to Indian society.

> In ancient India an elastic economy existed that supported the collective economic endeavors. In the Vedic Age the economic system of India evolved on the basis

of social classes (*varńa*). *Shúdras, kśatriyas, vipras* and *vaeshyas*—these four *varńas* evolved and they remained content with their work. One particular section farmed and the rest did other work. They didn't all rush toward agricultural work like today. This class system was hereditary and so there was less scope for economic imbalance.[10]

— Anandamurti

This ancient conception of the four fundamental social classes was essentially correct. However, it had nothing to do with blood or heritage but rather with mental tendency. Within a single family one may find all four mentalities, and as mentioned earlier, the mental color of a particular person can change over time depending on their actions and activities. The psychological basis of the *varńas* was understood in ancient India, at least in some circles, as evidenced in the Bhagavad Gita, which tells us that the *varńas* are evolved from the attributes arising from different activities.[11] Anandamurti dates the Bhagavad Gita, specifically the first eleven chapters,[12] to 3500 years ago, more than a century after Kapil systematized the Samkhya teachings, whose influence can be seen throughout the Gita. But by the time the Manusmriti, the Hindu social code, was composed some 1500 years later, this understanding was nowhere to be seen. From that time forward, the caste system became increasingly calcified, and this has led to greater and greater injustice and social discord. A division of labor that once had some social value became a destructive, antisocial institution and a source of enormous injustice. For the sake of human welfare, it is essential that the caste system be eliminated. Nevertheless, the fundamental principle behind the four *varńas*, the relationship between psychology, labor, and social class, continues to govern social dynamics, and we will look at the nature of that movement in subsequent sutras.

चक्रकेन्द्रे सद्विप्राश्चक्रनियन्त्रकाः ॥ २ ॥

V.2 *cakrakendre sadviprásh cakraniyantrakáh*

> *cakra*, cycle; *kendre*, in the nucleus, in the center; *sadviprah*, spiritual revolutionary; *niyantrakáh*, controller
>
> "*Sadvipras* control the social cycle from its nucleus."
>
> Those spiritual revolutionaries who work to achieve such progressive changes for human elevation on a well-thought, preplanned basis, whether in the physical, metaphysical or spiritual sphere, by adhering to the principles of *yama* and *niyama* [yogic code of ethics], are *sadvipras*.[13]
>
> — Anandamurti

For many if not most inhabitants of our planet, exploitation and injustice are major impediments to spiritual progress. Those who have had to struggle to put food on the table for themselves and their children, or to keep a roof over their heads, or who have had to face war or persecution or civil unrest, know how difficult it is under such conditions to pursue spiritual practices. Even those of us who are fortunate enough not to have had to face such extreme conditions still feel the weight of the endemic injustice and exploitation that is prevalent in even the most affluent societies. If we are to create an environment that fosters the spiritual growth of human beings, then it is essential that we do all we can to minimize injustice and exploitation, wherever it appears. It is, in effect, our collective responsibility.

Even a cursory study of history is enough to show that the degree of exploitation tends to increase as the dominant class becomes entrenched in positions of power. Institutions calcify and social structures and policies that were once beneficial gradually fall out of sync with the changing currents of social aspiration. What may have begun as a benevolent administration tends to turn increasingly exploitative over time, and as a consequence society suffers. Under such circumstances, the longer the dominant class remains in power, the more human suffering is prolonged. It thus becomes incumbent upon true well-wishers of humanity to put an end to injustice and exploitation by finding a way to engineer the removal of the dominant class, thereby breathing fresh life into society. Anandamurti refers to such champions of human progress as *sadvipras* because it requires a firm ethical foundation and an elevated spiritual consciousness to be able to discern the true goal of human evolution and to envision the path that will lead us there.

The word *vipra* means "intellectual," and *sat* means "true" or "immutable" (absolute truth is necessarily immutable). Thus the word *sadvipra*,[14] in Anandamurti's lexicon, refers to those human beings of enlightened intellect whose minds are illumined by the effulgence of spiritual elevation and who dedicate their efforts to human progress in the truest sense of the word. Such individuals, due to their ethical and spiritual development, have risen above the bondages and limitations of the four dominant class mentalities and yet retain those capabilities and skills. By virtue of their elevated minds and lack of class bias, they are uniquely positioned to promote the welfare of human society—not the welfare of any particular group but that of all human beings, along with all the other living beings with whom we share this planet. For that reason, Anandamurti places them at the center or nucleus of the social cycle, beyond the influence of the four quadrants or classes.

Unlike the previous sutra, this speaks more to the future than to the past, since we don't have any historical record as yet of *sadvipras* positioning themselves at the center of the social cycle and either nudging it or shoving it forward in order to put an end to rampant injustice—isolated examples, certainly, but not a concerted effort among spiritualists of different traditions to take up the reins of social welfare. Hence the concept of *sadvipra* encapsulates Anandamurti's vision for the developed spiritualists of the future, the placing of the mantle of social responsibility on their broad shoulders. Human society is the principal training ground for our spiritual evolution, and thus it behooves us that the best and wisest among us, the most ethically and spiritually developed, take up the reins of collective leadership, which rightfully belong in the hands of those who best understand the purpose of our human sojourn and who are most capable of making decisions that will promote the collective welfare of the entire human race, along with that of other living beings.

In the past, dedicated spiritualists tended to keep themselves apart from society, both figuratively and literally, often living in monasteries, ashrams, and hermitages without taking an active role in social construction or socioeconomic life. This tended to be true even when they resided in urban or suburban areas, for there was a prevalent conception in both East and West that society was a quagmire best avoided by those who wanted to achieve spiritual elevation. There have been some exceptions, but by and large, spiritual luminaries did not lend their wisdom and talents to the challenging work of social construction. In Anandamurti's view, however, the welfare of living beings cannot be assured in the absence of an ideal human society, a spiritually enlightened society, given how much impact human society has on both the animate and inanimate worlds, and hence it is his contention that it is the responsibility of all sincere spiritualists to take up the work of social development. If the welfare of others is our principle concern, if we truly want to combat suffering and help others along the path to liberation—which is, after all, our duty as ethical beings, something all authentic spiritual traditions recognize—then it is incumbent upon us to endeavor to construct a benevolent, universal society, one that will foster a propitious environment in which human beings can evolve without impediment and become true custodians of our planetary ecosystem.

By way of analogy, imagine a village beset by cholera. If we stay inside and lock our doors to escape the contagion, not only will we not be able to help anyone, thus depriving ourselves of the chance to do service, an essential prerequisite for spiritual liberation, but the contagion is likely to find its way past our doors despite our best efforts to the contrary. The proper response, the ethical response, the compassionate response, is to organize the villagers and institute proper sanitation so the disease cannot spread. In this way, everyone benefits, ourselves included. Thus Anandamurti's vision of the modern spiritualist is that of the spiritual revolutionary or *sadvipra* who applies their talents and wisdom toward the construction of an ideal human society that promotes the physical, mental, and spiritual welfare of all.

How then will these present and future *sadvipras* take responsibility for the onward march of human society? By placing themselves in the nucleus of the social cycle and from there taking what measures they deem necessary and feasible to eliminate injustice and foment all-around progress. Their position in the nucleus means not only that they will not belong to the dominant class but that they will not belong to any class, including the class that opposes the presumptive exploiters. Unlike Friedrich Engels, who came from a bourgeoisie family but was proud of his identification with the proletariat, they will not be influenced by class sentiment one way or the other—thus their position in the nucleus, no matter what class holds the reins of power. Free from the influence of class sentiment or class allegiance, they will fight against injustice and exploitation wherever it appears. If injustice rears its head within the opposition they will fight it, but most often that injustice and exploitation will be perpetrated by the dominant class, in which case they will be seen as revolutionaries supporting the opposition. If a military dictatorship suppresses individual freedoms to the point that society suffers, they will support the cause of intellectuals and artists who raise the banner of freedom. If at the end of the Vipra Age the dogmas propagated by the intellectual class, whether through religion or any other means, oppress society and the resultant injustice cannot be removed without a regime change, they will promote the cause of the *vaeshya* opposition. And at the end of the capitalist era they will promote the downfall of capitalism, thus ushering in the next rotation of the social cycle. The wheel will continue to turn with or without the *sadvipras*—that is the nature of social movement, and that movement is by and large beneficial for society—but when it becomes necessary, the *sadvipras* will hasten the turning of the wheel by helping to push one class out and the next class in, the strength of that push depending on the necessity of the hour and the nature of the conditions. With the change in leadership comes progressive ideas, fresh vigor, and ultimately a new social life. Everyone benefits, including the *sadvipras*, for their revolutionary social struggle speeds their progress toward the Divine. It becomes an essential part of their spiritual practice.

> By perfecting the ten weapons of *yama* and *niyama*, spiritual aspirants acquire force. The spiritual aspirant must

wage a constant war against crudeness. The attainment of Brahma is their goal, their object of ideation, the only ideal of their life. They wish to remove all the obstacles born of *avidyá* from this path of supreme attainment. They want to remove the clouds that hide the polestar of their life. They must fight like a hero against all these obstacles. The spiritual aspirant does not reform society for the sake of social reformation but for the defects that hinder the life of spiritual aspiration. They strive to build a harmonious society by fighting against all those defects that block the path that leads to that goal. For this very reason, they fight against the mud and mire they encounter in the psychic, economic, and other spheres of life. They do not fight for the sake of fighting, they do not fight for the sake of reform or correction—they fight to remove the thorns from the path. When those whose goal is social, psychic, or economic reform or correction achieve apparent success in their efforts, they take a seat in their weariness or become disoriented. But for a spiritual aspirant this is not an option.[15]

— Anandamurti

This sutra highlights the importance of leadership in society, regardless of era or of which class is dominant. Our modern capitalist society is a testament to the wealth of social problems and inequity that ensue when political leaders are chosen not for their moral integrity, spiritual wisdom, and practical abilities, but on the basis of how well they serve the vested interests of the powers-that-be. It is near impossible for society as a whole to be better than its leaders. If we wish to one day witness the emergence of an enlightened, benevolent society then we have no choice but to hand over the reins to enlightened, benevolent leaders. Without enlightened leadership, society will continue to suffer the convulsions of injustice and exploitation, and as a consequence we will continue to squander our enormous human potential.

शक्तिसम्पातेन चक्रगतिवर्धनं क्रान्तिः ॥ ३ ॥

V.3 *shaktisampátena cakragativardhanaṁ krántih*

shakti, force; *sampátena*, by the application of; *cakra*, cycle; *gati*, movement; *vardhanaṁ*, increase; *krántih*, transition, overcoming, forced evolution

"An acceleration of the movement of the social cycle by the application of force is called *kránti*."

These next two sutras highlight the role of the *sadvipra* in the forward movement of the social cycle. When the transition from one social class to another occurs by natural means it is called *svábhávika parivarttana* in Sanskrit, "natural change." By contrast, when force is applied to accelerate the transition from one *varṅa* to the next, rather than simply allowing this transition to occur on its own in the course of time, the word *kránti* is used, "forced evolution." As we saw in the previous sutra, it is the duty of the *sadvipra* to apply that force in order to accelerate the movement of the social cycle so that the rising tide of inequity and exploitation can be beaten back before it can do further harm to human society. If, for example, the *kśatriya* regime becomes tyrannical and unjust, as eventually happens with military dictatorships and other *kśatriya*-led societies, then the *sadvipras* will use whatever means are at their disposal to instigate a transfer of power to the intellectuals who oppose them, thereby ushering in the Vipra Age. If this can be accomplished purely through the mobilization of public protest and other forms of social pressure that eventually force the rulers to step aside, then it would be an example of *kranti*.

Any forward movement of the social cycle, regardless of which *varṅa* comes into power, brings new impetus to society, unleashing a wave of progress in different spheres of social life. This infusion of fresh ideas and fresh energy can last for an extended period of time, but eventually that surge of progress loses its momentum. The institutions of power, once so beneficial to society as a whole, begin to calcify, and the ruling class eventually becomes entrenched in the status quo, acting more to maintain their power and privilege than to benefit the populace. The more entrenched they become in the politics, economics, and social institutions that have proved so beneficial to them and to their predecessors, the more out of tune they become with the ever-changing needs and desires of the people. As a consequence, exploitation and injustice increase, which in turn gives rise to a growing opposition, consisting of those who are conscious of the weight of that injustice and who desire to set a new course for society by casting aside what increasingly appears to their eyes to be a moribund status quo.

This social dynamic, which has been around since the dawn of human society, generally goes under the rubric of "thesis, antithesis, and synthesis" in contemporary social discourse, terminology coined by Johann Fichte to describe the dialectical method of the German Idealist philosopher Georg Hegel and which Karl Marx later applied to social processes in his analysis of historical materialism (more commonly known as dialectical materialism). It is, however, an ancient idea that can be found in both the Hindu and Buddhist philosophical traditions. One idea or theory gathers strength until it is eventually opposed by a second idea or theory, and the resulting clash between the two gives birth to a synthesis, a new idea or theory that supersedes them both. This is a dynamic that applies as much to the world of social movements as it does to the world of mental constructs (the original Hegelian intent).

As with all movement in the manifest universe, this social dynamic is not linear but systaltic or pulsative. Whether it is a ray of photons traversing the universe or the flow of prana within the human body, movement is never linear but rather proceeds through a series of discrete jumps between alternating pauses.[16] In this it resembles our breathing or the beating of our heart. As we breathe in, our lungs expand, and this expansion continues until our lungs are filled with air. A diastolic pause ensues, after which we breathe out until we reach the systolic pause.[17] Unhindered expansion and unhindered contraction are both absent in the expressed universe, and it is a further characteristic of this systaltic movement that momentum is primarily accumulated during the systolic pause. This can be compared to a trek up and down a series of hills. We gain momentum during our pause in the valley and we use that accumulated force to climb to the top of the next hill, after which the descent begins, followed by a new pause and a new climb. Thus when a new synthesis is established in society, there is typically a great burst of energy and progress. Once that period of expansion reaches its peak, a slow decline begins. As the end of this decline approaches, an antithesis appears. The antithesis gathers force, opposes the declining thesis, and eventually overcomes it. In the process a new synthesis is born, injecting new life into society, and thus begins a new period of expansion and progress.

Up until now, the late stages of the previous eras in our different societies have all been witness to a prolonged period of exploitation and injustice. In the absence of *sadvipra* intervention, the wheel of social progress has turned with agonizing slowness, prolonging the suffering of the greater mass of humanity. The present era of late capitalism that reigns supreme in most parts of the globe is a testament to such prolonged exploitation. More than a century and a half has passed since Marx and other nineteenth-century reformers and social thinkers raised their voices against the outrages of *vaeshya* dominance, and the exploitation and injustice they spoke out against had already been in place well before their birth. Despite their efforts, however, it often seems like we are no closer in the early twenty-first century to getting out from under the yoke of capitalist oppression than we were in the late nineteenth century, perhaps because the nature of capitalist exploitation has become subtler and more difficult to identify, less ostensibly offensive to human dignity. There is no dearth of voices calling attention to the widespread ills that are a direct result of neocapitalist practices, but they often go unheard, or else these ills are attributed to other causes, and in the absence of enlightened and capable leadership, there are no visible signs on the horizon of the much-needed turning of the social wheel that will make possible the radical social change that is so patently necessary.

तीव्रशक्तिसम्पातेन गतिवर्धनं विप्लवः ॥ ४ ॥

V.4 *tiivrashaktisampátena gativardhanaṁ viplavah*

tiivra, intense; *shakti,* force, energy; *sampátena,* by the application of; *gativardhanaṁ,* acceleration; *viplavah,* revolution

"An acceleration of the movement of the social cycle by the application of intense force is called *viplava.*"

When a new age is ushered in within a very short span of time, or when the application of intense force is needed in order to remove the hegemony of the ruling class, it is termed *viplava* rather than *kránti,* revolution rather than forced evolution. The difference is a matter of degree. Even more so than with *kránti,* revolutions occur when the ruling class reaches the zenith point of degradation and exploitation, thus generating tremendous sentiment among the populace for radical change, a deeply felt pressure that makes the people ripe for overthrowing their governors by whatever means possible.

Revolutions play an important role in the dynamics of social change and have thus been the subject of much scrutiny. Not all historical revolutions, however, fit the Proutist criteria for *viplava.* There are many examples in history of putative revolutions that did not produce any revolutionary change, neither a change of *varńa* nor any of the far-reaching, radical changes in society that accompany a change of *varńa.* A mere seizure of power that lacks the characteristic influx of new ideas that leads to all-around progress in social life, and which does not put an end to the institutionalized exploitation and injustice perpetrated by the dominant class, cannot be considered a true revolution. Such coups or regime changes are examples of either palatial change—a new set of faces and new promises, but no substantive change to the dynamics of exploitation and thus no real benefit to the people—or pyramidical revolution, a top-down regime change resulting in an autocratic imposition of dogmatic ideas that only serves to thwart the aspirations of the masses or suppress them even further. By contrast, a true revolution inevitably results in a sweeping change in collective psychology and an end to the inertia that characterized the institutions and policies of the deposed ruling class. The status quo is swept away and the new collective psychology is given full rein to thrive and flourish.

In the past, the transition from one *varńa* to another occurred through the process of natural change as well as through *viplava* or *kránti*, revolution or forced evolution, but it seems unlikely going forward that future changes of *varńa* will occur through natural processes. The speed of social change has increased greatly in the past century, and that speed of change is expected to accelerate in the coming centuries as our collective human consciousness continues to expand at an ever-accelerating rate, and future changes of *varńa* are likely to be set in motion through conscious intervention.

Despite the much-needed change of *varńa* that authentic revolutions have brought in the past, they have by and large suffered from ideological defects as well as defects in the character of their leaders, the Russian Revolution being a case in point, and these defects tended to degrade the new social movements, thereby preventing them from realizing their full potential for social progress. With the emergence of *sadvipras*, Anandamurti envisions what he calls "nuclear revolution" to become the new norm, due to the highly evolved ethical and spiritual character of these spiritual revolutionaries:

> In nuclear revolution, every aspect of collective life—social, economic, political, cultural, psychic and spiritual—is completely transformed. New moral and spiritual values arise in society which provide the impetus for accelerated social progress. The old era is replaced by a new era—one collective psychology is replaced by another. This type of revolution results in all-round development and social progress. Nuclear revolution can only be brought about by *sadvipras* who reside in the nucleus of the social cycle. Through their concerted effort, moral and spiritual power, and all-round endeavor, they mobilize the exploited sections of society to overthrow the ruling class—the exploiters. This very struggle for mass upheaval liberates society from exploitation and ushers in a new era of peace and prosperity.[18]

In his writings, Anandamurti has detailed the necessary conditions under which such revolutions can take place, and how they can be successfully brought to fruition—leaving, in effect, a blueprint for social activists now and into the future. A detailed discussion of this blueprint is beyond the scope of this commentary, but it begins by creating ideological consciousness, first among intellectuals and activists, and later among the masses. From there it proceeds to other phases of revolutionary movement.

शक्तिसम्पातेन विपरीतधारायां विक्रान्तिः ॥ ५ ॥

V.5 *shaktisampátena vipariitadháráyáṁ vikrántih*

shakti, force; *sampátena*, by the application of; *vipariita*, contrary, reverse; *dháráyáṁ*, when the flow is; *vikrántih*, counter-evolution

The reverse movement of the social cycle by the application of force is called *vikránti*."

The natural movement of the social cycle is from the Shudra Age to the Kśatriya Age to the Vipra Age to the Vaeshya Age, but the contrary movement is also possible, backward instead of forward. A *vaeshya* society can follow the natural course and progress to the next *kśatriya* era after passing through a short-lived *shúdra* revolution, a phenomenon that will be discussed in sutra V.7, but it can also regress, so to speak, to a *vipra* society. In the same way, the Vipra Age will normally be followed by the Vaeshya Age, a transition that will be brought about either through natural change, forced evolution, or revolution, but in certain cases it may also regress to *kśatriya* rule. Such instances involving the backward movement of the social cycle are infrequent, and since such a change in *varńa* goes against the normal flow of social movement, it is invariably short-lived. For the same reason, it can only occur due to the application of force, not by natural change. As with any natural motion that is forcibly made to reverse course, as soon as the thwarting force weakens, the natural forward movement once again reasserts itself. While the counter-evolutionary movement may gain its impetus from anti-exploitation sentiment among the leaders and cadre of the incoming *varṅa*, it does not liberate society from the depredations of the ruling class but only alters the nature of that exploitation and injustice. Nor is such an unnatural change backed by the people, whose collective psychology is opposed to that of the new leaders, but is instead imposed from above. Eventually that dammed-up momentum finds its way past the barriers that have been erected in its path. The previous *varṅa* regains power and once again faces the pressures that will eventually bring its reign to a preordained end, an end that may come very quickly if the antithesis raised by the leaders of the next *varṅa* has already matured to a sufficient extent.

तीव्रशक्तिसम्पातेन विपरीतधारायां प्रतिविप्लवः ॥ ६ ॥

V.6 *tiivrashaktisampátena vipariitadhárayáṁ prativiplavah*

tiivra, intense; *shakti*, force; *sampátena*, by the application of; *vipariita*, contrary, reverse; *dhárayáṁ*, when the flow is; *prativiplavah*, counterrevolution

"The reverse movement of the social cycle due to the application of intense force is called *prativiplava*."

The backward or contrary movement of the social cycle can also be brought about by the application of great force, in which case it is termed *prativiplava* or "counterrevolution." There are numerous instances of counterrevolution in the annals of history and they have all been extremely short-lived, even more short-lived than counter-evolution, as is to be expected. Such a regressive change of *varṅa* is most often accompanied by new paradigms of institutionalized injustice, often more severe than that of the outgoing regime due to the ongoing use of force that is required to suppress the natural aspirations of the people. As a result, when the force that was applied in order to turn back the social cycle begins to wane, ie., when the vitality of the new regime diminishes sufficiently, the rising tide of opposition moves the social cycle forward once again, this time with redoubled force.

A careful study of the social history of the world will reveal that until now every attempt at *prativiplava* has not only caused enormous psychic and financial suffering and plunged humanity into the mire of gloom and despair, but has also lengthened the period of social contraction. This in turn, in the next phase, has helped to accelerate the speed of the period of social expansion.[19]

—Anandamurti

It is always difficult to analyze social changes without the benefit of sufficient hindsight, but if we go back far enough it is relatively easy to find obvious examples of *prativiplava*, as for instance in the historical annals of Medieval Europe, when certain *kśatriya* kings tried to forcibly wrest power back from the Church. In all such cases, whatever success they achieved was highly volatile and short-lived, while the damage they did left a lasting legacy.

पूर्णावर्तनेन परिक्रान्तिः ॥ ७ ॥

V.7 *púrńávartanena parikrántih*

púrńa, whole, full, complete; *ávartanena*, by a turning; *parikrántih*, perambulation, full evolutionary rotation

"A complete rotation results in *parikránti*."

One full rotation of the social cycle is considered complete when the Vaeshya Age or capitalist era comes to an end with a brief *shúdra* revolution and thereafter gives way to the subsequent Kśatriya Age. While prior changes of *varńa* can and have happened through *svábhávika parivarttana*, natural change, and *kránti*, forced evolution, the same cannot be said for the end of the Vaeshya Age, due to the distinct nature of late-capitalist exploitation. The degree of exploitation at the end of the Vaeshya Age is significantly greater than that of any of the previous eras, as is the control that the ruling class exerts over all facets of economic, political, and cultural life, and hence it is only through the application of great force that power can be wrested from the hands of the capitalists. It is termed a *shúdra* revolution, rather than a *kśatriya* or *vipra* revolution, because such a cataclysmic social change can only take place through the sheer force of the masses. Once the capitalists have been deposed, however, a Shudra Age does not ensue because the *shúdras*, by definition, do not have the requisite wherewithal to govern society (unless the brief and chaotic period of transition be considered a fleeting Shudra Age). A proletariat uprising of one form or another is necessary to overcome capitalist domination but a proletariat government can never be the fruit of that uprising, for the leaders of the revolution will always be those of *kśatriya* and *vipra* mentality. As was mentioned earlier, *shúdras* are those whose mental waves tend to be dominated by matter or are fully occupied with matter, and thus they possess neither the martial spirit nor the intellect and organizational capacity to lead a revolution. They make willing cadre when inspired by those of greater intellect or greater courage, but the *shúdra* revolution is instigated and led by those of *kśatriya* and *vipra* mentality who are able to arouse the masses on the basis of anti-exploitation sentiment, and it is they who assume the reins thereafter.

It is a peculiar phenomenon of the Vaeshya Age that as *vaeshya* dominance waxes and becomes increasingly intransigent and seemingly invincible, the *kśatriya* and *vipra* classes become increasingly subservient and somnolent. Despite their innate disposition toward the life of the mind and the attractions of heroic deeds, they are by and large reduced to leading lives of convenience and accommodation with the status quo, prime characteristics of the *shúdra* mentality. Anandamurti calls such members of the labor force *vikśubdha shúdras*, those who are not *shúdra* by mentality or predisposition but by force of circumstance. In the late Vaeshya Age, the military and police forces owe their allegiance not to career officers or heroic leaders but to capitalist interests, and the same is true of the intelligentsia, with educational institutions, the arts, science, engineering, and even religion marching to the drum of capitalist agendas. The *kśatriyas* and *vipras* become slaves to their salaries or to *vaeshya* patronage, becoming fully dependent for their economic well-being on those who hold the pursestrings, and the comfortable life they are offered in exchange for propping up the ruling class with their talents and effort is like a drug that deadens the better qualities of their respective *varṅas*.

The word *vikṣubdha* means "disgruntled" or "disturbed," and it serves to call attention to the mounting discontent among those of *kṣatriya* and *vipra* mentality in the late-capitalist era as the pressure of capitalist exploitation and control continues to grow, reducing them to the role of servile cogs in the capitalist machine. There is a general malaise among these sections of society, even if the majority are not fully conscious of the source of their discontent, a sense of alienation and cynicism that can be tied in part to the growth of materialism during this period in history, and this discontent continues to grow as their constraints tighten and their freedom becomes more and more circumscribed.[20] Those among them who have not succumbed to this state of somnolence, and who are acutely aware of the source of their discontent, will become the leaders of the coming antithesis. It is they who will promote the ideological education of their *kṣatriya* and *vipra* compatriots, bringing their attention to the nature and consequences of capitalist exploitation, and it is they who will stir the embers of ideological consciousness among the sleeping masses, a forerunner of the coming *shúdra* revolution.

As with any change in *varṅa*, the early capitalist era brings great benefit to society. The expanding role of commerce leads to rapid economic progress. The overall standard of living increases as the intellectuals of the age are rewarded for putting their intellect to work creating more attractive and useful consumer goods and public utilities, while the *kṣatriyas* are fruitfully employed in keeping order, so necessary for the free flow of goods and services. Political freedom also increases, since *vaeshyas* thrive best in democratic systems where their money can dictate policy from behind the scenes. But as time goes on, profit rather than progress becomes the prime mover. As a consequence, exploitation grows, and the exploitation of the late-capitalist era is greater than that of previous eras due to the nature of the capitalist mentality, which feeds on acquisition and accumulation. It is not so much the direct enjoyment of objects that *vaeshyas* seek as it is the possession of wealth and the power and prestige it bestows. More so than with any other *varńa*, the more the *vaeshyas* have, the more they want, and since material wealth is limited, their insatiable appetite for accumulation inevitably leads to widespread inequality and injustice, particularly in the economic sphere. The late-capitalist era is marked by the concentration of great wealth in the hands of the few, and it is the greater mass of humanity that bears the brunt of this disparity. This is not only evident in the extreme economic privations suffered by huge sectors of society—as of this writing, over 40% of the world's population lives on five dollars a day or less, while the richest 1% possesses over 40% of the world's wealth—but in a myriad other social ills as well. Capitalist exploitation is particularly prevalent in the psychic sphere—Anandamurti has written extensively on this subject, detailing the various stratagems that capitalists employ to create psychic stagnancy in the people and weaken their intellectual and cultural life—and also in the spiritual sphere, where the pervasive materialism that is so integral to the imposition of capitalist ideology has had a crushing effect on the human spirit.[21]

As capitalist society moves into its late stages, it eventually devolves into two classes, the exploiters and the exploited, which includes those of *kśatriya* and *vipra* mentality who have been reduced to being peons of the capitalists. Marx and Engels formulated their theory of a proletariat revolution based on their observations of late-capitalist exploitation, having been born at the beginning of the late-capitalist era, but their faith in the working class was essentially misplaced. They themselves were *vipras*, as were most social reformers at that time and into the present, and in order for public discontent to rise and eventually coalesce into an organized opposition, it must come from the mouths and minds of those same *vipras*, along with their *kśatriya* compatriots who supply the indispensable elements of energy, valor, and fighting spirit. Together they are the heart and soul of the opposition, the ideologues and the champions of justice, the ones who are able to discern the true nature of the exploitation that oppresses society without most people being aware of it and those who have the courage and vigor to raise their voices and agitate for social change.

The capitalists who control society are well aware of the danger that these *vikśubdha shúdras* pose to the perpetuation of their power, and thus they do everything possible to silence their voices,[22] but the finality of every capitalist society, sooner or later, is a *shúdra* revolution instigated and led by those same *vikśubdha shúdras*, which in turn ushers in the next *kśatriya* age, since the martial spirit so necessary to the successful removal of the capitalist regime belongs to the *kśatriya* leaders within the opposition. If the *vipra* voices among them are strong enough, it is possible that such a revolution can be pulled off without bloodshed, after which the *vipras* will wait their turn until the conditions are ripe for the next Vipra Age to emerge, but if the *kśatriya* elements dominate then such an outcome is unlikely,[23] and that has been the case in the *shúdra* revolutions that we have witnessed up until now. The Russian Revolution of 1917, according to many Proutist thinkers, was a prime example of this, when the Czarist world of late capitalism was supplanted by a *kśatriya* regime after a short and largely bloodless coup led by the *vipra* members of the rebellion. The *vipra* ideologues were critical to the initial success of the revolution but the *kśatriya*-minded revolutionaries quickly took control, and the civil war and purges that ensued were extremely bloody. It was these *kśatriya* elements who ruled the USSR in the decades that followed.

When Anandamurti first published his teachings on the Samaj Chakra in the late 1950s, it was his contention that the first Vaeshya Age was still going strong in most of the developed world. In some undeveloped or underdeveloped countries the first *kśatriya* or *vipra* ages were still in evidence, and in a few countries a second Kśatriya Age had emerged following a *shúdra* revolution, with some indications of a second Vipra Age on the horizon.[24] While there is a fair amount of debate among social theorists working within the Proutist model, Russia appears to be one of those countries that had moved into the second rotation of the social cycle by that time. Similarly, there were several societies in the 1950s that appeared to still be in the first Kśatriya Age. The Iranian revolution of 1979, for example, appears to have thrust what for centuries had been a largely agrarian society under *kśatriya* rule into a *vipra* era under the rule of the Islamic clerics. More than forty years later, that *vipra* era is still firmly in place in Iran, but there are growing signs among the Iranian populace of discontent with *vipra* rule and a collective desire to move toward a capitalist society under a democratic political structure.

While Anandamurti's theory of the Samaj Chakra will require a great deal of research and astute analysis by capable social thinkers before the class-wise movement of the different societies of the globe, both past and present, can be properly demonstrated, thus validating this theory in the realm of social discourse, it should be pointed out that the Indian philosophical tradition divides theories into two distinct classes, those in which theory precedes practice and those in which practice precedes theory. Some theories are first idealized in the mind and then an attempt is made to apply that theory to the manifest world, inevitably with mixed results, but the best theories are those that are based on careful observation of the manifest world. In effect, they are descriptions of reality, the mind's attempt to understand the underlying structures behind what the mind observes in praxis. The apple fell and on the basis of that observation Newton developed the theory of gravitational attraction—in effect, a description of observable fact. Anandamurti's Samaj Chakra belongs in this category, being a succinct description of social movement as it manifests in human society. Marxism, on the other hand, belongs to the first category. It was a noble attempt to formulate a theory of social movement for the purpose of human welfare that was unfortunately doomed to failure. Not only was it first idealized in the mind, rather than having been informed by a careful observation of history, it also failed to take into account some of the fundamental characteristics of human nature, most especially the key role that dharma plays in human motivation.

The fact that most of the world has yet to move into the second rotation of the social cycle may well be the reason why no social thinker before Anandamurti was able to recognize the universal nature of this class-wise movement. It is very difficult to step back and see something for what it is when you are still in the middle of it. But when the entire world has moved on to the second rotation of the social cycle, and in some places to the third, then the movement of the *varńas* should be far more clear to social theorists.

Chapter Five

वैचित्र्यं प्राकृतधर्मः समानं न भविष्यति ॥ ८ ॥

V.8 *vaecitryaṁ prákrtadharmah samánaṁ na bhaviśyati*

vaecitryaṁ, diversity; *prákrta*, natural; *dharma*, universal law or characteristic; *samánaṁ*, equal, same; *na*, not; *bhaviśyati*, will be

"Diversity is the natural law, not equality."

As we saw in Chapter Four, no two waves in the process of *sadrsha pariṅáma*, the sequential flow of curvature emanating from the Macrocosmic Mind, are ever the same. Similar, yes. Identical, no. Not only every wave, but every fragment of every wave is entirely unique. Thus, in the social sphere, the effort to impose artificial standards of equality in human affairs or human institutions is doomed to failure, since it goes against the laws of nature. It is yet another instance of a theory idealized in the mind that proves barren in the soil of practice. Karl Marx theorized about equality of outcome, and other social thinkers have emphasized equality of opportunity, but in the field of social welfare the understanding of diversity as it expresses itself in the world and in human nature must take precedence over any intellectual ideal of equality.

> Many theories sound very nice. These philosophies have spoken of equality for all, but in the practical world it has been seen that they don't work because the basic principles of these philosophies are contrary to the fundamental principles of the world as established by *prakrti*. *Vaecitryaṁ prákrtadharmah samánaṁ na bhaviśyati*. In other words, the world is a play of different forms, a pageant of different rhythms. This should never be forgotten—not now, not ever.[25]
>
> — Anandamurti

The recognition of diversity allows us to create systems of human affairs that can promote the maximum welfare of all of society's members, whereas efforts to impose unnatural standards of equality will in the long run prove to be an impediment to the pursuit of collective welfare. The idea of equal distribution on a large scale, for example, is detrimental to human welfare. Distribution, as we will examine in a later sutra, should be rational, not equal, and it should allow for the use of surplus wealth as an incentive.

युगस्य सर्वनिम्नप्रयोजनं सर्वेषां विधेयम् ॥ ९ ॥

V.9 *yugasya sarvanimnaprayojanaṁ sarveṣāṁ vidheyam*

yugasya, of the age or era; *sarvanimna*, minimum; *prayojanaṁ*, necessities; *sarveṣāṁ*, to all; *vidheyam*, should be provided

"The minimum requirements of the age should be guaranteed to all."

As was mentioned earlier in this chapter, the Sanskrit word for "society," *samāja*, means "to move together toward a common goal." The one common goal we all share is the attainment of happiness, which is itself predicated on the gradual expansion and ultimate liberation of consciousness. Thus the principle task of society is to promote the welfare of its members in such a way as to facilitate their forward movement along the path of spiritual evolution. Any and all impediments that block or constrain that forward movement, be they physical or psychic, must be removed if society is to be successful in the task of promoting human dharma, and the first and foremost of these impediments in the life of an individual is the failure to secure their minimum requirements. Whether or not we have experienced it directly, we can all appreciate just how difficult it is to achieve spiritual progress if the greater part of our energy is tied up in the struggle for economic survival. If we are not sure where our next meal will come from, if we don't have a roof over our head, proper clothing to protect against the elements, access to a quality education, or medical treatment in times of illness, whether for ourselves or for our family, it becomes exceedingly difficult to give sufficient time and energy to our spiritual life. Nor is it in any way indicative of a healthy human society when some of its citizens are caught up in the struggle for survival while others have the economic wherewithal to dedicate themselves to higher pursuits. With this in mind, it is incumbent on society to do all it can to remove those mundane obstacles so that each of us can move freely toward our spiritual goal, and this cannot be achieved without guaranteeing the minimum requirements for a productive life, a life that gives full scope for psychic and spiritual development, a life in which the primary obstacles are inside us rather than outside, forced upon us by a society that gives free rein to economic disparity and other forms of injustice.

Exactly what those minimum requirements are will differ from age to age, region to region, and even among individuals. A few centuries ago, for example, most people did not depend on a vehicle for their economic well-being, but nowadays a vehicle has become a necessity for most of us.[26] The housing, clothing, and alimentary requirements for people who live near the arctic circle is markedly different from those who live in the tropics, and in every society there are people with special needs. The determination of the minimum requirements will need to be made locally, in accordance with local needs and production, while taking into account any special needs that certain citizens may have. In conjunction with this, the production of essential goods, those that are involved in fulfilling the minimum requirements, should take priority in the local economy. In addition, it is the duty of society to make a continual effort to raise the minimum standard of its citizens in order to allow them to dedicate more of their time and energy to psychic and spiritual growth, as well as to keep pace with the inevitable changes that all societies undergo over time. At present, the minimum requirements are food, education, shelter, clothing, and medical treatment, and in most places, adequate transportation, but in the future those minimum necessities will surely increase. This should be a legal right for all citizens throughout the globe, and it should be enshrined in the constitution, whether it is the national constitution or the future world constitution.

How that legal right to the minimum requirements of life is guaranteed is also of critical importance. If the minimum requirements are given to people without any exchange of labor and skill then it is almost certain to lead to an increase in lethargy and idleness among a certain segment of the population. Moreover, it would require an unnecessary mobilization of state resources and the imposition of an unnecessary level of state control. Instead, each citizen should be guaranteed employment as a fundamental right, and the purchasing capacity provided by that employment must be sufficient for each household to comfortably secure their minimum requirements. Thus Anandamurti considers it the responsibility of the state to ensure 100% employment and for that employment to pay a living wage. This is an essential component of economic democracy, in which the economic power resides with the people, something that is far more important to social welfare and freedom from exploitation than political democracy.[27]

Anandamurti also extends the concept of the minimum requirements of life to other living creatures as well, in essence expanding our understanding of society to include the entire ecosystem:

> At present human beings are thinking about their own minimum requirements more than about the minimum requirements of animals and plants. A day is coming when some of the animals, if not all, will come within the realm of our social membership. Today we say that each and every human being will get the minimum requirements. Tomorrow we will say that the minimum requirements will also include the needs of dogs, cows, monkeys, etc. To fulfill these requirements, there should be more and more production. The earth is not only for human beings; it is for other living beings also.[28]

अतिरिक्तं प्रदातव्यं गुणानुपातेन ॥ १० ॥

V.10 *atiriktaṁ pradátavyaṁ guṅánupátena*

atiriktaṁ, surplus; *pradátavyaṁ,* should be given; *guṅa,* quality, merit; *anupátena,* by proportion

> "The surplus wealth should be distributed
> according to merit."

Our planet is capable of producing far more than the minimum necessities of life without compromising the environment or destroying the habitat of other living creatures. In the early 1960s, the eminent systems theorist R. Buckminster Fuller estimated that "Spaceship Earth," as he called it, was capable of supporting a population of ten billion people at middle-class American standards (a population total the UN forecasts we will reach by the end of the twenty-first century at present growth rates)—*if* the earth's resources were wisely used and equably distributed, without the prevalent disregard for the distinction between renewable and nonrenewable resources. And this estimation was made without taking into account future advances in technology. There will always be surplus wealth, even after guaranteeing the minimum requirements to all, and thus we need to see to it that this surplus wealth is distributed wisely.

In Anandamurti's view, surplus wealth should be used as an incentive to encourage people to utilize their skills and talents for the purpose of human development and to decrease the struggle for subsistence so that life can become increasingly productive and enjoyable. Karl Marx's famous slogan, "from each according to their ability, to each according to their needs," fails to take into account the physical, psychic, and spiritual longings of human beings. As people proceed on the path of evolution, their desire for happiness is expressed in different spheres of life, including the material sphere, where the unimpeded accumulation of wealth has been a principle factor in the unjust disparities that have plagued our race throughout the history of human civilization, never more so than in the present day. This physical longing must be controlled in order to ensure the welfare of all, but it cannot be unduly suppressed without creating widespread discontent. People need to have the scope to express their longing in the physical sphere as well as in the psychic and spiritual spheres—the widespread apathy among workers of different classes in the communist regimes of the last century is a testament to this—but that need should be met in such a way that it benefits the collective interest and contributes to the all-around development of the human race. This should be the guiding spirit behind the distribution of *atiriktam*. Distributing society's surplus wealth to those individuals who provide the greatest service to human society—such as doctors, scientists, and artists—provides an incentive for them to work hard to develop their talents and contribute to the tide of social progress.

In most cases, this can best be accomplished by awarding higher salaries to those whose contributions most benefit humanity. This will allow them to purchase the special amenities they need to develop their talents and pursue their professional ambitions, as well as allowing them to satisfy other longings, including the longing for specific comforts and possessions. In some cases, certain amenities may be provided by the state, such as access to the top labs for meritorious scientists and doctors, or to the best recording studios for important recording artists, but in general the incentive of a higher salary offers the most effective motivation for human beings who have not yet reached the point where they are motivated entirely by spiritual and humanitarian concerns. Naturally, as the spiritual standard of society increases, especially among intellectuals and otherwise talented individuals, the need for such incentives will gradually decrease.

The question of how large a gap should be fixed between the minimum and maximum salaries will have to be carefully considered, keeping in mind the changing conditions and changing needs in different parts of the globe. Included within the principle of *atiriktam* is the constant effort to minimize the gap between the minimum and maximum salaries without reducing the material incentive to providing greater service to humanity and always with a view toward promoting the physical, mental, and spiritual welfare of all. Not only should the minimum requirements gradually be raised as society progresses, there should also be a concurrent effort to provide maximum amenities to the general populace by increasing their purchasing capacity so that everyone's quality of life, as regards the mundane sphere, continues to improve. There are many material inventions and facilities that lie outside the scope of the minimum requirements but which make our lives easier and more enjoyable, thus lessening the physical obstacles that inhibit human progress. As long as these amenities are good for the physical or psychic development of human beings, society should make every effort to see to it that they are brought within the scope of everyone's purchasing power.

> The amenities of life are those things which make life easy. The word "amenity" comes from the Old Latin word *amoenus*, which means "to fulfill the desire" or "to make the position easy." Amenities mean physical and psychic longings. Whatever will satisfy the physical and psychic longings of the people will be the amenities of the age.[29]

सर्वनिम्नमानवर्धनं समाजजीवलक्षणम् ॥ ११ ॥

V.11 *sarvanimnamánavardhanaṁ samájajiivalakṣaṇam*

sarvanimna, minimum; *mána*, standard; *vardhanaṁ*, increase; *samája*, society; *jiiva*, life, vitality; *lakṣaṇam*, sign, indication

"An increase in the minimum standard of living is a sign of the vitality of society."

Like a chain that is only as strong as its weakest link, society as a whole can only be as strong as its most underprivileged or neglected members. Thus the constant effort to raise the minimum standard of living that was mentioned in the previous sutra in conjunction with the principle of *atiriktam* is also the principle indicator of the vitality of society, so much so that Anandamurti has stated that a politician who does not improve the living standard of his constituency should not be reelected. The biggest obstacle to spiritual growth on both an individual and collective level is the struggle for material and economic well-being, for it keeps the mind occupied with matter. Thus if society is to ensure that all of its members have the best, most propitious environment possible in which to pursue the path of spiritual evolution, then its first and foremost duty is to ensure the economic well-being of all, beginning with society's least privileged citizens. It is the responsibility of the state to create an educational and intellectual climate that fosters maximum psychic growth, and to promote the values of a universal spirituality while guaranteeing maximum access to the different avenues of spiritual growth, but neither psychic nor spiritual well-being is feasible for the majority of human beings if their physical well-being is not ensured. Thus the continual rise in the minimum standard of living, that which is guaranteed to all regardless of the social value of their work, is the most reliable measure of social progress and all-around social vitality.

As society progresses, what are considered special amenities in one age become part of the minimum requirements of life in a later age. Whereas nowadays a car may be considered a minimum necessity in most parts of the world and a private plane a special amenity reserved for the meritorious, a time will come when a plane is considered a minimum necessity and more advanced forms of transport a special amenity. This gradual rise in the minimum standard of living enables human beings to enjoy lives of greater ease and comfort, and this in turn frees them to turn their attention toward psychic and spiritual pursuits. As society advances in the material plane, work hours will diminish and people will have more time for personal development to go along with their increased affluence, and this will make them less likely to look toward the material world to satisfy their inner longings and more likely to direct their attention toward the psychic and spiritual worlds. When people feel materially deprived, it is only natural that they look toward the material world in order to fulfill that psychic hunger. But as that material deprivation diminishes, the understanding that material affluence cannot fulfill one's inner longing grows and the mind naturally turns toward subtler pursuits. Thus this increase in the minimum standard of living opens the door to progress in the higher spheres of life.

समाजादेशेन विना धनसञ्चयो ऽकर्तव्यः ॥ १२ ॥

V.12 *samájádeshena viná dhanasaiṇcayo 'kartavyah*

samája, society; *ádeshena*, by approval, by order; *viná*, without; *dhana*, wealth; *saiṋcayah*, accumulation; *akartavyah*, should not be done

"No individual should be allowed to accumulate any physical wealth without the clear permission or approval of the collective body."[30]

This is the first of the Five Fundamental Principles of Prout with which Anandamurti concludes *Ananda Sutram*. They are the guiding principles on which Proutist policies, plans, and programs should be based. The first of these five fundamental principles introduces a key concept in Proutist economics: the introduction of a wealth ceiling. The foremost duty of society is to promote the all-around elevation of its members, that is, of society as a whole, and thus, as a matter of principle, individual liberties should not be allowed to go against the collective interest. When an individual accumulates excess physical wealth to the detriment of others, their behavior becomes antisocial, and thus wealth accumulation, as a general principle, should be subject to the permission of the collective body, which is charged with the responsibility of overseeing collective welfare. Physical wealth is limited and excess accumulation in one sector of society inevitably leads to deprivation in others, an endemic form of injustice that must be eliminated if society as a whole is to thrive. As Anandamurti puts it, "can there be any justification for a situation in which some people are rolling in luxury while others are dying of starvation?"[31]

This idea is based on the principle of cosmic inheritance. The material universe is a thought projection within the Macrocosmic Mind evolved in the flow of *saiṋcara*, and thus there can be only one owner of the physical wealth of this universe: Brahma. This dictates that all material wealth be considered a common patrimony to be shared among the created beings in such a way that everyone benefits and no one is hindered in their evolution by the lack of the physical necessities of life.

> None of the movable or immovable property of this universe belongs to any particular individual; everything

is the common patrimony of all, and the father of all is Brahma. All living beings can enjoy their rightful share of this property, like members of a joint family in the Dayabhaga system. As members of a joint family, human beings should safeguard this common property in a befitting manner and utilize it properly. They should also make proper arrangements so that everyone can enjoy it with equal rights, ensuring that all have the minimum requirements of life to enable them to live in a healthy body with a sound mind.[32]

— Anandamurti

Human beings have a natural desire for physical pabula to fulfill both their physical needs and certain psychic longings related to their acquired and inborn *saṁskáras*,[33] and as long as the fulfillment of this desire does not affect collective welfare, there should be no bar to the exercise of individual liberty. But when a conflict arises between individual liberty and collective welfare, then collective welfare takes precedence in a Proutist system, since the fundamental individual interests, beginning with the minimum requirements of life, are guaranteed in the pursuance of collective welfare. The failure to place a ceiling on wealth accumulation has historically had a disastrous effect on society, benefiting a small percentage of the population while harming society as a whole. Overaccumulation by a small segment of society is the prime cause of wealth disparity, and this is not only fundamentally unjust, it is a direct cause of social conflict, which comes at a great cost to everyone, not only in the economic sphere but even more so in the psychic and spiritual spheres. The concentration of wealth in the hands of the few, so prevalent in our modern world, reduces the purchasing capacity of the majority and creates a class of have-nots, which further cripples economic life. This in turn leads to a myriad of social ills, from crime to social unrest to the balkanization of human society. Furthermore, the material benefits enjoyed by those who are guilty of overaccumulation are more than counterbalanced by the psychic and spiritual harm they accrue. Unbridled accumulation, apart from being fundamentally unethical for the reasons just described, increases one's desire for and preoccupation with material objects, and this in turn becomes an obstacle to psychic expansion and spiritual growth. In effect, the excessive desire for material accumulation is a psychic disease that in extreme cases requires the intervention of the collective body.[34] Given that the foremost duty of society is to promote the spiritual evolution of its members along with their physical and psychic well-being, it is in the best interests of the individual that the tendency for material accumulation be curbed—within reasonable limits.

The determination of that ceiling will depend on the particular society and the era in which it finds itself. Salaries should be set so that talented individuals will have sufficient incentive to cultivate their talents for the greater good, but they should not be so high that the *vaeshya* tendency of wealth accumulation is given free rein. There must be a gap between the minimum and maximum salaries, but after a certain point, additional wealth does not provide a real incentive for additional effort, and thus there comes a point of diminishing returns. Furthermore, the larger the gap, the lower the minimum salary will have to be, given the finite limits to wealth. At this juncture in the twenty-first century, those social analysts who support the idea of a wealth ceiling as well as a wealth floor typically suggest a difference somewhere between 500% and 1000%. From a Proutist perspective, the smaller the gap the better, as long as it does not hinder the effectiveness of the *atiriktam* incentive. If the annual minimum salary for an unmarried adult with no dependents is fixed at $50,000 in the United States, for example, then their maximum annual salary, in the view of these social theorists, should be somewhere between $250,000 and $500,000, a far cry from the top salaries that business magnates and certain professionals earn in that part of the world.

Naturally, the concept of a wealth ceiling is not limited to annual salary but encompasses all forms of wealth accumulation, including inherited wealth, property holdings, and speculative earnings. Apart from establishing a minimum and maximum salary, this first fundamental principle presupposes a fixed limit on net wealth as well. The transition to a global society in which there is a fixed limit to net wealth will entail the eventual appropriation by the collective body of excess wealth that is presently in the hands of the fortunate few, a transition that will have to be handled with forbearance and compassion, as Anandamurti has touched upon in his writings.

While material wealth is limited, there is no limit to what one can acquire in the psychic and spiritual realms, where the potential for human fulfillment is far greater—where it is, in fact, infinite. However, when intellectual property rights deprive others of the potential benefits of that intellectual wealth, they should be subject to the same prohibition, such as, for instance, the hoarding of patents, which deprives humanity of the potential of those inventions for collective welfare. The same principle holds for spiritual wealth, to ensure that spiritual teachings are freely available to the public rather than being limited to certain circles or communities, as has happened in the past.

स्थूलसूक्ष्मकारणेषु चरमोपयोगः प्रकर्तव्यो विचारसमर्थितं वण्टनं च ॥ १३ ॥

V.13 *sthúlasúkśmakáranesu caramopayogah prakartavyo vicárasamarthitam vantanam ca*

sthúla, crude, mundane; *súkśma*, subtle, supramundane; *káranesu*, in the causal, in the spiritual; *carama*, maximum; *upayogah*, utilization; *prakartavyah*, should be done strictly; *vicára*, rational judgement ; *samarthitam*, supported by; *vantanam*, distribution; *ca*, and

"There should be maximum utilization and rational distribution of all mundane, supramundane, and spiritual potentialities of the universe."

Our individual and collective development is dependent on both mind and matter, and hence it is incumbent upon human society to make the best possible use of all the resources available to us, in whatever sphere of life it may be, so that we can effectively promote the physical, mental, and spiritual welfare of all living beings. This best possible use can be reduced to the simple and succinct maxim of "maximum utilization and rational distribution."

The maximum utilization of resources, whether mundane, supramundane, or spiritual, may seem prima facie like an obvious concept and one that most capitalist enterprises would agree with, at least on the physical plane, but if we remove the profit motive from the equation and instead turn our focus to collective welfare, it becomes even more obvious that our current capitalist system, with its reliance on free markets, is responsible for the gross *mis*utilization of our planet's resources. While the previous *kśatriya* and *vipra* eras were also guilty of resource mismanagement, they didn't generate nearly the amount of waste or engage in the degree of misguided production that is so glaringly evident in our modern-day capitalist societies. The greater part of our world is rife with the overproduction of unessential goods, often at the cost of essential goods, such as medical supplies and even basic food items, and primarily because production is based on profit rather than universal welfare or collective need. How often do our modern business enterprises come out with new models of consumer goods for the sole purpose of inducing the consumer to spend money to replace slightly older but perfectly serviceable models that offer essentially the same functionality? How much money is wasted on consumer goods that offer no real value to human society, developed and sold by companies whose sole purpose is to increase their market share rather than to offer a product or service that will advance the cause of collective welfare? In the meantime, landfills swell with manufactured goods that would have made the world better by their absence. And almost all of it produced without factoring in the costs to the environment—air and water pollution, the destruction of wildlife habitat, the depletion of nonrenewable resources, and so on. Or the cost to our collective psyche as we are bombarded with advertising for those same products.

Prout looks at the universe through an entirely different lens, viewing it as a garden that must be carefully and wisely tended so that all living beings can enjoy their existence and realize their maximum potential as they wind their way along the pathways of spiritual evolution. As with any garden, we must consider not only the immediate mundane utility of its flowers and fruits but all that it has to offer in the supramundane and spiritual planes as well. Just as a garden may supply us with food, medicine, and plant fibers for clothes and construction — all vitally important to our physical well-being — it is also a source of aesthetic pleasure that helps us to develop an appreciation for beauty and harmony and to deepen our connection to the creation, qualities that are even more important to our spiritual development than the food and medicine with which we sustain our bodies. Society depends on a wide range of manufactured products for its material advancement, and these in turn depend on the harnessing of natural and man-made resources. This principle teaches us not only that we should harness those natural and man-made resources in an efficient and effective manner — ie., that we should do more with less, thus minimizing our environmental footprint — but that we should see to it that what we do produce serves to advance the cause of human progress to the greatest degree possible while at the same time promoting the health of our planetary ecosystem and the well-being and advancement of other, less developed life-forms. Maximum utilization must factor in not only material advancement but even more so psychic and spiritual advancement, for which the material plane serves as a base, not a be-all and end-all. Our modern computers and consumer electronics, to cite one example, are manufactured from a wide variety of minerals, too numerous to name. Computers and other electronics are fundamental to our way of life, but the indiscriminate mining of those minerals comes at a terrible cost to the environment — not just an economic cost, such as that measured by the longterm costs of pollution and the loss of nonrenewable resources, but an aesthetic and spiritual cost as well, when we factor in the aesthetic treasures that are destroyed or depleted by such indiscriminate mining and the numerous other benefits of nature that are lost to us forever, an undocumented and unappreciated deprivation that is shared by the living creatures that depend on those habitats for their existence and who have no voice with which to protest their loss.

The maximum utilization of mundane resources thus presupposes a commitment to sustainability and a focus on renewable resources, as well as a careful examination and mitigation of all the possible negative effects that the extraction of those resources might have on human society, the environment, and other living beings. The natural resources we harness—I hesitate to use the word "exploit," because the word itself implies a lack of universal outlook—are all integral residents of the biosphere that Buckminster Fuller called Spaceship Earth, from the living trees we cut for wood, fellow creatures on the path of *pratisaiñcara*, leaning toward perfection, to the seemingly inert minerals, metals, and stones that also vibrate with an inherent albeit dormant intelligence and which will one day cross the border from *saiñcara* into *pratisaiñcara*. All this has to be carefully considered before we can decide on the maximum utilization of the different mundane or material resources that have been provided to us by the Cosmic Mind, whether on land, in the sea, or in outer space. How can those resources best be utilized so that they can further the all-around progress of the human race without adversely affecting the rest of the animate and inanimate worlds?

The same holds true for the maximum utilization of our supramundane resources. These include the natural beauty of our planet, the healthful atmosphere and other supramundane benefits afforded us by our treasure trove of lakes and rivers, mountains and plains, as well as our man-made supramundane resources—our historical sites, our art and architecture and inventions, our different cultural traditions from around the globe, the vast compendium of human knowledge bequeathed to us by our predecessors. The hills that we quarry for stone have an aesthetic charm that we cannot neglect with impunity, a supramundane resource that is lost to humanity forever once that hill is destroyed, as is that habitat to the living creatures who call it home, and the same is true for the cultural heritage that we pave over in our quest for material advancement, the languages we allow to die out along with their unique perspective of the world, the ancient arts and wisdom traditions that we fail to keep alive. How can all these best be preserved and utilized for the benefit of all without unduly compromising our mundane requirements?

And finally, how do we make the best use possible of our spiritual resources: the spiritual teachings and philosophies that have been handed down to us by the sages of the past, our religious landmarks and pilgrimage sites, the valleys and hills and hermitages where great saints have achieved liberation, leaving an enduring vibration that aids the spiritual progress of anyone who meditates there? How can each of these best be utilized for the welfare of all, while at the same time recognizing that every resident of Spaceship Earth, both animate and inanimate, has not only a utility value, their contribution to the health and progress of the biosphere, but an existential value as well, a right to live out their natural lives on the planet on which they have incarnated in the flow of cosmic evolution?

In short, the maximum utilization of our resources, if this principle is to be properly understood, must be seen through a single lens that comprehends the spiritual and supramundane value of those resources as well as their mundane value and which measures maximum utilization by the greatest good it can do for the material progress, psychic expansion, and spiritual evolution of the human race without neglecting the welfare of all those who are rightfully under our care—recognizing that as the highest evolved beings we are ipso facto custodians of our planetary garden and are thus responsible for the well-being and progress of all other life-forms and for the care and nurturing of the inanimate orb that is carrying us through space and time.

Maximum utilization is not enough to promote maximum welfare, however, if the necessary resources do not reach those who need them, and in a just proportion, that is, if it is not coupled with rational distribution—not equal distribution, or indiscriminate distribution, or unjust distribution, as is so often the case, but rational distribution, a distribution that takes into account the different needs of all segments of society, on both the individual and collective levels, and which measures the fulfillment of those needs in terms of all-around welfare, physical, mental, and above all, spiritual. This rational distribution in turn depends on the implementation of the three principles discussed in sutras V.9–V.12. First of all, everyone must be guaranteed their minimum requirements so that there is no undue impediment to their all-around progress. By guaranteeing a living wage to all, we can ensure that everyone has access to the natural and man-made resources they need to lead a healthy and productive life. Secondly, the surplus wealth must be directed toward those members of society who perform the greatest service to society as a whole—not to those who run after profit but to those who run after universal welfare—and this includes ensuring that they have the facilities they need to develop their talents and maximize their potential for service. And finally, there must be a ceiling on wealth accumulation so that the distribution of the world's resources is not jeopardized by overaccumulation or hoarding. Rational distribution also includes guaranteeing universal access to all available educational resources, both locally and globally, and ensuring that everyone will have ample access to the myriad supramundane and spiritual treasures of our planet through a constant commitment to expanding public facilities and programs in all spheres of cultural life, along with making parks, nature preserves, and areas for contemplation and spiritual pursuits available to communities throughout the globe. Our planetary resources should be rationally, efficiently, and equably distributed, and no system of distribution can be considered rational if it is not designed to effect the greatest good in all three planes of existence, with the sole motive of increasing individual and collective welfare.

व्यष्टिसमष्टिशारीरमानसाध्यात्मिकसम्भावनायां चरमोपयोगश्च ॥ १४ ॥

V.14 *vyaśtisamaśtisháriiramánasádhyátmikasambhávanáyáṁ caramopayogash ca*

vyaśti, individual; *samaśti*, collective; *sháriira*, physical body; *mánasa*, mind, psychic body; *ádhyátmika*, spiritual; *sambhávanáyáṁ*, potentialities, possibilities; *carama*, supreme, maximum; *upayogah*, utilization; *ca*, and

"There should be maximum utilization of the physical, metaphysical, and spiritual potentialities of the unit and collective bodies of human society."

The sole purpose of the collective body of society is to ensure the physical, mental, and spiritual welfare of each of its members, and hence this third fundamental principle of Prout hinges upon the relationship between the individual and society. Society must endeavor to create the most propitious conditions possible for individual growth and happiness, but at the same time it must maintain a balance between individual and collective welfare by ensuring that individual liberties do not have a negative impact on society by weakening the collective spirit or by impinging on the growth and well-being of others. The promotion of individual welfare is the basis of collective welfare, but if the collective body is not strong, harmonious, and just, it will stunt the growth of the individual. Thus it is the duty of society to make ongoing efforts to instill in the collective mind a sense of social consciousness and a spirit of service.

However independent and self-reliant we may wish to be or think ourselves to be, we depend in large part on society for the fulfillment of our physical, mental, and spiritual aspirations, a simple truth that the spirit of individualism fails to recognize. Without society we wouldn't have the homes we live in, the food we eat, the clothes we wear, or the doctors we run to when we fall sick. We wouldn't have the education we need to make our way through the world, and we wouldn't have the spiritual teachings we depend on to guide us to our ultimate liberation. Nor can we overestimate the impact of cultural evolution on human development, being arguably the most complex phenomenon in the known universe.[35] Anandamurti frequently reminds us in his writings that humanity is one and indivisible. We all walk the path of spiritual evolution together, and if we are to go beyond our limited ego in the quest for supreme fulfillment, then we must extend our sense of identity to all of humanity, and eventually to the entire universe. This sense of social awareness begins by looking at humanity as a single extended family. When one member in a family is suffering or is deprived, then the whole family suffers with them and does everything in their power to help them. The more this sense of collective spirit grows, the more everyone benefits. At the same time, however, if undue weight is given to the collective, it can have a negative impact on individual welfare, as was painfully evident in the communist societies of the twentieth century where the pursuit of the collective at the expense of the individual led to wide-scale suppression of individual liberties and individual potential that eventually undermined society as a whole.[36]

This principle is a corollary of the previous one. While the second fundamental principle focuses on the maximum utilization of resources in the three spheres of existence, this third principle focuses on the maximum utilization of our human potential, both individual and collective, in those same three spheres. The one cannot be divorced from the other because the maximum utilization and rational distribution of resources depends on the maximum utilization of our human potential. It is, after all, human beings who explore and develop the world around us and put it to the work of collective welfare, and it is human beings who have to decide what constitutes physical, psychic, and spiritual progress and how best to achieve it.

On the physical plane, we need to explore all possible avenues, over and above guaranteeing the minimum requirements to all, to ensure that we are able to get the most out of our physical bodies for as long as we are on this planet. For example, apart from providing health care to all through some form of universal health care, society should promote health consciousness and healthy lifestyle choices through appropriate education and various forms of incentives. In addition to guaranteeing full employment, society should make efforts to promote labor productivity at all levels of economic life. This will increase individual satisfaction (a natural byproduct of productive labor) and allow society to provide more and more amenities and conveniences to the general population, thus easing our mundane burdens. In time, this increase in efficiency coupled with technological advancement and the elimination of the profit motive will lessen the dependence on manual labor and lead to a decrease in working hours, thereby freeing up more time for higher pursuits, which will in turn fuel the psychic and spiritual progress of the human race.

On the psychic plane, every effort should be made by the collective body to develop the all-around intellectual standard of its members and to foster the talents of those who show an aptitude or attraction for the sciences, the arts, and other intellectual pursuits. In our present age, the abilities of many promising artists and intellectuals go to waste for lack of opportunity, especially in the more disadvantaged parts of the globe. Talented musicians and writers are forced to take a day job to pay the rent, and many intellectually gifted individuals are herded into jobs they either don't like or which greatly underutilize or misutilize their potential. This is a gross waste of human ability that hampers the growth of those individuals and deprives the society of the full benefits of their talents. This principle demands that our educational system, economy, and social institutions be designed so that these psychic potentialities can be fully developed and utilized. It is our collective responsibility to see to it that everyone has the opportunity to discover and develop their latent talents, as well as the chance to pursue a career in the field that most attracts their interest, and our economy needs to be structured so that they can make a living in their chosen field once their education is complete. By doing so, the entire society will benefit from the fruits of their labors.

As with the overaccumulation of material wealth, which must be curtailed in order to protect the economic rights of others, society also has a duty to curtail or regulate those psychic activities or pursuits that impinge upon the material or psychic well-being of others, even when this involves restrictions on individual liberties. The freedom to produce or sell child pornography, for example, is one individual liberty that is almost universally proscribed in our modern societies due to the negative impact it has on the well-being of others. But where the psychic interests of the individual do not detract from collective welfare, then every effort should be made by the collective to facilitate the pursuit of those interests.

Finally, in the absence of spiritual and ethical elevation at a collective level, any advances we make in the other spheres of life will be hollow, since they will fail to promote the fulfillment of mankind's deepest urge, the desire for unbounded happiness that can only be fully satisfied through spiritual development. Thus every effort should be made by the collective body to foster the spiritual elevation of human society through education, the arts, the state support of spiritual institutions, making spiritual tools such as yoga and meditation freely available in the workplace and other public venues, and so on. In addition, those individuals who show an aptitude to be spiritual teachers should be afforded every opportunity to work in this field. Just as we currently give grants to especially gifted artists and scientists so that their talents won't be sacrificed at the altar of economic survival, the spiritual talents of such individuals should be encouraged and supported by society in the interest of both individual and collective welfare, since it is they who will do the work of elevating the overall spiritual standard of the collective.

> The development of the collective body, collective mind, and collective spirit must be ensured. Collective welfare lies in the individual and individual welfare lies in the collective. This must not be forgotten.[37]
>
> — Anandamurti

स्थूलसूक्ष्मकारणोपयोगाः सुसन्तुलिता विधेयाः ॥ १५ ॥

V.15 *sthúlasúkśmakáraṅopayogáh susantulitá vidheyáh*

sthúla, crude, material; *súkśma*, subtle, psychic, supramundane; *káraṅa*, causal, spiritual; *upayogáh*, utilization; *susantulitáh*, well-balanced; *vidheyáh*, should be done

> "There should be a proper adjustment among these physical, metaphysical, mundane, supramundane, and spiritual utilizations."
>
> "A galaxy is very vast and extends a very great distance. An ant is extremely small. But both are equally important in maintaining the balance of the universe. If an ant dies before its appointed hour, then that mishap will disturb the balance of the entire universe."[38]
>
> — Anandamurti

In 1981 Alain Aspect and his colleagues at the University of Paris-South conducted an experiment that proved the contention of quantum mechanics that the connection between quantum particles was nonlocal in character. They sent paired photons in opposite directions and showed that if the polarization of one photon was changed, the other photon instantaneously changed its polarization as well. Somehow the two photons maintained their connection even though any physical communication or link between the two was impossible given the parameters of the experiment. Thus the connection could only be nonlocal in character, a phenomenon known as "entanglement." This demonstration, impossible to explain within the framework of Newtonian physics, highlights an aspect of the universe that has been known to Tantric yogis for millennia—that everything in this universe is inextricably connected. The fabric of space-time is in essence a surging ocean of Consciousness, set in motion by its own inherent momentum, and every tremor in that fabric, every ripple that arises in the ocean of Consciousness, is felt everywhere, even if its effect remains by and large imperceptible to the human mind. Thus every decision we make concerning our use of the world's resources and that of our human potential must be examined in the context of its effect on all the other arenas of individual and collective life so that a harmonious balance can be maintained. If one utilization, as useful as it may initially seem, causes another to wobble, then the whole vehicle will wobble and the forward progress of society will be compromised.

In Anandamurti's social philosophy this concept of integral balance is called *pramá*, and ideally it should be applied within each sphere of existence as well as between spheres. For example, to achieve *pramá* in the economic sphere, the minimum requirements of life must be guaranteed to all, but if those minimum requirements were to be supplied without a corresponding exchange of labor, then balance would be lost both in individual life, due to the tendency of handouts to promote lethargy and a lack of initiative, and in collective life, since that same indolence and lack of initiative, even if it is only in a relatively minor portion of society, would impede the forward progress of the collective. Another example of *pramá* in the economic sphere is the effort to strike a harmonious balance between our utilization of the earth's mundane resources and the possible costs to our planetary ecosystem, and by extension to human society. Insufficient industrialization, for example, leads to economic underdevelopment and a lower standard of living for the local people, while overindustrialization places undue stress on the environment and leads to increases in social tensions. The ripples in one sphere of life inevitably affect other spheres; hence the decisions we make in the agricultural sector are bound to affect the industrial sector, which in turn affects commerce, which affects the health care system, which affects psychic well-being, which affects our spiritual life—every ripple in the fabric of existence affecting everything else. We must also balance present needs with future needs, acknowledging our responsibility for the welfare of future generations; mundane progress and technological advancement with psychic well-being and spiritual growth; the health of the biosphere with the growth of human society; the development of one region of the globe with that of other regions, and so on. In short, this principle promotes balance in and between every sphere of life, and these adjustments must be of a dynamic nature so that they can keep pace with the changes that inevitably accompany the growth of any living system. It therefore becomes the duty of the collective body to devise social policies that take into account the effect of those policies on all aspects of individual and collective life, now and into the future, and which strive to achieve a harmonious balance in the web of interrelated effects. Needless to say, our modern capitalist societies have failed miserably in this regard, from the indiscriminate burning of coal and fossil fuels for energy, with their terrible cost to the environment that will have to be borne by future generations, to the endemic wealth inequality that has led to so much psychic suffering and social conflict.

Another important aspect of *pramá* is the relative weight that is given to the three planes of existence, physical, psychic, and spiritual, not only as regards the integral development of the individual but also as a key component of social planning. While the state should do all it can to promote a harmonious balance between the physical, psychic, and spiritual growth of its citizens, it should also encourage those who are both physically talented and intellectually developed to dedicate more of their time and energy to the intellectual sphere, due to the comparative rarity of intellectual ability and its greater potential for promoting collective welfare. For the same reason, it should encourage those who are physically, intellectually, and spiritually developed to devote more of their time to spiritual work, less to intellectual work, and still less to physical work. Naturally, there will always be some people with particular talents who prefer not to pursue them, a math savant, for instance, who feels happier doing manual labor, and while this seemingly goes against the spirit of this sutra, the first and foremost human need at the psychic level is happiness, however that is measured, and thus society has a responsibility to create a social environment and social structure that fosters individual happiness and mental contentment. This includes the freedom to pursue a profession that does not fully utilize one's talents, as well as the opportunity to pursue a profession that does, although society can and should encourage such individuals through appropriate ethical and spiritual education to find avenues that allow them to render the greatest possible service to society without sacrificing their psychic well-being.

Inevitably, the successful application of this fourth fundamental principle will depend upon enlightened leadership. The all-important decisions governing the adjustments between the different spheres of life should be made by those who are best capable of making them, ie., those who have the requisite vision and the necessary skills to ensure that our various social policies promote collective welfare in all spheres of life and that these social policies work together in a harmonious, balanced way. Thus the leadership of society, regardless of which *varńa* is in ascendance, should be entrusted to the *sadvipras*, to those who have developed the best qualities of all four *varńas*—physical skills, courage and boldness, intellectual acumen, and spiritual maturity—and whose ethical firmness and spiritual wisdom will ensure that the journey of human society will not get derailed as it has so often in the past.

देशकालपात्रैरुपयोगाः परिवर्त्तन्ते त उपयोगाः प्रगतिशीला भवेयुः ॥ १६ ॥

V.16 *deshakálapátraer upayogáh parivarttante ta upayogáh pragatishiilá bhaveyuh*

desha, place; *kála*, time; *pátraeh*, person; *upayogáh*, utilization; *parivarttante*, changing; *te*, those; *pragatishiiláh*, progressive; *bhaveyuh*, should be

> "The method of utilization should vary in accordance with changes in time, place, and person, and the utilization should be of progressive nature."

The five fundamental principles of Prout are meant to provide a compass by which social policymakers can guide their decisions and ensure that they reflect the underlying spirit of individual and collective welfare that Anandamurti's social philosophy was designed to promote, and this fifth fundamental principle is meant to ensure that this compass will never get stuck pointing in an outmoded direction but will continue to show society its true north. The nature of the universe is constant change. Wave after inimitable wave surges forth from the wellsprings of the Cosmic Imagination, fashioned by the dexterous hand of *prakrti*, the Magna Mater. Human society is part of that endless flow, and thus nothing in human society can remain static. Every expression of social life is constantly changing, and if society is to retain its dynamism and continue to move forward in a balanced, productive manner toward the goal of collective welfare, then its social institutions and policies must be ready to adapt to the changes in the three relative factors of time, space, and person in order to maintain their ability to respond to the ever-evolving needs of the people.

Up until now, however, human society has been plagued to a greater or lesser extent by a lack of adaptability, and this has invariably proved an obstacle to human progress. Resistance to change is a part of human nature. We tend to cling to the past, to old behaviors, institutions, and traditions, to the familiar and the easy, the path of least resistance—in effect, old *saṁskáras*—but this limits our growth and contributes to our suffering. The tendency to resist change is equally true of societies, and the consequences are equally devastating. Institutions that resist change invariably fall out of step with the world around them. Due to their inability to adapt to the changing conditions or the changes in collective psychology, they gradually decay from within and increasingly fail to promote collective welfare. This is true of social institutions, religious institutions, cultural traditions—in short, of all aspects of collective life—and history teaches us that this tendency becomes more and more pronounced toward the end of any era as the dominant *varńa* loses its dynamism and grows increasingly rigid and exploitative. Those in power cling to the forms that served them in the past, whether out of self-interest or ignorance or both, failing to realize that it is not the forms that matter but the inherent forward dynamism that those forms originally embodied.

Tantra recognizes the dynamic nature of the evolutionary process and teaches us to welcome change for the challenges it provides, the opportunity to break through the shell of the past and into the free air of our untapped potential. Obstacles are our friends, not our enemies, and the challenge of meeting the demands of changing circumstances fosters our growth, both individual and collective. Thus it is incumbent upon policymakers and social leaders to recognize these changes and adapt their policies and institutions in order to maintain the dynamic equilibrium upon which social progress is dependent. What is good for one era may not be good for the next, and what is beneficial for one region or community may not benefit another. Change is inevitable and thus the utilizations in the physical, psychic, and spiritual spheres will have to keep pace with a changing world. Not all change is progressive, however, and thus it is the responsibility of decision-makers to ensure that the changes they institute continue to maintain contact with the touchstone of true progress.

The Sanskrit word for "progress," *pragati*, literally means "forward movement," as does its English equivalent, but in Tantra *pragati* implies movement toward the spiritual goal — that is, progress is only progress when it involves the expansion of consciousness. In this sense, movement that does not foster spiritual evolution cannot be considered real progress.

From the philosophical point of view, freedom cannot be achieved in either the physical or psychic planes, since both remain forever under the bondage of *prakrti*, and thus to talk of physical or psychic progress in an absolute sense is a misnomer. Every advancement in the physical and psychic planes is invariably accompanied by some negative consequence that serves to maintain the balance of the universe. The move from horse-drawn carts to automobiles and other forms of modern transport is understandably considered to be a noteworthy sign of progress, but while this technological development has certainly contributed to an increase in productivity and convenience, it has also led to a corresponding increase in accidents and fatalities, as well as contributing significantly to the air pollution that is depleting the ozone layer, fueling global warming, and compromising our health. The human race is generally hailed as having made tremendous psychic or intellectual progress since the days of those horse-drawn carts, but with the increased intellectual complexity of the modern mind has come a corresponding increase in psychological complexes and existential angst. When all factors are taken into consideration, the result is a net gain of zero, as dictated by the laws of *prakrti,* where freedom in the physical and psychic spheres is ultimately impossible to achieve.[39] Freedom is only possible in the spiritual plane, for the very reason that real freedom means freedom from the bondage of *prakrti,* and thus true progress is only possible in the spiritual sphere, where the individual's forward movement is not counterbalanced by any negative consequence.

In the relative sense, however, there is a way to measure progress in the physical and mental spheres: by the degree to which movement in those spheres facilitates expansion in the spiritual sphere. A human being's spiritual growth depends on a firm base in the relative world, and this in turn depends on the physical and psychic resources at our disposal. A healthy body and a healthy mind, for example, are prerequisites for spiritual development, and both depend on a balanced economy that provides our minimum necessities, on access to health care and proper education, including spiritual teachings, and on many other relative factors. Deficiencies in either of these spheres will hamper our growth, and thus for maximum utilization in all spheres of life to be achieved, social construction must center around creating a psychophysical environment that fosters maximum spiritual growth. To cite another example, the overuse of some technologies, such as smartphones and other handheld devices, has compromised certain mental faculties that are integral to spiritual development. Digital distraction is ubiquitous in our current cultural milieu and this has led to a well-documented decrease in attention span, so important to spiritual meditation, and a corresponding increase in mental turbulence. And yet these same devices have also benefited human society in numerous ways. Thus it becomes our duty to determine how to use that technology in such a way that we can maximize its benefits while minimizing its negative effects.

> Spiritual progress depends on the support of a physical and mental base. For this reason, this physical and mental base has to be progressively adjusted to the changing conditions of time and space in order to maintain balance. Spiritual aspirants have to devise ways to protect themselves from the reactions in the physical and intellectual spheres...The only true progress for human beings is spiritual progress. For this reason, a wise person's main concern should be the spiritual sphere. One should only work in the remaining two spheres, the physical and intellectual spheres, for the purpose of attaining spiritual progress.[40]
>
> — Anandamurti

Anandamurti concludes this final chapter of *Ananda Sutram* with the following Sanskrit dictum: *pragatishiila upayogatattvam idaṁ sarvajanahitārthaṁ sarvajanasukhārthaṁ pracáritam*—"this is the Progressive Utilization Theory, propounded for the happiness and welfare of all." It is happiness that is the goal of our individual journey as incarnate beings, a journey that eventually culminates in the attainment of the Infinite, and thus it is happiness that must be the goal of our collective journey as well, the journey of society. Hence, Anandamurti's social philosophy, Prout, is the logical conclusion to a modern-day spiritual philosophy that builds on its predecessors to create something entirely new and perfectly suited to the spiritual era that is getting ready to appear on the horizon. A spiritual philosophy that recognizes that everything is divine, that the entire cosmos is designed to promote the liberation of the living being, and that the pursuit of liberation cannot be separated from the effort to create a universal human society—dedicated to the happiness and welfare of all.

Afterword

IN HIS ANALYSIS OF the various factors that will be necessary in order to establish a truly universal human society, Anandamurti emphasizes the need for a common philosophy of life.[1] As he is wont to do in his writings, he uses the word "ideology" in that same discussion as a synonym that expands the reach of what we normally think of as philosophy. He does not use the word, however, in the same way that we commonly do. For Anandamurti, the word "ideology" carries with it an implicit spiritual sense that is largely absent in our modern use of the word:

> This state is called samadhi. Here the psychic waves have attained a parallelism with the spiritual waves of the atman. This psycho-spiritual parallelism is known as "idea," or *bháva*. When this *bháva* or idea is conceived on the psychic level, it is "ideology." Ideology, therefore, is the conception of idea and nothing else. Hence when we call some materialistic or political principles of a person, party, nation or federation an "ideology," it is a wrong use of the term. "Ideology" involves in it a spiritual sense; it is an inspiration which has a parallelism with the Spiritual Entity.[2]

In short, the true meaning of human life can only be found in the journey of spiritual evolution that leads to our merger with Brahma, and the effort to imbue all aspects of our life with that ultimate meaning, to orient all facets of our life toward the attainment of that ultimate goal, is what Anandamurti refers to as "ideology." Thus ideology in this sense is not only spiritual in nature, it is inherently universal.

The effort to give voice to a universal human ideology has been around for thousands of years, and it has proved critical to the development of the human race by sowing in our minds the noblest of ideas by which to live our lives. It can be seen in the Bhagavad Gita and in the six classical systems of Indian philosophy, in Buddhism and the other heterodox philosophies, and above all in the Tantras, as well as in the work of saints and sages from beyond the Indian subcontinent. In India, Hinduism is often referred to as *sanatana* dharma, the eternal dharma, but a universal spiritual ideology cannot be Hindu, it cannot be Indian. It must be all-embracing and all-encompassing, and it must meet the needs of human beings in all spheres of human life if it is to help us progress toward our ultimate goal. By definition, human truth can only be one, and thus in the deepest sense there can be only one human ideology — that which encapsulates the essence and purpose of the human incarnation — although there can be different iterations of that universal human ideology as the ages pass and human understanding continues to expand in order to keep pace with the ever-evolving manifestations of *prakrti*.

Ananda Sutram, the latest staging point in the river of Indian spiritual thought, represents the philosophical nexus of Anandamurti's lifelong effort to present humanity with an embodiment of this universal human ideology consonant with our modern age, an ideology that looks toward the future of our race, toward a universal society that will personify the best of who we are, while recognizing that our individual search for fulfillment cannot be divorced from the social context in which we live. The ultimate meaning of life, both individual and collective, must in the final analysis be a discovery of each individual human soul as we make our way toward perfection. It must be a matter of direct experience rather than a product of the intellect. But without an accurate map of the territory that lies in front of us, the journey becomes immeasurably more difficult. *Ananda Sutram*, along with all of Anandamurti's work throughout an extraordinarily productive life, proposes to make that journey easier by lending a modern voice to that universal ideology, a voice that helps us to plumb its depths, to manifest it in our lives, and to spread that living flame to future generations.

It is my hope that this commentary will play a small part in that ongoing effort by helping to make this extraordinary map of reality a little bit easier to read.

Ananda Kiirtana,

August 28, 2021

Bibliography

This bibliography is not a complete list of the works I have consulted in the preparation of this commentary but it does include those that have figured substantively in my research, and I hope that it can also serve as a convenient source list for those who would like to read more extensively on particular topics.

Apte, V. M. *Brahma-Sutra Shankara-Bhasya: Badarayana's Brahma-Sutras with Shankaracharya's Commentary*. Bombay: Popular Book Depot, 1960.

Acosta, Devashish Donald. *Anandamurti: The Jamalpur Years*. San Germán: Innerworld Publications, 2010.

Acosta, Devashish Donald. *When the Time Comes: Conversations with Acharya Chandranath Kumar*. San Germán: Innerworld Publications, 1998.

Avadhutika Ananda Mitra Acarya. *The Spiritual Philosophy of Shrii Shrii Anandamurti: A Commentary on Ananda Sutram*, 2nd ed. Kolkata: Ananda Marga Publications, 1998.

Berman, Bob. *Earth-Shattering: Violent Supernovas, Galactic Explosions, Biological Mayhem, Nuclear Meltdowns, and Other Hazards to Life in Our Universe*. New York: Little, Brown and Company, 2019.

Bjonnes, Ramesh. *A Brief History of Yoga: From its Tantric Roots to the Modern Yoga Studio*. San Germán: Innerworld Publications, 2018.

Bjonnes, Roar. *Principles for a Balanced Economy*. Copenhagen: Prout Research Institute, 2012.

Brown, Colum and Kevin Laland. *Fish Cognition and Behaviour*. Edited by Jens Krause. Oxford: Blackwell Publishing, Ltd, 2011.

Bryant, Edwin. *The Yoga Sutras of Patanjali*. New York: North Point Press, 2009. Epub.

Bryson, Bill. *A Short History of Nearly Everything*. New York: Ramdom House, 2003.

Chaisson, Eric J. *Cosmic Evolution: The Rise of Complexity in Nature*. Cambridge: Harvard University Press, 2001.

Chamovitz, Daniel. *What a Plant Knows: A Field Guide to the Senses*. New York: Scientific American/Farrar, Straus and Giroux, 2012.

Durant, Will. *The Story of Philosophy*. New York: Simon and Schuster, Inc., 1927.

Feynman, Richard, Robert Leighton, and Matthew Sands. *The Feynman Lectures of Physics: Volume 1*. New York: Basic Books, 2010.

Feynman, Richard, Robert Leighton, and Matthew Sands. *The Feynman Lectures of Physics: Volume 2*. New York: Basic Books, 2010.

Feynman, Richard, Robert Leighton, and Matthew Sands. *The Feynman Lectures of Physics: Volume 3*. New York: Basic Books, 2010.

Geddes, Patrick. *The Life and Work of Sir Jagadis C. Bose*. London: Longmans, Green, and Co., 1920.

Greene, Brian. *The Fabric of the Cosmos: Space. Time. And the Texture of Reality*. New York: Alfred A. Knopf, 2004.

Nagel, Thomas. *Mind and Cosmos: Why the Materialist Neo-Darwinian Conception of Nature is Almost Certainly False*. New York: Oxford University Press, 2012.

Pagels, Heinz. *Perfect Symmetry: The Search for the Beginning of Time*. New York: Bantam Books, 1985.

Prasada, Rama, Trans. *Patanjali's Yoga Sutras with the Commentary of Vyasa and the Gloss of Vachaspati Misra*. New Delhi: Munshiram Manoharlal Publishers Pvt. Ltd., 1998.

Ricard, Matthieu and Trinh Xuam Thuan. *The Quantum and the Lotus: A Journey to the Frontiers Where Science and Buddhism Meet*. Translated by Ian Monk. New York, Three Rivers Press, 2001.

Rovelli, Carlo. *The Order of Time*. Translated by Simon Carnell and Erica Segre. New York: Riverhead Books, 2018. Epub.

Rovelli, Carlo. *Reality is Not What it Seems*. Translated by Simon Carnell and Erica Segre. New York: Riverhead Books, 2017. Epub.

Rovelli, Carlo. *Seven Brief Lessons on Physics.* Translated by Simon Carnell and Erica Segre. London: Penguin Random House, 2015. Epub.

Sri Swami Satchidananda. *The Yoga Sutras of Patanjali.* Buckingham, Virginia: Integral Yoga Publications, 2012. Epub.

Swami Niranjanananda Saraswati. *Samkhya Darshan: Yogic Perspective on Theories of Realism.* Munger: Yoga Publications Trust, 2008.

Swami Virupakshananda. *Samkhya Karika of Isvara Krsna with the Tattva Kaumudi of Sri Vacaspati Misra.* Madras: Sri Ramakrishna Math, 1995.

Tignath PhD, Pandit Rajmani. *Seven Systems of Indian Philosophy.* Allahabad: Himalayan Institute India, 2011.

Urry, Lisa, Michael Cain, Steven Wasserman, Peter Minorsky, and James Reese. *Campbell Biology*, 11th ed. New York: Pearson, 2017.

Vivekananda, Swami. *Patanjali Yoga Sutras.*

Wohlleben, Peter. *The Hidden Life of Trees.* Translated by Jane Billinghurst. Vancouver: David Suzuki Institute, 2016.

Woodroffe, John. *Kularnava Tantra.* Delhi: Motilal Banarsidass Publishers, 1965.

Woodroffe, John. *Shakti and Shakta: Essays and Addresses on the Sakta Tantrasastra.* Leeds: Celephais Press, 2009.

Woodroffe, John. *The Serpent Power*, 4th ed. Madras: Ganesh & Co., 1950.

Woodroffe, John. *The World as Power: Reality, Life, Mind, Matter, Causality and Continuity*, 2nd ed. Madras: Ganesh & Co., 1957.

Yogananda, Paramhansa. *Autobiography of a Yogi.* 13th ed. Los Angeles: Self-Realization Fellowship, 1998.

List of Anandamurti's Works Cited in this Commentary:

English:

Electronic Edition of the Works of P. R. Sarkar, Version 9.0.6.122 (Abbreviated as EE9)

Sarkar, Shrii Prabhat Ranjan, *Idea and Ideology*, 7th ed. Calcutta: Ananda Marga Publications, 1993. [Compiled from the disciples's notes of Anandamurti's classes in the summer of 1959.

The lectures were given in a mixture of English and Hindi, and the original manuscript was published in English.]
Sarkar, Shrii Prabhat Ranjan, *Shabda Cayaniká Part 1*. Translated by Devashish Donald Acosta. Calcutta: Ananda Marga Pracarika Samgha, 1996.
Sarkar, Shrii Prabhat Ranjan, *Varńa Vijiṋána: The Science of Letters*. Translated by Devashish Donald Acosta. Calcutta: Ananda Marga Pracarika Samgha, 2000.

Bengali (translated by the author):

Anandamurti, Shrii Shrii, *Ánanda Márga*. Jamalpur: Ánanda Márga Pracárika Saḿgha, 1955.
Anandamurti, Shrii Shrii, *Ánanda Sútram*. Calcutta: Ánanda Márga Pracárika Saḿgha, 2007.
Anandamurti, Shrii Shrii, *Ánanda Vacanámrtam 1–3*. Calcutta: Ánanda Márga Pracárika Saḿgha, 1997.
Anandamurti, Shrii Shrii, *Ánanda Vacanámrtam 6*. Calcutta: Ánanda Márga Pracárika Saḿgha, 1998.
Anandamurti, Shrii Shrii, *Ánanda Vacanámrtam 7–9*. Calcutta: Ánanda Márga Pracárika Saḿgha, 1998.
Anandamurti, Shrii Shrii, *Ánanda Vacanámrtam 10*. Calcutta: Ánanda Márga Pracárika Saḿgha, 1980.
Anandamurti, Shrii Shrii, *Jiivana Veda*. 6th ed. Calcutta: Ánanda Márga Pracárika Saḿgha, 1991.
Anandamurti, Shrii Shrii, *Namah Shiváya Shántáya*. Calcutta: Ánanda Márga Pracárika Saḿgha, 1982.
Anandamurti, Shrii Shrii, *Subháśita Saḿgraha 1–3*. Calcutta: Ánanda Márga Pracárika Saḿgha, 1998.
Anandamurti, Shrii Shrii, *Subháśita Saḿgraha 2*. Jamalpur: Ánanda Márga Pracárika Saḿgha, 1957.
Anandamurti, Shrii Shrii, *Subháśita Saḿgraha 3*. Jamalpur: Ánanda Márga Pracárika Saḿgha, 1958.
Anandamurti, Shrii Shrii, *Subháśita Saḿgraha 4*. Anandanagar: Ánanda Márga Pracárika Saḿgha, 1971.
Anandamurti, Shrii Shrii, *Subháśita Saḿgraha 5*. 2nd ed. Anandanagar: Ánanda Márga Pracárika Saḿgha, 1977.
Anandamurti, Shrii Shrii, *Subháśita Saḿgraha 6*. Anandanagar: Ánanda Márga Pracárika Saḿgha, 1971.

Anandamurti, Shrii Shrii, *Subháśita Saḿgraha 7*. Anandanagar: Ánanda Márga Pracárika Saḿgha, 1979.
Anandamurti, Shrii Shrii, *Subháśita Saḿgraha 8*. Calcutta: Ánanda Márga Pracárika Saḿgha, 1980.
Anandamurti, Shrii Shrii, *Subháśita Saḿgraha 9*. Calcutta: Ánanda Márga Pracárika Saḿgha, 1982.
Anandamurti, Shrii Shrii, *Subháśita Saḿgraha 10*. Calcutta: Ánanda Márga Pracárika Saḿgha, 1984.
Anandamurti, Shrii Shrii, *Subháśita Saḿgraha 11*. Calcutta: Ánanda Márga Pracárika Saḿgha, 1980.
Anandamurti, Shrii Shrii, *Subháśita Saḿgraha 12*. Calcutta: Ánanda Márga Pracárika Saḿgha, 1981.
Anandamurti, Shrii Shrii, *Tantre Dárshanikatá*, Calcutta: Ánanda Márga Pracárika Saḿgha, 1981.
Anandamurti, Shrii Shrii, *Tattva Kaomudi 1*. Anandanagar: Ánanda Márga Pracárika Saḿgha, 1978.
Anandamurti, Shrii Shrii, *Tattva Kaomudi 2*. Anandanagar: Ánanda Márga Pracárika Saḿgha, 1978.
Sarkar, Shrii Prabhat Ranjan, *Abhimata 4*. Calcutta: Ánanda Márga Pracárika Saḿgha, 1985.
Sarkar, Shrii Prabhat Ranjan, *Ájker Samasyá*. Jamalpur: Ánanda Márga Pracárika Saḿgha, 1958.
Sarkar, Shrii Prabhat Ranjan, *Buddhir Mukti-Navyamánavatáváda*. Calcutta: Ánanda Márga Pracárika Saḿgha, 1982.
Sarkar, Shrii Prabhat Ranjan, *Kańikáya Navyamánavatáváda 1*. Calcutta: Ánanda Márga Pracárika Saḿgha, 1987.
Sarkar, Shrii Prabhat Ranjan, *Kańikáya Prout 4*. Calcutta: Ánanda Márga Pracárika Saḿgha, 1987.
Sarkar, Shrii Prabhat Ranjan, *Kańikáya Prout 6*. Calcutta: Ánanda Márga Pracárika Saḿgha, 1987.
Sarkar, Shrii Prabhat Ranjan, *Kańikáya Prout 7*. Calcutta: Ánanda Márga Pracárika Saḿgha, 1987.
Sarkar, Shrii Prabhat Ranjan, *Kańikáya Prout 13*. Calcutta: Ánanda Márga Pracárika Saḿgha, 1988.
Sarkar, Shrii Prabhat Ranjan, *Manasa Sádhanár Staravinyása*. Calcutta: Ánanda Márga Pracárika Saḿgha, 1981.
Sarkar, Shrii Prabhat Ranjan, *Mánuśer Samája 2*. Anandanagar: Ánanda Márga Pracárika Saḿgha, 1970.

Glossary of Sanskrit Terms

ahamtattva, aham = ego principle, doer-I
ánanda = bliss
átmá = atman, individual consciousness, soul
avidyá = ignorance
avidyámáyá = extroversive or centrifugal force of *prakrti*
bhúta = fundamental factor
Brahma = Supreme Consciousness
buddhi = intellect
buddhitattva = pure I-feeling, synonym for *mahat*
citta = objectivated I, mind-stuff
guńa = binding rope, quality, force of *prakrti*
jiiva = living being
jiivátmá = individual consciousness, soul
kśatriya = warrior, warrior class
mahat = pure I-feeling
nirguńa = without *guńa*, unmanifest
nirvikalpa = objectless and subjectless, indeterminate
parama puruśa = Supreme Consciousness
paramátmá = Supreme Consciousness
prakrti = causal matrix, the creative force of Consciousness
práńa = energy
práńah = vital energy, the ten vital airs
pratisaiṇcara = introversive or incoming phase of creation, evolution
puruśa = consciousness
puruśottama = Supreme Consciousness
rajaguńa, rajas = mutative force of *prakrti*
sadguru = true guru
sadhaka = spiritual aspirant
sadvipra = spiritual revolutionary
saguńa = with *guńa*, manifest

saiṇcara = extroversive or outgoing phase of creation, involution
saṁskára = reactive momenta, reaction in potentiality
sattaguṅa, sattva = sentient force of *prakrti*
savikalpa = determinate, with subject and object
Shakti = creative matrix, energy
Shiva = Consciousness
shúdra = laborer, laboring class
tamoguṅa, tamas = static force of *prakrti*
vaeshya = merchant, capitalist, capitalist class
varṅa = color, letter, social class
vidyá = knowledge
vidyámáyá = introversive or centripetal force of *prakrti*
vipra = intellectual, intellectual class
vrtti = mental tendency or propensity
yama and *niyama* = the yogic code of ethics, consisting of ten principles

Roman Sanskrit Key

IAST equivalents, where they differ from Anandamurti's romanization, have been placed in parentheses.

Vowels

अ a	आ á (ā)	इ i	ई ii (ī)	उ u	ऊ ú (ū)
ऋ r (ṛ)	ॠ rr (ṝ)	ऌ lr (ḷ)	ॡ lrr (ḹ)	ए e	ऐ ae (ai)
ओ o	औ ao (au)	अं aṁ (ṃ)	अः ah (ḥ)		

Consonants

क ka	ख kha	ग ga	घ gha	ङ uṇa (ṅa)
च ca	छ cha	ज ja	झ jha	ञ iṇa (ña)
ट ta (ṭ)	ठ tha (ṭh)	ड da (ḍ)	ढ dha (ḍh)	ण ńa (ṇa)
त ta	थ tha	द da	ध dha	न na
प pa	फ pha	ब ba	भ bha	म ma
य ya	र ra	ल la	व va	
श sha (śa)	ष śa (ṣa)	स sa	ह ha	क्ष kśa (kṣa)

Conjuncts

ज्ञ jiṇa (jña)

Notes

(AT = Author's translation)

1. Anandamurti, *Naman Shiváya Shántáya*, 199. AT

Introduction

2. *Á – drsh + ghain = ádarsha*: that which we keep in front of us or watch, and follow while we act. ...Whenever some person or individual was held up before others so that they could watch him and do as he did, or try to emulate him, then that individual was called *ádarsha puruśa*. In the Vedic language, *adarsha* means "mirror". In comparatively recent Sanskrit the word *ádarshii* was more common, but that is not to say that the word *ádarsha* was not used at all. (Anandamurti, *Shabda Cayaniká, Part 1*, 143.)

3. Readers interested in his life can see my biography of this twentieth-century spiritual master, *Anandamurti: The Jamalpur Years*.

4. According to Tantric tradition, Shiva was the father of Tantra and its first great master, though it is said that Tantra already existed in a rudimentary form when he was born. Exactly when that was cannot be ascertained by modern scholarship, and the same is true for the contention that he was a historical figure. According to Anandamurti, however, Shiva was indeed a historical figure who was born approximately 7000 years ago in Northern India (a date and locale that other Indian sages, such as Swami Shivananda of Rishikesh, and some Indian historians also accept) and who systematized the Tantric teachings as we now know them. For the purposes of this text, and in accordance with *aptávákya*, which considers the words of an enlightened sage to be the highest expression of truth, the dating of the Indian historical record will follow the indications given by Anandamurti in his written texts.

5. Although there is still a great deal of debate about the conclusions that can be drawn from recent genetic studies, the evidence increasingly supports a series of migrations into India from Central Asia and Europe, consistent with Anandamurti's historical writings on the subject. The following is a quote from the American geneticist

NOTES (INTRODUCTION) 337

Dr. Spencer Wells:

"The Aryans came from outside India. We actually have genetic evidence for that. Very clear genetic evidence from a marker that arose on the southern steppes of Russia and the Ukraine around 5,000 to 10,000 years ago. And it subsequently spread to the east and south through Central Asia reaching India. It is on the higher frequency in the Indo-European speakers, the people who claim they are descendants of the Aryans, the Hindi speakers, the Bengalis, the other groups. Then it is at a lower frequency in the Dravidians. But there is clear evidence that there was a heavy migration from the steppes down towards India." https://www.rediff.com/news/2002/nov/27inter.htm

6. The modern reductionist model of the universe is also a map of reality. It is not the territory but a description of the territory, one with glaring defects, for the very reason that it removes consciousness from the equation, despite depending on consciousness for its existence. There are many scientists, however, who do not ascribe to this model, at least not fully, especially those who are strongly influenced by the findings of quantum mechanics, which has demonstrated that the observer cannot in fact be taken out of the equation.

7. The word *sádhaná* literally means "effort to complete." It is commonly used to refer to spiritual practice in toto and sometimes to meditative practice in particular. The word *shástra* is commonly translated as "treatise" or "scripture."

8. As far as we know from the history of spiritual sadhana, Sadashiva was the first to propound it. He gave this spiritual path the name Tantra. Tantra was the secret behind spiritual progress. The scriptural definition of Tantra is *tam jadyat tarayet yastu sah tantrah parikirttitah*. That which delivers a person from the seed of staticity, *tam*, that is, through whose blessing one is liberated from the noose of staticity, is Tantra. Tantra can also be explained in another way. The Sanskrit verbal root *tan* means "to expand," that is, the process of sadhana that leads to the expansion of consciousness and consequently to emancipation is called Tantra. Thus we see that the sadhana of liberation is called Tantra; in other words, sadhana and Tantra are inseparable. Strictly speaking, book knowledge cannot be called Tantra. Tantra is something practical. Hence in Tantra, book knowledge is altogether secondary.

The practical process of Tantra begins at the physical level. The body and mind must be trained, then the mind and the *átmá*, and finally one must be established in consciousness. Tantra was mainly practical, and thus great emphasis was placed on the guru-disciple relationship. The Tantric, learning with great care from the mouth of the guru and putting those teachings into practice, must prove their mastery at every step. For this reason Sadashiva didn't want the Tantric teachings to be written down. However, in the course of time, due to a lack of competent preceptors and disciples, Tantra was about to vanish. It therefore became necessary to put the teachings in writing to save them from total extinction. There are presently sixty-four written Tantric texts. (Anandamurti, *Subhásita Samgraha 8*, 25. AT)

9. The Vedas suffered a similar fate due to a prevalent superstition.

> They believed that since their forefathers had not written down the Vedas then it would have been unjust and undesirable for them to write them down. Actually they conveniently forgot that written script had not been invented at that time. It was only later on, when the Kashmir pandits of northwest India began to write in Sáradá script, that they realized the impossibility of committing the four Vedas to memory. Not only that, out of the 108 extant parts of the Vedas, fifty-two had vanished. Thus they decided to write down the Vedas, thinking that if they delayed much longer the Vedas might all disappear. So they wrote down the remaining portions of the Vedas in Sáradá script. Those parts that had vanished were never written down and no matter how much effort is expended those lost portions will never be recovered. (Sarkar, *Varńa Vijińána*, 74.)

10. One of those advantages stemmed from the rarity of books and the scarcity of writing materials in the ancient world. Books were rare commodities fashioned by hand that required a lot of time and effort to make, and the condensed character of the sutra form allowed for easier preservation and dissemination of those teachings.

11. A strong case can and has been made for placing both the Samkhya and Yoga philosophical systems outside the orthodox Vedic tradition, for both these closely related doctrines appear to be more closely aligned with Tantra.

12. Acosta, *The Jamalpur Years*, 259.

13. Professor Indradeva Gupta, a prominent early disciple of Anandamurti, wrote a short English commentary in 2007 that was never published but which is available in electronic format.

14. Panini's work has been variously dated by different historians to somewhere between the fourth and seventh centuries BCE.

15. Professor Indradeva Gupta was an accomplished Sanskritist. He recounted that he approached Anandamurti with a proposal for the addition of sandhi and other minor orthographic changes to the sutras. Anandamurti approved his proposal, but those alterations were never added to the published text.

Chapter One

1. *Accent Magazine*, "The Hidden World of Mind," Oct. 1972, New Delhi, India.

2. Vishvasára Tantra.

3. This should not be taken as a slight against Descartes, who was a spiritually minded philosopher and scientist, the founder of analytic geometry. After several days of increasingly ecstatic feelings in November of 1619, Descartes had a series of three mystical dreams, which then became the foundation of his philosophical and scientific endeavors. Regarding these insights, he is quoted as saying "that human intelligence had played no part in it." (*que l'esprit humain n'y avoit aucune part.*) There are many examples in history of persons who had mystical experiences but were unable to discern the difference between consciousness and mind, indicative of the difficulty of achieving this level of discernment.

4. Shiva and Shakti are the two aspects of the same reality. Shakti is not a separate entity: Shakti is the immanent principle and Shiva the transcendental. "Shakti" means Operative Principle. In every action, two principles are required, one cognitive and another operative. (Anandamurti, *Subhásita Samgraha Part 18*, chap. 11. EE9)

5. In Sanskrit the root *kr* means "that by which objects change place," are moved from one place to another. This nearby pillow is in one place; I move it from here to there. What happened? I have performed an action. That by which the object changes its place I call an action. The root *kr* is used in this sense. In this sense *puruśa* is *akartá*. It does not make the object change its place. So who makes it change its place? That is *paramá prakrti*, the operative force or creative faculty. That is what the word *prakrti* means. *Pra – kr + ktin*, that is, *prakrti* is that whose nature is to cause an action or bring about an action. (Anandamurti, *Ánanda Vacanámrtam 10*, 84. AT)

6. In this universe of ours, two forces are working side by side—the sentient and the static. Sometimes the sentient force and at other times the static force dominates. There is no scope for a pact between these forces. Human beings will have to march ahead amidst the ceaseless struggle of these opposite forces. (Sarkar, *Prout in a Nutshell Part 18*, chap. 1. EE9)

7. In every object of the universe, there is an incessant struggle between *rajoguña* and *tamoguña*. As long as *rajoguña* prevails, there is the sweet revelation of *sattva*. Look at a flower bud. As long as it is blooming, that sweet display is increasing moment by moment; that is, the victory of *rajoguña* is evident in the struggle with *tamoguña*. But when the force of *rajoguña* is spent, then the dominance of *tamoguña* increases at every moment. The flower gradually withers, the glow of *sattva* wanes, and in the end, the all-devouring hunger of *tamoguña* transforms it into a state of crudeness. In other words, it dies. From sprout to leaf to autumn defoliation, from infancy to youth to old age—all are variegated expressions of the struggle between *rajoguña* and *tamoguña*, the war between creator and destroyer, Hari and Hara. (Anandamurti, *Subhásita Samgraha 1–3*, 7–8. AT)

8. Anandamurti dates the Mahabharata war to approximately 1500 BCE. As mentioned in the notes to the introduction, this commentary uses Anandamurti's dating of historical events wherever possible.

9. Due to the lack of historical records from ancient India and the mythological overlay that surrounds Kapil, thanks in large part to the Puranas, there is considerable debate among scholars, especially Western scholars, whether or not Kapil was a historical figure. Anandamurti, however, is quite clear on this point:

> He wanted to get to the bottom of the mystery of creation and bring the causal factors of the universe within a framework of a theory of numbers. We in today's world cannot imagine how much self-confidence and inner daring it took for a person to do this. Maharshi Kapil was born in a certain place near Jhalda in Ráŕh. He came to the highest philosophical realization at Gangasagar, on the Bay of Bengal, at the furthest extremity of Samatat in Ráŕh. (Anandamurti, *Rarh*, chap. 2. EE9)

According to Anandamurti, Kapil was born before Krishna but his teachings were not widely disseminated and studied until after the Mahabharata.

10. Our modern conception of the workings of the physical universe, from Newton's laws of motion to classical electromagnetism, from rel-

ativity theory to quantum mechanics, is defined by the mathematical formulas of modern physics. These are commonly thought of as the laws of nature—the law of gravitation, the laws of motion, the laws of thermodynamics, and so on. However, from the standpoint of philosophy, these are better thought of as descriptions of the workings of *prakrti*. Mathematics is a language and this language is particularly apt at describing the different forces of the manifest universe. These "laws" do not govern the workings of *prakrti* or nature (which Anandamurti calls the "style" of *prakrti*), but rather they describe the nature of *prakrti's* expression within the realms of matter and energy.

11. The twenty-four enumerates or *tattvas* are *prakrti, mahat, aham, manas*, the five *bhútas*, the five *tanmátras*, and the five sensory and five motor organs. Some commentators on Samkhya include *puruśa* as a factor or *tattva* and thus give Samkhya twenty-five enumerates but rightly speaking, *puruśa* is not a *tattva*.

12. Typically in Indian art, when Shiva is lying down with Kali dancing on his chest, his eyes are open, looking at Kali, witness to the dance of creation performed by his Shakti.

13. Being essentially a dualist philosophy, Samkhya did not recognize *puruśa* as the fundamental substance of creation. Rather it assigned that role to *prakrti*. It reasoned that the effect must be of the same nature as the cause, and since everything in the manifest universe is an expression of the three *guńas* in varying proportions, then the three *guńas* of *prakrti* must be both the material and efficient causes. They used the analogy of thread being woven into cloth (a poetically evocative analogy since the word *guńa* also means "thread"), contending that there is essentially no difference between the thread and the cloth, and so the material and efficient causes of the fabric of creation must be the three threads of *prakrti*.

This Samkyan analysis of cosmic causation influenced subsequent schools of Indian philosophy and can even be found in some later Tantric texts, most likely influenced by Vedanta. Anandamurti, however, directly contradicts this Samkyan conception of causation in his commentary to this sutra by recognizing consciousness as both the fundamental substance of the universe and the sovereign cause at whose behest *prakrti* performs her magic act.

14. The electron's motion was filmed for the first time in Sweden in 2008 using a quantum stroboscope. It is the closest we have come to direct observation of an electron, though their existence and properties have been known for more than a century.

15. Yogananda, *Autobiography of a Yogi*, 79.

16. Geddes, *Sir Jagadis C. Bose*, 96.

17. Ibid., 97.

18. Anandamurti, *Ánanda Sútram*, 4. AT

19. The mind's conception of the motivity of action is called time; the measurer of this motivity with the help of the mind is person; and that which establishes the relation between time and person is space. The existence of these three is dependent on mental activity, i.e., on the flow of thought or *oṅmkára*. (Anandamurti, *Subháśita Saṁgraha* 2, 132. AT)

20. Where the active force is dormant, motionless or quiescent, there are no waves of expression, and there is no swelling of life and spirit. Consciousness is lying in blessedness as if it were a serene and silent ocean. When the bosom of the ocean is beset by storms, then surging waves are created. Hence, when the unmanifest Consciousness is tossed by the storms of *prakrti*, the diverse splendor of expression arises. This universe, full of fleeting shows and wonders, is its crude manifestation, and behind this crudeness lies that subtle causal entity—it is the result of the influence of *prakrti* over *puruśa*. (Anandamurti, *Subháśita Saṁgraha* 1-3, 20. AT)

21. The twin nature of *avidyámáyá*, composed of *avaranii shakti* and *viksepii shakti*, and *vidyámáyá*, composed of *samvit shakti* and *hládinii* or *rádhiká shakti*, are ancient ideas that were popularized by Shankaracharya in his *Vivekachudamani*. Anandamurti has provided these concepts with fresh insights, which can be found in various discourses. In the case of *avidyámáyá*, for example:

> First of all, let us take the case of the eccentric force. The eccentric force is called *avidyá shakti*. This *avidyá shakti* has two kinds of influence on the *jiiva*. One is spirituo-psychic and the other is psycho-physical. The spirituo-psychic influence of the eccentric force on the human entity, on the *jaevii* entity [i.e., the *jiiva*, the unit being], is called *vikśepa shakti*. *Vikśepa* means "the drifting away of the entity from the hub," that is, increasing its radius. This *vikśepa shakti* teaches a person to keep away from the Father.
>
> And another influence is psycho-physical. The psycho-physical influence is called *ávaraṅii shakti*. In Sanskrit, *ávaraṅa* means "to cover." That is, one tries to cover one's eyes so as not to see the Lord. One's intention is that one will not see the Lord, that

is why one covers one's eyes. It is just like a rabbit that thinks that because it closed its eyes with the help of its ears and is not able to see the hunter, the hunter will not see it either. This is the effect of *ávaranii shakti* on the *jiiva's* mind. While committing anything antisocial, committing a sin, a person is influenced by this *ávaranii shakti* of *avidyámáyá*. He or she thinks, "This particular action of mine is not being witnessed by the Supreme Father." This is *ávaranii shakti*. (Anandamurti, *Subháśita Samgraha Part 24*, chap. 1. EE9)

22. This shortening of the wavelength as matter becomes denser refers to the five *bhútas*, or five fundamental factors, which will be analysed in Chapter Two.

23. Everywhere change goes on imperceptibly but effectively and all the face of the Earth is changed and re-changed. Egypt is the work of the Nile, and the product of its deposits through the centuries. Here the sea encroaches upon the land and the land reaches out timidly into the sea. New continents and oceans rise and old continents and old oceans disappear, and all the face of the Earth is changed and re-changed in a great systole and diastole of growth and dissolution. (Durant, *The Story of Philosophy*, 76.)

24. A depraved person, a degenerated person, all of a sudden one fine morning starts thinking, "What have I done in this life? I have been given a human structure, a human body, a human mind, a human soul, but I haven't yet utilized that structure. What have I done? I have misused my human potentiality." This idea is created by the concentric force. It is physico-psychic. *Ávaranii* was psycho-physical, and this one is physico-psychic—moving from physicality towards the realm of mentality. This *samvit shakti* creates the urge in the human mind to do something noble, to do intuitional practice. "Now I must not waste my time. I should do something noble, something concrete." After that, what does it do at that moment? It gets His *krpá* [grace]. And one gets the chance to know, to do, to practice, intuitional science. So what will be the next phase? In the next phase one is helped, one gets help from, the concentric force in the form of *hládinii shakti*. *Hládinii shakti* means the *shakti* that helps, that propels, that directs, the *jiiva* towards the realm of supreme beatitude. This is *hládinii shakti*. *Hládinii shakti* is also known as *rádhiká shakti* in Sanskrit, and the Supreme Hub is called Krśńa. *Rádhiká shakti* helps the *jiiva* in coming in contact with Krśńa. Then there will be union of Krśńa and Rádhá [the unit entity]. (Anandamurti, *Subháśita Samgraha Part 24*, chap. 1. EE9)

25. The third type of conscience is *átmánátma viveka*. The sadhana of this type of conscience is to discern whether that eternal, nondual Entity is Consciousness (*átmabháva*) or nonconsciousness (*anátmabháva*). Everything in this universe is a metamorphosed manifestation of Consciousness. This metamorphosis takes place due to the influence of the force of *prakrti*. *Prakrti's* form-creating activity flows in waves; thus the different forms of the world of form are realized through motion. Form is the *prakrti*-bound manifestation of the formless. Consciousness is turned into solid matter, witness-ship taking the form of a perceptible object, and thus Consciousness is converted into nonconsciousness. From mind to solid matter there is nonconsciousness and hence the existence of the three factors—the knower, the knowing, and the known. When a spiritual aspirant applies *átmánátma viveka* to their own mind they can easily discern these three factors and come to the realization that all three are changeable and perceptible—they are nonconsciousness. And the eternal, nondual witnessing Entity that is above these three factors is nothing but Consciousness. (Anandamurti, *Subháśita Saṁgraha 6*, 81. AT)

26. Two birds—*jiivátmá* and *Paramátmá*—are perched on the same tree. Due to the influence of reactive momenta the *jiivátmá* has to undergo suffering, bent double under the tremendous weight of afflictions. It appears to be inseparably associated with the unit being's sense of individual identity. Although, the *jiivátmá* is not the original author of actions—it is just the witness—it appears to be caught up in the cycle of action and reaction. Human beings call some *jiivátmás* mahatma (high soul), some *punyatmá* (pious soul) and some *papátmá* (wicked soul), but in fact it contains neither sin nor virtue, neither good propensity nor bad. It is forced to assume these epithets because of its supposed association with the psychic propensities. (Anandamurti, *Subháśita Saṁgraha 5*, chap. 2. EE9)

27. See sutra II.17 of the Yoga Sutras, where the conjunction between the seer and the seen is identified as the cause of suffering.

28. This is not to imply that mind and consciousness are truly separate. Mind is differentiated from consciousness but it can never be separated, for it is evolved from consciousness and its existence requires the substantiation of consciousness. The same is true for matter.

29. This *jaḋasphoṫa* is nothing but the recoiling of the thought waves of the Cosmic Mind. These recoiling waves are freed by the explosion. (Anandamurti, *Subháśita Saṁgraha 5*, 72. AT)

30. Anandamurti considers this to be the eventual fate of all celestial bodies:

> Under these circumstances the planet will gradually get condensed. As its hydrosphere vanishes, its size will become infinitesimally small. As a result of its atmosphere and thermosphere becoming so dense,* it becomes so small that one day it will be difficult to even conceive that it was once a huge planet. If its internal ethereal factor reaches the nadir of crudity, it will appear to be nonexistent, and in this *jaḋasphoṫa* state it will undergo a great explosion. As a result of this explosion, the immense energy in that infinitesimal dense matter converts it back into ethereal factor. All those celestial bodies in this universe that have become unfit to support life are moving forward through a process of *jaḋasphoṫa*, hurtling toward their death through a violent explosion. This is the natural finality of every celestial body. (Anandamurti, *Subháśita Saṁgraha* 5, 71–72. AT)
>
> *Here "thermosphere" does not refer to the fourth layer of Earth's atmosphere but to a planet's luminous factor.

31. The Big Bounce is one of several cyclical cosmological models in which the present period of expansion, originating with the Big Bang, was preceded by a period of contraction, leading to a model where periods of contraction are followed by periods of expansion in an eternal cyclical universe. Current work in loop quantum gravity tends to support the collapse of a previously existing universe prior to the Big Bang. This cyclical cosmological model has been compared to the nights and days of Brahma from Hindu mythology.

32. Because along with progress and due to psychic clash in the vast cosmic body, the expression of *rajoguńa* increases. Hence, it is not possible for all parts of creation to have a uniform temperature or undergo a thermal death. When the energy of the material structure gets concentrated in its center due to extreme crudity, *jaḋasphoṫa* occurs. This releases vast amounts of energy, thus helping in particular to maintain the thermal disparity of the universe and the continued flow of the cosmic imagination. That is why the fear of some scientists that the universe will meet a thermal death is unfounded. In this universe some particular place or some particular form may indeed undergo destruction, but there will never be any collective thermal death of the universe. (Anandamurti, *Subháśita Saṁgraha* 5, 78. AT)

33 There are considerable differences of opinion regarding entropy among contemporary physicists. For many, the idea of the universe

reaching a state of maximum entropy has already been proved to be untenable, due to the ever-increasing gap between the actual and maximum entropies, since in an expanding universe the actual entropy increases less rapidly than the maximum possible entropy: "... it is this inability of the cosmos to ever reach true maximum disorder that allows order, or lack of disorder, to emerge in localized open systems." (Chaisson, *Cosmic Evolution*, 29). In other words, the very expansion of the universe creates the necessary conditions for the emergence of star systems and eventually of life.

Indeed, life itself is the quintessential expression of negative entropy. The more complex the life-form (and any life-form, no matter how primitive, is more complex, more ordered, than any inanimate structure), the greater the expression of structural organization. Complex living organisms are veritable storehouses of low entropy and concentrated energy. They are the universe's greatest expression of order and organization, nowhere more so than in the human being and human brain, but despite complex living organisms being the quintessence of negative entropy, they do not violate the second law of thermodynamics, due to the entropy they generate in order to maintain their level of organization.

34. Actually, whatever we consider to be the fundamental material of the world, be it atoms, molecules, electrons, or etherons, they are but a manifestation of energy, different forms of energy. Matter is nothing but bottled-up energy—this statement is quite correct. And energy also is not a fundamental entity. It is also but a special expression of the binding power of *prakrti* over Consciousness. Thus if objectivity is to be correctly comprehended, then one will have to arrive at the theory of Brahma as being composed of *puruśa* and *prakrti*. (Anandamurti, *Subhásita Samgraha 3*, 110–111. AT)

35. Rovelli, *Seven Brief Lessons*, chap. 4.

36. The present dating of the oldest known traces of life is 3.85 billion years ago, almost immediately after the earth's crust turned solid some 3.9 billion years ago and the first oceans formed. The oceans formed once atmospheric temperatures dropped below the boiling point of water. Prior to this the Earth's water was in a gaseous state.

37. Biochemical evolution focuses on how the molecules of life could have "evolved" under primeval conditions; however, the molecules of life cannot be equated to life any more than chemical events in the brain can be equated to consciousness, something the scientists working in this field have seemingly failed to comprehend.

38. When the *práńashakti*, due to the complexity of its physical structure, takes the individual mind as the apparent source of its actional flow, then that *práńashakti* is called *práńáh* (life or vital energy). This *práńáh* is the collection of ten *váyus*, which is why in Sanskrit it is always used in the plural. In the modern Indian languages descended from Sanskrit we use the word *práńa* in the sense of *práńáh*. That microcosm or material entity that directs its overall structure with the help of *práńáh* we call a living being. *Práńa* originates after the emergence of the five fundamental factors in the phase of *saiṋcara*, not before. The origin of *práńáh* marks the beginning of *pratisaiṋcara*. (Anandamurti, *Subháśita Saḿgraha 5*, 65. AT)

39. See the preceding endnote.

40. No living creature can survive for an extended length of time in a true vacuum, unless they go into a state of suspended animation, as is the case with spores, for example, which have no active expression of *práńáh*. A similar principle is at work when living cells are frozen. They can be revived under certain conditions but while they are frozen there is no appreciable expression of *práńáh*.

41. Three anaerobic species belonging to phylum Loricifera were discovered in 2010 buried in sediment under the Mediterranean seafloor. They were the first anaerobic metazoans, or multicellular lifeforms, ever to be discovered. They use hydrogenosomes, organelles resembling mitochondria that are found in various microorganisms, to generate energy using hydrogen.

42. Anaerobic respiration evolved in the Earth's first life-forms under conditions in which oxygen was not available in the atmosphere. It is, however, far less efficient than aerobic respiration and this is thought to have greatly impeded the progress of biological evolution until the early cyanobacteria were able to sufficiently oxygenate the atmosphere, thus paving the way for more energy-efficient aerobic life-forms.

43. Anaerobic lifeforms display an astounding variety of adaptive processes that allow them to generate energy under the most inhospitable conditions. From the deep-water hydrothermal vents, where certain bacteria and archaea thrive at temperatures approaching the boiling point of water and feed off of hydrogen sulphide (as well as free hydrogen and CO_2 bubbling up from the Earth's molten core), to ancient endoliths living inside rocks that consume so little energy they are thought to reproduce only once every ten thousand years, life persists where it is almost impossible to imagine its presence.

However, in all cases they must be able to absorb hydrogen in one form or another, whether from the Earth's most abundant substance, water, or in some other form.

Hydrogen is required not only for anaerobic respiration but also for the generation of energy in aerobic cells through the proton motive force, which is now thought to be fundamental to the production of energy in all forms of life. The proton motive force was first proposed by Peter Mitchell in 1961 as being responsible for the synthesis of ATP in cellular respiration, due to the accumulation of hydrogen ions on the outside of the cellular membrane during electron transport, thus setting up an electrochemical potential. While his theory was not particularly well received at the beginning, evidence validating his ideas continued to accumulate and in 1978 he was awarded the Nobel Prize in Chemistry for his discovery.

44. This does not prohibit asteroids from carrying life with them in protected pockets as they journey through space, one of the theories of the advocates of panspermia, but only the appearance of life under those conditions.

45. Bryson, *A Short History*, 172.

46. Complete cessation, however, is contrary to the principle of movement, because nothing in this universe can stop moving. Actually, there is no such thing as absolute pause or absolute speed. All pause and speed is relative, but this cessation is contrary to relativity because time, space, and person are functioning between these two stages. It is due to the influence of these three factors that the next stage arises; that is, it is due to the impact of the three factors of time, space, and person that the preceding stage is transformed into the subsequent stage. This is how the play of creation proceeds — in matter, in mind, and in consciousness. When the movement reaches the maximum point of crudification, then the relative factors give it a jolt, but there is no scope for it to become any cruder because that movement has reached its final point. This state is known as *svayambhú*. That jolt then takes it in the direction of consciousness. (Anandamurti, *Subháśita Saṁgraha 9*, 26–27. AT)

47. With the development of the mind, the physical structure becomes more complex. It can be put in another way: the physical structure grows in complexity in order to serve as a proper vehicle for the expression of a developed mind. (Anandamurti, *Subháśita Saṁgraha 7*, chap. 3. EE9)

48. The Himalayas do not know that they exist but a tiny fly does ... when *citta* emerges as a result of clash, then this existential awareness slowly awakens, and with the development of *aham* and *mahat*, existential awareness becomes evident. In the end the role of the I becomes paramount. (Anandamurti, *Subhásita Saṁgraha 8*, 6–7. AT)

49. Anandamurti defines human beings as those beings whose *mahat*, or self-awareness, has evolved to the point that they have the conscious ability to go against the flow of *pratisaiṇcara*, an ability no other living being has. He dates this development to approximately one million years ago. Though hominins were around long before that, including Homo erectus, who may have been the direct ancestor of Homo sapiens, the possession of an anatomical structure similar to modern humans is not enough to merit consideration as a human being. It is the evolution of the mind that is the determining factor.

50. The terms that Kapil used for his Samkhya philosophy, such as *puruśa*, *prakrti*, the three *guńas*, the five *mahábhútas*, and the five *tanmátras*, were current in the Tantric teachings that were still oral at that time. Like Patanjali, who synthesized the ancient traditions of yoga into a single coherent system, Kapil synthesized Tantric concepts that were prevalent during his time and added his own unique insights to formulate his Samkhya teachings. As mentioned in a previous endnote, Anandamurti places Kapil's birth before that of Krishna and the events of the Mahabharata. The Samkhya philosophy is mentioned by name a number of times in the Bhagavad Gita, and its core concepts, such as *prakrti* and the three *guńas*, are fundamental to the teachings of the Gita.

51. There are significant differences between Anandamurti's analysis of the three functional layers of the mind and Kapil's. The differences between the two conceptions of *mahat* is explained in sutra I.18. Regarding the difference between *citta*, as explained by Anandamurti, and the *manas* of Kapil, Samkhya attributes to *manas* first of all the recognition of impressions (being the mental seat of the organs), which are then presented to the *ahaṁkára* after analysis and identification (*manas* literally means "thinking"). According to Anandamurti, the process of analysis is performed by *ahaṁtattva*, not by the *citta* or *manas*. A further difference is that the Samkhya conception of *manas* does not account for the formation and accumulation of *saṁskáras* (though the idea of *saṁskára* plays an important role both in Samkhya and Yoga), and this may be why Shankaracharya felt it necessary to add a fourth compartment or layer in his Advaita Ve-

danta, for which he used the traditional word *citta*, which in Yoga was used as a general word for the mind. In his explanation, he compares *manas* to the surface of the ocean of mind when it is tossed by waves, those waves corresponding to the mental activity of *manas*, whereas the impressions that result from the activity of *manas* are then stored in the *citta*, as if they were the sediment or residue of those waves sinking into the depths.

52. Hidehiro Watanabe, Makoto Mizunami, "Pavlov's Cockroach: Classical Conditioning of Salivation in an Insect," *PLOS Sustainability and Transformation*, https://doi.org/10.1371/journal.pone.0000529

53. See *Fish Cognition and Behaviour*, Colum Brown, Kevin Laland, and Jens Krause, Ed. 2011, Blackwell Publishing, LTD.
   For rodent learning there are numerous sources. Rats, for instance, improve their foraging capabilities by observing other rats.

54. For undeveloped entities whose *citta* is larger than *aham* enjoyment of crude matter is the goal of life, because their mental power moves within the arena of the crude mind. ...And when there arises a subtler "I" feeling in the *citta* which does something more than merely establish a link with matter, that is, which acquires the capacity to direct matter according to its own desire, it is termed *buddhi* [intellect]. (Anandamurti, *Neohumanism in a Nutshell Part 1*, Chap. 9. EE9)

55. Just as the intellect's movement toward the crude mind gives rise to the material sciences, in the same way, when it seeks to move in the intellectual sphere it gives birth to philosophy. In other words, philosophy emerges at the point where the crude mind ends and intellect begins. That is, philosophy is confined to the intellectual field. (Anandamurti, *Subháśita Saṁgraha 8*, 12. AT)

56. This independence is of course relative, being only valid from the microcosmic point of view. From the macrocosmic standpoint, nothing within the Macrocosmic Mind can be truly independent.

57. What is knowledge? *Satyam jiṋánamanantam brahmah*. *Paramátmá* is the embodiment of knowledge. Every particle of the universe is the manifestation of *paramátmá*. This is the essence of knowledge. What is the sadhana of knowledge? When one starts realizing that every mundane objectivity is the manifestation of *paramátmá* one comes from the sphere of theory to practice. The realization that the universe is the manifestation of *paramátmá* is *siddhi* or achievement in *jiṋána sádhaná*. (Anandamurti, *Subháśita Saṁgraha 19*, chap. 1. EE9)

58. In classical Samkhya, as it has come down to us, *mahat* or *buddhi* is characterized by reflective discernment and it manifests in eight different forms: dharma (virtue, psycho-spiritual urge), *jiṋána* (knowledge), *vairágya* (nonattachment), and *aeshvarya* (the eight occult powers) when *sattva* dominates, and their opposites when *tamas* dominates, ie., ignorance, attachment, etc. (*Sáṁkhya Káriká* XXIII). While these eight forms of expression have been interpreted differently by different commentators, they all concur in attributing a certain degree of authorship to *mahat* that according to Anandamurti rightly belongs to *aham*. For example, when the *buddhi* is overcome by *tamoguńa* and becomes subject to ignorance, this lack of discrimination or *viveka* is a function of *aham*, rather than *mahat*, as the Samkhya philosophers understand it to be.

According to tradition, Kapil, the original propounder of Samkhya, wrote two separate treatises, the *Sáṁkhya Pravachana Sutra* and the *Tattva Samasa Pravachana Sutra*, both of which have been lost. Thus we cannot be certain about Kapil's original conception of *mahat*. The oldest extant Samkhya text is the *Sáṁkhya Káriká* of Ishvara Krishna, composed more than a millennium and a half after Kapil and from which comes our modern understanding of Samkhya's conception of *mahat*.

59. For example, if a teacher of Bhopal is asked, "How many ants are there in the city?" or "How many bricks are there in the buildings?" they will not be able to answer. It is impossible to answer because the external objectivities have not been subjectivized. Where it is possible to do so, there is no necessity of reading books. The person can see the object reflected in the atman and can form an exact conception of the object. What is this, what is that, who has done this and when have they done it—all of this is known. This is the only knowledge; everything else is the mere shadow of knowledge. (Anandamurti, *Subháśita Saṁgraha 9*, 45. AT)

60. (Anandamurti, *Ánanda Vacanámrtam Part 12*, chap. 32. EE9)

61. When the intellect is transcended and intuition blossoms, then human beings realize beyond any shadow of a doubt that a living being cannot attain supreme blessedness through material science or philosophy—only intuition can reach that Supreme Entity. Supreme blessedness is hidden in intuition. (Anandamurti, *Subháśita Saṁgraha 8*, 13. AT)

62. With the exception of the aforementioned sponges and bivalves.

63. There are numerous studies on the sensory abilities and mechanisms of plants. For an in-depth look at how plants experience the world, see *What Plants Know* (2012) by Daniel Chamovitz, Ph.D., who was Chair of the Department of Plant Sciences at Tel Aviv University when he wrote the book.

64. Within cells, electrical signals are conveyed along the cell membrane. For communication between cells, electrical signals are generally converted into chemical signals that are conveyed by neurotransmitters.

65. One example of this similarity is the role of glutamate receptors in cell-to-cell communication. Glutamate receptors in the human brain play a key role in neural communication, and recent studies have shown that glutamate receptors play a similar role in cell-to-cell signaling in plants. (for more details, see Chamovitz, *What a Plant Knows*, chap. 6.)

66. According to Tantra, sound is the subtlest of the five inferences, and thus it stands to reason that the perception of the sound inference will be the least developed of the five sensory capabilities in plants.

67. Plants use statoliths to sense gravity, just as we use otoliths in our inner ears. Statoliths are dense ball-like structures that change their position in the cell depending on the plant's spacial orientation, like marbles rolling to the bottom of a jar. They are essentially gravity receptors and are what allow for the phenomenon of gravitropism. (for more details, see Chamovitz, *What a Plant Knows*, chap. 5.)

68. Murphy et al., "Kin recognition: Competition and cooperation in Impatiens (Balsaminaceae)," *American Journal of Botany*, 2009; 96 (11): 1990 DOI: 10.3732/ajb.0900006

69. The offspring of plants who have made new DNA combinations in response to environmental stresses have been shown to make these same new combinations even though they have not been exposed to those environmental stresses. This is a form of transgenerational memory. (for more details, see Chamovitz, *What a Plant Knows*, chap. 6.)

70. http://hdl.handle.net/10355/6759

71. There is a theory in evolutionary biology that life took so long to evolve into more complex forms because Earth's early atmosphere did not allow for aerobic organisms. It took approximately two billion years for the early cyanobacteria to oxygenate the atmosphere

to modern levels, and those cyanobacteria's modern relatives are considered by many biologists to be Earth's slowest-evolving lifeforms. However, this theory does not accord with *Ananda Sutram*, where evolution is not seen as a physical process but a mental process. It took nearly two billion years for the first eukaryotes to appear and another billion or so after that till the first metazoans precisely because the *citta* mind of those early unicellular organisms was so rudimentary and hence so slow to evolve.

72. Perry et al., "Unexpected rewards induce dopamine-dependent positive emotion-like state changes in bumblebees," *Science* 30 Sep 2016: Vol. 353, Issue 6307, pp. 1529-1531 DOI: 10.1126/science.aaf4454

73. There are a number of great apes, including chimpanzees, orangutans, gorillas, and bonobos, who have learned some form of sign language or symbolic language based on images to communicate with humans. Koko the gorilla and Kanzi the bonobo are two of the most well known. While Koko was more famous, Kanzi is the better conversationalist. There are some scientists who push back against the conclusion that the great apes can use language as humans do, albeit in a very simple form, but the evidence is overwhelming.

74. Anandamurti has used the term *sattá bodha* (entitative or existential awareness) in Bengali to refer to the awareness of existence that is present in an incipient form in organisms possessing only *citta* and which becomes evident in beings that possess *aham*, the sense of individuation bereft of self-awareness or *mahat*.

> The principle difference between animate and inanimate entities is that an animate entity has existential awareness (*sattá bodha*) whereas inanimate entities lack this feeling. A piece of iron or a grain of sand does not know that it exists but even an undeveloped living being like an earthworm knows that it exists. The Himalayas do not know that they exist but a tiny fly does …When *citta* emerges as a result of clash, then this existential awareness slowly awakens. With the development of *aham* and *mahat*, existential awareness becomes evident, and in the end the role of the I becomes predominant. (Anandamurti, *Subhásita Samgraha 8*, 6–7. AT)

75. Alice Walker, *Living by the Word: Selected Writings 1973–1987* (New York: Harcourt Brace Jovanovich, Publishers, 1989), 3.

76. One study of metacognition in rats was conducted by the neuroscientist Jonathon Crystal of the University of Georgia at Athens and

his graduate student Allison Foote and published in March, 2007 (https://www.ncbi.nlm.nih.gov/pmc/articles/PMC1861845/). There are numerous studies of empathy in rats, including a well-known study at the University of Chicago conducted by Peggy Mason, Jean Decety, and Inbal Ben-Ami Bartal and published in the December 7, 2011 issue of *Science*.

77. The atman is not only in human beings and animals; it is also in plants, for they too have minds, they too have existential awareness (*astitva bodha*). The fact that trees and plants had minds was known to the ancient sages and this fact was proved scientifically by Acharya Jagadish Chandra Bose. (Anandamurti, *Subhásita Samgraha 5*, 39. AT)

78. When Anandamurti visited the Philippines in 1969, he often sat with a group of disciples under a particular banyan tree. The disciples would sit and meditate in front of the master, often entering into trance states, and they would also sing kirtan. When they would sing kirtan, the leaves of the banyan tree would start to shiver, and it appeared almost as if the leaves were dancing along with the devotional chanting. Later Anandamurti related that the collective effect of the disciples meditating and singing kirtan under that tree vibrated its unexpressed *samskáras*.

> "It liked the vibration of that kirtan. When those vibrations struck its crude mind, its mind quickly elevated. Plants and animals feel pleasure and pain; they have some of the characteristics of higher life." Baba then said emphatically, "So after the death of that banyan tree it will not remain in an undeveloped body. It will get a developed body. It will get a double promotion. It will get a human body." (Acarya Nityasatyananda Avadhuta, *Tumi Nije Ele Dhará Dile* (Kolkata: Ananda Marga Publications, 2016), 199. AT)

79. In this way, as plant life progresses on the path of evolution, it reaches a point where plant life ends and animal life begins. With the progressive expression of intelligence in animals, they also reach a point that we can call the terminal point of animality and the beginning point of humanity. (Anandamurti, *Abhimata 4*, 50. AT)

80. Modern hardwood trees first appear in the fossil record approximately fifty million years after the first mammals, and there is a great deal of ongoing research into their behaviors and social interactions, especially in the context of both old-growth and newly planted forests. A highly readable account of some of this research can be found

in *The Hidden Life of Trees* by Peter Wohlleben.

81. Anandamurti, *Ánanda Vacanámrtam Part 10*, chap. 10. EE9

82. Heather Salazar and Roderick Nicholls, eds., *The Philosophy of Spirituality: Analytic, Continental and Multicultural Approaches to a New Field of Philosophy*. (Boston: Brill Rodopi, 2019), 15.

83. During the first stage of *savikalpa* samadhi the sense of "I" feeling still exists and so also does the process of cosmic imagination of the universe in its vastest scope. But when the *sádhakas* attain the zenith of this state, they gradually enter a realm beyond the reach of action and thought. (Anandamurti, *Subhásita Saḿgraha* 2, chap. 4. EE9)

"The entire cosmos, gently luminous, like a city seen afar at night, glimmered within the infinitude of my being. The dazzling light beyond the sharply etched global outlines faded somewhat at the farthest edges; there I saw a mellow radiance, ever-undiminished. It was indescribably subtle; the planetary pictures were formed of a grosser light.

The divine dispersion of rays poured from an Eternal Source, blazing into galaxies, transfigured with ineffable auras. Again and again I saw the creative beams condense into constellations, then resolve into sheets of transparent flame. By rhythmic reversion, sextillion worlds passed into diaphanous luster; fire became firmament.

I cognized the center of the empyrean as a point of intuitive perception in my heart. Irradiating splendor issued from my nucleus to every part of the universal structure. Blissful *amrita*, the nectar of immortality, pulsed through me with a quicksilverlike fluidity. The creative voice of God I heard resounding as *Aum*, the vibration of the Cosmic Motor." (Yogananda, *Autobiography of a Yogi*, 167)

84. *Citta* can be concentrated on anything, on matter or on an idea. It may flow toward emancipation (*kaevalya*) or it may move toward the mundane world. Hence it is said that the river of *citta* can flow both ways. When it flows toward *kaevalya* it is called *kalyána vahá* (flowing toward benevolence), and when it runs toward matter it is called *pápa-vahá* (flowing toward sin). When the *citta's kalyáná-vahá* stance becomes fixed it is called *savikalpa* samadhi. This *savikalpa*, or in strict philosophical language, *samprajiṇáta* samadhi is also marked by certain signs:

1) Realization of the Absolute. When a spiritual aspirant realizes their oneness with the Absolute, which is the root substance of every object of the world, then they experience the supreme truth of every-

thing. For this reason, they have no need to study books or to make any other kind of effort.

2) The second sign is the waning of afflictions. The afflictions caused by defective cognition rapidly disappear as a result of attaining this samadhi.

3) The third sign is the loosening of the bondages of action. Every living entity is under the bondage of action. Even after attaining *savikalpa* or *samprajiṋáta* samadhi, one continues to perform actions but does not get entangled in them. At this stage their ideation is:

> *Kámato' kámato vápiyat karomi shubbháshubham*
> *Tatsarvaḿ tvayi sannyástaḿ tatprayuktah karomyahaḿ*
>
> [Whatever I do, good or bad, with or without desire, I offer unto you.]

4) And the fourth sign is the movement towards the undifferentiated state of cognition. This state is called *samprajiṋáta* samadhi because self-knowledge is fully expressed. (Anandamurti, *Subháśita Saḿgraha 8*, 55–56. AT)

85. What is omniscience? Knowledge of the past, present, and future is called omniscience. The seed of omniscience lies in every human being, but the degree of its expression varies — in some it is ripe, in others less so. In *samprajiṋáta* samadhi this seed fully ripens and in continuous *savikalpa* it assumes vast proportions. In that state one's object no longer remains limited to the objects of the individual mind but becomes as vast as the Macrocosm. One's potentiality becomes immeasurable. (Anandamurti, *Subháśita Saḿgraha 8*, 70. AT)

86. The chakras are the subtle centers that control the flow of psychic energy in the human being, of which there are seven principle chakras. There are many different types of samadhi described in the yogic literature, but one way of classifying those samadhis is according to the ascent of the kundalini, which reaches the second, third, fourth, and fifth chakras before reaching the sixth chakra and *savikalpa* samadhi.

> When the *sadhaka* [spiritual aspirant] by dint of his or her sadhana, intuitional practice, exalts that *kulakuńḋalinii*, and when the *kulakuńḋalinii* crosses the *svádhiśthána cakra*, the next higher *cakra*, the *sadhaka's* feeling, his or her expression, his or her status, is known as *sálokya*. It is the first stage of samadhi. A *sadhaka* by constant practice is sure to attain that status. ... *Sálokya* means that the *sadhaka* feels that in the stratum, or

sphere, where he or she is, where that person's exalted mind is, he or she is not alone; the Supreme Father is also there.

Then when this coiled serpentine, sleeping divinity, crosses the *mańipura cakra*, just near the hub, the controlling point, of the pancreas, the person enjoys another sort of pleasure, and that pleasure is called *sámiipya* samadhi. *Sámiipya* is a Sanskrit word. It means "proximity." That is, the *sadhaka* feels his or her proximity to the Supreme Father.

In the first stage, the *sadhaka* felt that the Supreme Father was there in the same status. He is not in the sky, he is everywhere, He is with you. If you are here and He is in the sky, then you are alone here, and He is also alone there. No, no, no, no. In the first phase the feeling was that "Where I am, He is also with me." And in the second phase, "I have come very close, very near that Supreme Father; I am in close proximity to the Supreme Progenitor. By dint of my sadhana, the gap between my Father and myself is being bridged." It is the second phase, known as *sámiipya*. *Sámiipya* means "proximity."

Then when that sleeping divinity, that *kulakuńḍalinii*, crosses the *anáhata cakra*, this plexus, this "solar plexus" (in Latin), the *sadhaka's* feelings are known as *sáyujya*. *Sáyujya* means "in close contact." In Sanskrit *sáyujya* means "close contact, just side by side, just touching." In *sálokya* He is with you. In *sámiipya* you feel the proximity, the nearness. And here in *sáyujya* what do you feel? A tactual experience. You get a tactual experience.

Then when by dint of your sadhana the divinity, the sleeping divinity, the *kulakuńḍalinii*, crosses this point [the throat], one will experience another sort of sadhana, a subtler sadhana. And that one is called *sárúpya*. In *sárúpya* the feeling is "I am one with Him." "I am one with Him"—not close contact, but oneness. "I am one with the Supreme Progenitor, I am one with the Supreme Cognition." This is *sárúpya*.

Then by still more sadhana, when the sleeping divinity crosses this point [between the eyebrows], the controlling point of the pituitary gland, the *ájiṋá cakra*, the *sadhaka's* feelings, or experiences—another sort of sadhana, still more high—are known as *sárśti* in Sanskrit. At that point, the feeling is that "I am He;" that is, "I" and "He", these two entities, have become one. "I am," but "He" and "I" have coincided. (Anandamurti, *Ánanda Vacanámrtam Part* 23, chap. 12. EE9)

87. Mahendranath Gupta, *The Gospel of Sri Ramakrishna*, Translated by Swami Nikhilananda (Chennai: Sri Ramakrishna Math, 1996), 197.

88. (Anandamurti, *Subháśita Saṁgraha 1–3*, 240–241. AT)

89. To meditate on *nirguńa* is not possible; one can only meditate on Saguńa or Táraka Brahma. Meditation can only occur when both subject and object exist. (Anandamurti, *Subháśita Saṁgraha 8*, 73. AT)

90. Liberation means liberation from the *guńas* of *prakrti*. Only Nirguńa Brahma is free from the *guńas* of *prakrti*, hence it alone is emancipated. But Nirguńa Brahma cannot be the cause of liberation because it is devoid of the *guńas*. (Anandamurti, *Ánanda Márga*, 189. AT)

Whatever one may or may not get from meditating on that which has no experience and no mind, they will not get grace. How can the eternally free *nirguńa puruśa* have the right to bestow grace on human beings? That right belongs to those free souls who at one time were bound, that is, Saguńa Brahma and Táraka Brahma, whose mind is established at the tangential point between *saguńa* and *nirguńa*. Those beings who were once bound and are now free, and who will never again be bound, they become equal to Saguńa Brahma and are thus called *mahápuruśa* (great soul). They also have the right to bestow grace. (Anandamurti, *Subháśita Saṁgraha 8*, 74. AT)

91. For this reason it is said in the Tantras that while *savikalpa* is theoretically possible to achieve through one's own efforts, *nirvikalpa* is only possible through the medium of the *sadguru*, the enlightened teacher.

92. Sarkar, *Idea and Ideology*, 46.

93. *Mahá* is a substitute for *mahat* in certain Sanskrit compounds.

Chapter Two

1. Indeed, energy can only be detected through the presence of matter. Electromagnetic energy is detected through the excitation of electrons, heat through the agitation of atoms and molecules, and so on. This is because energy requires the container of matter.

> By splitting up the atom immense energy is released. This is due to the fact that the energy which is packaged up in matter comes out. To claim that energy is obtained due to the destruction of matter is theoretical and not physically proven. In fact, the energy comes out from within the store of the atom.

Energy always requires a material shelter—a container. After the destruction of the container, the immense released energy moves very fast with tremendous speed in all directions in search of some or other material shelter. (Anandamurti, *Microvitum in a Nutshell*, chap. 21. EE9)

2. The type of vibration that arises in the mind through the intake of *tanmátras* or ideas that are congenial to one's *vrttis* will be just opposite to the vibrations that arise due to the intake of uncongenial *tanmátras* or ideas. The former will be pleasant and the latter will be painful. Generally, the easier we can assimilate the impact of vibrations, the more pleasant they are, and the more difficult the vibrational intake, the more painful we find it. Thus in general, the vibrational state in which the *citta* seeks to remain is called *sukha*, and that in which it does not want to remain is called *duhkha*. (Anandamurti, *Subhásita Samgraha 1–3*, 248–249. AT)

3. For Anandamurti's discussion of Patanjali's classification of the *vrttis*, found in Book Two of the Yoga Sutras, see the discourse "Psychic Force and Cognitive Practice" in *Subhasita Samgraha Part 8* as well as "The Cardinal Attributions of God" in *Ananda Vacanamrtam Part 2*. For his discussion of Patanjali's classification of the different samadhis, found in Book One of the Yoga Sutras, see the discourse "Psychic Assimilation in Psycho-Spiritual Practice" from *Subhasita Samgraha Part 8*.

4. A list of the fifty principle *vrttis* can be found in Anandamurti's discourse "Plexi and Microvita" (*Yoga Psychology*) as well as in certain Tantric texts (see Woodroffe, *The Serpent Power*, 138). Each of the fifty *vrttis* has an associated *biija mantra*, or acoustic root, which is represented by one of the fifty sounds of the Indo-Aryan alphabet. For an in-depth analysis of these fifty *biija* mantras, see "The Acoustic Roots of the Indo-Aryan Alphabet" (Anandamurti, *Discourses on Tantra Volume One*).

> People's thought processes are becoming more and more complicated, and so this may happen. It is not that the number of *vrttis* will be limited to fifty. Just imagine the situation. As a result of humanity's thirst for knowledge, the nerve cells are becoming more complex. In order to accommodate that complexity, the nervous system needs to become more powerful. Consequently, the human cranium will become larger in the future; the brain will gradually become larger, and due to the increased size of the cranium, the head will also

gradually become larger. (Anandamurti, *Ánanda Vacanámrtam 7–9*, 100. AT)

5. According to Tantra, the subtle anatomy of the human body contains thousands of psychic nerves, or *náḍiis*, through which the psychic energy flows, some major, some minor (some traditional yogic texts number them at seventy-two thousand). The principal *náḍiis* flow into and out of the chakras and thus that vibrational energy forms shapes that reminded the early yogis of petals coming out from the circular center of the chakra, the controlling center of the *náḍiis* and of the *vrttis*. Because the energy of the different "petals" vibrates at different frequencies, and since all vibration emits both color and sound, each of these petals has their respective color and sound.

6. Each unit being is by nature subject to attraction, but the cause is not found in the attraction itself but in the urge for self-preservation. It is only because of this that they run after crude, subtle, or causal expressions, and this urge arises because they want to survive in order to attain happiness. Thus it is seen that behind the attraction between one entity and another, to which we give the name *káma*, lies the pure desire to attain happiness. (Anandamurti, *Subháśita Saṁgraha 1–3*, 280–281. AT)

7. There are documented instances where a dog has sacrificed their life to save their master. It is debatable, however, whether or not they realized that they were about to sacrifice their life. What is not debatable is that in that instance they showed a high level of *mahat* and were perhaps close enough to human life that that act might have pushed them over the edge.

8. Everyone wants to preserve their existence, and they want to do so in order to attain happiness. People do not want to die, for they know happiness cannot be achieved after death. This is the main cause behind the fear of death. For this reason, you will see that those who do not find any of the ingredients for happiness in their life, or who do not see even the possibility thereof, become weary of their life, thinking it to be a burden, and thus commit suicide. It is because they no longer regard life as a means of attaining happiness that they destroy it. People commit suicide for the same reason that people under normal conditions seek to destroy those factors that are detrimental to their happiness, considering them to be their enemies. (Anandamurti, *Subháśita Saṁgraha 4*, 47–48. AT)

9. It is primarily in the Tantras and to a certain extent in Vaishnavism

and the bhakti cults in general that we find this embracing of *sukha* as a motive force in spiritual evolution.

10. *The Nyāya-sūtras of Gautama with the Bhāṣya of Vātsyāyana and the Vārttika of Uddyotakara*, Delhi: Motilal Banarsidass, 1984.

11. Edwin Bryant, *The Yoga Sutras of Patanjali*, chap. 2.

12. *Sukha* denotes a congenial mental state whereas *ánanda* is a metempirical state that overflows the mind — it can be called neither congenial nor uncongenial. *Ánanda* is metempirical because it is limitless. (Anandamurti, *Tattva Kaomudi 1*, 46. AT)

13. Anandamurti, *Ánanda Sútram*, chap. 2. EE9

14. The individual self is incomplete. As long as it does not become established in the Infinite Entity, its suffering cannot be removed. (Anandamurti, *Subhāśita Saṁgraha 2*, 9. AT)

15. The word *brahma* in Sanskrit means "great, absolute." He is the greatest of all — *brhattvád Brahma*. Is that all? By ideating on him, all become Brahma, that is, he has the capacity to make all Brahma — *brṁhanatvád brahma*. (Anandamurti, *Subhāśita Saṁgraha 1–3*, 162. AT)

16. Concomitant with a fully reflected *mahat*, which confers the ability to go against the flow of *pratisaiṇcara*, comes the first conscious inkling that there may be a cosmic power behind our existence and that of the universe in which we find ourselves, a thought that by itself separates human beings from animals. In 1969 Anandamurti conducted a demonstration for the disciples in Ranchi in which he asked Vijay Kumar to close his eyes and bring his mind to a particular chakra. Anandamurti then asked him to look into the mind of the person sitting next to him and tell him what he saw. This was a common type of demonstration in which Anandamurti would temporarily give whomever he chose as the subject the ability to see the past lives of the other person. After a brief pause, Vijay started seeing a goat walking along the embankment of a rapidly rushing river. At a certain moment the embankment gave way. The goat fell into the river and was swept away. Vijay described its thoughts and emotions as it struggled without success to reach the riverbank, until its energy was spent and it realized that it could not save itself. Its last thought before it died was, "If I am going to survive there must be something greater than me that can save me." "Yes," said Anandamurti, bringing the demonstration to a close, "that was the thought that propelled that mind into a human body in its next life."

From very ancient times, human beings slowly started to realize that behind whatever they knew and whatever they obtained, behind their every action, there was a great force at work. From then on the desire awakened in them to find out how to reach that great force, how to get that great force. It was through this longing to know, this longing to obtain, that the spiritual intellect (*dharmabuddhi*) of human beings first arose. It can be said that from the very day that this *dharmabuddhi* arose, human beings became human. Before that they were the same as other animals and birds. (Anandamurti, *Ánanda Vacanámrtam 6*, 44. AT)

17. The word *sádhaná* literally means "the effort to complete." When that effort is directed toward the attainment of the Supreme then it is *dharma sádhaná*. The word *sádhaná* is commonly used in yoga as a synonym for meditation or for spiritual practice in general.

18. *Pranidhána* is to bring all those propensities to a particular point i.e., the entire ectoplasmic structure of the microcosm is to be apexed to a particular point and from that point the resultant is to move forward towards the Cosmic Self. This movement of that apexed resultant is called *Pranidhána*. (Anandamurti, *Subhásita Samgraha Part 18*, chap. 10. EE9)

19. The division of *bhagavad* dharma into *vistára*, *rasa*, and *sevá* is unique to Anandamurti's philosophy.

20. *Iishvara* means "controller" or "Supreme Being." When a human being knowingly tries to attain the Great and does *iishvara pranidhána* for that purpose, that mental attitude is known as dharma and that effort is known as *dharma sádhana*. (Anandamurti, *Ánanda Sútram*, 19. AT)

Pranidhána means to understand clearly or to adopt something as a shelter. Therefore *iishvara pranidhána* means to establish oneself in the cosmic idea—to accept Iishvara as the only ideal of life. The physical body fashioned from the five fundamental factors does not go against the *saincara* or *pratisaincara* movement of Iishvara's thought projection—your mind does, and as a result the individual consciousness degenerates, because the individual consciousness is a reflection in the mind. So *iishvara pranidhána* means to rush toward him in order to establish the mind in that Supreme Shelter. (Anandamurti, *Jiivana Veda*, 46. AT)

21. If your individual flow does not maintain adjustment with the macrocosmic flow, your desires will never be fulfilled. You want so

much but how many of these desires are actually realized? Do you know the reason? If your desires do not accord with the cosmic waves, your actions will not be successful... When human beings are bound to Parama Puruśa through divine love, then they come to know his nature, and accordingly they follow his will. As a result, such individuals become unrivaled and victorious in the world. Other people think, "What a great personality!" But *sádhakas* know the cause behind their success, how they have become successful. Thus the fundamental spirit of *rasa sádhaná* is to direct one's individual desires toward Parama Puruśa. (Anandamurti, *Subháśita Saḿgraha 8*, 113–114. AT)

22. Edward O. Wilson, *On Human Nature*, 2nd edition (Boston: Harvard University Press, 1994)

23. The *muládhára* is the first chakra at the base of the spine and the *sahasrára* chakra is the seventh chakra at the crown of the head. The kundalini, the human being's psychic force, is dealt with in Chapter Four.

24. You need not do anything for *vastu* dharma, because it is automatic. Nor need you do anything for *jaeva* dharma, because it is automatic. You feel hungry before a meal, so you feel the urge to satisfy your hunger; you feel thirsty before drinking water, and that is why you try to quench your thirst. You need not do anything particularly for that purpose. But for *bhágavata* dharma you have to do. That is why it has been said above, "Ensconce thyself in Me, come under My [shelter], that is, follow the path of *bhágavata* dharma." (Anandamurti, *Subháśita Saḿgraha Part 21*, chap. 6. EE9)

25. This idea has been echoed in numerous Indian scriptures. The following is one oft-quoted example:

*Áhára-nidrá-bhaya-maethunaiṋca
Sámányametad pashubhirnaránám;
Dharmo hi teśám adhiko visheśah
Dharmena hiináh pashubhih samánáh*

"Food, sleep, fear, procreation—these are the common properties of humans and animals. But humans possess an especial dharma, in the absence of which they are as bad as animals." (*Hitopadesha* verse 0.25)

A human being who behaves like an animal goes against the very spirit of expansion and is no better than an animal. ... That sort of dharma is not meant for human beings. It is easy, no doubt, but it is not meant for humans. (Anandamurti, *Ánanda Vacanámrtam Part 4*, chap. 12. EE9)

26. Are the individual consciousness and the Supreme Consciousness two separate entities? No, they are not. As long as the individual consciousness is bound by *saṁskáras*, it remains subject to birth and death, moving round in the wheel of samsara. But when the objective mind, through sadhana, exhausts all its acquired reactive momenta, it becomes one with the Supreme Consciousness. In fact, apart from the difference engendered by *saṁskára* and *upádhi* (extra qualification), there is no difference between them. (Anandamurti, *Tattva Kaomudi 2*, 23–4. AT)

27. Nevertheless if this shadow-entity can be clearly seen and understood, one can get a glimpse of the actual moon. But that's all; the real moon cannot be attained through this. So if one knows the *jiivátmá*, one can indeed know the *paramátmá*; if one knows the I, then he can be known, but one cannot attain him or get established in him. Thus, even though the fullness of knowledge can be gained from the lesser samadhis, it does not established one in Brahma. (Anandamurti, *Subháśita Saṁgraha 4*, 104. AT)

28. Although the *jiivátmá* is not the original author of actions—it is just the witness—it appears to be caught up in the cycle of action and reaction. Human beings call some *jiivátmás mahátma* (high soul), some *punyatmá* (pious soul) and some *papátmá* (wicked soul), but in fact it contains neither sin nor virtue, neither good propensity nor bad. It is forced to assume these epithets because of its supposed association with the psychic propensities. (Anandamurti, *Subháśita Saṁgraha Part 5*, chap. 2. EE9)

29. Genuine spiritual practice is that which does away with the mirror of *buddhitattva* in order to merge the shadow-entity *jiivátmá* into the *paramátmá*, the original entity. (Anandamurti, *Subháśita Saṁgraha Part 1–3*, 94. AT)

30. Anandamurti, *Ánanda Vacanámrtam Part 34*, chap. 2. EE9

31. Now there may be a question, can *antarátmá*, the spirit, or the *jiivátmá*, exist only in living beings? *Sarvabhúta* means stone, metal, wood, everything—whatever has been created comes within the scope of *bhúta*. So the question is, is there any *antarátmá* or *jiivátmá* in all those inanimate beings? Certainly there is, but due to their undeveloped stage of mind, undeveloped condition of mind, the *jiivátmá*, or *antarátmá*, is not in a dominating role, is not in a prominent role. But the *jiivátmá* is there. Because of the mind being in a dormant form, the expression of *jiivátmá* is not clear, is not in a dominant

form, in a dominating form. (Anandamurti, *Ánanda Vacanámrtam Part 3*, chap. 20. EE9)

32. Anandamurti, *A Few Problems Solved Part 3*, chap. 6. EE9

33. Apart from being a philosopher, Kanada was also a great scientist who propounded the world's first atomic theory. To their credit, some of Kanada's Greek contemporaries also believed that the universe was composed of atoms, an idea thought to have been first proposed among the Greeks by Democritus, but they did not advance an atomic theory, per se.

34. In reality, there are other factors in play, thus the use of the word "simplistic."

35. The law of cause and effect, as understood in Tantra, should not be confused with determinism or with the linear understanding of cause and effect in classical Newtonian physics, nor is there any conflict with quantum indeterminacy. Determinacy cannot be equated with predictability or computability. The web of cause and effect is far too complex to be predictable or computable, even in theory, and Kanada's contention of cause and effect is in perfect accord with the indeterminacy of quantum theory.

36. Anandamurti, *Subháśita Saṁgraha Part 10*, chap. 3. EE9

37. I must say at the very outset that accident can never be the primary cause of evolution or of the cycle of creation. *Káraṅábhávát karyábhávah*; that is, "Without a cause there can be no effect." When we come across an effect and along with it we get acquainted with its causal factor, we then call that effect an "incident." But when, due to ignorance, we cannot know the cause of the effect, or when the causal factor gets transformed suddenly into the effect factor, we call that effect an "accident." But in the universe there is no such thing as an accident. It is only to cover up one's ignorance of the real cause that one talks about an "accident." (Anandamurti, *Subháśita Saṁgraha Part 24*, chap. 2. EE9)

38. The movement and nature of everything in the world—big or small, great or insignificant—is governed by this cause-and-effect theory. When we look at a tree, we realize that there must have been a seed behind its growth. Again, when we look at a seed, we realize that it must have come from a tree. If we trace this backwards—from tree to seed, from seed to tree, and so on—then we will arrive at a stage where the Mind becomes the effect, but as its cause we find

only the absence of Mind. In other words, what was the cause at one stage was the effect at the previous stage, and this effect had a cause at a still earlier stage. If we proceed backwards along the line of cause and effect—if we move on from the tree to the seed and so on—finally we will get the tree as the effect. While looking for the seed [i.e., its own seed], the mind that is looking for its effective cause arrives at a stage where the mind does not exist. How can the mind understand or experience something at a stage wherein the mind itself is not functioning? To attempt to think about something or argue about something at a stage wherein the mind does not exist is known as *anavasthá dosa*, that is, the fallacy of infinite regression. (Anandamurti, *Shabda Cayaniká Part 4*, chap. 2. EE9)

39. If someone considers himself or herself to be very wise and traces different causes behind different effects, that person will still not be able to reach the first cause, because the theory of causality works only in the arena of mind and the arena of time, space, and person. So when at the last point the effect is found within the scope of time, space, and person, but the cause remains beyond that spatio-temporo-personal boundary, one will not be able to catch the cause, as one's mind will not work there—the cause has gone beyond the boundary of the mind. The theory of causality was founded by Maharshi Kanada. Kanada said, *káranábhávat káryábhávah*—"Where there is no cause there is no effect." The theory is correct, but a human can only find those causes which are within the scope of the mind—that which is beyond the scope of the mind cannot be found. (Anandamurti, *Subháśita Samgraha Part 21*, chap. 7. EE9)

40. The word "quinquelemental" was coined by Anandamurti to refer to the world of the five fundamental factors. *Quinque* means "five" in Latin and "element" comes from the Latin word *elementum*, which refers to the four fundamental elements of earth, water, fire, and air. "Quinquelemental" is the English equivalent of *páińcabhaotika*, "made of the five *bhútas*."

41. Anandamurti, *Ánanda Vacanámrtam Part 12*, chap. 9. EE9

42. Then human beings began their long circumambulation. Having emerged from Brahma where can they go? They cannot go outside of the entity beyond whom there is nothing. Parama Puruśa cannot tell anyone to get out. If Parama Puruśa tells someone, "I don't like you, you're a scoundrel, get out," then that person can say, "Oh Lord, you're telling me to get out, but where can I go? There is nothing outside you. So wherever I go, I will still be inside you. So kindly tell

me, where should I go? What place must I go to? And if you can't kindly tell me where I should go, then please do one thing: change your name. If that's the case, then you are no longer infinite." (Anandamurti, *Subhāśita Saṁgraha 11*, 104. AT)

43. A short description of the "grand system of *ābhāsa*," as it has been called, can be found in chapter nineteen of John Woodroffe's *The Garland of Letters*, as well as in Christopher Wallis's *Tantra Illuminated*, to name two easily accessible sources.

44. Sir Arthur Eddington, *The Nature of the Physical Universe*. (London: Cambridge University Press, 1928), xvi, 276. (from the introduction to the written form of his 1927 Gifford lectures)

45. Shankaracharya went to great lengths to establish the supremacy of his doctrine over the Mayavada of the Buddhists, who were in ascendance in Hindu society in the eighth century. His debates with Buddhist philosophers were legendary and were instrumental in the revival of the study of classical Indian philosophy that took place at that time.

46. This aphorism predates Shankaracharya by at least a millennium, being found in the Niralamba Upanishad. Shankaracharya incorporated it in verse 20 of his *Brahmajiṇānāvaliimālā* (ब्रह्मज्ञानावलीमाला), and it has since been inseparably associated with his Advaita Vedanta:

ब्रह्म सत्यं जगन्मिथ्या जीवो ब्रह्मैव नापरः ।
अनेन वेद्यं सच्छास्त्रमिति वेदान्तडिण्डिमः ॥ २०॥

*brahma satyaṁ jaganmithyā jiivo brahmaeva nāparah
anena vedhaṁ sacchāstramiti vedāntadiṅdimah* (verse 20)

"Brahma is real, the world is false, the living being is none other than Brahma itself.
    This should be understood as the true scripture, being proclaimed by Vedanta."

47. Anandamurti, *Subhāśita Saṁgraha Part 10*, chap. 5. EE9

48. "Buddha at the Gas Pump," interview 197, 10/12/2013. https://batgap.com/david-godman/

49. Sri Nisargadatta Maharaj, *I am That: Talks with Sri Nisargadatta Maharaj*, Translated by Maurice Frydman (Durham, The Acorn Press, 1988), 16.

50. There are certain logical fallacies in Shankara's explication of his doctrine of maya. Among them is that he depends upon the existence of mind (and by extension the body) both to advance his reasoning and for his reasoning to be understood. This and other perceived defects forced him to resort to a kind of verbal jugglery, a philosophical sleight of hand, to defend his position. When confronted with the argument that if only Brahma exists then maya cannot exist, and if maya exists then maya must be real, he answered that maya is neither real nor unreal. "Maya is most strange;" he continued, "her nature is inexplicable." An answer that fails to answer. As was his contention that maya was both real and unreal.

In *Namámi Krśńa Sundaram*, Anandamurti tells this story about Shankaracharya without mentioning him by name:

> Once a certain *mahápuruśa* who happened to be an orthodox *máyávádin* was walking along the road in Kashi [adjacent to Varanasi]. The popular saying goes that Kashi is famous for four things, for *śáńŕ, ráńŕ, sinŕi, sannyásii*—the bulls which throng the streets; the many widows; the stairs which one has to climb up or down every few meters; and the thousands of itinerant monks—and that in Kashi one should carefully avoid these four things. Anyway, one morning a wild bull suddenly started to charge that *mahápuruśa*, so he ran away as fast as his legs could carry him. A logician who happened to be standing nearby asked the *mahápuruśa*, "Well sir, if you say that this world is unreal, then the bull is also unreal, so why are you running in fear?" That *mahápuruśa* would not accept any defeat in logic and replied, "My running away is also unreal." This is the way things went on for many centuries. (Anandamurti, *Namámi Krśńa Sundaram*, chap. 10. EE9)

51. The Sháunkar Darshan [philosophy of Shankaracharya] made people apathetic about the world. Too much apathy makes people cynical. (Anandamurti, *Rarh: The Cradle of Civilization*, chap. 2. EE9)

This nihilistic philosophy has made the people of India and Southeast Asia averse to reality and has been the cause of untold misery in their lives. (Anandamurti, *Namámi Krśńasundaram*, chap. 13. EE9)

It is fairly safe to assume, however, that Shankaracharya's intention was not to promote apathy or nihilism but rather that it was an unintended effect. He was a metaphysician trying to explain an inexplicable reality in terms of what had come before him, and this included his efforts to defeat the Buddhist philosophers of his day, whose own version of Mayavada was extremely influential at the time.

52. *andhaṁ tamah pravishanti ye'vidyámupásate | tato bhúya iva te tamo ya u vidyáyáṁ ratáh ||*

They enter into blinding darkness who worship *avidyá*; into still greater darkness, as it were, do they enter who delight in *vidyá*.
— Isha Upanishad verse 9

The traditional explanation of this verse is that the adverse consequences of negative actions is greater for advanced spiritualists due to their higher state of spiritual elevation—in other words, because they should know better—and the conscious failure to maintain a proper adjustment with the material world, ie., the neglect of one's duties in the world, is considered to be a negative action.

53. Is *puruśa* a disinterested witness in this playful creation of *prakrti*? Does *prakrti* act alone? Is this great dance the sole responsibility of *prakrti*? *Puruśa* is not at all a disinterested witness. When creation is in an unexpressed state, *prakrti's* dance remains under the hypnotic spell of *puruśa*, that is, it is from *puruśa's* hypnotic power that *prakrti* receives the inspiration to dance. (Anandamurti, *Subháśita Saṁgraha 8*, 1. AT)

54. Hence *Puruśa Bhava* is also known as a principle which is *Citi Shakti*. It is because in his absense *Karma Shakti* can't get expression. This *Karma Shakti* or *Prakrta Shakti* is a principle within the *Citi Shakti*. Where *Citi Shakti* is the vibrator (*pratisamvedii*), there alone action is expressed. And where *Citi Shakti* assimilates (*grasa*) *Prakrta Shakti*, there *Prakrta Shakti* is *avyakta* (unexpressed). Therefore the vibration (*pratisamvedan*) is only due to *Citi Shakti*. So the *Citi Shakti* is the Supreme Vibrator (*parama pratisamvedii*). (Anandamurti, *Subháśita Saṁgraha Part 20*, chap. 2. EE9)

55. In other words, whatever there is in this universe will work and function so long as there is *Citi Shakti*. If *Citi Shakti* is not there, no work will be done. The reason is that the creative power which is expressed in the form of nature is basically a blind power. Unless *Citi Shakti* guides it, nothing can happen. Take electric power, for instance. This is a blind power. So long as people's *prajiṇá* (*Citi Shakti*) does not work behind it, nothing can happen. Thus, what we call energy in the crude world is known as *kriyá shakti* in Hindi. This energy cannot do anything until it gets the approval of the *prajiṇá*. In the same way, until the subtler power, the ectoplasmic flow that pervades the supramundane sphere, gets the approval of *prajiṇá*, no

progress is possible. We observe that whatever happens in the supramundane sphere follows a system of laws. And it can function according to this system only when *prajiná* is behind it.(Anandamurti, *Ánanda Vacanámrtam Part 5*, chap. 4. EE9)

56. Parama Puruśa is not only the Cognitive Faculty, he is more than that. He exists not only in the manifest world, but in the unmanifest world as well. Here, the "manifest world" refers to that part of the creation that is vibrated by the three *guńas* of *prakrti*. And that portion of the creation that is not vibrated by the *guńas* is also within his mind. Thus Parama Puruśa is not only in the manifest world, he is also in the unmanifest world. Philosophy is silent regarding the presence of Parama Puruśa in the unmanifest world. Philosophy is only able to comment on Parama Puruśa in the manifest world. So if philosophy says that he is only the Cognitive Faculty, that applies only to the manifest world, not to the unmanifest world. Thus it is mere foolishness to say that Parama Puruśa is only the Cognitive Faculty. … He is also Iisháńa. One name of Parama Puruśa is Iisháńa. *Iisháńa* means "controller." It is not enough to create something—one will also have to control it. *Prakrti* is only able to create. It is not able to control. Parama Puruśa is that controller. (Anandamurti, *Subháśita Samgraha Part 12*, 94–96. AT)

57. Anandamurti's position on this question is a significant departure from that of Samkhya. In verse 20 of the Samkhya Karika we find:

tasmáttatsamyogádacetanam cetanávadiva liṅgam |
guńakartrtve-api tathá karteva bhavatúdásínah ||

"Therefore, through this union, the insentient evolute appears as if it were conscious; similarly, from agency belonging to the *guńas*, consciousness appears as if it were the agent."

Here the insentient evolute refers to all the manifestations or evolutes of *prakrti*. The mind appears to be conscious due to its union with consciousness, and consciousness appears to be the agent due to its union with the *guńas* of *prakrti*. While in Samkhya it is admitted that *prakrti* cannot act without inspiration from *puruśa* (it has been compared in Samkhya to a magnet infusing iron with its force), Samkhya did not accept the idea that Consciousness could be the controller of the *guńas*, and thus by extrapolation it did not accept the idea of a supreme controller—*iishvara*, or God. By the same token, Anandamurti, by citing the actionless *puruśa* as the controller of the *guńas*, places the Supreme Consciousness at the center of the creation as the Supreme Controller, thus paving the way for the centrality of devotion.

58. Generally speaking, he has already supplied us with everything we need. Look at this created universe. It has everything we need, but due to our own folly and mismanagement we suffer. In society there are certain rules. If we follow them then everything is peaceful. But when antisocial elements rise up they disturb the entire society. Whose creation is this? It is the human beings' own creation. We do wrong and we suffer for it. So I should not blame him, or claim that we are tools and that he is making us dance as he wishes. No. Lord Krishna has said, "Neither do I do anything, nor do I make anybody do anything; it is the law of nature that is taking its course." And what is that law? Action and reaction. If somebody puts their hand in the fire their hand will burn because this is the law of nature. You cannot blame the fire or blame God for having burnt your hand. It is your own action that is the cause of your hand being burnt. So a person should be careful while acting, and then alone can that person be considered a wise person. (Acosta, *When the Time Comes*, 77.)

59. Mental actions that are purely instinctual do not involve the *aham* and thus remain confined to the *citta*, the instinctual mind. This will be addressed in sutra III.4 in the context of generating *saṁskáras*.

60. Studies have shown that sensory centers in the brain continue to function under general anesthesia, albeit in an impaired or altered manner.

61. Anandamurti, *Ananda Marga Elementary Philosophy*, chap. 5. EE9

62. According to both science and logic, every action has a reaction that is equal to the original action, whether the action be an action in the physical world or only an internal psychic vibration. For example, suppose you have stolen something with your own hands. In this instance there is no doubt that you have committed an act of theft. But supposing that for fear of public scandal or fear of punishment, you didn't carry out the theft but had someone do it for you, or else you stole mentally. In this case also, have you not committed an act of theft? If you think that you will not reap the consequences for a theft committed mentally, you are wrong. (Anandamurti, *Subháśita Saṁgraha 1–3*, 21. AT)

63. Unlike in the physical plane, where the reaction is equal and opposite to the action, in the psychic plane the requital to an action may in some cases be more intense due to changes in the relative factors,

especially that of time.

> Next comes *vipáka*. Vi - pac + ghaiṇ = *vipáka*. *Vipáka* means "reaction" or "result." Whenever a person does an action it gives rise to an equal and opposite reaction. This is the rule. But to state this is not enough. Something more must be added: "provided the three factors—time, space, and person—remain unchanged." If a change occurs in the three relative factors of time, space, and person, the reaction will not be equal and opposite. It will be slightly more or less. For example, suppose Mr. X borrowed two thousand rupees from Mr. Y one evening at seven o'clock. If Mr. X returns the amount right away, he will not be required to pay anything extra. But if not, if he returns the amount at a later date, then due to the lapse of time he will have to pay a certain amount as interest along with the principal. Similarly, if someone commits some unjust or undesirable action, then the *vipáka* will not be exactly the same as the original action because the reaction is not expressed immediately after the original action is performed; it usually takes place after several hours or several days. It may even take place after a number of decades. Due to this, the person who has committed that improper action will have to undergo a reaction that is greater in degree than the original action. They will have to undergo some extra suffering as interest to the original action. This is *vipáka*. (Anandamurti, *Subháśita Saṁgraha 10*, 102–104. AT)

64. ...the movement of human beings toward matter in the path of negative *pratisaiṇcara* is called "hell." When the mind advances in the path toward the attainment of Brahma through positive *pratisaiṇcara*, we can call that movement heaven-ward or upward movement. (Anandamurti, *Subháśita Saṁgraha 7*, 93. AT)

65. *The Dhammapada: A New Translation of the Buddhist Classic with Annotations*, Translated by Gil Fronsdal (Boston: Shambala Publications, Inc., 2006), 1.

66. https://elpais.com/diario/1999/09/05/sociedad/936482411_850215.html

67. https://www.kosmosjournal.org/article/integral-spirituality-2/

68. Anandamurti, *Mánuśer Samája 2*, 94. AT

69. Our sense of spatial awareness depends on gravity, which is itself space.

70. In this connection it is good to keep in mind that the philosophical term *bhúta* is different from the scientific term "element." The Sanskrit equivalent for "element" is *maolika padártha*, while by *bhúta* we normally mean "that which has been created." From the philosophical point of view, *bhúta* is that which is recognized as a *tattva*. The English synonym for *tattva* is "factor." In the world there are many elements, but the *bhútas* are fundamentally five. (Anandamurti, *Subháśita Samgraha Part 7*, 53–54. AT)

71. *Merriam-Webster's Collegiate Dictionary, Eleventh Edition* (Springfield: Merriam Webster, Incorporated, 2008), 403. or https://www.merriam-webster.com/dictionary/element

72. The Planck length is approximately 10^{-33} centimeters.

> To give an idea of the smallness of the scale we are discussing: if we enlarged a walnut shell until it had become as big as the whole observable universe, we would still not see the Planck length. Even after having been enormously magnified thus, it would still be a million times smaller than the actual walnut shell was before magnification. At this scale, space and time change their nature. They become something different; they become "quantum space and time," and understanding what this means is the problem.
>
> Matvei Bronštejn understands all of this in the 1930s and writes two short and illuminating articles in which he points out that quantum mechanics and general relativity, taken together, are incompatible with our customary idea of space as an infinitely divisible continuum. (Rovelli, *Reality Is Not What It Seems*, chap. 5.)

73. Rovelli, *Reality Is Not What It Seems*, chap. 6.

74. This description of the universe as the cosmic egg implies, as some physicists believe, that if a person started traveling in one direction in the universe they would in theory eventually wind up where they started from.

> I used the words "cosmic spirit" because as you know our universe is very big but it is not infinite. ... wherever there is the binding influence of the static principle, the objectivity, that is, the phenomenal counterpart of the noumenal subjectivity,

becomes limited. A line of demarcation, a boundary line, is created. And where there is a boundary line, it cannot be infinite. It may be very, very big, but it is not infinite. And it is to some extent, not exactly, elliptical—oval shaped—and that is why in Sanskrit it is called *brahmáńda*—*brahma* plus *ańda*—"the oval creation of Brahma." *Brahma* means the creative faculty of *parama puruśa*. (Anandamurti, *Subháśita Saḿgraha* Part 21, chap. 8. EE9)

75. Due to its extreme subtleness the *vyomatattva* is able to prove its existence only through its sound *tanmátra*. In order to understand this *vyomatattva* or its sound-waves or its sound-radiation, a special type of scientific instrument is necessary. Except for this *vyomatattva*, the remaining four elements you can easily make out with the help of your crude organs. (Anandamurti, *Subháśita Saḿgraha Part 3*, chap. 4. EE9)

The ethereal body, despite belonging to the five fundamental factors, is almost beyond the scope of human perception; that is, it requires a sharp intellect and scientific efforts to be grasped or understood. (Anandamurti, *Subháśita Saḿgraha 5*, 50. AT)

76. The following is a short account of a demonstration that Anandamurti performed through one of his disciples, Dasarath, which shows the ability of an advanced mind to directly perceive the sound inference, even in this case when the sounds were four centuries old:

> Baba once did a demonstration in which he asked Dasarath to concentrate in sadhana and describe what he heard. He described a beautiful female voice singing a devotional song in a language he couldn't completely understand, but which seemed to be a dialect of Marathi. Baba said that it was the Braj language and explained that he was hearing Mirabai singing one of her songs some four hundred years earlier. He said that the sound was still traveling in the cosmos and that one day scientists would develop instruments that would be able to record such phenomena. (Anandamurti, *The Jamalpur Years*, 407.)

77. ... there is no difference between the crudest state of the Cosmic Mind and the subtlest state of the ethereal factor. The ethereal factor is also not an unchanging state; it also varies in the degree of subtlety and crudity. Just as the subtlest state of the ethereal factor is nothing but the crudest state of the Cosmic Mind, similarly the crudest state

of the ethereal factor is no different from the subtlest state of the subsequent aerial factor. (Anandamurti, *Subháśita Saḿgraha 7*, 51–52. AT)

78. We find the luminous factor in the various celestial bodies of outer space. Due to their being relatively condensed, these celestial bodies have assumed a particular shape, despite not being, for the most part, solid or liquid entities. After advancing further in the path of *saiṋcara*, these luminous entities assume a liquid form in which the intermolecular spaces decrease even further. Thus their internal friction increases and as a result of the contraction of their internal space, having assumed a particular size and shape, they develop an even greater capacity to resist the exterial force. When burning celestial bodies congeal in the process of *saiṋcara* they are converted into liquid oceans of fire. The Earth, after its dissociation from the burning, predominantly luminous-factor Sun, was in a liquid state for some time. When this liquid factor reaches the nadir point in the flow of *saiṋcara*, its molecules and atoms reach the zenith point of proximity. Within that body there arises intense agitation, its material flow becomes perceptible to all the sense organs, and its capacity to fight against the exterial force becomes tremendous. (Anandamurti, *Subháśita Saḿgraha 5*, 62–63. AT)

79. The same three factors are equally present in modern physic's understanding of time. Space-time, as it is explained in contemporary physics, is explained from the standpoint of the observer.

80. From the cosmic point of view there is no time and no individual entity in this eternal play in the bosom of the Infinite. ... We cannot say that something that has slipped out of the palm of a person's hand, which has gone out of a person's reach, is lost forever. For the Supreme Cognition, there is no bondage of relativity. What is considered past to the people of this relative world remains forever with Sadashiva, the Infinite Consciousness. That child is beaming with laughter for all eternity on the lap of Sadashiva — his eternal, cherished child, dancing forever on the lap of the Supreme Father. "It was never lost, it is never lost, it never will be lost." (Anandamurti, *Namah Shiváya Shántáya*, 167–168. AT)

81. Anandamurti, *Idea and Ideology*, 20.

82. Every *bhúta* from the ethereal to the solid is in an eternal flow. The very existence of *bhútatattva* is just a pattern of waves, a microscopic fraction of waves taken in a collective form by the sensory-organs-cum-citta. These microscopic fractions carried through waves

are called *tanmátras*. Hence *tanmátras* are nothing but the waves produced by the objects concerned as a result of reflection of the subtler *bhúta* on the cruder ones. *Tanmátras* in the mathematical sense are not something homogeneous. They are heterogeneous in character and their heterogeneity gives rise to the varieties in the perceptible external world. This heterogeneity is specialized by the difference in wavelengths amongst different *tanmátras* within or without the scope of any particular *bhúta*. (Anandamurti, *Idea and Ideology*, 20.)

83. Anandamurti, *The Jamalpur Years*, 247.

84. The evidence gathered from seismic waves shows the earth's outer core to be a liquid, and based on a number of educated deductions it is assumed that its composition is mostly iron with approximately 10% of a lighter element, likely oxygen, and a small amount of nickel (4%). Leaving aside the likelihood of these being the elements that make up the outer core, the determination of whether or not it was *apatattva*, liquid factor, would depend on whether or not it carried the smell *tanmátra*. It can be surmised that the extreme heat and pressure in that environment would not allow for the transmission of smell.

85. The composition of the earth's inner core has been deduced from seismometers. The most common assumption based on the data is that it is primarily composed of a nickel-iron alloy; however, an extremely dense plasma, such as that in a star, would show similar properties but would better explain the apparent thermodynamics of the inner core. If it is indeed predominantly luminous factor, then it would not carry the taste *tanmátra*.

> The above formations are not abrupt but gradual. The intermediate stage between *citta* and ether is neither an abstract nor matter. Similarly the sun is at an intermediate stage between the aerial and the luminous factors. The earth in its infancy was in a stage that can be termed neither luminous nor liquid. Gradually it was converted into a liquid body and slowly the outer surface was turned into solid. In its inner body the earth is still in liquid form; and in the more interior portion the luminous and gaseous factors are being slowly converted into liquid. (Anandamurti, *Idea and Ideology*, 19).

86. The ethereal factor is the most expansive and subtlest of the five fundamental factors. ... Earlier I said that the subtler an object, the less the organs are able to perceive it, and so if it is to be understood, there is a need for sadhana and a sharp intellect. For this reason, hu-

man beings try to understand subtler objects with the help of their minds. What is beyond the perceptual capacity of the ears and eyes and other crude organs can often be easily understood with the help of the internal ears and eyes, or the introversial mind. (Anandamurti, *Subhásita Saṁgraha 5*, 50–51. AT)

87. The word *vyavadhi* means "size" or "extension." Even though a particular object can be seen through the form *tanmátra*, its size, its largeness or smallness, cannot be grasped in this way. That through which the largeness or smallness of size is determined is called *vyavadhi*. We receive the *tanmátras* through the organs, but it is through the *práńáh* that the mind forms a conception of *vyavadhi*. (Anandamurti, *Subhásita Saṁgraha 8*, 48. AT)

88. The wave by which your acceptance or rejection of the *tanmátras* takes place cannot be a perpetual flow, because were it a perpetual flow that would preclude the possibility of sensing. If the eyes could apprehend form waves continuously, or if the form waves were themselves continuous, then due to their lack of division, the object to be held by the *práńáh* could not have a place in the apperceptive plate (*sthirabhúmi*) of the *citta*. In order to effect breaks in the waves, the eyes blink, and the stream of waves is also interrupted by pauses. Energy in motion is not continuous but flows in definite little jumps. Thus the stream of action has been called "systaltic" in the scriptures. This applies equally to all inferential flows, and you receive them during the contractive phase of those flows or motion—with the help of the *práńáh* they are captured by *citta's sthirabhúmi*. So the more steadiness one can create in the *práńáh*, the firmer will be one's power of receptivity. (Anandamurti, *Subhásita Saṁgraha 4*, 19. AT)

This principle has also been recognized in modern physics. Photons, for example, have been shown to move in discrete jumps. Research into quantum gravity suggests that the same is true for time, and physicists working in this field have fixed a minimum quantity for the smallest discrete measurement of time, Planck time.

89. In our daily life the experiences of soft and hard, melodious and harsh, hot and cold are being experienced by our *práńendriya*. These experiences do not come within the scope of the five fundamental perceptions of *shravańa* (hearing), *sparshana* (feeling by touch), *darshana* (vision), *ashvádana* (taste) and *ághráńa* (smell). The aforesaid subtler experiences, not coming within the jurisdiction of crude fundamentality, are felt by the sixth organ—*práńendriya*. The special function of *práńendriya* is to recognize the objectives from dif-

ferent experienced sense perceptions and innate psychic projections. *Práńendriya* also works as an auxiliary force in some of the internal mental activities, and with the help of this *práńendriya* one feels that a particular person is very kind and affectionate, or a particular person is unkind and antipathetic. (Such an experience is based more on a subjective feeling than on any outer objective correlation.) (Anandamurti, *Idea and Ideology*, 28.)

90. Just as you feel the heat or coldness of things through *sparsha tanmátra*, similarly you know their hardness and softness with the help of *práńáh*. Suppose there is a piece of cotton and a piece of gold of equal temperature. The sensory organ of the eyes will see them, the sensory organ of the skin will feel their hotness or coldness, and the *práńáh* will feel the hardness of the gold and the softness of the cotton. The sensory organ of the ear will hear the song and the *práńáh* will perceive its sweetness. The ears will hear the scandal and the *práńáh* will capture its harshness or severity, and hearing this the *práńáh* will be hurt—anguish will awaken in the *práńáh*, that heartache is held in the *práńáh*. This receptive capacity of the *práńáh* we call the "core of the heart." When you call a particular person "hard" or "soft" based on the hardness of iron or the fluidity of water, that is also a product of your *práńáh-bodha* or vital sense. A "hard" man does not mean that the man is hard to the touch. That person's speech or behavior as received through any of the other organs creates a hard sensation in the *práńáh* similar to the sensation in the *práńáh* when the skin organ touches something hard. Then you call that person "hard." Indeed, in the same way you also call many people "soft." (Anandamurti, *Subháśita Saḿgraha 4*, 17–18. AT)

91. Anandamurti, *Subháśita Saḿgraha Part 21*, chap. 1. EE9

Chapter Three

1. The *kośas* are not mentioned at all in the philosophical systems of Samkhya and Yoga. They are first mentioned in Vedanta but they are not elaborated to any great extent after the Taittiriya Upanishad. Even Shankaracharya only gave them a cursory glance, essentially summarizing what is found in the Taittiriya Upanishad. This is not surprising, since the focus of Vedanta lies elsewhere, in pure philosophy rather than psychology, and in liberation from the influence of maya.

2. The development of the *kośas* during the evolutionary process is also absent from the Vedanta system.

3. The primary meaning of the word *prájiṋa* is "cognition," but it has many different meanings and has been used in many different contexts in the Indian spiritual tradition. Here it is used in a specific philosophical context to refer to the microcosmic consciousness when it is directly occupied with matter, that is, when it is cognizing the external world through the *kámamaya kośa*.

> When the Cosmic Consciousness is in a dormant state or under the influence of *tamoguńa*, it is called *prájiṋa*. Iishvara is a special state of *puruśottama*, so he is not required to practice sadhana. But *prájiṋa*, being dominated by *tamoguńa*, has to wage war against dullness. *Prájiṋa* here does not mean "wise"; it refers to the *jiivátmá* that is dormant in the spiritual sense. In fact, although *prájiṋa* has the full capability to know and understand each and every object, it cannot do so due to the influence of *avidyá*. *Prájiṋa* will fight to save itself from the hands of *tamoguńa*. It will have to fight against its negative propensities. When *prájiṋa* attains victory in this battle it becomes one with *paramátmá*. (Anandamurti, *Tattva Kaomudii* 2, 13–14. AT)

In the Upanishads the word *prájiṋa* has been used to refer to the microcosmic witnessing consciousness during deep sleep. While some commentators equate this state with the subtlest causal mind, Anandamurti points out that in deep sleep the individual mind is actually in a state of dullness or staticity in which its consciousness or *prájiṋa* is dormant.

> The reason for calling the *puruśa* in the egocentric sleep state *prájiṋa* is that the seed of omniscience is hidden in this state. There is knowledge and the potential for awakening, but due to darkness there is no discrimination—such is the state of sleep. (Anandamurti, *Subháśita Saṁgraha 1–3*, 207. AT)

4. The word *taejasa* is also used in both the Upanishads and the Tantras to refer to the witnessing consciousness during the dream state. Not coincidentally, *kámamaya kośa* is suspended during the dream state and *manomaya kośa* is active. Here the mutative force of *prakrti* is dominant.

5. Clever scientific studies involving beepers and diaries suggest that an average daydream is about fourteen seconds long and that we have about two thousand of them per day. In other words, we spend about half of our waking hours—one-third of our lives on

earth—spinning fantasies. We daydream about the past: things we should have said or done, working through our victories and failures. We daydream about mundane stuff, such as imagining different ways of handling a conflict at work. But we also daydream in a much more intense, storylike way. We screen films with happy endings in our minds, where all our wishes—vain, aggressive, dirty—come true. And we screen little horror films, too, in which our worst fears are realized. (Jonathan Gottschall, *The Storytelling Animal: How Stories Make us Human* (New York: Houghton Mifflin Harcourt Publishing Company, 2012), chap. 1. Epub)

This wandering tendency of the mind is of course greatly diminished by the regular practice of meditation and other spiritual disciplines.

6. The term *vishva* is also used in the Upanishads to refer to the microcosmic consciousness during the waking state. Here the sentient force of *prakrti* is dominant.

> The *puruśa* of the ego-bound waking state of living beings is called *vishva* (a philosophical word) or subjectivated *puruśa*. Because the proper enjoyment of objects through the sense organs is possible only in the waking state, the *puruśa* of this state is called the subjectivated *puruśa*. Similarly, the *puruśa* of the dream state of the ego-bound living being is called *taejasa* and the ego-bound *puruśa* of the deep-sleep state is called *prájińa*. (Anandamurti, *Subháśita Saḿgraha 1–3*, 175. AT)

7. Has anyone at the close of the nineteenth century any clear perception of what the poets of strong ages called inspiration? If not, I will describe it. Possessing only the smallest remnant of superstition one would hardly be able to reject the idea that one is nothing but a medium for super-mighty influences. That which happens can only be termed revelation, that is to say, that suddenly, with unutterable certainty and delicacy, something becomes visible and audible and shakes and rends one to the depths of one's being. One hears, one does not seek; one takes; one does not ask who it is that gives; like lightning a thought flashes out, out of necessity, complete in form—I have never needed to choose. It is a rapture, the enormous excitement of which sometimes finds relief in a storm of tears; a state of being entirely outside oneself with the clearest consciousness of fine shivering and a rustling through one's being right down to the tips of one's toes; a depth of joy in which all that is most painful and gloomy does not act as a contrast but as a condition for it, as though demanded, as a necessary colour in such a flood of light....Everything

happens in the highest degree involuntarily, as in a storm of feeling of freedom, of power, of divinity. (F. Nietzsche, *Werke* (Taschenausgabe), vol. VII, pp. xxiv.)

8. But the division of the microcosm into a causal portion is merely a theoretical proposition. There is no separate existence of the unit causal mind from the cosmic causal mind. In case the crude and subtle portions of the unit mind suspend their work by the process of sadhana or otherwise, the causal portion of the unit mind will not be able to maintain its separate identity; only the seed of past action will remain just to differentiate the microcosm from the Macrocosm. By a process of correct sadhana, the *sádhaka* will feel that there is one causal mind in the universe. (Anandamurti, *Idea and Ideology*, 35.)

9. Yogananda, *Autobiography of a Yogi*, 169.

10. The water-moon cannot be clearly seen or understood due to waves or impurities in the water. Similarly, due to the waves of *vrttis* or the impurities of *saṁskáras* on the mental canvas, the reflection of *paramátmá* on that canvas (i.e., the *jiivátmá*) is not properly understood. That was why I said that in the lower *kośas*, where the expression of the *vrttis* or the impurities of the *saṁskáras* are more manifest, the spiritual self is correspondingly unmanifest...

If the mind is to be converted into a real mirror, then every *kośa* has to be made transparent. The inclinations of the lower *kośas* have to be sublimated into the higher *kośas*, and those higher *kośas* have to be made even more transparent through sadhana, through the impact of the *sattvaguńa* force, and merged into the still higher *kośas*. Thus through the medium of this *kośa*-wise sadhana, the higher the sphere a spiritual aspirant attains, the more their entire being will be filled with divine radiance, with divine bliss. After the last trace of impurities have been wiped clean from the *buddhitattva*, the atman that will manifest in that purified *buddhi* will be the *puruśottama* itself, the nucleus of Saguńa Brahma, for there remains no small I in that purified reflector of the *buddhi*. And when, by jumping over the *buddhitattva* wall of maya, one races toward the true existence, free from desire for any reflection in the *buddhi*, then one's entire being along with their *buddhi* merges into and becomes one with that selfsame Consciousness. That unreflected atman is the pure *nirguńa*. This state is the unquestionable establishment in *satyaloka*. (Anandamurti, *Subháśita Saṁgraha* 4, 104–105. AT)

11. The Rigveda is the oldest literature known to man. Its composition took place over several millennia and was completed nearly ten

thousand years ago according to Anandamurti, some six millennia before the composition of the Bhagavad Gita.

12. A lengthy description of these astral and causal worlds can be found in Chapter 43, "The Resurrection of Sri Yukteshwar." The chapter focuses principally on what Sri Yukteswar calls the Hiranyaloka, which would be the equivalent of the *taparloka* in Anandamurti's system, essentially the *hirańyamaya kośa* of the Macrocosm, although Sri Yukteswar's interpretation of this plane of existence, as recounted by Yogananda, is very different than Anandamurti's.

13. In volume one of his *Letters on Yoga*, Sri Aurobindo draws a parallel between the Puranic conception of the *lokas* and the different planes that he outlines in his system of yoga.

14. There may be many interpretations of the word *iishvara*. But more or less it means "controller." The one who controls the thought waves of this universe is *iishvara*. Therefore, *iishvara* is not exactly the same as *puruśottama*. In philosophy the word *iishvara* has one more meaning. It refers to the ego-bound *puruśa* where the static principle of *prakrti* is dominant, the witness of the causal ocean, the cosmic stance of *prájińa*. *Puruśa* when free of all bondages is also known as *iishvara* in philosophical language. (Anandamurti, *Jiivana Veda*, 45. AT)

Some Vedanta commentators use the term *iishvara* to refer to the witness of the cosmic causal mind.

15. In the same way, when *prakrti's* mutative influence waxes, the *puruśa* in its macrocosmic stance is called *hirańyagarbha*, and in its microcosmic stance, *taejasa*. The universe is in essence swaying with the vibrations of *hirańyagarbha*. You should not confuse this *hirańyagarbha* with the *hirańyagarbha* that is the metamorphosed form of Saguńa Brahma—this *hirańyagarbha* is nothing but a philosophical term that doesn't have any relevance for spiritual practitioners. Anyhow, this *hirańyagarbha* dominated by the mutative principle was created after *prakrti* exerted its *sattvaguńii* influence on Brahma, that is, the cosmic existential "I" was also the witness of the origin of *hirańyagarbha*. (Anandamurti, *Subhásita Saḿgraha 5*, 74–75. AT)

16. Traditionally, the names Viráta or Vaisvánara, Hirańyagarbha, and Iishvara have been used in the Upanishads to refer to the Cosmic Consciousness as the witnessing counterpart of the physical universe, the mental plane, and the causal plane respectively, paralleling the waking state, the dream state, and deep sleep in the microcosm. This usage, with some exceptions, is reversed in the Tantras,

with Iishvara, the creator, being the witness of the physical universe and Viráta the witnessing Consciousness of the causal plane.

17. The *vijiṋánamaya kośa* or *janarloka*, being involved with the I-feeling (*asmitá*), also has impurities. Although it is very elevated, it is not free from the possibility of downfall. In this *loka* the mind experiences the semblance of bliss, but stimulated by its *saḿskáras* it may also move toward crudeness — although both of these happen somewhat unconsciously. Thus someone who is somewhat acquainted with this *loka* becomes rather self-forgetful, whether they do good actions or bad actions. Its other name in Sanskrit is *gandharvaloka*. The semblance of happiness that comes from music and the other fine arts belongs to this *loka*. In English we can call it the "subliminal sphere." Due to the influence of *asmitá* this *loka* lacks perfection, so while one may indeed attain a semblance of happiness by the cultivation of the fine arts alone, one cannot become fully established in divine bliss — in order to achieve this, one must do Brahma sadhana. (Anandamurti, *Subhásita Saḿgraha 4*, 109. AT)

18. Anandamurti, *Idea and Ideology*, 38.

19. Association by proper adjustment and parallelism between the psychic and physical bodies causes life, and dissociation under adverse conditions results in death. (Anandamurti, *Idea and Ideology*, 52.)

20. If a psychic clash with higher thought brings about the better wavelength and thereby becomes the cause of a more evolved physical body, contact and clash with meaner thought will lessen the wavelength of the mental waves. Here, as well, the loss of parallelism shall occur and the physical and psychic bodies shall dissociate from each other. For example, if the mental wavelength of a person cannot adjust properly with the human body, the psychic body of the person will have to be associated with a properly adjustable physical structure, which may be of an inferior animal, a plant or still cruder matter. The symbolic story of the epic Ramayana, wherein Ahalya, the wife of Gaotama Muni, was transformed into stone for some sin done by her, is just to illustrate the process of negative *pratisaiṋcara*. The imbibing of waves of higher wavelengths can rarefy the psychic body of a lower animal or plant, so that it can have an association with the human physical structure, and vice versa, if the wavelength is made cruder by inculcating meaner thoughts. (Anandamurti, *Idea and Ideology*, 51.)

21. Of the ten *váyus*, one *váyu*—*dhanainjaya*, the *váyu* responsible for sleep and drowsiness—remains associated with the body until it is cremated or until it decomposes sufficiently. For this reason, the bodiless mind remains in the vicinity of the body and cannot reincarnate until *dhanainjaya* is released. However, it cannot function in this condition, since it is no longer associated with the brain.

22. It is said in the scriptures that the disembodied soul with its *samskáras* first accepts a suitable sperm with the help of the Cosmic Mind. Then that sperm unites with a suitable ovum to produce an embryo that is suitable for the expression of its *samskáras*. As the embryo grows, it acquires psychic nourishment on the one hand, and on the other hand it experiences its *samskáras* at the same time. Until the mind is sufficiently developed to act according to the dictates of its I-feeling, it will have no recourse but to experience the afflictions that stem from being the subject of reactive actions (*samskára múlaka karma*). As soon as the nerve cells acquire the capacity to work according to the developed I-feeling, it also starts to perform original actions (*pratyaya múlaka karma*). (Anandamurti, Subháśita Saṁgraha 5, 106–107. AT)

23. There is a fair amount of debate, both scientific and philosophical, over the nature of mental activity in the developing embryo. The embryo does not begin forming brain cells until the fourth week, and it is only in the sixth week that there is any sign of electrical brain activity, though not the kind of brain activity consistent with the presence of sensation, much less thought. It is in the second trimester that the fetus's nascent brain begins to emit brain waves that are consistent with sensation and thought and thus the beginning of the formation of the *kámamaya* and *manomaya kośas*, which may suggest that the mind of the fetus does not become active until the eleventh week. However, a case can be made that the causal mind is active well before the emergence of the *kámamaya* and *manomaya kośas*.

24. So I say that death too is a benevolent system. (Anandamurti, Subháśita Saṁgraha Part 3, chap. 4. EE9)

25. Generally, the bundle of *samskáras* does not ripen during a person's life unless there is a disconnection of the sensory organs, motor organs, and *práńendriya* from the mind. Thus the reactions to the actions performed in this life are not ordinarily seen in this life. ... Ordinarily, the bundle of actions from this life becomes well formed once the mind disassociates from the sensory organs, motor organs, and the *práńendriya* at the time of death and in the next life takes the

form of reactions. Since it is quite natural for the results of action to be experienced in the next life, at the time of experiencing the reaction, the original action is forgotten. Since the original action cannot be seen, human beings often blame God for their fate. (Anandamurti, *Subhásita Samgraha 8*, 95–96. AT)

26. The human mind is sentimental—full of love, affection, camaraderie, etc. People have a deep attraction to this world; they remain preoccupied throughout their lives with fears and anxieties for the safety of their families. So many problems have to be confronted. The problems of one life alone are enough to make people restless. If they had to face the problems of several lives, they would be unable to lead a natural life. The problems of the past lives, compounded by the strife of the present life, would drive them to the brink of insanity. Secondly, it is difficult for people to be detached from love and attachment for one life. So much effort is required to overcome the bondages of attachment and march towards Parama Puruśa. If the memory of the past lives is revived, the bondage of attachment will tighten its grip, putting a halt to spiritual advancement. One will be caught in the grip of worldly attachment. Thus the decree of merciful Providence is, "Let human beings be oblivious of their past lives." (Anandamurti, *Tattva Kaomudi Part 2*, chap. 13. EE9)

27. When a person is struck by a serious disease, bereavement, or fainting spell as a painful consequence of their original actions, or else due to the awakening of *kulakuńdalinii* caused by association with a great soul, then the mind may become temporarily detached from the sensory organs, motor organs, and *práńendriya*, and as a result, the bundle of *samskáras* becomes well formed and the reactions of one's previous life start to express themselves during the present life. This kind of karma is known as *dŕśta vedaniiya* karma. In other words, in the case of *dŕśta vedaniiya* karma, good or bad actions along with the good or bad reactions they engender occur in the same life. ...

Generally one does not reap in this life the consequences of the actions performed in this life. If the actions of this life are similar to the bundle of *samskáras* from the past life, however—that is, if the karmic waves of both lives are of the same type—then the reactions to the *samskáras* from both lives may easily be experienced concurrently. But if the karmic waves of this life conflict with the karmic waves of the past life, then the reactions of the two lives will generally not occur concurrently. In the latter case, one will reap the consequences of the actions of the previous life. (Anandamurti, *Subhásita Samgraha 8*, 86–87. AT)

28. Action is of two kinds—original (*pratyayamúlaka*) and reactive (*samskáramúlaka*). *Samskáras* accumulate through original actions and they are exhausted through reactive actions. Thus in the case of original actions the living being has freedom, but not in the case of reactive actions. (Anandamurti, *Subhásita Samgraha 4*, 108. AT)

29. This potentiality of reaction or *samskára* that you earn through physical or mental action will have to be served by means of another action. So you see, the experience of the results of action is served through a special type of action. But when you perform an action in order to reap the consequence of a previous act, then you do not have the power to act independently. At that time you are forced to act mechanically, and as a result you may be obliged to do some undesirable act that brings you disgrace, reproach, and affliction. You upbraid yourself and tell yourself, "What have I done?" But there is no way to avoid that action; it is as if your hands and feet were tied. (Anandamurti, *Subhásita Samgraha 1*, 28. AT)

30. These original actions (*pratyayamúlaka* karma) are performed in the waking state, whether they be actions or thoughts. Thoughts in a dream, in most cases, if not all, are nothing but the tightly-woven expressions of the dreamer's *samskáras*. Since the *kámamaya* and the *manomaya kośas* have no direct authorship in the dream state, original action is not possible. (Anandamurti, *Subhásita Samgraha 4*, 8. AT)

31. Even if you do not harm anyone physically but you think of harming someone, that kind of *samskára* will be created inside you. Whatever feelings you may have for a person, good or bad, will also engender a reaction, which will result in the formation of a *samskára* in the subtle mind. For this reason, wise people look upon the entire universe with equanimity and wish for the welfare of all. *Sarvesám maungalam káunkśe*. Otherwise one will have to suffer endlessly for one's mean-mindedness. (Anandamurti, *Subhásita Samgraha 8*, 78–79. AT)

32. Emerson's verse paraphrases nearly identical verses from the Buddha and Lao Tze.

33. In the case of Tibetan Buddhist practice and the transition through the bardos, it can be contended that the main import of these practices, rituals, and the guidance they involve is to prepare the mind of the dying person before it actually disincarnates, to help that person use their death as a springboard to further evolution.

34. It is likely that there are some cases in yogic and spiritual literature

where *devayonis* have been mistakenly identified as astral beings.

I say "being" because it is difficult for me to say that they are living beings or that they are dead beings. (Anandamurti, *Ánanda Vacanámrtam* Part 3, chap. 17. EE9)

Any entity containing solid and liquid factors will certainly require food and drink, because solid factor is mainly food and liquid factor is mainly water. But if the body is such that it has luminous, aerial, and ethereal factors but no solid or liquid, then we can call that type of body a *devayoni*. These *devayonis* do not have nerves because nerves are composed of the five fundamental factors; they do not have nerve cells because nerve cells are composed of the five fundamental factors. By means of nerve cells, the mind operates within a physical body, but here there are three factors. Just as the nerves create the sense of objects through the inferences of smell, form, sound, and so on, similarly the nerve cells either capture those inferences or project them externally. Since they don't have these, they cannot function properly. However, as in auto-suggestion, they can to some extent create a vibration within their structure and experience some type of feeling or sensation.

These luminous bodies are not ghosts. They have no connection with ghosts, nor are they created by any kind of auto-suggestion or outer-suggestion. But under certain circumstances, if someone happens to see this kind of luminous body, they may think they are seeing a ghost. But they are not seeing a ghost at all — they are seeing a *devayoni*. It is not possible to see luminous bodies in broad daylight; it may be possible during the darkness of night, but not everywhere.

It is said that there are seven kinds of luminous bodies: *yakśa, siddha, gandharva, kinnara, vidyadhara, prakrtiliina* and *videhaliina*. They are categorized on the basis of their respective psychologies. (Anandamurti, *Abhimata* 5, 75–76. AT)

... *devayonis* are composed of three fundamental factors — ethereal, aerial and luminous. The solid and liquid factors are left on the earth after the death of the physical body. (Anandamurti, *Microvitum in a Nutshell*, chap. 15. EE9)

35. Anandamurti, *Ánanda Vacanámrtam* Part 7, chap. 5. EE9

36. This can happen in two ways. First, the *atimánas kośa* of the person having the positive hallucination may unintentionally exert an influence over the *manomaya kośa* of the onlooker, inducing that person to see the same image that is present in the subconscious mind

of the first person. Even more rare is when the mental force of the first person is so strong that a visible image takes shape in the atmosphere for a short period of time.

37. Through the concentrated state of this telepathic vision, when the conscious mind is more calm and sedate, people can visualize events concerning their distant beloved ones, enacted before their eyes in the external world or feel as if they are seeing them; this is called "telepathic clairvoyance." Mistaking such acts as those of spirits many people come to believe in spiritism. Truly speaking such incidents have no connection at all with spirits or ghosts. Telepathic vision and telepathic clairvoyance are intrinsically the same as supramental vision. They are born of the inspiration of the unconscious mind, the knower of the universe. To believe in ghosts and spirits is merely to perpetuate the cowardly mentality of the pre-historic people. (Anandamurti, *Subhásita Samgraha Part 2*, chap. 5. EE9)

Visions of gods and goddesses or so-called saints is the same type of thing as possession by ghosts. Don't *vipra* priests really know that those who receive medical guidance or divine revelations by prostrating themselves before a temple or a saint's mausoleum for days together without taking food and water, actually experience nothing more than the workings of their own intuition? Had the *vipras* not known this, they would not have persistently stressed the importance of faith to their followers. Vipras understand that when through faith the crude mind reaches the realm of the subtle mind and the subtle mind reaches the realm of the intuition, it is the intuition, the innate repository of infinite knowledge, that enlightens the intellect. But the person who receives the medical guidance or divine revelation believes that it comes from the deity he or she was worshipping. If one's faith is not strong enough there will be a lack of concentration and the intellect will not be able to cross the threshold of the *aham* and enter the realm of the intuition. Consequently it will not be possible for the person to receive medical guidance or a divine revelation from his or her so-called deity. (Anandamurti, *Human Society Part 2*, chap. 2. EE9)

38. Possession is similar to seeing a ghost, or a god or goddess. The difference is that the person becomes absorbed in the imagined object, merging their sense of individuality with it, and as a result they believe themselves to be that ghost or god or goddess and act according to that *samskára*. There is a greater expression of knowledge and energy in that thought vibration, and hence the person in that state

of absorption displays new convictions and acts unnaturally. When a process is followed to bring the nervous system back to a normal state, then gradually the influence of the ghost or god or goddess disappears. (The exorcist and the doctor perform the same task; the difference is that the doctor does so in a simple and straightforward manner, while the exorcist invokes the spirit's name and using their so-called mantric power inspires blind belief in the patient's mind.) (Anandamurti, *Tattva Kaomudi 1*, 31–32. AT)

39. Exorcists tell stories about the various supernatural activities of ghosts or about offering food to manes at Gaya to make a patient concentrate his or her mind. The patient's concentrated mind may then break the branch of a tree or crack a parapet of the roof, but the *vipra* exorcists claim that such occurrences are caused by the fleeing ghost and are proof of the power of their mantras. Actually ghosts never kill people, only *vipras* do. (Anandamurti, *Human Society Part 2*, chap. 2. EE9)

40. Anandamurti, *Under the Fathomless Depths of the Blue Sea*. EE9.

41. Anandamurti, *Tattva Kaomudi Part 2*, chap. 1. EE9

42. Bhagavad Gita, chapter 4, verse 24

43. Anandamurti, *Ánanda Márga*, 190–191. AT

44. Sri Nisargadatta Maharaj, *I Am That: Talks with Sri Nisargadatta Maharaj* (Durham: The Acorn Press, 1973), 145.

45. As long as one does not remove the shackles from one's own hands and feet, how can they remove another's shackles? Thus the person who is not emancipated cannot be the cause of another's emancipation. For that reason, no one other than a liberated soul (*muktapuruśa*) can be the cause of another's liberation. Only a *muktapuruśa* is capable of being a guru. (Anandamurti, *Ánanda Márga*, 189. AT)

46. One who has reached *nirguńa* through sadhana, and who through their own wish comes under the influence of *prakrti* for a predetermined length of time for the welfare of living beings, is a *muktapuruśa* (liberated soul) or *nirmmańcitta* guru. They remain under the influence of *prakrti* for the time that they take a body, but as soon as they leave that physical body they attain supreme liberation, merging with Nirguńa Brahma. (Anandamurti, *Ánanda Márga*, 189–190. AT)

47. Arthur Avalon (Sir John Woodroffe), *Kularnava Tantra* (Delhi, Motilal Banarsidass Publishers, 1965), 77.

48. Ram Dass, *Miracle of Love: stories about Neem Karoli Baba* (Nainital, Sri Kainchi Hanuman Mandir & Ashram, 1995), 398.

49. Anandamurti, *Subháśita Saṁgraha 11*, 77. AT

50. In its attempts to subdue *avidyámáyá*, sadhana will naturally meet resistance from the crudifying force of *avidyámáyá*. Obstacles in sadhana should be regarded as an indication of one's success in one's attempt to remove *avidyámáyá*. Obstacles are not created by God or the *sadguru*, as they wish every one of the units to become emancipated like themselves. They are created by *prakrti*, against whom one is waging war. If one is to win, *prakrti* has to be defeated with the weapon of sadhana, against which *avidyámáyá* defends itself by placing obstacles in one's way. Obstacles in sadhana should be regarded as good signs, indicating that the influence of *avidyámáyá* is beginning to wane. (Anandamurti, *Ananda Marga Elementary Philosophy*, chap. 8. EE9)

51. Sadhana is the microcosm waging war against infinite *prakrti* and becoming liberated by winning this war. *Prakrti* is a force (*shakti*), hence sadhana means defeating that force and becoming free so that Shakti and its *guńas* cannot exert their influence. Earlier it was said that *puruśa* and *prakrti* can never be apart, so if *prakrti* is defeated in this war will it remain with *puruśa*? Before the war *prakrti* was like the master, in that it directed *puruśa* according to its wish, but when it loses the war then *puruśa* becomes the master, that is, *puruśa* gains control over the infinite Shakti. So it is seen that when Shakti is defeated in sadhana one gains mastery over Shakti, in that it can no longer exert its influence. Thus if a person does sadhana they become the master of Shakti. (Anandamurti, *Ánanda Márga*, 183–184. AT)

52. Dalai Lama, *The Art of Happiness: A Handbook for Living* (London, Hodder and Stoughton, 1998), 148-9.

53. Anandamurti, *Tantre Dárshanikatá*, 88. AT

54. One prays to God for something which one does not possess or thinks one does not possess. One asks God for these favors with the faith that he alone can bestow everything and by His mere wish all wants can be satisfied. By prayer or by begging one wants to awaken his wish so that one may be granted the things one lacks. Does not

one's attempt to rouse the wish of God to fulfill these needs, upon careful and rational thinking, appear to be a reminder to God to give one something of which God has kept one deprived? It would otherwise not be necessary to remind him in prayer of that thing or to try to arouse his wish to give. For instance, if one is in need of money, one would, with the faith that God alone can give, pray to him for the favor of giving one money. Does not this request show God's fault in keeping one in want of money, when he alone can give it? God alone is blamed for it, and by praying to him for money one is precisely pointing out to him his partiality in not giving one the money one needed. Therefore, prayer or asking for favors from God is only pointing out to the Sole Giver his mistakes in the distribution of his favors. It only presumes lack of impartiality in him, and that is why he is blamed for making some very rich and others very poor. Praying to God for favors is only to bring to his notice the charge of partiality leveled against him. When prayer leads to such a conclusion, it is only ignorance to ask for favors. One who performs actions will also bear the consequences, and blaming God for it as his partiality is not going to save one from bearing the consequences. (Anandamurti, *Ananda Marga Elementary Philosophy*, chap. 6. EE9)

55. This is one traditional classification of bhakti. The different classifications of bhakti go back to the Bhagavad Gita, which divided devotion into *pará* bhakti and *apará* bhakti. In his writings, Anandamurti adds his own interpretation to these traditional classifications.

56. To speak plainly, *stuti* is flattery. Whom do we flatter and why? We flatter those from whom we want to receive something. In *stuti* we sing of the Lord's qualities, such as, "O Lord, you are merciful, you are omnipotent, you are gracious." On closer examination, are we not flattering God? Does God not know that he is merciful or omnipotent or gracious? Doesn't praising him in this way mean that you are reminding him of his qualities? Is it not flattery when a person reminds another person that they are endowed with such wonderful qualities? When a hymn sings of God's qualities, can it be called anything but flattery? We flatter someone when we hope they will do something for us. So we see that behind *stuti* is concealed a prayer. Earlier we saw that prayer is a waste of time, and when the purpose of *stuti* is to want something or receive something is it not also useless? (Anandamurti, *Ánanda Márga*, 162–163. AT)

57. Anandamurti, *Namah Shiváya Shántáya*, chap. 15. EE9

58. Now, bhakti means withdrawing the mind from crude objec-

tivities. The psychological principle for attaining salvation is also that—that is, withdrawing the mind and guiding it unto the Supreme Self. So fundamentally there is no difference. (Anandamurti, *Subhāśita Saṁgraha Part 24*, chap. 5. EE9)

59. Although the mind is very powerful it has one great defect: it cannot think of two things at the same time. When it thinks, it has only one object, but it works so quickly that we don't realize this. While I am doing something I also hear someone speaking. Actually that is due to the mind's fleetness. Due to this power of the mind, our flow of thought seems continuous. For example, in the cinema I see the images and also enjoy the dialogue, but if we examine this with due attention we can understand how the mind works. The point is that the mind can only do one thing at a time. For this reason, worldly acts and ideation on Brahma cannot be done simultaneously. (Anandamurti, *Subhāśita Saṁgraha 1*, 95. AT)

60. In order to preserve our corporeal existence, we have to maintain adjustment with the phenomenal world, and thus the mind must think if it is to perform its various duties, which subjects it to the bondage of *prakrti*. That bondage can be counteracted, however, by the practice of *madhuvidya*, the cultivation of the awareness that everything is a manifestation of the Divine. Nevertheless, in order to enter the *nirvikalpa* state this awareness of the divine nature of phenomenal existence must also be transcended.

61. The word *bhāva* has a number of different meanings. It is sometimes translated as "attitude" or "mood" when referring to the five *bhāvas* or sentimental attitudes of traditional Vaishnavism that a devotee adopts in their devotional relationship with the Divine. According to the Vaishnava teachings, a devotee can relate to God in five different ways: by looking upon God as one's lover (*madhura bhāva*), as one's master (*dasya bhāva*), as one's friend (*sakhya bhāva*), as one's child (*vātsalya bhāva*), or by maintaining a peaceful attitude (*shānta bhāva*). Sri Ramakrishna also referenced an additional *bhāva, santāna bhāva,* in which one relates to the Divine as a child to their father or mother.

62. For example, in the Bhagavad Gita, verse II.66.

63. *Dhyāna kriya* means withdrawing the mental propensities from all external entities, and then collecting those withdrawn mental propensities and directing them toward the one and only Supreme Entity. If there is no sincere love for the Supreme Entity, how will the mind move toward Parama Puruśa? So without love for God, *dhyā-*

na becomes meaningless. *Dhyána* comes from the root *dhae*, which means to withdraw the mental propensities and direct them toward Parama Puruśa. So if there is no love or attraction toward the Great, *dhyána* will not be successful. On the other hand, if there is just a wee bit of attachment, not even a lot, a little amount of love, then one will attain God. (Anandamurti, *Ánanda Vacanámrtam 1–3*, 55–56. AT)

64. मोक्षकारणसामग्र्यां भक्तिरेव गरीयसी ।

mokśakáranasámagryáṁ bhaktireva gariiyasii

"Of all things that lead to liberation, bhakti is supreme." (verse 31)

65. Brother Lawrence, *The Practice of the Presence of God: The Best Rule of Holy Life* (London: The Epworth Press), 5.

66. Philosophy says that the controlling point of this universe is *parama puruśa*, he who is situated in the nucleus of the cosmological order. But the philosophical Consciousness, the hub of the universe, is a formless, impersonal entity. Human beings want a personal God whom they can love, and to whom they can narrate the pleasures and pains and joys of their life. Human beings cannot feel extreme love and affection toward an impersonal entity of philosophy, because that is something abstract, and the human heart cannot fully identify with something abstract. People cannot express the stories of their joys and sorrows, their pains and pleasures, the affection and happiness they may feel, to an abstract idea. They want a personal God to whom they can fully convey their inner longings. Thus the necessity for a personal God. Human beings do not search for God in distant nebulae and meteors—they search for God where they are, in their very midst. They want to make him the sole shelter of their life. In the play of imagination people may derive some temporary peace and happiness but not lasting peace. The God of philosophy cannot provide complete fulfillment to people's internal urges. They want one to whom they can open their hearts. That is one's *iśt́a*. (Anandamurti, *Subhásita Saṁgraha 12*, 97–98. AT)

67. Anandamurti, *Subhásita Saṁgraha 7*, 74–75. AT

Chapter Four

1. There are various interpretations of *kalá*, *náda*, and *bindu* in Kashmiri Shaivism. In one of these, the creation emerges out of a point, *bindu*, the primordial seed. This gives rise to *náda*, the primordial

vibration, which is expressed as the sound of creation, or Om, and from this comes the manifest universe, or *kalá*. This is seen by some modern writers as an implied reference to the Big Bang.

2. These laws were first apprehended through intuition and only afterward were they symbolized in the intellect through the language of mathematics. Einstein understood the nature of relativity in a flash of intuitive insight but he had to labor hard for a number of years to develop the equations to express his intuition. Likewise, Farraday understood the field nature of the fabric of space through intuition and James Clerk Maxwell then had to labor to give expression to that intuition through the equations that defined the nature of the electromagnetic field.

3. In the Supreme Puruśa, a countless number of linear waves are emanating in the different flows of the sentient, mutative and static principles. These triple-attributional flows are running from all sides in infinite directions. When they run parallel, no figure is formed. But when they lose parallelism, they form multi-conical or polygonal diagrams. All these forces are belligerent in nature. *Prakrti* here is called *anucchúnyá* (unmanifested) and Brahma here is objectless (*niskala*), because there is no question of subjectivation or objectivation. Brahma is *nirguńa* here because the balanced *prakrti* has not been able to influence Brahma. Later on, these polygonal diagrams gradually get transformed into triangles of forces due to homomorphic evolution, or *svarúpa parińáma*. This triangle of forces is endless and is flowing eternally.

In the initial stage, there is balance in the triangular figure. The reason for formation of triangular figures is this, that when more than two forces act at a place, the figure of forces tends to become triangular in shape. The multi-conical figures have been transformed into a triangle of forces, but no resultant is formed, because of proper adjustment. (Anandamurti, *Ánanda Vacanámrtam Part 33*, chap. 9. EE9)

4. There is no evidence that Kapil used the term *svarúpa parińáma* in this sense, nor Ishvara Krishna, the author of the Samkhya Karika (the term does not appear in the Samkhya Karika), but this is how later commentators have described it.

5. Anandamurti, *Subháśita Saḿgraha 7*, 101–102. AT

6. ... though no resultant force has formed, there is a theoretical difference between the *puruśabháva* in the first stage, when *prakrti* was *anucchúnyá* (unexpressed), and the *puruśabháva* in the second stage

when *prakrti* has shaped Herself into a triangle of forces. In the later stage, not only is *puruśa* in a theoretical bondage of the three principles, but also there is a chance of His getting expression. *Puruśa* has not yet metamorphosed due to equilibrium of the triangle of forces, but the chance of metamorphosis is imminent, and so in spite of the fact that *puruśa* here is unaffected, there is a theoretical speciality in *puruśa* at this stage. (Sarkar, *Idea and Ideology*, 59.)

7. While operating on the same side, one *guńa* is converted into another as a result of the fluctuation in their waves. When the three principles, due to their mutual conflict, exert a varying influence on a vertex of the triangle, a resultant *guńa* emerges. This resultant *prakrti* or *guńa* cannot continue to flow within the triangle but emerges from one of the vertices and moves outwardly. This extroversive movement of the resultant Shakti is a sign of a loss of balance in the triangle of forces...When the *tamoguńa* force begins to move in a straight line (not as a wave) in the path of manifestation we can call it the second stage in the play of creation and the first stage of expression. This stage is full of manifestative potentiality and is hence dominated by *sattvaguńa*. Since this movement is linear, it is called *náda*. It seeks greater and greater expression. It wants to create sound in the deep silence. (Anandamurti, *Subháśita Saḿgraha 7*, 102,104. AT)

8. *Kala* means "sprout." *Sakala* means "that from which the sprout has emerged," in other words, that which is manifest or expressed. Everything in this universe is a manifest entity. For example, in philosophy it is called *sakala* Brahma, that is, manifest Brahma. When unmanifest it is *niśkala* Brahma or Nirguńa Brahma. (Anandamurti, *Varńa Vijińána*, chap. 18. EE9)

9. The extroversive waves of Shakti that emerge from a vertex of the triangle gradually exert their influence over *puruśa*, so we can call this point the unexpressed seed of the expressed universe (the noumenal cause of the phenomenal universe). Although it appears as if a change is effected in the body of *puruśa* by the waves that are produced from this seed point, the correct conclusion is that *puruśa* does not and cannot undergo any alteration as a result of these waves. *Puruśa* under all circumstances remains unaltered. In reality, the apparent change that is seen in the body of *puruśa* is nothing but the changing wavelengths in the forces of *prakrti*. (Anandamurti, *Subháśita Saḿgraha 7*, 103. AT)

10. Anandamurti, *Subháśita Saḿgraha 3*, 139–140. AT

11. Actually the unfolding of the creation begins from this *kalá*. As long as *kalá* has not arisen, there is only the Causal Brahma (Kárana Brahma). The Effect Brahma (Kárya Brahma) can only arise when there is *kalá*, thus Saguńa Brahma, which is the composite of Kárana Brahma and Kárya Brahma, can also be called Sakala Brahma or Sakala Dev. In this analysis Nirguńa Brahma is also called Niskala Brahma. (Anandamurti, *Subháśita Samgraha 7*, 105. AT)

12. Parama Puruśa's *icchá shakti* or *kámabiija* is eternally active behind the creation of this universe. This *icchábiija* of Parama Puruśa is termed *shambhúliungá* in philosophy. (Anandamurti, *Subháśita Samgraha 8*, 77. AT)

13. *Bindu* is *iccháshakti* (will force), *náda* is *jińánashakti* (cognitive force), and *kalá* is *karmashakti* (actional force). The origin of the flow of creation is Brahma's *iccháshakti*. (Anandamurti, *Subháśita Samgraha 7*, 106. AT)

14. Over the last eight years of his life, Anandamurti composed 5018 devotional songs, the vast majority in Bengali, with the remainder divided among Hindi, Sanskrit, English, Urdu, Magahi, Maithili, and Angika. This phrase is taken from one of those songs.

15. Anandamurti, *Subháśita Samgraha Part 19*, chap. 6. EE9

16. Non-qualified liberation, or *mokśa*, is, however, only possible if the mental body, starting from the crudest mental subjectivity of the physical body, can, by any force, retrace against the singular positive force emanating due to the thought-projection of the Macrocosm. This force against the singular positive force must be a negative one. Hence the path of non-qualified spiritual practice which can reach final *mokśa* is always the path of negativity. The theoretical negative force with its fundamental negativity, which tends towards the final merger into *puruśa* for attaining *mokśa*, is called *kulakuńdalinii*—the "coiled serpentine."

Since *kulakuńdalinii* is the negative force of the unit body, it is different for each individual. As the sadhana is more or less for a psycho-physical liberation in the initial stage, its starting point must be in the crudest manifestation. It must reside in that portion of the physical body from which the crudest matter (*kśititattva*) of the body is controlled. The starting point of the *kulakuńdalinii*, therefore, is in the *múládhára*. It is fundamentally negative in character, and its starting point is the negative *kámabiija* of the living being, just as the point from which the positive resultant force of *prakrti* got expression is the *kámabiija*, or *icchábiija*, of the Cosmic Being.

The arena in which the *kulakuńḍalinii* resides is known as *kámapiitha*. The starting point of the fundamental positivity, that is, the *kámabiija* of the Cosmic Being, is on the back of *shambhúliuṋgá*, and that of negativity on the back of *svayambhúliuṋga*. Within the self of the yoga *sádhaka*, or one who practices the scientific method of spiritual approach with the help of this *kulakuńḍalinii*, the force of fundamental negativity fights out and aggressively rises up against the force of *avidyámáyá* and thereby gets domination over the flow of fundamental positivity. This path of non-compromising aggressive spirituality is the only way to ultimate oneness with Infinite Consciousness. (Sarkar, *Idea and Ideology*, 61–62.)

17. Jacob Boehme, *The Confessions of Jacob Boehme*, ed. W. Scott Palmer (Evinity Publishing Inc., 2009), chap. 2. https://www.sacred-texts.com/eso/cjb/cjb04.htm

18. Anandamurti, *Subháśita Saḿgraha Part 19*, chap. 6. EE9

19. Gopi Krishna, *Kundalini: The Evolutionary Energy in Man* (Boston: Shambhala, 1997), 12–13.

20. However there is no fixed rule that one will have to achieve these samadhis in order to reach the highest spiritual stage. For example, passengers on a train traveling from Delhi to Calcutta may be able to see the cities of Jamalpur or Bhagalpur as they pass, but if for some reason the doors and window shutters are closed then the passengers may not know that they are passing through Jamalpur or Bhagalpur. Even if the passengers are unaware of the towns they are passing through, they still reach their destinations at the same time. In the world of sadhana as well, a spiritual aspirant, while ideating on the Supreme, may not know when they pass through many stages of spiritual realization. (Anandamurti, *Tattva Kaomudi 2*, 19–20. AT)

21. In the US federal prison system, levels one and two are considered minimum security, levels three and four are medium security, and levels five and six are maximum security. Level-six prisoners, who are considered a danger to the guards and other prisoners, are only allowed out of their cell one hour a week for solitary exercise, and their only human contact during the week is when the guard passes their food through a small slot in their cell door three times a day. This is analogous to the human mind in a state of maximum spiritual bondage or spiritual ignorance.

Chapter Five

1. Anandamurti, *Subhásita Samgraha Part 6*, chap. 2. EE9

2. *Samánam ejati iti samájah*. That is, when everyone makes a unanimous decision that they will move together, that they will stay together in good times and in bad, then their collective name is *samája* (society). Some may have moved far ahead; others may have lagged behind. Some may be unable to walk due to pain in their legs; others may have fallen face down. Those who have moved ahead without looking after them are not members of society. Society must move in unison, and if it is to move, it has an increased responsibility for them. That person who is unable to move must be carried so that the rhythm of movement remains unbroken. ... What are we seeing? In some homes people are rolling in luxury while others are dying of starvation. One portion of society is strolling about freely in the outside air while another portion, perhaps half the population, has been kept confined to their homes. One portion does whatever they please and no one denounces them, while society treats the other portion extremely harshly if they make a mistake, even unknowingly. This simply will not do. (Sarkar, *Kańikáya Prout 13*, 1–2. AT)

3. According to Anandamurti, "The first human beings evolved one million years ago in Rárh. These first humans were no better than animals. They had only one occupation and that was physical." (Sarkar, *Prout in a Nutshell Part 16*, chap. 8. EE9) By evolution, he is referring to the point when the minds of those early hominids became recognizably human in terms of the evolutionary flow of *pratisaiṇcara*, that is, when they became capable of truly independent action, of going against the flow of *pratisaiṇcara*, something their immediate ancestors were incapable of.

4. When the waves of the individual mind try to keep pace with the waves of matter without attempting to assimilate them, then this effort eventually makes the individual mind materialistic. This individual mind, which dwells on matter and in which the darkness of *tamoguńa* is greater, I call *shúdra*, and the collective name of those who move ahead with a *shúdra* mentality is the "*shúdra* society." (Sarkar, *Mánuśer Samája 2*, 12–13. AT)

5. Sarkar, *Mánuśer Samája 2*, 17–18. AT

6. Anandamurti, *Human Society Part 2*, chap. 1. EE9

7. Sarkar, *Idea and Ideology*, 68.

8. Another important meaning of the word *varńa* is "letter," which is also based on its original meaning of "color." Letters represent sounds, and sounds are vibrational frequencies and are thus chromatic in nature. According to modern physics, all material vibrations emit color—every atom for example emits characteristic color frequencies, its spectrum, which in turn allows for the analysis of the atmosphere of distant planets by color spectrometry—and according to Tantra the same is true for all psychic vibrations. All vibration, whether psychic or material, emits color, as well as sound and form.

> All forms in the universe are chromatic and the distinction between objects is indicated through color. Color is indicative of attributional difference. The three binding principles of Saguńa Brahma are also characterized by color. Despite being chiefly *sattva*, Saguńa Brahma is all three, *sattva*, *rajas*, and *tamas*. Whenever there is an excess of *sattvaguńa* in any particular entity, the vibrations emanated by that object will be sentient, and that particular object or thought is known through the medium of those waves. If you perceive those sentient vibrations with your eyes, or through any other means, you will find that they have created a white color in your *citta*, that is, it appears white to your eyes. So you can see what a close relationship there is between attribution and color. The waves of color indicate the attributes of an entity. *Sattva* is white, *rajas* is red, and *tamas* is black. The greater the degree of purity, the more *sattvaguńa* predominates and also the whiter it is. That is why in India whiteness and purity are often used synonymously. What is white? White is no color; the combination of all colors is white. What is black? Black is no color; the want of color is black. That is why black is the symbol of inertia, the semblance of *tamoguńa*. It is due to the absence of vibration or to one's inability to apprehend the vibration that an object appears black. Since the vibrational expression of the form *tanmátra* is indistinct in the dark, we see black. (Anandamurti, *Subhásita Samgraha* 3, 260–261. AT)

9. The traditional colors assigned to the four *varńas*—black, red, white, and yellow—are largely symbolic.

10. Sarkar, *Kańikáya Prout 7*, 60. AT

11. *cháturvarńyam mayá srśtam guńakarmavibhágashah*

The four *varńas* have been created by me based on the division of *guṅa* and karma, qualities and actions.

— Bhagavad Gita IV.13

The Gita also says that the four *varṅas* are evolved from the differences in attributes and activities. The differences in attributes account for the differences in activities, and the differences in activities account for the differences in *varṅa*. With a change of attributes or activity, the *varṅa* also changes. Hence the distinction of *varṅa* in social life is not an unchangeable or inviolable institution. You have created it through your actions and you can change it through your actions. (Anandamurti, *Subhāśita Saṁgraha 3*, 264–265. AT)

12. It has been reported that Anandamurti privately told a small group of disciples that the original Gita ended with Krishna showing his *vishvarupa* or universal form (Chapter 11). The subsequent chapters were added later during the Vaishnava period. This is evidenced by certain stylistic differences in the Sanskrit.

13. Sarkar, *Idea and Ideology*, 71.

14. The word *sadvipra* first appears in the Rigveda, verse 1.64.46, but with a different meaning: *ekaṁ sadviprā bahudhā vadanti,* which is commonly translated as "the truth is one but is called by different names." Anandamurti's use of the word is entirely new.

15. Anandamurti, *Subhāśita Saṁgraha 5*, 96. AT

16. Movement only appears to be linear due to our limited perceptual ability. This has been amply demonstrated by modern physics, and this understanding of the discrete nature of *prakrti* has been extended to time, an inevitable development since time is our mental measurement of movement.

17. The terms "systolic" and "diastolic," which are normally used to refer to the beating of our heart, are used here as translations for the Bengali words *saṁkocátmaka,* "contractive," and *vikáshátmaka,* "expansive."

18. Sarkar, *Prout in a Nutshell Part 21*, chap. 3. EE9

19. Sarkar, *Human Society Part 1*, chap. 1. EE9

20. As a result of *vaeshya* exploitation, those having *kśatriya* or *vipra* mentalities are transformed into the disgruntled slaves of the *vaeshyas*. They have no alternative but to toil at the behest of the *vaeshyas* to fill their bellies. Those *kśatriyas* and *vipras* who are turned into *shúdras* under circumstantial pressure carry a simmering discontent

in their hearts. This group are known as the *vikśubdha shúdras* or the "disgruntled workers." These disgruntled workers—the exploited *vipras* and *kśatriyas*—give systematic expression to the frustrations of the masses to end *vaeshya* exploitation. This is the class with revolutionary distinction. (Sarkar, *Prout in a Nutshell Part 21*, chap. 3. EE9)

21. Anandamurti's teachings on this subject are scattered throughout his Prout writings, but of particular interest is the article "Capitalism in Three Spheres" (*Prout in a Nutshell Part 13*, 8.) and "Various Forms of Exploitation" (*Prout in a Nutshell Part 18*, 8.). For example, in his enumeration of the different forms of psychic exploitation prevalent in capitalism, he discusses what he calls psycho-economic exploitation, which seeks to weaken and paralyze the people in various ways so that they can be more easily exploited. In the colonial form of capitalist hegemony, the suppression of indigenous language and culture and the imposition of the conquerors' language and culture is one example of psycho-economic exploitation.

22. From the outset, those who exploit human beings, who cheat them to serve their own self-interests, do not want them to have socioeconomic freedom. And so that they don't have it, they exploit them subtly in the psycho-economic sphere. They do not exploit them directly in the social sphere, but they do it in the psycho-economic sphere in such a clever way that you are not even aware of it and are unable to properly develop your *yatamána*.* Moreover, you are also unable to develop economically because they control the economy in a subtle way. When those vested interests see that they are no longer able to keep obstructing them in the psycho-economic sphere because a good number of intelligent people who see through their tricks have emerged from the exploited masses—yes, the media may be in their hands, but these people have seen through them, and as result, they start a kind of whispering campaign, and this also has a price—then they get active in the intellectual sphere so that the people cannot gain their intellectual freedom. And what do they do so that people cannot be intellectually free? They control the educational system, the media, the propaganda machine, and public relations departments in a final effort so that their sandbags can keep the Damodar River from flooding. (Sarkar, *Manasa Sádhanár Staravinyása*, 11–12. AT)

* the first stage of spiritual sadhana

23. While this is true at this stage in the development of human society, it can be hoped that in the future, due to the ethical and spiritual de-

velopment of the human race, that such a change of *varṅa* can and will occur without bloodshed, even when the *kśatriya* elements dominate.

24. Today, in the modern world, the Kśatriya Age and the Vipra Age are still evident in some undeveloped countries. In most developed countries the Vaeshya Age is prevalent. In a few countries a new Kśatriya Age has emerged following *shúdra* revolution, and in one or two places we can even see indications of the emerging Vipra Age. (Sarkar, *Problems of the Day*, section 1, 35. EE9)

25. Sarkar, *Buddhir Mukti-Navyamánavatávúda*, 3. AT

26. In ancient times, people were satisfied with a dhoti, a shirt and a pair of wooden sandals. Not only that, they did not even feel the need for shoes. But today a suit is an absolute necessity. In olden days people would travel long distances on foot, but today a cycle or motor car has become essential. (Sarkar, *Prout in a Nutshell Part 6*, chap. 2. EE9)

27. To make democracy successful, economic power must be vested in the hands of the common people and the minimum requirements of life must be guaranteed to all. This is the only way to ensure the economic liberation of the people. Prout's slogan is: "To end exploitation we demand economic democracy, not political democracy."…The first requirement for economic democracy is that the minimum requirements of a particular age—including food, clothing, housing, education, and medical treatment—must be guaranteed to all. Not only is this an individual right, it is also a collective necessity, because the easy availability of the minimum requirements will increase the all-round welfare of society. The second requirement for economic democracy is that increasing purchasing capacity must be guaranteed to each and every individual. (Sarkar, *Prout in a Nutshell Part 21*, chap. 5. EE9)

28. Sarkar, *Prout in a Nutshell Part 17*, chap. 4. EE9

29. Sarkar, *Prout in a Nutshell Part 17*, chap. 4. EE9

30. The Five Fundamental Principles of Prout were originally dictated by Anandamurti in English in 1959 for inclusion in his book *Idea and Ideology*, and only two years later did he compose the Sanskrit equivalents for Chapter Five of *Ananda Sutram*. The translations of sutras V.12–V.16 included in this commentary are not direct translations of the Sanskrit sutras but the original English versions that appeared in *Idea and Ideology*.

31. Sarkar, *Ájker Samasyá*, 2. AT

32. Sarkar, *Problems of the Day*, Section 1. EE9.

33. The word *pabula* is the nominative plural of the Latin "pabulum," meaning "food" or "sustenance," whether physical or mental. Anandamurti commonly used this word when speaking English to make up for its lack in the English lexicon.

34. The desire to become rich by exploiting others is a kind of psychic disease. In fact, if the infinite hunger of the human mind does not find the correct path to fulfillment through psychic and spiritual wealth, it becomes engaged in accumulating surplus wealth in the physical world by depriving others. If any member of an extended family appropriates food from the family stock by using physical or intellectual force and keeps that food for themselves, they become a cause of suffering to others. A similar thing happens when capitalists say, "We have amassed wealth by our intellect and hard work; if others have the capacity and diligence, let them do the same, no one is stopping them," they do not want to understand that the quantity of commodities on this earth is limited, while the need is common to all. Excessive individual affluence, in most cases, forces others into bare subsistence. (Sarkar, *Ájker Samasyá*, 5–6. AT)

35. Cultural evolution is much faster than biological evolution — information and the fruits of experience are passed on much faster through communication than through genes. Thus the role of cultural evolution cannot be neglected in any analysis of human spiritual evolution. Our gene pool is virtually the same as that of Cro-magnon man, but the advances that the human mind has made since then due to the effects of cultural evolution have been astronomical.

36. The lack of motivation among workers in communist countries due to the suppression of individual liberties and the failure to satisfy individual longings has been well documented. In the West, the scale has long been tipped in the opposite direction. Western society as a whole is justifiably accused of being too individualistic, which has led to numerous social problems. Most of the blame for this tends to be laid at the feet of our modern capitalist culture, which promotes individuality, materialism, and ultimately selfishness, but there are some thinkers, such as the Italian philosopher Umberto Galimberti, who trace the pervasiveness of individualism in the West back to the rise of Christianity, which puts the salvation of the soul, an individual affair in the Christian view, above collective welfare. This led Rousseau to say that a Christian in

principle is not a good citizen. He can be in practice but not in principle, because what interests him is the salvation of his soul.

37. Anandamurti, *Ananda Sutram*, 43. AT

38. Anandamurti, *Subháśita Saṁgraha 9*, 7. AT

39. In the vibrational field, balance is maintained by the conjunction of two opposites, the positive and the negative. In other words, when happiness arises, then unhappiness increases in equal proportion. Thus we see that in the physical stratum so-called scientific progress is responsible for both happiness and unhappiness. For example, the use of cars in place of bullock carts makes for greater physical comfort but also for a greater risk of accidents. The use of airplanes increases the ease of travel and the risks in equal proportion. Thus we find that the enjoyment of material possessions in the physical sphere is balanced out by painful or negative experiences. ...

In the psychic sphere, the main feature is the increase of mental hunger. However this increase is not quantitative. Thus *anukúla vedaniiyam* in the psychic sphere refers to that state in which the mind wants more psychic pabula. Naturally *pratikúla vedaniiyam* also increases so that the balance among mental waves may be maintained. This can be illustrated through an example. In ancient times, when human beings were intellectually backward, they also had less emotional disturbances. Those who are intellectually lacking are also less susceptible to anxiety. Intellectually developed people are more sensitive in the emotional sphere. They create unnecessary problems for no reason and lose sleep night after night. Thus in the intellectual sphere as well, balance is maintained with the help of *anukúla vedaniiyam* and *pratikúla vedaniiyam*. (Sarkar, *Kańikáya Prout 6*, 92–93, 95. AT)

40. Sarkar, *Kańikáya Prout 6*, 81–82. AT

Afterword

1. (2) Common Philosophy of Life:

People unite on the basis of a common ideology. As long as the inhabitants of this vast planetary world do not accept a living ideology, there is very little possibility of social synthesis. In its absence, strife arises among human beings. Hence a common philosophy of life is absolutely necessary. (Sarkar, *Kańikáya Prout 4*, 30. AT)

2. Anandamurti, *Idea and Ideology*, 63.

About The Author

Devashish holds an MFA in fiction from San Diego State University. He divides his time between Ananda Kirtana, a spiritual community in the Brazilian countryside, and his farm in Puerto Rico, where he has a yoga center and a tropical-fruit plantation. You can reach him at:

www.devashishdonaldacosta.com

www.ingramcontent.com/pod-product-compliance
Lightning Source LLC
Chambersburg PA
CBHW022210090526
44584CB00012BA/374